Study Guide to Accompany

QUANTITATIVE METHODS FOR BUSINESS

Sixth Edition

DAVID R. ANDERSON
UNIVERSITY OF CINCINNATI

DENNIS J. SWEENEY
UNIVERSITY OF CINCINNATI

THOMAS A. WILLIAMS
ROCHESTER INSTITUTE OF TECHNOLOGY

PREPARED BY

JOHN LOUCKS
ST. EDWARD'S UNIVERSITY

JOHN LAWRENCE
CALIFORNIA STATE UNIVERSITY - FULLERTON

BARRY PASTERNACK
CALIFORNIA STATE UNIVERSITY - FULLERTON

WEST PUBLISHING COMPANY
MINNEAPOLIS/ST. PAUL NEW YORK LOS ANGELES SAN FRANCISCO

WEST'S COMMITMENT TO THE ENVIRONMENT

In 1906, West Publishing Company began recycling materials left over from the production of books. This began a tradition of efficient and responsible use of resources. Today, up to 95% of our legal books and 70% of our college texts and school texts are printed on recycled, acid-free stock. West also recycles nearly 22 million pounds of scrap paper annually—the equivalent of 181,717 trees. Since the 1960s, West has devised ways to capture and recycle waste inks, solvents, oils, and vapors created in the printing process. We also recycle plastics of all kinds, wood, glass, corrugated cardboard, and batteries, and have eliminated the use of Styrofoam book packaging. We at West are proud of the longevity and the scope of our commitment to the environment.

Production, Prepress, Printing and Binding by West Publishing Company.

610 Opperman Drive
P.O. Box 64526
St. Paul, MN 55164–0526

Printed in the United States of America
02 01 00 99 98 97 96 95   8 7 6 5 4 3 2 1 0

ISBN 0–314–04973–8

Table of Contents

Preface

The *Study Guide to Accompany Quantitative Method for Business, 6th ed.* has been written with several goals in mind. Its objectives are:

1. To *provide an outline of the material* in the parent text via an opening key concepts page from which the student may design a course of study of the individual techniques and concepts of each chapter.

2. To *organize and summarize the material* in the parent text in a structured review section.

3. To *illustrate the basic concepts* of the parent text in detail through the presentation of 111 illustrated problems.

4. To *reinforce the basic concepts* by providing 179 additional problems and 270 true/false questions whose answers are in the back of the book.

5. To *challenge the student* by giving several problems requiring more than simple, straightforward application of the techniques of the chapter.

6. To *expand the coverage* of certain areas beyond the parent text by offering additional insights and algorithms to assist in the solution strategy.

7. To *illustrate business applications* areas in the management sciences to which the quantitative techniques may be applied.

To accomplish these goals, each chapter has been divided into five basic parts:

1. Key Concepts Cover Page:
   This page notes the main topic areas of each chapter and denotes which problems illustrate the concept, and which answered problems require the use of the concept in its solution.
   Every major concept of the text is illustrated in at least one problem worked out in detail and in at least one answered problem with its answer provided in the back of the book.

2. Review Section:
   This section summarizes point by point the theoretical foundations, the definitions, and the approaches of every topic area of the chapter. This provides an excellent check-list for understanding the essential points of the chapters.
   A categorical list of important formulas is included in this section where applicable.
   Major algorithms are described in sentence form and with flow charts at the end of this section where applicable.

3. Illustrated Problems:
   These are problems worked out in full, giving the cumbersome step-by-step details as the problem is worked through to fruition.

4. Answered Problems:
   These problems are for the student to do on his/her own with the answers provided in the back of the book. This enables the student to test him/herself on the individual concepts with brief answers to validate his results.

5. True/False Questions:
   Each chapter contains fifteen questions designed to reinforce the theoretical concepts of the chapter. The answers are provided in the back of the book.

In addition, note boxes appear throughout the study guide mentioning students' common errors and misconceptions and providing helpful tips and reminders.

Again, every major concept of the text is covered in at least one illustrated problem and at least one answered problem. Through the use of the Key Concepts page, the student may select the topic area he wishes to study and see the concept demonstrated in an illustrated problem, and/or he may test himself on the concept by solving a corresponding answered problem.

We hope you find this study guide instructive and a useful supplement in your study of quantitative methods for business.

John Loucks
John Lawrence
Barry Pasternack

Chapter 1
Introduction

KEY CONCEPTS

CONCEPT	ILLUSTRATED PROBLEMS	ANSWERED PROBLEMS
Management Science Approach	1,2	6,7
Mathematical Models Development	3,4	8,9,10,11,12
Cost, Volume, Profit Analysis	5	13
Marginal Analysis	5	13
Breakeven Analysis	5	13

REVIEW

1. Management science is a quantitative approach to decision making based on the scientific method of problem solving. A synonymous term is operations research. It had its early roots in World War II and is flourishing in business and industry with the aid of computers in general and the microcomputer in particular.

2. Problem solving is a process designed to better a current state of affairs, It consists of two phases: (1) decision making; and (2) implementation and evaluation.

3. The decision making process involves: (1) structuring the problem; and (2) analyzing the problem.

4. Structuring the problem includes: (1) defining the problem; (2) identifying the alternatives; and (3) choosing the criteria (single or multiple) to be used to evaluate the alternatives.

5. Analyzing the problem consists of: (1) qualitatively and quantitatively evaluating the alternatives; and (2) making a decision recommendation (choosing an alternative).

6. Evaluating alternatives is often accomplished by experimenting with a model. A model is a representation of a real object or situation. Generally, experimenting with a model is less costly, requires less time, and involves less risk.

7. Three forms of models are iconic, analog, and mathematical. Iconic models are physical replicas (scalar representations) of real objects. Analog models are physical in form, but do not physically resemble the object being modeled.

8. Mathematical models (also called symbolic models), represent real world problems through a system of mathematical formulas and expressions. They are idealizations of real-life problems based on key assumptions, estimates, "guesstimates", and/or statistical analyses.

9. After the problem has been structured, the steps in the quantitative analysis are: (1) mathematical modeling; (2) data preparation; (3) model solution (and refinement); and (4) report generation.

10. Mathematical models relate decision variables (or controllable inputs) with fixed or variable parameters (or uncontrollable inputs). Frequently mathematical models seek to maximize or minimize some objective function subject to constraints.

11. If any of the uncontrollable inputs is subject to variation the model is said to be stochastic. Otherwise the model is said to be deterministic. Generally, stochastic models are more difficult to analyze.

12. The values of the decision variables that provide the mathematically-best output are referred to as the optimal solution for the model.

13. Cost/benefit considerations must be made in selecting an appropriate mathematical model. Frequently a less complicated (and perhaps less precise) model is more appropriate than a more complex and accurate one due to cost and ease of solution considerations.

14. Quantitative analysis should be used as one of many input factors for managerial decision making. It is not a replacement for human decision making.

15. Primary reasons for the use of quantitative analysis are: (1) the problem is complex; (2) the problem is important and/or the decision must be thoroughly justified; (3) the problem is new and there is little or no previous experience to rely on; (4) the problem is repetitive (with varying uncontrollable input values) and time-consuming; and (5) what-if questions need to be answered in an efficient manner.

16. Quantitative methods can be combined with computer-based systems to enhance the decision-making process. Two such computer-based systems are decision support systems and expert systems.

17. A decision support system (DSS) usually contains four components: an interactive capability, a data management system, a modeling subsystem, and a output generator.

18. Expert systems (ES) apply knowledge from specific fields of expertise to make recommendations in problem solving and decision making. An ES includes a knowledge base, an inference engine for selecting and applying information from the knowledge base, and a user interface for introducing new information and outputting conclusions/recommendations

19. Break-even analysis uses a basic mathematical model of the relationship between a volume variable and cost, revenue, or profit. The break-even point is the volume that results in total revenue equaling total cost.

20. Some of the primary applications areas of management science are forecasting, production scheduling, inventory control, capital budgeting, and transportation.

21. Statistical analysis, simulation, linear programming, PERT/CPM, and queueing theory are among the most frequently used quantitative techniques in business.

ILLUSTRATED PROBLEMS

> **NOTE:** Certainty about almost any uncontrollable input is rare. Unfortunately, stochastic models are generally more difficult to analyze than are deterministic models. So, models are often simplified out of necessity. The challenge lies in simplifying a model without significantly reducing its effectiveness in helping to solve a real problem.

PROBLEM 1

Consider a construction company building a 250-unit apartment complex. The project consists of hundreds of activities involving excavating, framing, wiring, plastering, painting, landscaping, and more. Some of the activities must be done sequentially and others can be done simultaneously. Also, some of the activities can be completed faster than normal by purchasing additional resources (workers, equipment, etc.).

a) How could management science be used to solve this problem?

b) What would be the uncontrollable inputs?

c) What would be the decision variables of the mathematical model? the objective function? the constraints?

d) Is the model deterministic or stochastic?

e) Suggest assumptions that could be made to simplify the model.

SOLUTION 1

a) Management science can provide a structured, quantitative approach for determining the minimum project completion time based on the activities' normal times and then based on the activities' expedited (reduced) times.

b) Normal and expedited activity completion times; activity expediting costs; funds available for expediting; precedence relationships of the activities.

c) Decision variables--which activities to expedite and by how much, and when to start each activity; objective function--minimize project completion time; constraints--do not violate any activity precedence relationships and do not expedite in excess of the funds available.

d) Stochastic--activity completion times, both normal and expedited, are uncertain and subject to variation; activity expediting costs are uncertain; the number of activities and their precedence relationships might change before the project is completed due to a project design change.

e) Make the model deterministic by assuming normal and expedited activity times are known with certainty and are constant. The same assumption might be made about the other stochastic, uncontrollable inputs.

PROBLEM 2

Consider a department store that must make weekly shipments of a certain product from two different warehouses to four different stores.

a) How could management science be used to solve this problem?

b) What would be the uncontrollable inputs for which data must be gathered?

c) What would be the decision variables of the mathematical model? the objective function? the constraints?

d) Is the model deterministic or stochastic?

e) Suggest assumptions that could be made to simplify the model.

SOLUTION 2

a) Management science can provide a systematic, quantitative approach for determining a minimum shipping cost from the warehouses to the stores.

b) Fixed costs and variable shipping costs; the demand each week at each store; the supplies each week at each warehouse.

c) Decision variables--how much to ship from each warehouse to each store; objective function--minimize total shipping costs; constraints--meet the demand at the stores without exceeding the supplies at the warehouses.

d) Stochastic--weekly demands fluctuate as do weekly supplies; transportation costs could vary depending upon the amount shipped, other goods sent with a shipment, etc.

e) Make the model deterministic by assuming fixed shipping costs per item, that demand is constant at each store each week, and that the weekly supplies in the warehouses are also constant.

PROBLEM 3

An auctioneer has developed a simple mathematical model for deciding the starting bid he will require when auctioning a used automobile. Essentially, he sets the starting bid at seventy percent of what he predicts the final winning bid will (or should) be. He predicts the winning bid by starting with the car's original selling price and making two deductions, one based on the car's age and the other based on the car's mileage. The age deduction is \$800 per year and the mileage deduction is \$.025 per mile.

a) Develop the mathematical model that will give the starting bid (B) for a car in terms of the car's original price (P), current age (A) and mileage (M).

b) Suppose a four-year old car with 60,000 miles on the odometer is up for auction. If its original price was \$12,500, what starting bid should the auctioneer require?

c) The model is based on what assumptions?

SOLUTION 3

a) The expected winning bid can be expressed as:

$$P - 800(A) - .025(M)$$

The entire model is:

$$B = .7(\text{expected winning bid}) \quad \text{or}$$
$$B = .7(P - 800(A) - .025(M)) \quad \text{or}$$
$$B = .7(P) - 560(A) - .0175(M)$$

b) $B = .7(12{,}500) - 560(4) - .0175(60{,}000) = \$5460.$

c) The model assumes that the only factors influencing the value of a used car are the original price, age, and mileage (not condition, rarity, or other factors). Also, it is assumed that age and mileage devalue a car in a linear manner and without limit. (Note, the starting bid for a very old car might be negative!)

PROBLEM 4

A firm manufactures two products made from steel and just received this month's allocation of b pounds of steel. It takes a_1 pounds of steel to make a unit of product 1 and it takes a_2 pounds of steel to make a unit of product 2. Let x_1 and x_2 denote this month's production level of product 1 and product 2 respectively.

Denote by p_1 and p_2 the unit profits for products 1 and 2, respectively. The manufacturer has a contract calling for at least m units of product 1 this month. The firm's facilities are such that at most u units of product 2 may be produced monthly.

a) Write a mathematical model for this problem.

b) Suppose $b = 2000$, $a_1 = 2$, $a_2 = 3$, $m = 60$, $u = 720$, $p_1 = 100$, $p_2 = 200$. Rewrite the model with these specific values for the uncontrollable inputs.

c) The optimal solution to (b) is $x_1 = 60$ and $x_2 = 626\ 2/3$. If the product were engines, explain why this is not a true optimal solution for the "real-life" problem.

SOLUTION 4

a) The total monthly profit = (profit per unit of product 1) x (monthly production of product 1) + (profit per unit of product 2) x (monthly production of product 2) $= p_1x_1 + p_2x_2$.

The total amount of steel used during monthly production
= (steel per unit of product 1) x (monthly production of product 1)
+ (steel per unit of product 2) x (monthly production of product 2)
$= a_1x_1 + a_2x_2$.

This quantity must be less than or equal to the allocated b pounds of steel: $a_1x_1 + a_2x_2 \leq b$.

The monthly production level of product 1 must be greater than or equal to m: $x_1 \geq m$.

The monthly production level of product 2 must be less than or equal to u: $x_2 \leq u$.

The production level for product 2 cannot be negative: $x_2 \geq 0$.

Thus, the model is:

$$\begin{aligned} \text{MAXIMIZE} \quad & p_1x_1 + p_2x_2 \\ \text{S.T.} \quad & a_1x_1 + a_2x_2 \leq b \\ & x_1 \geq m \\ & x_2 \leq u \\ & x_2 \geq 0 \end{aligned}$$

b) Substituting, the model is:

$$\begin{aligned} \text{MAXIMIZE} \quad & 100x_1 + 200x_2 \\ \text{S.T.} \quad & 2x_1 + 3x_2 \leq 2000 \\ & x_1 \geq 60 \\ & x_2 \leq 720 \\ & x_2 \geq 0 \end{aligned}$$

c) One cannot produce and sell 2/3 of an engine. Thus the problem is further restricted by the fact that both x_1 and x_2 must be integers. They could remain fractions if it is assumed these fractions are work in progress to be completed the next month.

PROBLEM 5

Ponderosa Development Corporation (PDC) is a small real estate developer operating in the Rivertree Valley. It has seven permanent employess whose monthly salaries are given in the table below:

Employee	Monthly Salary
President	$10,000
VP, Development	6,000
VP, Marketing	4,500
Project Manager	5,500
Controller	4,000
Office Manager	3,000
Receptionist	2,000

PDC leases a building for \$2,000 per month. The cost of supplies, utilities, and leased equipment runs another \$3,000 per month.

PDC builds only one style house in the valley. Land for each house costs \$55,000 and lumber, supplies, etc. run another \$28,000 per house. Total labor costs are figured at \$20,000 per house. The one sales representative of PDC is paid a commission of \$2,000 on the sale of each house. The selling price of the house is \$115,000.

a) Identify all costs and denote the marginal cost and marginal revenue for each house.

b) Write the monthly cos function c(x), revenue function r(x), and profit function p(x).

c) What is the breakeven point for monthly sales of the houses?

d) What is the monthly profit if 12 houses per month are built and sold?

SOLUTION 5

a) The monthly salaries total \$35,000 and monthly office lease and supply costs total another \$5,000. This \$40,000 is a monthly fixed cost. The total cost of land, material, labor, and sales commission per house, \$105,000, is the marginal cost for a house. The selling price of \$115,000 is the marginal revenue per house.

b) $c(x)$ = variable cost + fixed cost = 105,000 + 40,000
$r(x) = 115{,}000x$
$p(x) = r(x) - c(x) = 10{,}000x - 40{,}000$

c) $r(x) = c(x)$ or $115{,}000x = 105{,}000x + 40{,}000$. Solving $x = 4$.

d) $p(12) = 10{,}000(12) - 40{,}000 = \$80{,}000$ monthly profit.

ANSWERED PROBLEMS

PROBLEM 6

Zipco Printing operates a shop that has five printing machines. The machines differ in their capacities to perform various printing operations due to differences in the machines' designs and operator skill levels.

At the start of the workday there are five printing jobs to schedule. The manager must decide what the job-machine assignments should be.

a) How could management science be used to solve this problem?

b) What would be the uncontrollable inputs for which data must be collected?

c) Define the decision variables, objective function, and constraints to appear in the mathematical model.

d) Is the model deterministic or stochastic?

e) Suggest some simplifying assumptions for this problem.

PROBLEM 7

Zizzle Company is a new small local company that is about to manufacture Zizzle briefcases in three styles. The company wants to determine how to use its resources most efficiently to get the product mix that will maximize its profits.

One manager has advocated hiring an outside consulting firm to analyze sales potentials and customer preferences. He suggests doing a complete time and motion study of the production process and analyzing the potential for acquiring additional manpower and material resources. In short, he is advocating an extremely accurate but complex study.

A second manager suggests a simplified model using "best guess", rough approximations and simplifying assumptions as a starting point. The data for this model can be obtained in a short period of time, and the model can be solved in-house at a fraction of the cost of the more complex model.

a) Which manager's advice would you follow? Explain.

b) Would your answer change if Zizzle Company were a large national conglomerate which plans to market tens of thousands of briefcases?

PROBLEM 8

A client of an investment firm has $10,000 available for investment. He has instructed that his money be invested in three stocks so that no more than $5,000 is invested in any one stock but at least $1,000 is invested in each stock. He has further instructed the firm to use its current data and invest in a manner that maximizes his expected overall gain during a one-year period. The stocks, the current price per share, and the firm's projected stock price a year from now are summarized in the following table.

Stock	Current Price	Projected Price 1 Year Hence
James Industries	$25	$35
QM Inc.	$50	$60
Delicious Candy Co.	$100	$125

a) Let s_j = the number of shares of stock j purchased for j = 1 (James), 2 (QM), 3 (Delicious). Formulate a mathematical model for this problem using these decision variables.

b) Let x_j = the number of dollars invested in stock j. Reformulate this mathematical model in terms of these decision variables instead of those used in part (a).

c) If both models were solved using management science techniques, how would you expect the results of the models to compare?

PROBLEM 9

Bank Guard Company provides security service for banks and savings and loan companies during business hours. The number of guards supplied is a function of the average number of people in the facility. One guard is provided for an average of 25 customers. Let L = the average number of customers in the facility, C_g = the hourly cost per guard, N = the number of guards required, and C = the daily cost for guard service (based on an 8-hour day).

a) Develop a mathematical model for N in terms of L. Then develop a mathematical model for C in terms of N and C_g. Finally, express C in terms of L and C_g.

b) If night guard service costs a flat $$C_n$, develop a mathematical model for 24 hour guard service. Discuss the results with C_g = $10 per hour, C_n = $100 per night and L = 50. Discuss the results with L = 65.

PROBLEM 10

Comfort Plus Inc. (CPI) manufactures a standard dining chair used in restaurants. The demand forecasts for quarter 1 (January-March) and quarter 2 (April-June) are 3700 chairs and 4200 chairs, respectively. CPI has a policy of satisfying all demand in the quarter in which it occurs.

The chair contains an upholstered seat that can be produced by CPI or a subcontractor. The subcontractor currently charges $12.50 per seat, but has announced a new price of $13.75 effective April 1. CPI can produce the seat at a cost of $10.25.

Seats that are produced or purchased in quarter 1 and used to satisfy demand in quarter 2 cost CPI $1.50 each to hold in inventory.

a) What are the controllable inputs?

b) Develop a mathematical model for the total cost (objective) function.

PROBLEM 11

Continuing with problem 9, consider the following additional information. CPI's seat-producing capacity is 3800 seats per quarter. CPI cannot hold more than 300 seats in inventory from quarter to quarter.

a) Complete the mathematical model started in problem 9 by modeling the constraints in the problem.

b) Is the model stochastic or deterministic?

c) How would adding a third quarter to the problem change the model?

PROBLEM 12

A retail furniture store has set aside 800 square feet to display its new 18th Century Collection of sofas and chairs. Considering aisle space, it is estimated that each sofa utilizes 50 sq. ft. and each chair utilizes 30 sq. ft. At least five sofas and at least five chairs are to be displayed.

a) Write a mathematical model representing the store's constraints.

b) Suppose the profit on sofas is $200 and on chairs is $100. On a given day, the probability that a displayed sofa will be sold is .03 and that a displayed chair will be sold is .05. Mathematically model each of the following objectives:
   1) Maximize the total pieces of furniture displayed.
   2) Maximize the total expected number of daily sales.
   3) Maximize the total expected daily profit.

PROBLEM 13

Universal Computer is considering producing the new UC15 computer. Its components cost $630 and it will take 1/2 hour to assemble and 1/4 hour to pack. Skilled workers assemble the computer and make $16 per hour. Unskilled laborers pack the computers and make $4 per hour. Packaging material cost $11 per computer.

The computer will be produced in a plant located on Harbor Blvd. and leased for $3,100 per month. Utilities, supplies, insurance, etc. are expected to run another $1,900 per month regardless of the quantity of computers produced. Based on current market conditions, Universal assumes it can sell at $700 each all units it produces.

a) Identify the variable and fixed costs for Universal. Let x = the monthly producion quantity of UC15s. Express the monthly cost function in terms of x.

b) Express the revenue function in terms of x.

c) What is the breakeven point?

d) What is the marginal cost of a computer?

e) What will be the monthly profit with a production schedule for UC15 computers of 500 per month?

TRUE/FALSE

14. The optimal solution to a mathematical model is always the policy that should be implemented by the company.

15. A problem to decide monthly shipping patterns is dependent on the amount of product available at the factory. This amount can be modeled by a normal distribution. Thus, this is a stochastic mathematical model.

16. Microcomputers have made most management science techniques more accessible to even moderate size firms.

17. The three most commonly used management science techniques are statistical analyses, simulation, and linear programming.

18. A company seeks to maximize profit subject to limited availability of man-hours. Man-hours is a controllable input.

19. Past data might be used to test the validity of a mathematical model.

20. A toy train layout designed to represent an actual railyard is an example of an analog model.

21. A feasible solution is one that satisfies at least one of the constraints in the problem.

22. The terms stochastic and deterministic have the same meaning in management science.

23. If you are deciding whether to buy machine A, B, or C with the objective of minimizing the sum of three costs (labor, material and utilities), you are dealing with a multicriteria decision.

24. If your decision alternatives for dealing with increased product inventory are: (1) build another warehouse, (2) reduce the production rate, and (3) increase the sales rate, you are dealing with a multicriteria decision.

25. Model development should be left to management scientists; the model user's involvement should begin at the implementation stage.

26. The volume that results in marginal revenue equaling marginal cost is called the break-even point.

27. In quantitative analysis, the optimal solution is the mathematically-best solution.

28. Problem solving is narrower in scope than decision making.

Chapter 2
Introduction to Probability

KEY CONCEPTS

CONCEPT	ILLUSTRATED PROBLEMS	ANSWERED PROBLEMS
Experiments, Sample Spaces, Counting Rule	1	7,12
Assignment of Probabilities	1-4	13
Probability Relationships: Complement Union Intersection Mutually Exclusive Addition Law Conditional Probability Joint Probability Marginal Probability Multiplication Law	1-4	8,9,14,15,16
Bayes' Theorem	5,6	10,11,17

REVIEW

1. Probability is concerned with the study of uncertain or random events. It is a numerical measure of the chance that a particular event will occur. It provides a mechanism for developing a mathematical model which enables an analysis of the uncertainties of future events. Such an analysis is important for decision making concerning these events.

2. An experiment is any process that generates well-defined outcomes.

3. A sample space consists of all outcomes of interest to the experimenter. For example, if one observes the number of foreign cars in a sample of 20, the sample space consists of 21 sample points: E_1 = (0 foreign cars observed), E_2 = (1 foreign car observed), ..., E_{21} = (20 foreign cars observed).

4. Probabilities are non-negative values between 0 and 1 assigned to each sample point. The probabilities of all the sample points in the sample space must sum to 1.

5. The basis for assigning probabilities to outcomes is an attempt to assign to each outcome a numerical value which reflects its likelihood of occurrence.

6. There are three methods for assigning probabilities to sample points:
   (1) If all outcomes are equally likely (e.g. the flip of a fair coin), the classical method assigns to each possible outcome an identical probability.
   (2) If evidence suggests that all outcomes are not equally likely to occur, the relative frequency method assigns the probability based on evidence.
   (3) When neither the classical nor the relative frequency methods can be applied, the subjective al nor the relative frequency methods can be applied, the subjective method may be used. This assigns the probabilities based on the experimenter's belief concerning the likelihood of each outcome occurring.

7. Events are sets of sample points which are of interest to the experimenter. For example, using the example above, the event, "fewer than three foreign cars" is a set of the sample points consisting of $\{E_1, E_2, E_3\}$. Since events are sets, set operations such as union, intersection, and complementation may be applied.

8. The probabilities for <u>sample outcomes</u> are used to determine the probability for events. The probability of any event is equal to the sum of the probabilities of the sample points in the event. (For example, if a fair die is rolled, the probability of each of the six sample points is 1/6. Thus the probability of the event {rolling a number higher than a 3} will be the sum of the probabilities of {rolling a 4}, {rolling a 5}, or {rolling a 6}. This equals 1/6 + 1/6 + 1/6 = 1/2.)

9. Given an event, A, the <u>complement</u> of A, denoted A^C is defined as consisting of all sample points not in A.

10. The <u>union</u> of two events, A and B, denoted $A \cup B$, is defined as the set of all sample points in A or in B or in both A and B.

11. The <u>intersection</u> of two events, A and B, denoted $A \cap B$, is defined as the set of all sample points in both A and B.

12. Two events, A and B, are said to be <u>mutually exclusive</u> if the events do not have any sample points in common. (A and A^C are mutually exclusive.)

13. One method frequently used for visualizing relationships between event sets is the <u>Venn diagram</u>. This is a picture with a rectangle representing the entire sample space, S, and event sets represented by circles within the rectangle. If events are not mutually exclusive, then corresponding circles will overlap in the Venn diagram.

14. The <u>addition law of probability</u> states that for two events, A and B, $P(A \cup B) = P(A) + P(B) - P(A \cap B)$. Note that if A and B are mutually exclusive, then $P(A \cap B) = 0$ and $P(A \cup B) = P(A) + P(B)$.

15. The probability of the complement of the event A is $P(A^C) = 1 - P(A)$.

16. In certain instances, one may be interested in the probability of one event, A, given knowledge concerning a second event, B. This <u>conditional probability</u> of event A given event B has occurred is written as $P(A|B)$ and its probability is given by: $P(A \cap B)/P(B)$.

17. For mutually exclusive events $P(A|B) = P(B|A) = 0$, (e.g. the probability a coin comes up heads given it comes up tails is 0.)

18. The <u>multiplicative law</u> is derived from the definition of conditional probability and states: $P(A \cap B) = P(A|B)P(B) = P(B|A)P(A)$.

19. Two events, A and B, are said to be <u>independent</u> if $P(B|A) = P(B)$ or $P(A|B) = P(A)$. Then $P(A \cap B) = P(A)P(B)$.

20. Often the *joint probability* of events A and B, $P(A \cap B)$ will be written in a *joint probability table*. The row sums and the column sums of this table are referred to as *marginal probabilities*.

21. *Bayes' Theorem* is used to update the probability of events to account for new information concerning the events of interest. Consider the sample space being partitioned among n mutually exclusive and collectively exhaustive events, $A_1, A_2, \ldots, A_n$. Initially, *prior probabilities*, $P(A_1), P(A_2), \ldots, P(A_n)$ are assumed. Additional information (such as market surveys, experiments, etc.) is obtained, the result being event being event B.

    Bayes' Theorem then gives a formula for revising the estimates for the probabilities of events A_1, A_2, etc. These *posterior probabilities*, $P(A_i|B)$, are given by:

$$P(A_i|B) = \frac{P(A_i)P(B|A_i)}{P(A_1)P(B|A_1) + P(A_2)P(B|A_2) + \ldots + P(A_n)P(A_n|B)}$$

22. An easy way to compute the posterior probabilities using Bayes' Theorem is through the tabular approach. In this method five columns are prepared listing:
    (1) the mutually exclusive events possible
    (2) the prior probabilities for the events
    (3) the given conditional probabilities
    (4) the joint probabilities (Column (2) x Column (3))
    (5) the posterior probabilities (Column (4) divided by the sum of the entries in Column (4)).

    For example:

(1) Event A_i	(2) Prior Probabilities $P(A_i)$		(3) Conditional Probabilities $P(B\|A_i)$		(4) Joint Probabilities $P(A_i \cap B)$	(5) Posterior Probabilities $P(A_i\|B)$
		x		=		
A_1						
A_2						
.						
.						
A_n						
				P(B) =	------------	

ILLUSTRATED PROBLEMS

PROBLEM 1

A market study taken at a local sporting goods store showed that of 20 people questioned, 6 owned tents, 10 owned sleeping bags, 8 owned camping stoves, 4 owned both tents and camping stoves, and 4 owned both sleeping bags and camping stoves.

Let: Event A = owns a tent
Event B = owns a sleeping bag
Event C = owns a camping stove

and let the sample space be the 20 people questioned.

a) Find P(A), P(B), P(C), $P(A \cap C)$, $P(B \cap C)$.

b) Are the events A and C mutually exclusive? Explain briefly.

c) Are the events B and C independent events? Explain briefly.

d) If a person questioned owns a tent, what is the probability he also owns a camping stove?

e) If two people questioned own a tent, a sleeping bag, and a camping stove, how many own only a camping stove? In this case is it possible for 3 people to own both a tent and a sleeping bag, but not a camping stove?

SOLUTION 1

a) Using the relative frequency method, the probability equals the number of sample points in the event divided by the number of sample points in the sample space.

Thus, P(A) = 6/20 = .3
P(B) = 10/20 = .5
P(C) = 8/20 = .4

$P(A \cap B)$ = P(owns a tent and owns a camping stove) = 4/20 = .2
$P(B \cap C)$ = P(owns a sleeping bag and owns a camping stove) = 4/20 = .2

b) Events B and C are not mutually exclusive because there are people (4 people) who both own a tent and a camping stove.

c) To see whether events B and C are independent, check to see if $P(B \cap C) = P(B)P(C)$. Since $P(B \cap C) = .2$ and $P(B)P(C) = (.5)(.4) = .2$, then these events are independent.

d) Here the probability that a person owns a camping stove given he owns a tent or $P(C|A)$ must be determined. Using conditional probability,

$$P(C|A) = P(A \cap C)/P(A) = .2/.3 = .667.$$

e) Using a Venn diagram gives the following:

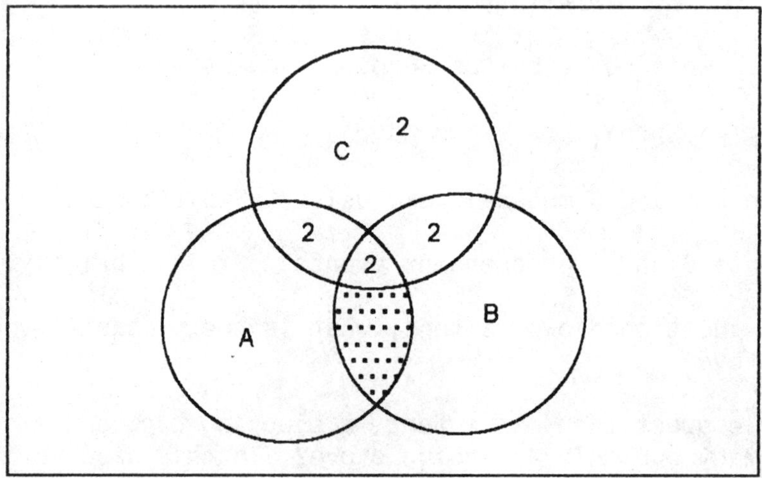

Note that two people own only a camping stove.

To determine whether it is possible for three people to own both a tent and a sleeping bag, but not a camping stove, note that the total size of event A is 6. Therefore the shaded area above could not have a value of three.

PROBLEM 2

The Bidwell Valve Company requires all prospective employees to be interviewed by a three man personnel committee. Each member of the committee votes individually for or against a recommendation of employment. Upon examining the company's records over the past year, the personnel director has noted the following probabilities for eight possible outcomes:

	VOTE OF MEMBER			
OUTCOME	1	2	3	PROBABILITY
E_1	for	for	for	.20
E_2	for	for	against	.14
E_3	for	against	for	.12
E_4	for	against	against	.07
E_5	against	for	for	.08
E_6	against	for	against	.11
E_7	against	against	for	.06
E_8	against	against	against	.22

Denote the following events:

A = Member 1 votes for employment
B = Member 2 votes for employment
C = Member 3 votes for employment

a) Find P(A), P(B), and P(C).

b) Which sample outcomes correspond to the event $D = A \cup B$ (Member 1 or Member 2 votes for employment)? Find P(D).

c) Which sample outcomes correspond to the event $G = A \cap B$ (Member 1 and Member 2 vote for employment)? Use the addition law of probability to find P(G).

d) Let the event $F = B^c \cap C$ (Member 2 votes against employment and Member 3 votes for employment). Draw a Venn diagram to represent the event $G \cup F$.

e) If a new employee is hired only if a majority of the committee members vote for employment, what is the probability that a prospective employee is hired? Does a job applicant stand a better or worse chance of being employed going before the committee than one of the individuals?

SOLUTION 2

a) Find the outcomes corresponding to events A, B, and C.

$A = \{E_1, E_2, E_3, E_4\}$. Thus $P(A) = P(E_1) + P(E_2) + P(E_3) + P(E_4)$
$= .20 + .14 + .12 + .07 = .53.$

$B = \{E_1, E_2, E_5, E_6\}$. Thus $P(B) = P(E_1) + P(E_2) + P(E_5) + P(E_6)$
$= .20 + .14 + .08 + .11 = .53.$

$C = \{E_1, E_3, E_5, E_7\}$. Thus $P(C) = P(E_1) + P(E_3) + P(E_5) + P(E_7)$
$= .20 + .12 + .08 + .06 = .46.$

b) The event D corresponds to all sample points which are either in event A or event B or both. Thus $D = \{E_1, E_2, E_3, E_4, E_5, E_6\}$.

$P(D) = P(E_1) + P(E_2) + P(E_3) + P(E_4) + P(E_5) + P(E_6)$
$= .20 + .14 + .12 + .07 + .08 + .11 = .72.$

c) The event G corresponds to sample points in both event A and event B. Thus $G = \{E_1, E_2\}$.

The addition law states: $P(A \cup B) = P(A) + P(B) - P(A \cap B)$
or in this case: $P(G) = P(A) + P(B) - P(D) = .53 + .53 - .72 = .34.$

Note that this checks with $P(G) = P(E_1) + P(E_2) = .20 + .14 = .34.$

d) Event $B^c = \{E_3, E_4, E_7, E_8\}$. $F = B^c \cap C$ = the events common to both B^c and $C = \{E_3, E_7\}$.

The Venn diagram for $G \cup F$ is:

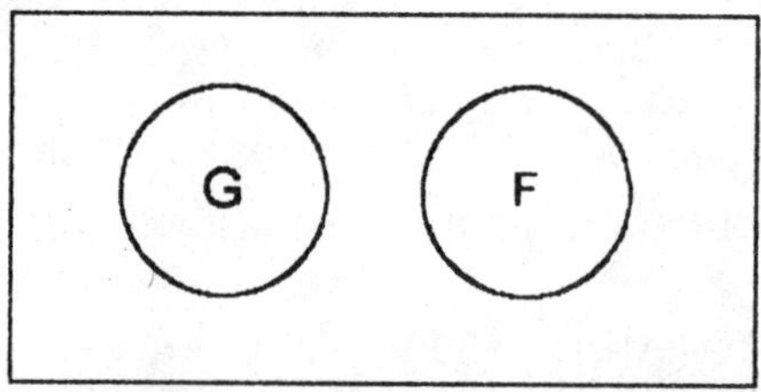

e) Let event L = the event that the majority of the committee members vote for employment, i.e. two or three vote for employment.
Thus, $L = \{E_1, E_2, E_3, E_5\}$. $P(L) = P(E_1) + P(E_2) + P(E_3) + P(E_5)$. Thus $P(L) = .20 + .14 + .12 + .08 = .54.$
Since this is higher than P(A), P(B), and P(C), the job applicant has a better chance of being employed by going before the committee.

PROBLEM 3

Harry owns shares of stock in both Bidwell Valve Company and Mini Car Motors, Inc. Harry has recorded the performance of these shares on each day for a 200 day period as to whether the price has risen, fallen or remained unchanged. Harry's data is as follows:

Event	Bidwell	Mini Car	# of Days
E_1	Rise	Rise	40
E_2	Rise	Unchanged	14
E_3	Rise	Fall	20
E_4	Unchanged	Rise	18
E_5	Unchanged	Unchanged	12
E_6	Unchanged	Fall	14
E_7	Fall	Rise	28
E_8	Fall	Unchanged	16
E_9	Fall	Fall	38

a) Using this data and the relative frequency approach, find the following probabilities:
   (1) a rise in the price of Bidwell stock
   (2) a fall in the price of Mini Car stock
   (3) a rise in Bidwell <u>and</u> a fall in Mini Car stock
   (4) a rise in Bidwell <u>or</u> a fall in Mini Car stock (Use the addition law.)

b) Suppose Harry is told that Bidwell stock has risen. What is the probability that Mini Car stock has fallen?

c) Suppose Harry is told that Mini Car stock has fallen. What is the probability that Bidwell stock has risen?

d) Are the events "a rise in Bidwell stock" and "a fall in Mini Car stock" independent?

SOLUTION 3

Let: event A = "rise in Bidwell stock" = $\{E_1, E_2, E_3\}$
event B = "fall in Mini Car stock" = $\{E_3, E_6, E_9\}$

Using the relative frequency approach,

$$P(E_1) = 40/200 = .20$$
$$P(E_2) = 14/200 = .07$$
$$P(E_3) = 20/200 = .10$$
$$P(E_4) = 18/200 = .09$$
$$P(E_5) = 12/200 = .06$$
$$P(E_6) = 14/200 = .07$$
$$P(E_7) = 28/200 = .14$$
$$P(E_8) = 16/200 = .08$$
$$P(E_9) = 38/200 = .19$$

(1) $P(A) = P(E_1) + P(E_2) + P(E_3) = .20 + .07 + .10 = .37$
(2) $P(B) = P(E_3) + P(E_6) + P(E_9) = .10 + .07 + .19 = .36$
(3) $P(A \cap B) = P(E_3) = .10$
(4) $P(A \cup B) = P(A) + P(B) - P(A \cap B) = .37 + .36 - .10 = .63$

b) $P(B|A) = P(A \cup B)/P(A) = .10/.37 = .27$.

c) $P(A|B) = P(A \cup B)/P(B) = .10/.36 = .28$.

d) There are several ways to check if events A and B are independent. One method is to see if $P(A|B) = P(A)$. Since $P(A|B) = .28$ and $P(A) = .37$, these events are <u>dependent</u>.

PROBLEM 4

The Board of Directors of Bidwell Valve Company have made the following estimates for the upcoming year's annual earnings:

P(earnings lower than this year) = .30
P(earnings about the same as this year) = .50
P(earnings higher than this year) = .20

After talking with union leaders, the personnel department has drawn the following conclusions:

P(Union will request wage increase¦lower earnings next year) = .25
P(Union will request wage increase¦same earnings next year) = .40
P(Union will request wage increase¦higher earnings next year) = .90

a) Are the probabilities developed by the directors and personnel manager based on the classical, relative frequency, or subjective method?

b) Calculate the following probabilities:
(1) The company earns the same as this year and the union requests a wage increase
(2) The company has higher earnings next year and the union does not request a wage increase
(3) The union requests a wage increase

SOLUTION 4

a) Since the predicted outcomes of earnings and wage increase requests have unequal probabilities, they are not based on the classical method. Similarly, since the outcomes arise from a unique situation, the relative frequency method is not applicable. Instead, the probabilities stated reflect the judgment of the individuals involved, and hence are developed by the subjective method.

b) Define the following events: L = lower earnings next year; S = about the same earnings next year; H = higher earnings next year. Further define R = union requests a pay increase next year, so R^c = union does not request a pay increase next year.

(1) This is $P(S \cap R)$. Now, $P(S) = .50$ and $P(R|S) = .40$.
Thus, $P(S \cap R) = P(S)P(R|S) = (.50)(.40) = .20$

(2) This is $P(H \cap R^c)$. Now, $P(H) = .20$ and $P(R^c|H) = 1 - P(R|H) = .10$
Thus, $P(H \cap R^c) = P(H)P(R^c|H) = (.20)(.10) = .02$.

(3) This is P(R). $P(R) = P(R|H)P(H) + P(R|S)P(S) + P(R|L)P(L) =$
$(.25)(.30) + (.40)(.50) + (.90)(..20) = .455$

PROBLEM 5

An accounting firm has noticed that of the companies it audits, 85% show no inventory shortages, 10% show small inventory shortages and 5% show large inventory shortages. The firm has devised a new accounting test for which it believes the following probabilities hold:

P(company will pass test|no shortage) = .90
P(company will pass test|small shortage) = .50
P(company will pass test|large shortage) = .20

a) If a company being audited fails this test, what is the probability of a large or small inventory shortage?

b) If a company being audited passes this test, what is the probability of no inventory shortage?

SOLUTION 5

a) Let: A_1 = no inventory shortage
A_2 = small inventory shortage
A_3 = large inventory shortage

P = company passes test
F = company fails test

Using the tabular approach and $P(F|A_i) = 1 - P(P|A_i)$:

Event	Prior Probabilities $P(A_i)$	x	Conditional Probabilities $P(F|A_i)$	=	Joint Probabilities $P(A_i \cap F)$	Posterior Probabilities $P(A_i|F)$
A_1	.85		.10		.085	.486 (=.085/.175)
A_2	.10		.50		.050	.286
A_3	.05		.80		.040	.229
					P(F) = .175	

The probability of a large or small shortage = .286 + .229 = .515.

b)

Event	Prior Probabilities $P(A_i)$	x	Conditional Probabilities $P(P|A_i)$	=	Joint Probabilities $P(A_i \cap P)$	Posterior Probabilities $P(A_i|P)$
A_1	.85		.90		.765	.927
A_2	.10		.50		.050	.061
A_3	.05		.20		.010	.012
					P(P) = .825	

The solution is $P(A_1|P)$ = .927. Note that P(P) + P(F) = 1.

PROBLEM 6

An investment advisor recommends the purchase of shares in Probaballisitics, Inc. He has made the following predictions:

P(Stock goes up 20%|Rise in GNP) = .6
P(Stock goes up 20%|Level GNP) = .5
P(Stock goes up 20%|Fall in GNP) = .4

An economist has predicted that the probability of a rise in the GNP is 30%, whereas the probability of a fall in the GNP is 40%.

a) What is the probability that the stock will go up 20%?

b) We have been informed that the stock has gone up 20%. What is the probability of a rise or fall in the GNP?

SOLUTION 6

a) Since P(Rise in GNP) = .3 and P(Fall in GNP = .4), then the P(Level GNP) = 1 - .3 - .4 = .3.

Now, P(Stock goes up by 20%)
= P(Stock goes up by 20%|Rise in GNP) x P(Rise in GNP)
+ P(Stock goes up by 20%|Level GNP) x P(Level GNP)
+ P(Stock goes up by 20%|Fall in GNP) x P(Fall in GNP)
= (.6)(.3) + (.5)(.3) + (.4)(.4)
= .49

b) From Bayes' Law,
P(Rise in GNP|Stock goes up by 20%)
= P(Stock goes up by 20%|Rise in GNP)P(Rise in GNP)/P(Stock goes up 20%)
= (.6)(.3)/.49
= .367

P(Fall in GNP|Stock goes up by 20%)
= P(Stock goes up by 20%|Fall in GNP)P(Fall in GNP)/P(Stock goes up 20%)
= (.4)(.4)/.49
= .327

Thus, the probability of a rise or fall in the GNP is .367 + .327 = .694.

ANSWERED PROBLEMS

PROBLEM 7

Providence Land Development Company has just hired four new salespersons. After six months on the job each salesperson will be rated as either poor, average or excellent and will be compensated accordingly. Assume that Providence is concerned with the number of salespersons in each category.

a) List the outcomes of this experiment.

b) Let the event A = at least two salespersons are rated average and let event B = exactly one salesperson is rated poor. List the outcomes in $A \cap B$.

c) Let the event C = exactly two salespersons are rated excellent. List the outcomes in $D = B \cap C$.

d) Are events D and A mutually exclusive?

e) Are events D and A collectively exhaustive?

f) Let the event E = at most one salesperson is rated average. Are events A and E mutually exclusive and collectively exhaustive?

PROBLEM 8

Global Airlines operates two types of jet planes: jumbo and ordinary. On jumbo jets, 25% of the passengers are on business while on ordinary jets 30% of the passengers are on business. Of Global's airfleet, 40% of its capacity is provided on jumbo jets.

a) What is the probability a randomly chosen business customer flying with Global is on a jumbo jet?

b) What is the probability a randomly chosen nonbusiness customer flying with Global is on an ordinary jet?

PROBLEM 9

The following probability model describes the number of snow storms for Washington, D. C. for a given year:

# of Snowstorms	0	1	2	3	4	5	6
Probability	.25	.33	.24	.11	.04	.02	.01

The probability of 7 or more snowstorms in a year is virtually 0.

a) What is the probability of more than 2 but less than 5 snowstorms?

b) Given this a particularly cold year (in which 2 snowstorms have already been observed), what is the conditional probability that 4 or more snowstorms will be observed?

c) If at the beginning of winter there is a snowfall, what is the probability of at least one more snowstorm before winter is over?

PROBLEM 10

Safety Insurance Company has compiled the following statistics. For any one year period:

P(accident|male driver under 25) = .22
P(accident|male driver over 25) = .15
P(accident|female driver under 25) = .16
P(accident|female driver over 25) = .14

The percentage of Safety's policyholders in each category are:

Male Under 25	.20%
Male Over 25	.40%
Female Under 25	.10%
Female Over 25	.30%

a) What is the probability that a randomly selected policyholder will have an accident within the next year?

b) Given that a driver has an accident, what is the probability that the driver is a male over 25?

c) Given that a driver has no accident, what is the probability the driver is a female?

d) Does knowing the fact that a driver has had no accidents give us a great deal of information regarding the driver's sex?

PROBLEM 11

Consider the Bidwell Valve Company of problem 4. The directors believe that the probability of strong first quarter earnings is dependent on the full year's earnings. They estimate:

P(Strong first quarter earnings | lower earnings next year) = .10
P(Strong first quarter earnings | same earnings next year) = .30
P(Strong first quarter earnings | higher earnings next year) = .70

a) Using this data together with data in problem 4, find the probabilities of the company earnings being higher, lower, and the same as this year's given the company has strong first quarter earnings.

b) Using these new posterior probabilities, compute the probability that the union requests a wage increase given the company has a strong first quarter.

c) Compute the probability that the union requests a wage increase given the company does not have a strong first quarter.

PROBLEM 12

Mini Car Motors offers its luxury car in three colors: gold, silver and blue. The vice president of advertising is interested in the order of popularity of the color choices by customers during the first month of sales.

a) How many sample points are there in this experiment?

b) If the event A = gold is the most popular color, list the outcome(s) in event A.

c) If the event B = blue is the least popular color, list the outcome(s) in $A \cap B$.

d) List the outcome(s) in $A \cap B^c$.

PROBLEM 13

Sales of the first 500 luxury Mini Cars were as follows: 250 gold, 150 silver, and 100 blue. Assume the relative frequency method is used to assign probabilities for color choice and the color of each car sold is independent of that of any other car sold.

a) What is the probability that the next two cars sold will both be gold?

b) What is the probability that neither of the next two cars sold will be silver?

c) What is the probability that of the next two cars sold, one will be silver and the other will be blue?

PROBLEM 14

The sales manager for Widco Distributing Company has estimated demand for a new combination microwave oven and color television will be between 0 and 2 units per day. He believes the probability of selling no units is .65, of one unit is .25, and two units is .10. The company is interested in sales over a two day period.

a) What is the probability of selling no units during the two days?

b) What is the probability of selling one unit during the two days?

c) What is the probability of selling three or more units during the two days?

d) What is the probability of selling two units during the two days?

PROBLEM 15

Super Cola sales breakdown as 80% regular soda and 20% diet soda. While 60% of the regular soda is purchased by men, only 30% of the diet soda is. If a woman purchases Super Cola, what is the probability that it is a diet soda?

PROBLEM 16

Stanton Marketing conducted a taste preference test among married and single persons for the Super Cola Company. Among single people, 11% of the sample questioned preferred Super Cola over all other brands. For married people the data was:

	Wife Prefers	Wife Does Not Prefer
Husband Prefers	.08	.06
Husband Does Not Prefer	.07	.79

a) Using this study as a basis for a probability measure, find the probability that if two single people are questioned: (1) they both prefer Super Cola, (2) they both do not prefer Super Cola, and (3) one prefers Super Cola and the other does not

b) What is the probability that a married female prefers Super Cola?

c) Given that a husband prefers Super Cola, what is the probability his wife will prefer Super Cola?

d) Is the event "husband prefers" independent of the event "wife prefers"?

e) Do married people prefer Super Cola more than single people?

PROBLEM 17

Higbee Manufacturing Corp. has recently received 5 cases of a certain part from one of its suppliers. While the defect rate for the parts is normally 5%, the supplier has just notified Higbee that one of the cases shipped to them has been made on a misaligned machine that has a defect rate of 97%. Learning this, the plant manager selects a case at random and tests a part.

a) What is the probability that the part tested is defective?

b) Suppose the part is defective, what is the probability that this is from the case made on the misaligned machine?

c) Given that the first part was defective, suppose a second part from the case is tested and found to be good. What is the probability that the two parts are from the defective case?

d) Would you obtain the same posterior probabilities as in part (c) if the first part was not found to be defective but the second part was?

e) Suppose the plant manager was 80% certain, based on other evidence, this case was the one made on the misaligned machine. How would your answer to part (b) change?

TRUE/FALSE

18. Two events that are mutually exclusive cannot be independent.

19. $P(A|B) = P(B|A)$ for all events A and B.

20. $P(A|B) = 1 - P(B|A)$ for all events A and B.

21. $P(A|B) = 1 - P(A^c|B)$ for events A and B.

22. One would use the classical method to assign probabilities for customers' preference of automobile models.

23. The intersection of A and A^c is the entire sample space.

24. If A and B are mutually exclusive, $P(A) + P(B)$ must equal 1.

25. If A and B are mutually exclusive, $P(A \cap B) = 0$.

26. Using Bayes' Theorem, if A_1 and A_2 are prior events, then $P(A_1 \cap A_2) = 0$.

27. $P(A|B) + P(A|B^c) = 1$ for all A and B.

28. If A and B are independent, $P(A \cap B) = 0$.

29. A joint probability can have a value greater than 1.

30. The probability of at least one head in two flips of a coin is 0.75.

31. Two events that are dependent cannot be mutually exclusive.

32. Posterior probabilities are conditional probabilities.

Chapter 3
Probability Distributions

KEY CONCEPTS

CONCEPT	ILLUSTRATED PROBLEMS	ANSWERED PROBLEMS
Continuous and Discrete Random Variables	1-3	9,10
Expected Value and Variance	3	9,10,15
Discrete Distributions		
Relative Frequency	3	15
Binomial	4	11,16
Poisson	6	17,21
Continuous Distributions		
Uniform	5	13,18
Normal	7	12,14,19,20
Exponential	6,8	21

REVIEW

1. The result of an experiment can be defined so that each possible outcome generates one numerical value. The result of such an experiment is called a random variable.

2. A random variable which may only take on a countable number of values is called a discrete random variable.

3. Associated with each discrete random variable is a probability distribution, f(x), defining the probability of the random variable being equal to the specific value x.

4. The expected value or mean of a random variable (designated μ) is a weighted average of all possible values of the variable, with the weights being the probabilities. Hence, for discrete random variables, $\mu = \Sigma x f(x)$. The expected value can be interpreted as the long run average value for the experiment.

5. The variance, (denoted σ^2) of a random variable is a measure of dispersion of the variable about its mean. The formula used to calculate the variance for discrete random variables is:

$$\sigma^2 = \Sigma(x-\mu)^2 f(x)$$

6. The standard deviation of a variable is the square root of its variance.

7. A Bernoulli Process is a sequence of independent trials with two possible outcomes (success, x = 1 and failure, x = 0) and the probability of success (denoted by p) remains constant.

8. The binomial distribution is the probability distribution of the number of successes, x, in n independent Bernoulli trials. This distribution's mean $\mu = np$ and its variance $\sigma^2 = np(1-p)$. The probability distribution for the binomial distribution of x successes in n trials is:

$$f(x) = \frac{n!}{x!(n-x)!} p^x (1-p)^{n-x}$$

Appendix A provides a table of binomial probabilities for various values of n and p for $p \leq .50$. If p is greater than .50, then one can use the table by focusing on the number of failures as follows: the probability of a single failure is 1-p (a number less than .50), and if x denotes the number of successes, then the number of failures is (n-x).

9. The Poisson probability function is often used for describing the number of occurrences of an event over a specified interval of time. If the average number of events in the specified time interval is denoted by λ, then its mean, $\mu = \lambda$, and variance $\sigma^2 = \lambda$. The Poisson distribution for x events occurring in the time interval is given by:

$$f(x) = \frac{\lambda^x e^{-\lambda}}{x!}$$

Selected Poisson probabilities are given in Appendix B while values for $e^{-\lambda}$ are tabulated in Appendix D.

10. A process can be defined by the Poisson distribution if the following three assumptions hold:
    1) In any short interval there can be at most one occurrence of the event;
    2) The probability of an occurrence of the event is the same for any two intervals of equal length;
    3) The occurrence or nonoccurrence of the event in any interval is independent of the occurrence or nonoccurrence of the event in any other interval.

11. A random variable which, at least theoretically, may take on any possible value within an interval (e.g. time, distance, weight, etc.) is called a continuous random variable.

12. Probabilities for continuous random variables are defined over intervals by a probability density function, f(x) with the following properties:
    (1) $f(x) \geq 0$ for all x;
    (2) The total area under the curve f(x) is equal to 1;
    (3) The probability that the random variable takes on a value between two values a and b, is equal to the area under the curve, f(x), between the points a and b.

13. For continuous random variables, (3) implies the probability of any specific value is equal to 0. This is not to say that such events are impossible, however, the probability is defined this way so as to be mathematically consistent.

14. If a random variable is restricted to be within some interval and the probability density function is constant over the interval, (a,b) the continuous random variable is said to have a uniform distribution between a and b. Its density function is given by:

$$f(x) = 1/(b-a) \quad \text{for } a \leq x \leq b, \text{ and } = 0 \text{ outside this interval.}$$

15. The normal distribution is perhaps the most widely used distribution for describing a continuous random variable. Its probability density function is a bell shaped curve which is symmetric about the mean and defined over all values of x.

16. A continuous random variable which has a normal distribution with a mean of 0 and a standard deviation of 1 is said to have a standard normal distribution. Because of the complexity of the density function for the normal distribution, random variables with a normal distribution are transformed to a standard normal distribution, for which tables are readily available (Appendix C). For a normal random variable with mean = μ and standard deviation = σ, a value x is transformed to its standard normal value, z, by: $z = (x - \mu)/\sigma$.

17. A continuous probability distribution frequently used for computing the probability of the time to complete a task is the exponential distribution. If the average time to complete a task is denote by m, then the probability density function for the amount of time, x, to complete the task is given by:

$$f(x) = (1/\mu)e^{-(x/\mu)} \quad \text{for } x \geq 0 \text{ and } \mu > 0.$$

From this distribution, the probability a task is completed within a specified time, x_0, is:

$$P(x < x_0) = 1 - e^{-(x_0/\mu)}$$

18. If customers arrive according to a Poisson distribution with a mean of λ customers, then the interarrival times of customers follows an exponential distribution with $\mu = 1/\lambda$.

ILLUSTRATED PROBLEMS

PROBLEM 1

Dollar Department Stores is planning to open a new store on the corner of Main and Vine Streets. It has asked the Stanton Marketing Company to do a market study of randomly selected families within a five mile radius of the store. Among the questions it wishes Stanton to ask each homeowner are: (a) family income; (b) family size; (c) distance from home to the store site; and, (d) whether or not the family owns a dog or a cat.

For each of the four questions, develop a random variable of interest to Dollar Department Stores. Denote which of these are discrete and which are continuous random variables.

SOLUTION 1

Question	Random Variable	Discrete/ Continuous
(a) Family income	x = Annual dollar gross income the family reported on their tax return	Discrete
(b) Family size	x = Number of dependents in the family reported on their tax return	Discrete
(c) Distance from home to store	x = The distance in miles from home to the store site	Continuous*
(d) Dog/Cat	x = 1 if own no pet; = 2 if own dog(s) only; = 3 if own cat(s) only; = 4 if own dog(s) and cat(s)	Discrete

* This is a continuous random variable even though it will appear to be discrete due to the limits in accuracy of measurement.

PROBLEM 2

Stanton Marketing reported back to Dollar Department Stores the following information. Out of 400 families surveyed, 260 owned no pet, 120 owned dogs and 50 owned cats.

a) On the basis of this information, find the probability distribution for the random variable x, defined in (d) in problem 1.

b) Dollar is considering opening a pet department if the expected number of families owning pets shopping at its store exceeds 4,000. If Dollar expects to serve 12,000 families, should it open a pet department?

SOLUTION 2

Since 260 owned no pets, 140 owned pets. Since 120 owned dogs and 50 owned cats (total = 170), then 30 must own both dogs and cats.

a) Since 120 owned dogs and 30 owned dogs and cats, 120 - 30 = 90 own dogs only. Similarly, 50 - 30 = 20 own cats only. Using the relative frequency method to calculate f(x):

$$f(1) = 260/400 = .65 \qquad f(3) = 20/400 = .05$$
$$f(2) = 90/400 = .225 \qquad f(4) = 30/400 = .075$$

b) The probability of owning a pet = 1 - the probability of not owning a pet = 1 - f(1) = 1 - .65 = .35. Multiply this probability by the total number of families Dollar expects to serve to obtain the expected number of families owning pets = (.35)(12,000) = 4,200. Since this is greater than 4,000, Dollar should open a pet department.

PROBLEM 3

The salespeople at Gold Key Realty sell up to 9 houses per month. the probability distribution of a salesperson selling x houses in a month is as follows:

Sales (x)	0	1	2	3	4	5	6	7	8	9
Probability f(x)	.05	.10	.15	.20	.15	.10	.10	.05	.05	.05

a) What is the mean number of houses sold by a salesperson per month?

b) What is the standard deviation for the number of houses sold per month by a salesperson?

c) Any salesperson selling more houses than the amount equal to the mean plus two standard deviations receives a bonus. How many houses per month must a salesperson sell to receive a bonus?

SOLUTION 3

a) The mean, $\mu = \Sigma xf(x) = (0)(.05) + (1)(.10) + (2)(.15) + (3)(.20) + (4)(.15) + (5)(.10) + (6)(.10) + (7)(.05) + (8)(.05) + (9)(.05) = 3.9.$

b) The variance, $\sigma^2 = \Sigma(x - \mu)^2 f(x) = (0 - 3.9)^2 (.05) + (1 - 3.9)^2 (.10) + (2 - 3.9)^2 (.15) + (3 - 3.9)^2 (.20) + (4 - 3.9)^2 (.15) + (5 - 3.9)^2 (.10) + (6 - 3.9)^2 (.10) + (7 - 3.9)^2 (.05) + (8 - 3.9)^2 (.05) + (9 - 3.9)^2 (.05) = 5.49$. Since σ is the square root of σ^2, $\sigma = 2.34$.

c) The number of houses a salesperson must sell to be two standard deviations from the mean is $\mu + 2\sigma = 3.9 + (2)(2.34) = 8.58$ or 9 houses.

PROBLEM 4

Ralph's Gas Station is running a giveaway promotion. With every fillup of gasoline, Ralph gives out a lottery ticket which has a 25% chance of being a winning ticket. Customer who collect four winning lottery tickets are eligible for the "BIG SPIN" for large payoffs.

What is the probability of qualifying for the big spin if a customer fills up: (a) 3 times; (b) 4 times; (c) 7 times?

SOLUTION 4

a) If a customer fills up only three times there is no possibility of 4 winning lottery tickets. Hence the probability is 0.

b) If a customer fills up 4 times, he must obtain 4 winning tickets in 4 tries. From the binomial table, $n = 4$, $x = 4$, $p = .25$, this probability is .0039.

c) If a customer fills up $n = 7$ times, he will qualify for the big spin if he has $x = 4$, $x = 5$, $x = 6$, or $x = 7$ winning tickets. From the tables with $p = .25$ this is $= (.0577) + (.0115) + (.0013) + (.0000) = .0705$.

PROBLEM 5

Suppose a random variable x has a continuous uniform distribution with values ranging from 5 to 15.

a) What is the probability that x has a value between 8 and 10?

b) What is the probability that the value for x is less than 7 or greater than 12?

c) What is the probability that x has a value less than 20?

d) What is the probability that x equals 11?

SOLUTION 5

Since x has a uniform distribution between 5 and 15,

$$f(x) = 1/10 \text{ for } 5 \leq x \leq 15$$

$$= 0 \text{ elsewhere.}$$

a) To find the probability x has a value between 8 and 10, multiply the interval width (2) by f(x). This equals (2)(.1) = .2.

b) The event "7 or less" is the interval between 5 and 7 = 2, and "greater than 12" is between 12 and 15 = 3. The total interval width of the event is 3+2 = 5. Hence its probability is 5(.1) = .50

c) Since x can only be 15 or less, the probability $x \leq 20$ is 1.

d) The probability that x exactly equals 11 is 0 by definition.

PROBLEM 6

Telephone calls arrive at the Global Airline reservation office Lemonville according to a Poisson distribution with a mean of 1.2 calls per minute.

a) What is the probability of receiving exactly one call during a one minute interval?

b) What is the probability of receiving at most 2 calls during a one minute interval?

c) What is the probability of receiving at least two calls during a one minute interval?

d) What is the probability of receiving exactly 4 calls during a five minute interval?

e) What is the probability that at most 2 minutes elapse between one call and the next?

SOLUTION 6

a) In this problem λ = 1.2/minute. $f(1) = \dfrac{1.2^1 e^{-1.2}}{1!} = (1.2)(.3012)/1 = 36.$

b) The probability of receiving at most two calls is f(0) + f(1) + f(2).

$$f(0) = \frac{(1.2)^0 e^{-1.2}}{0!} = .30 \qquad f(2) = \frac{(1.2)^2 e^{-1.2}}{2!} = \frac{(1.44)(.3012)}{2} = .22$$

Hence the probability is .30 + .36 + .22 = .88.

c) The probability of receiving at least two calls is 1 - the probability of receiving at most one call = 1 - f(0) - f(1) = 1 - .30 - .36 = .34.

d) First calculate λ for a 5-minute interval. This is simply 5(1.2) = 6. Hence,

$$f(4) = \frac{6^4 e^{-6}}{4!} = \frac{(1296)(.0025)}{24} = .135.$$

e) To find the probability that at most two minutes elapse between two calls, use the exponential distribution with $\mu = \lambda = 1.2$.

$$P(x \leq 2) = 1 - e^{(-1.2)(2)} = 1 - e^{-2.4} = 1 - .0907 = .9093.$$

PROBLEM 7

The time at which the mailman delivers the mail to Ace Bike Shop follows a normal distribution with mean 2:00 PM and standard deviation of 15 minutes.

a) What is the probability the mail will arrive after 2:30pm?

b) What is the probability the mail will arrive before 1:36pm?

c) What is the probability the mail will arrive between 1:48pm and 2:09pm?

SOLUTION 7

The mail delivery time follows a normal distribution with mean μ = 2:00pm and σ = 15 minutes. To transform any time x to a standard normal random variable z, $z = (x - \mu)/\sigma$.

a) The probability that the mail arrives after 2:30 is the probability that z is greater than (2:30 - 2:00)/15 or the $P(z > 2)$. See figure below. From Appendix C, $P(0 < z < 2) = .4772$. Hence, $P(z > 2) = .5000 - .4772 = .0228$.

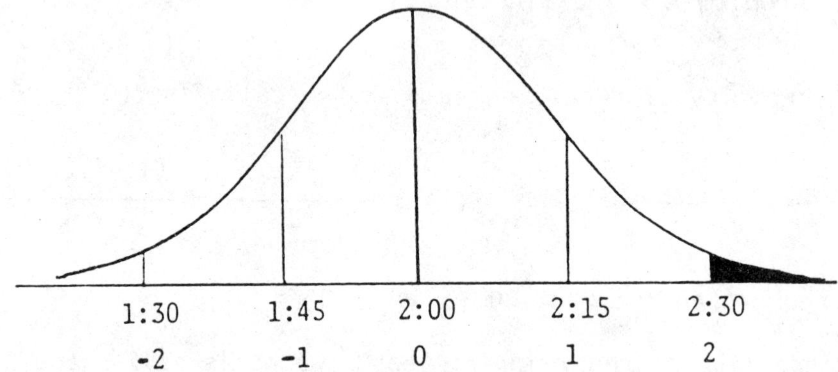

b) The probability the mail will arrive before 1:36pm is equivalent to the P(z < (1:36 - 2:00)/15) = P(z < 24/15) = $P(z < -1.6)$ = .5000 - P(z is between -1.6 and 0) = .5000 - .4452 = . 0548.

c) The probability that the mail arrives between 1:48pm and 2:09pm is the same as the sum of the probabilities between 1:48pm and 2:00pm and between 2:00pm and 2:09pm. 1:48 has a z-value of (1:48 - 2:00)/15 = -0.80 and 2:09 has a z-value of (2:09 - 2:00)/15 = 0.60. From the table these two areas sum to .2257 + .2881 = .5138.

PROBLEM 8

A light bulb manufacturer claims his light bulbs will last 500 hours on the average. The lifetime of a light bulb is assumed to follow an exponential distribution.

a) What is the probability that the light bulb will have to replaced within 500 hours?

b) What is the probability that the light bulb will last more than 1000 hours?

c) What is the probability that the light bulb will last between 200 and 800 hours?

SOLUTION 8

a) As the average life of a light bulb is 500, using the exponential distribution with m = 500, gives

$$P(x \leq 500) = 1 - e^{-(500/500)} = 1 - e^{-1} = 1 - .368 = .632.$$

b) $P(x > 1000) = e^{-(1000/500)} = e^{-2} = .135.$

c) $P(200 \leq x \leq 800) = P(x > 200) - P(x > 800)$

$$= e^{-(200/500)} - e^{-(800/500)} =$$

$$= e^{-.4} - e^{-1.6} = .670 - .202 = .468.$$

ANSWERED PROBLEMS

PROBLEM 9

Ace Mopeds sells mopeds which on which it gives a one month warranty. Over a one year period the following data was compiled.

Month	Number Sold	Number Returned For Warranty Service	Month	Number Sold	Number Returned For Warranty Service
Jan	4	1	Jul	20	4
Feb	6	2	Aug	20	4
Mar	3	0	Sep	20	4
Apr	20	1	Oct	16	3
May	10	2	Nov	16	3
Jun	16	4	Dec	10	3

a) Based on this data determine the probability distribution for: (1) the number of mopeds sold in a month; (2) the number of mopeds returned for warranty in a given month; (3) the percentage of mopeds returned for warranty in a given month.

b) Which of these distributions are for discrete and which are for continuous random variables?

c) Which distribution would be of concern to (1) the quality control engineer at the moped factory; (2) the sales department at Ace; and (3) the service department at Ace?

d) What is the probability that the percentage of Mopeds returned for service in a randomly selected month is between 10% and 21%?

e) What is the probability that the number of mopeds returned for service in a randomly selected month is greater than 1 and less than 4?

f) What is the expected number of mopeds Ace sells in a month?

g) What is the expected number of mopeds returned for service in a month?

h) What is the expected percentage of mopeds returned for service in a month?

i) Is the answer to part (h) equal to the answer in part (g) divided by the answer to part (f)?

PROBLEM 10

Two headache remedies, Relief and Comfort are waging an advertising campaign. Each claims it eliminates a headache faster. The data compiled by an independent testing agency is as follows:

Time (in minutes) after taking remedy	Percentage of Headaches Cured at That Time Using Relief	Comfort
5	.60	0
10	0	.10
15	0	.75
20	0	.15
25	0	0
30	.40	0

a) What are the means and variances of the time until headache cure (1) using Relief; (2) using Comfort?

b) Which remedy has the maximum probability of relieving a headache within 10 minutes?

c) Which remedy has the maximum probability of relieving a headache within 20 minutes?

PROBLEM 11

Sandy's Pet Center grooms large and small dogs. It takes Sandy 40 minutes to groom a small dog and 70 minutes to groom a large dog. Large dogs account for 20% of Sandy's business. Sandy has 5 appointments on August 15.

a) What is the probability that all 5 dogs are small?

b) What is the probability that two of the dogs are large?

c) What is the expected amount of time to finish all five dogs? (Hint: Find the expected number of small and large dogs and multiply by the time required for grooming.)

PROBLEM 12

The township of Middleton sets the speed limit on its roads by conducting a traffic study and determining the speed (to the nearest 5 miles per hour) at which 80% of the drivers travel at or below. A study was done on Brown's Dock Road which indicated that driver's speeds follow a normal distribution with a mean of 36.25 miles per hour and a variance of 6.25.

a) What should the speed limit be?

b) What percent of the drivers travel below that speed?

PROBLEM 13

The Harbour Island Ferry leaves on the hour and at 15 minute intervals. The time, x, it takes John to drive from his house to the ferry has a uniform distribution with x between 10 and 20 minutes. One morning John leaves his house at precisely 8:00am.

a) What is the probability John will wait less than 5 minutes for the ferry?

b) What is the probability John will wait less than 10 minutes for the ferry?

c) What is the probability John will wait less than 15 minutes for the ferry?

d) What is the probability John will not have to wait for the ferry?

e) Suppose John leaves at 8:05am. What is the probability John will wait (1) less than 5 minutes for the ferry; (2) less than 10 minutes for the ferry?

f) Suppose John leaves at 8:10am. What is the probability John will wait (1) less than 5 minutes for the ferry; (2) less than 10 minutes for the ferry?

g) What appears to be the best time for John to leave home if he wishes to maximize the probability of waiting less than 10 minutes for the ferry?

PROBLEM 14

Dollar Department Stores has compiled the following data concerning its daily sales. The sales for each day of the week are normally distributed with the following parameters:

Day	Mean (μ)	Standard Deviation (σ)
Monday	$120,000	$20,000
Tuesday	$100,000	$25,000
Wednesday	$100,000	$10,000
Thursday	$120,000	$40,000
Friday	$140,000	$20,000
Saturday	$160,000	$50,000

For each day of the week, find the probability that the store sales are between $110,000 and $150,000.

PROBLEM 15

June's Specialty Shop sells designer original dresses. On 10% of her dresses, June makes a profit of $10, on 20% of her dresses she makes a profit of $20, on 30 of her dresses she makes a profit of $30, and on 40% of her dresses she makes a profit of $40.

a) What is the expected profit June earns on the sale of a dress?

b) On a given day, the probability of June having no customers is .05, of one customer is .10, of two customers is .20, of three customers is .35, of four customers is .20, and of five customers is .10. June's daily operating cost is $0 per day. Using your answer to (a), find the expected net profit June earns per day. (Hint: To find the expected daily gross profit, multiply the expected profit per dress by the expected number of customers per day.)

c) June is considering moving to a larger store. She estimates that doing so will double the expected number of customers. If the larger store will increase her operating costs to $100 per day, should she make the move?

PROBLEM 16

Chez Paul is an exclusive French restaurant that seats only 10 couples for dinner. Paul is famous for his "truffle salad for two" which must be prepared one day in advance. The probability of any couple ordering the salad is .4 and each couple orders independently of other couples.

a) What is the expected number of "truffle salads for two" that Paul serves per dinner? What is the variance?

b) What is the probability that on a given evening, at most three couples want a "truffle salad for two"?

c) How many salads should Paul prepare if he wants the probability of not having enough salads for all customers who desire one to be no greater than .10?

d) If there is a 70% chance a couple will order coffee after dinner, what is the probability that on a given evening exactly eight out of ten couples will order coffee?

PROBLEM 17

The number of customers at Winkies Donuts between 8:00am and 9:00am is believed to follow a Poisson distribution with a mean of 2 per minute.

a) During a randomly selected one minute interval during this time period, what is the probability of 6 customers arriving to Winkies?

b) What is the probability that at least 2 minutes elapse between arrivals?

PROBLEM 18

Delicious Candy markets a two pound box of assorted chocolates. Due to natural production variation, the actual weight of the chocolate has a continuous uniform distribution ranging from 31.8 to 32.6 ounces.

a) Define a probability density function for the weight of the box of chocolate.

b) What is the probability that a box weighs (1) exactly 32 ounces; (2) more than 32.3 ounces; (3) less than 31.8 ounces?

c) The government requires that at least 60% of all products sold weigh at least as much as the stated weight. Is Delicious violating government regulations?

PROBLEM 19

Mark Investment Service is currently recommending the purchase of shares of Dollar Department Stores selling at \$18 per share. Mark estimates that in one year the price of the shares will be at x, where x is a random variable which is approximately normally distributed with mean of \$20 and a standard deviation of \$2.

a) What is the probability that in a year the shares will be selling for (1) exactly \$20; (2) more than \$20; (3) less than \$20; (4) less than \$18?

b) What is the expected profit per share within a year?

PROBLEM 20

Joe's Record World has two stores. The sales at each store follow a normal distribution. For store 1, μ = \$2,000 and σ = \$200 per day. For store 2, μ = \$1,900 and σ = \$400 per day.

a) Which store has the higher average daily sales?

b) What is the probability that daily sales are greater than \$2,200 for store 1? for store 2?

c) Is there a contradiction between parts (a) and (b)? Explain.

PROBLEM 21

During lunch time, customers arrive at Bob's Drugs according to a Poisson distribution with λ = 4 per minute.

a) During a one minute interval, determine the following probabilities: (1) no arrivals; (2) one arrival; (3) two arrivals; and, (4) three or more arrivals.

b) What is the probability of two arrivals in a two minute period?

c) What is the probability that no more than 30 seconds elapses between customer arrivals?

TRUE/FALSE

22. A probability distribution's variance will always be greater than its mean.

23. If a random variable can take on a countable infinite number of values, one would use a discrete distribution.

24. If one wanted to find the probability of ten customer arrivals in an hour at a service station, one would generally use the Poisson distribution.

25. To use the standard normal distribution, one subtracts the mean from the variable value and divides this result by the variance.

26. The variance of a random variable will always be greater than its standard deviation.

27. An arrival process follows a Poisson distribution with a mean of 5 per hour. The probability of no arrivals in an hour is the same as the probability of the interarrival time being at least an hour when calculated using an exponential distribution with $\mu = 5$.

28. The probability of exactly 3 heads in 6 tosses of a fair coin is 1/2.

29. Suppose the weight of adult males follows a normal distribution with a mean of 160 lbs. and a standard deviation of 15 lbs. Then the probability that a randomly selected male weighs exactly 160 is .50.

30. If the lifetime of an appliance follows an exponential distribution with a mean of 10 years, the probability it will fail within 10 years is .50.

31. Suppose that the arrival time for the next bus at a bus stop is uniformly distributed between 1 and 25 minutes. The probability that the bus will arrive within the next 5 minutes is 1/6.

32. The binomial distribution is most symmetrical when p equals 0.5.

33. An exponential distribution, like the poisson distribution, can be described by a single parameter.

34. Each of the five probability distributions studied can be classified as always left-skewed, always right-skewed, or never skewed.

35. A Bernoulli process is a sequence of independent trials with two possible outcomes whose probabilities can change between trials.

36. The probability of a continuous variable having any specific value is 0.

Chapter 4
Decision Analysis

KEY CONCEPTS

CONCEPT	ILLUSTRATED PROBLEMS	ANSWERED PROBLEMS
Payoff Tables	1,2,3	6-14
Nonprobabilistic Decision Criteria: Optimistic, Conservative, Minimax Regret Approaches	1,2	6,7,8,10,13
Probabilistic Decision Criteria: Expected Monetary Value, Expected Opportunity Loss	1-4	6-14
Decision Trees	1,3,4	8-14
Expected Value of Perfect Information	1,3	7,8,9,11,12,14
Bayes' Rule: Revising Probabilities	3,4	9,11,12,14
Expected Value of Sample Information	3	9,11,12,14
Efficiency	3	9,11
Sensitivity Analysis	5	9

REVIEW

1. A decision problem is characterized by decision alternatives, states of nature, and resulting payoffs.

2. The decision alternatives are the different possible strategies the decision maker can employ.

3. The states of nature refer to future events, not under the control of the decision maker, which may occur. States of nature should be defined so that they are mutually exclusive and collectively exhaustive.

4. For each decision alternative and state of nature, there is a resulting payoff. These are often represented in matrix form called a payoff table.

5. A decision is said to dominate another decision if the payoffs for every state of nature for one is at least equal to the corresponding payoffs for the other and is greater for at least one state of nature.

6. One way to solve a complex decision problem is by the use of a decision tree. This is a chronological representation of the decision problem.

7. Each decision tree has two types of nodes. Round nodes correspond to the states of nature while square nodes correspond to the decision alternatives. The branches leaving each round node represent the different states of nature while the branches leaving each square node represent the different decision alternatives.

8. At the end of each limb of a decision tree are the payoffs attained from the series of branches making up that limb. To solve the problem one "folds back the tree", working backwards from the ends of the branches towards the root node of the tree.

9. Decision making under certainty occurs when the decision maker knows with certainty which state of nature will occur.

10. If the decision maker does not know with certainty which state of nature will occur, then he is said to be doing decision making under uncertainty.

11. Three commonly used criteria for decision making under uncertainty when probability information regarding the likelihood of the states of nature is unavailable are: (1) the optimistic, (2) the conservative, and (3) the minimax regret approach.

12. The optimistic approach would be used by an optimistic decision maker. The decision with the largest possible payoff is chosen. (If the payoff table was in terms of costs, the decision which had the lowest cost would be chosen.)

13. The conservative approach would be used by a conservative decision maker. For each decision the minimum payoff is listed. Then the decision corresponding to the maximum of these minimum payoffs is selected. Hence, the minimum possible payoff is maximized. (If the payoff was in terms of costs, the maximum costs would be determined for each decision. The decision selected would be the one which had the minimum of these maximum costs.)

14. The minimax regret approach requires the construction of a regret table or an opportunity loss table. This is done by calculating for each state of nature the difference between each payoff and the largest payoff for that state of nature. Then, using this regret table, the maximum regret for each possible decision is listed. The decision chosen is the one corresponding to the minimum of the maximum regrets.

15. If probabilistic information regarding he states of nature is available, one may use the expected value (EV) approach. Here the expected return for each decision is calculated by summing the products of the payoff under each state of nature and the probability of the respective state of nature occurring. The decision yielding the best expected return is chosen.

16. Sensitivity analysis can be used to determine the probability range over which a decision will remain optimal. Such an analysis can provide a better perspective on management's original judgment regarding the state of nature probabilities.

17. Frequently information is available which can improve the probability estimates for the states of nature. The expected value of perfect information (EVPI) is the increase in the expected profit that would result if one knew with certainty which state of nature would occur. This quantity provides an upper bound on the expected value of any sample or survey information. EVPI can be calculated as follows:
    (1) determine the optimal return corresponding to each state of nature;
    (2) compute the expected value of these optimal returns;
    (3) Subtract the EV of the optimal decision from the amount determined in step (2).

18. Knowledge of sample or survey information can be used to revise the probability estimates for the states of nature. Prior to obtaining this information, the probability estimates for the states of nature are called prior probabilities. With knowledge of conditional probabilities for the outcomes or indicators of the sample or survey information, these prior probabilities can be revised by employing Bayes' Theorem. The outcomes of this analysis are called posterior probabilities.

19. Posterior probabilities are calculated as follows:
   (1) For each state of nature, multiply the prior probability by its conditional probability for the indicator -- this gives the joint probabilities for the states and indicator.
   (2) Sum these joint probabilities over all states -- this gives the marginal probability for the indicator.
   (3) For each state, divide its joint probability by the marginal probability for the indicator -- this gives the posterior probability distribution.

20. The expected value of sample information (EVSI) is the additional expected profit possible through knowledge of the sample or survey information. EVSI is calculated as follows:
   (1) determine the optimal decision and its expected return for the possible outcomes of the sample or survey using the posterior probabilities for the states of nature;
   (2) compute the expected value of these optimal returns;
   (3) Subtract the EV of the optimal decision obtained without using the sample information from the amount determined in step (2).

21. Efficiency of sample information is the ratio of EVSI to EVPI. As the EVPI provides an upper bound for the EVSI, efficiency is always a number between 0 and 1.

ILLUSTRATED PROBLEMS

PROBLEM 1

Consider the following problem with three decision alternatives and three states of nature with the following payoff table representing profits:

		States of Nature		
		s_1	s_2	s_3
Decisions	d_1	4	4	-2
	d_2	0	3	-1
	d_3	1	5	-3

a) What is the optimal decision if the decision maker were conservative?

b) What is the optimal decision if the decision maker were optimistic?

c) What is the optimal decision using the minimax regret approach?

d) Use a decision tree to find the optimal decision if $P(s_1) = .20$, $P(s_2) = .50$, $P(s_3) = .30$.

e) Given the probabilities in (d), calculate the EVPI.

SOLUTION 1

a) A conservative decision maker would use the conservative approach. List the minimum payoff for each decision. Choose the decision with the maximum of these minimum payoffs.

Decision	Minimum Payoff	
d_1	-2	
d_2	-1	<==== maximum, choose d_2
d_3	-3	

b) An optimistic decision maker would use the optimisitic approach. All we really need to do is to choose the decision that has the largest single value in the payoff table. This largest value is 5, and hence the optimal decision is d_3.

c) For the minimax regret approach, first compute a regret table by subtracting each payoff in a column from the largest payoff in that column. In this example, in the first column subtract 4, 0, and 1 from 4; in the second column, subtract 4, 3, and 5 from 5; etc.

The resulting regret table is:

	s_1	s_2	s_3
d_1	0	1	1
d_2	4	2	0
d_3	3	0	2

Then, for each decision list the maximum regret. Choose the decision with the minimum of these values:

Decision	Maximum Regret	
d_1	1	⟸ minimum, choose d_1
d_2	4	
d_3	3	

d) The tree diagram looks as follows:

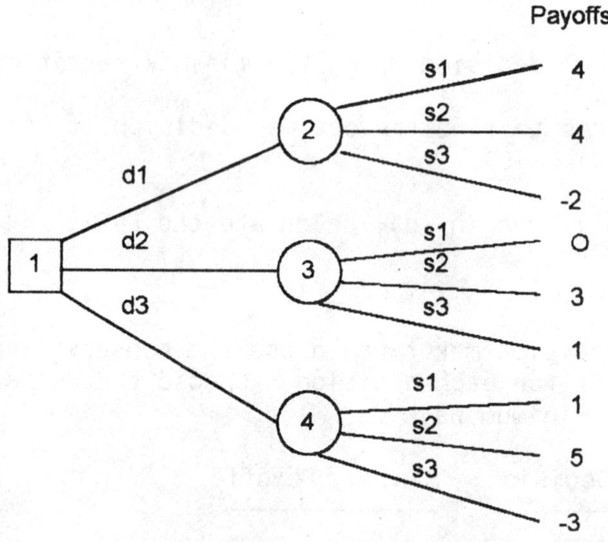

To calculate the expected values at nodes 2, 3, and 4, multiply the payoffs by the corresponding probabilities and then sum. The decision with the maximum expected value of 2.2, d_1, is then chosen.

EV(Node 2) = .20(4) + .50(4) + .30(-2) = 2.2 ⟸ maximum, choose d_1
EV(Node 3) = .20(0) + .50(3) + .30(-1) = 1.2
EV(Node 4) = .20(1) + .50(5) + .30(-3) = 1.8

e) The EVPI is calculated by multiplying the maximum payoff for each state by the corresponding probability, summing these values, and then subtracting the expected value of the optimal decision from this sum. Thus, the EVPI = [.20(4) + .50(5) + .30(-1)] - 2.2 = .8

PROBLEM 2

Jim has been employed at Gold Key Realty at a salary of $2,000 per month during the past year. Because Jim is considered to be a top salesman, the manager of Gold Key is offering him one of three salary plans for the next year: (1) a 25% raise to $2,500 per month; (2) a base salary of $1,000 plus $600 per house sold; or, (3) a straight commission of $1,000 per house sold.

Over the past year, Jim has sold up to 6 homes in a month.

a) Compute the monthly salary payoff table for Jim.

b) For this payoff table find Jim's optimal decision using: (1) the conservative approach, (2) minimax regret approach.

c) Suppose during the past year the following is Jim's distribution of home sales. If one assumes that this a typical distribution for Jim's monthly sales, which salary plan should Jim select?

Home Sales	Number of Months
0	1
1	2
2	1
3	2
4	1
5	3
6	2

SOLUTION 2

a) There are three decision alternatives (salary plans) and seven states of nature (the number of houses sold monthly).

	Number of Homes Sold						
	0	1	2	3	4	5	6
Plan I	2500	2500	2500	2500	2500	2500	2500
Plan II	1000	1600	2200	2800	3400	4000	4600
Plan III	0	1000	2000	3000	4000	5000	6000

b) (1) Conservative Approach

Decision	Minimum Payoff	
Plan I	2500	⟸ choose Plan I
Plan II	1000	
Plan III	0	

(2) Minimax Regret Approach

Construct a regret table by subtracting all numbers in a column from the maximum number in the column:

Regret Table

	Number of Homes Sold						
	0	1	2	3	4	5	6
Plan I	0	0	0	500	1500	2500	3500
Plan II	1500	900	300	200	600	1000	1400
Plan III	2500	1500	500	0	0	0	0

Choose the decision with the minimum of the maximum regrets.

Decision	Maximum Regret	
Plan I	3500	
Plan II	1500	⟸ minimum,
Plan III	2500	choose Plan II

c) Use the relative frequency method for determining the probabilities:

Homes Sold	Frequency	Probability
0	1	1/12
1	2	2/12
2	1	1/12
3	2	2/12
4	1	1/12
5	3	3/12
6	2	2/12

Use the expected value (EV) approach:

EV(Plan I) = 1/12(2500) + 2/12(2500) + 1/12(2500) + 2/12(2500) + 1/12(2500) + 3/12(2500) + 2/12(2500) = 2500

EV(Plan II) = 1/12(1000) + 2/12(1600) + 1/12(2200) + 2/12(2800) + 1/12(3400) + 3/12(4000) + 2/12(4600) = 3050

EV(Plan III) = 1/12(0) + 2/12(1000) + 1/12(2000) + 2/12(3000) + 1/12(4000) + 3/12(5000) + 2/12(6000) = 3417

Choose Plan III, the plan with the highest EV.

PROBLEM 3

Burger Prince Restaurant is contemplating opening a new restaurant on Main Street. It has three different models, each with a different seating capacity. Burger Prince estimates that the average number of customers per hour will be 80, 100, or 120. The payoff table for the three models is as follows:

	Average Number of Customers Per Hour		
	$s_1 = 80$	$s_2 = 100$	$s_3 = 120$
Model A	\$10,000	\$15,000	\$14,000
Model B	\$ 8,000	\$18,000	\$12,000
Model C	\$ 6,000	\$16,000	\$21,000

Burger Prince estimates the probability of 80 customers per hour is the same as the probability of 120 customers per hour and twice as much as the probability of 100 customers per hour.

a) What is the optimal decision using the expected value approach?

b) What is the expected value of perfect information?

c) Burger Prince must decide whether or not to purchase a marketing surveyfrom Stanton Marketing for \$1,000. The results of the survey are "favorable" or "unfavorable". The conditional probabilities are:

$$P(\text{favorable} \mid 80 \text{ customers per hour}) = .2$$
$$P(\text{favorable} \mid 100 \text{ customers per hour}) = .5$$
$$P(\text{favorable} \mid 120 \text{ customers per hour}) = .9$$

Should Burger Prince have the survey performed by Stanton Marketing?

d) What is the efficiency of the survey?

SOLUTION 3

a) (1) Determine the probabilities for 80, 100, and 120 customers:

Given: $P(80) = P(120)$
$P(80) = 2P(100)$.
$P(80) + P(100) + P(120) = 1$

Thus: $P(80) + .5P(80) + P(80) = 1$
$2.5P(80) = 1 \text{ --> } P(80) = .4 \text{ --> } P(100) = .2,\ P(120) = .4.$

(2) Calculate the expected value for each decision. The following decision tree can assist in this calculation. Here d_1, d_2, d_3 represent the decision alternatives of models A, B, C, and s_1, s_2, s_3 represent the states of nature of 80, 100, and 120.

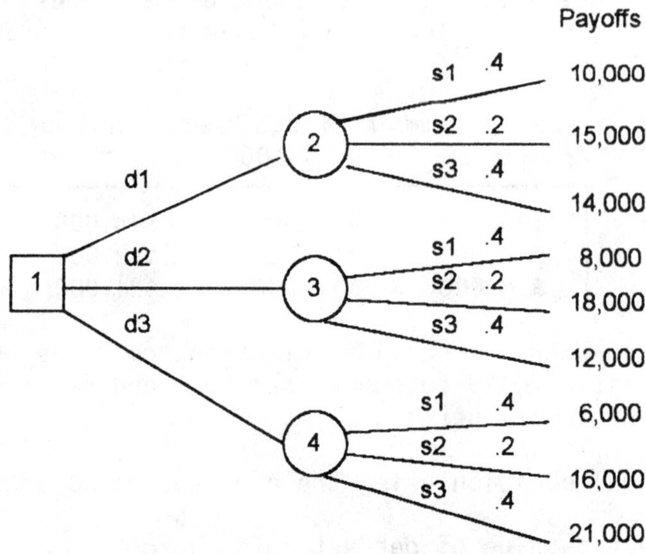

Calculating the expected value for each decision gives:

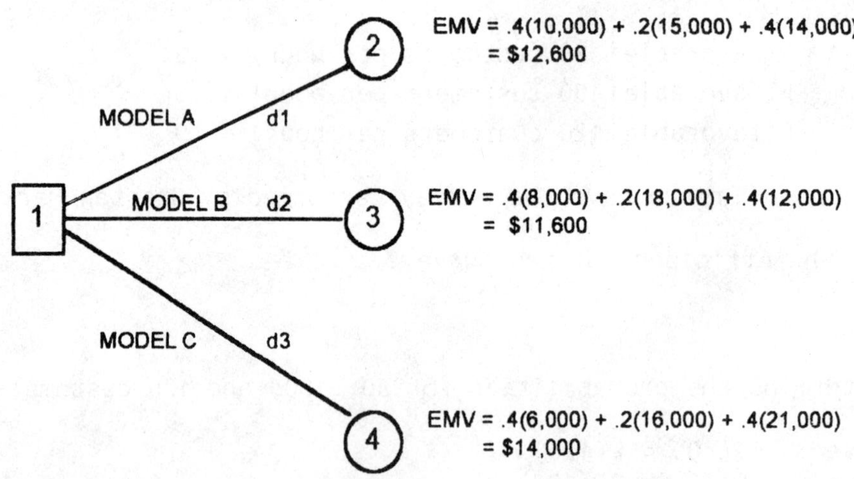

(3) Choose the model with largest EV -- Model C.

b) Calculate the expected value for the optimum payoff for each state of nature and subtract the EV of the optimal decision: EVPI= .4(10,000) + .2(18,000) + .4(21,000) - 14,000 = $2,000.

c) Find the posterior probabilities:

Favorable

State	Prior	Conditional	Joint	Posterior*
80	.4	.2	.08	.148
100	.2	.5	.10	.185
120	.4	.9	.36	.667
		Total	.54	1.000

Unfavorable

State	Prior	Conditional	Joint	Posterior*
80	.4	.8	.32	.696
100	.2	.5	.10	.217
120	.4	.1	.04	.087
		Total	.46	1.000

Note:
* Posterior probability
  = (Joint Probability)/(Sum of Joint Probabilities)

The decision tree for this problem is on the next page.

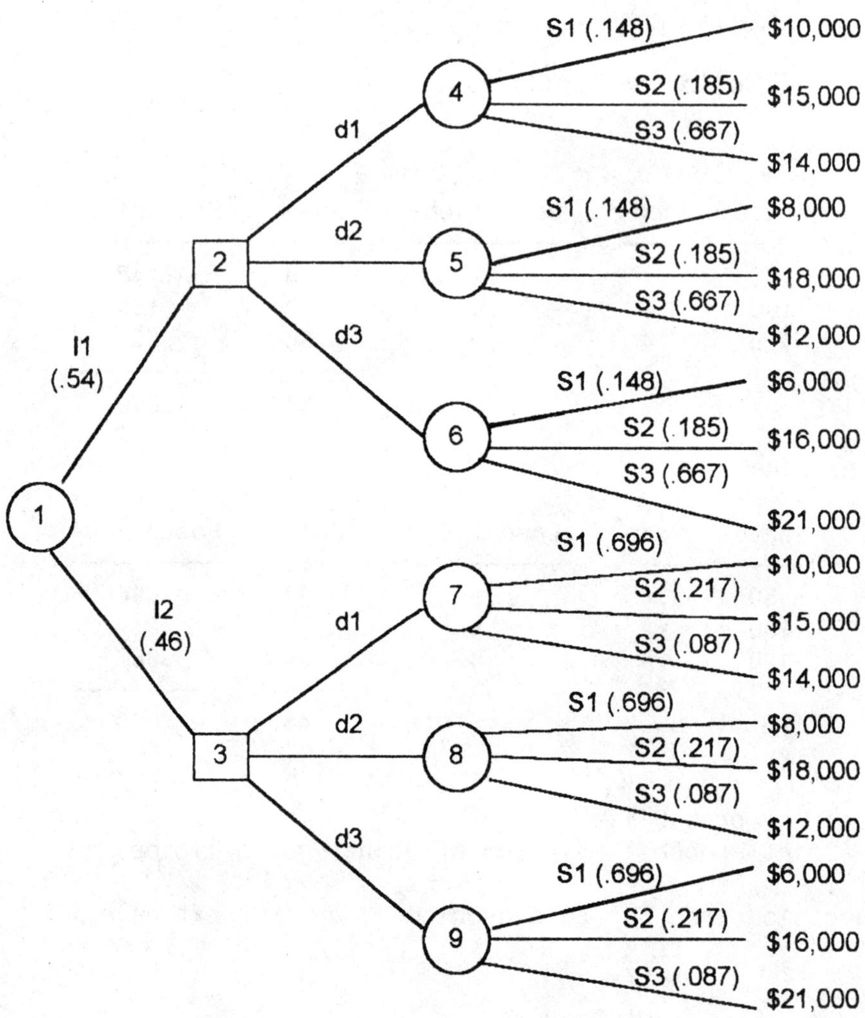
1
I1
(.54)
I2
(.46)
2
3
d1
d2
d3
d1
d2
d3
4
5
6
7
8
9
S1 (.148)
S2 (.185)
S3 (.667)
S1 (.148)
S2 (.185)
S3 (.667)
S1 (.148)
S2 (.185)
S3 (.667)
S1 (.696)
S2 (.217)
S3 (.087)
S1 (.696)
S2 (.217)
S3 (.087)
S1 (.696)
S2 (.217)
S3 (.087)
$10,000
$15,000
$14,000
$8,000
$18,000
$12,000
$6,000
$16,000
$21,000
$10,000
$15,000
$14,000
$8,000
$18,000
$12,000
$6,000
$16,000
$21,000

Calculate expected values

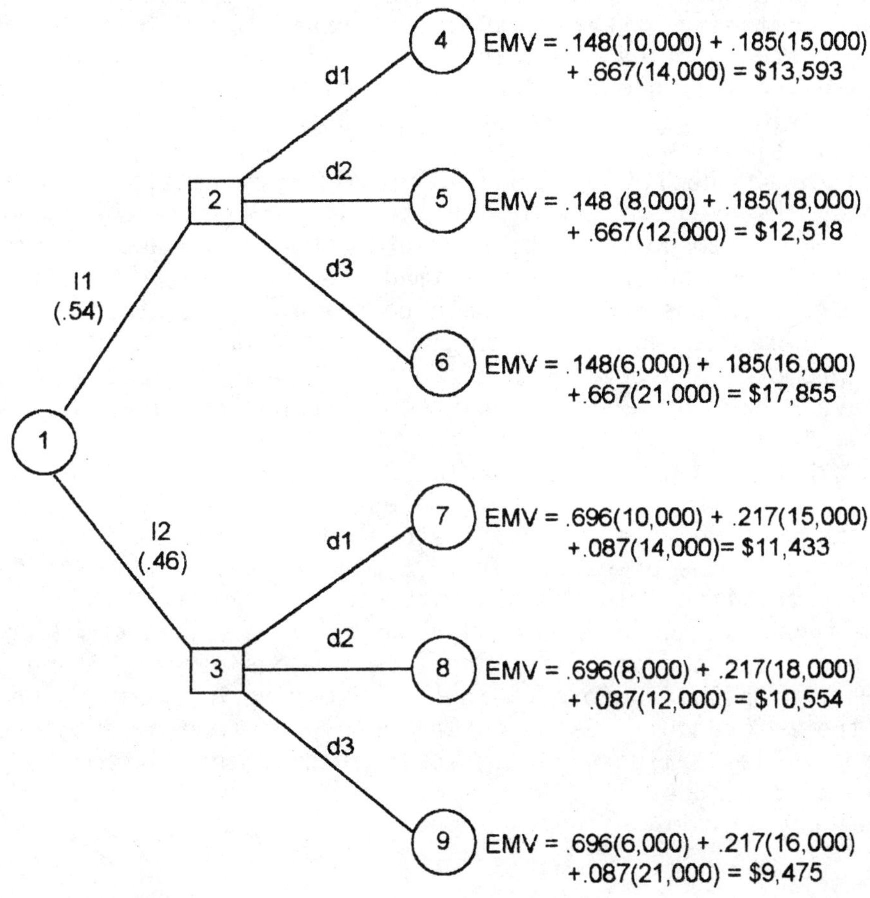

Hence, if the outcome of the survey is "favorable" choose Model C. If it is unfavorable, choose model A.

$$\text{EVSI} = .54(\$17,855) + .46(\$11,433) - \$14,000 = \$900.88$$

Since this is less than the cost of the survey, the survey should not be purchased.

d) The efficiency = EVSI/EVPI = ($900.88)/($2000) = .4504.

PROBLEM 4

The past few years have seen a general decline in the economic conditions of the resort community of Pacific City. Certain town officials, as well as other interested parties from Las Vegas, believe that the legalization of casino gambling will greatly improve the city's future. They have succeeded in having a gambling referendum placed on the ballot in next month's special election.

One effect of the declining economic condition of Pacific City has been the bankruptcy last year of the St. Carlton Inn, the city's largest hotel. The St. Carlton is scheduled to be sold at a sealed bid auction next week. The terms of the auction call for an immediate 10% down payment by the highest bidder, with the remaining balance due in two months.

One party interested in bidding on the St. Carlton is Justin Thyme, a real estate promoter and publisher of Fantasy Magazine. Justin has learned from associates that there are at least three other parties interested in the property, including a syndicate from Chicago.

Justin has decided that if he submits a bid it will be for $5 million for the property. If he bids $5 million, he estimates that he has a 40% chance of winning the auction. He also estimates that if the gambling referendum passes, he can sell the property for $7.5 million. If the initiative fails, he will sacrifice his 10% deposit.

Justin believes, based on polls taken to date, that the gambling referendum has a 30% chance of passing. He is considering hiring the noted pollster, Harris Gallup, before the auction to give his opinion on the outcome of the referendum. Based on Gallup's past record, Justin estimates that the probability Gallup will correctly predict the outcome is .8. Gallup's fee is $100,000.

What should Justin do?

SOLUTION 4

To solve this problem, first construct a tree diagram with possible courses of actions and outcomes properly sequenced.

Justin's first decision is whether or not to hire Gallup. If he does, then he will either obtain a prediction from him that the referendum will pass or fail. At that point, or if he does not hire Gallup, he must decide whether or not to bid.

Following this, he will learn if his bid is a winning one. If it is, then he will next be concerned with whether the referendum passes or not. If it does, he sells his property for $7.5 million. If it does not pass, he sacrifices his $.5 million deposit.

The tree diagram is presented on the next page including returns and probabilities.

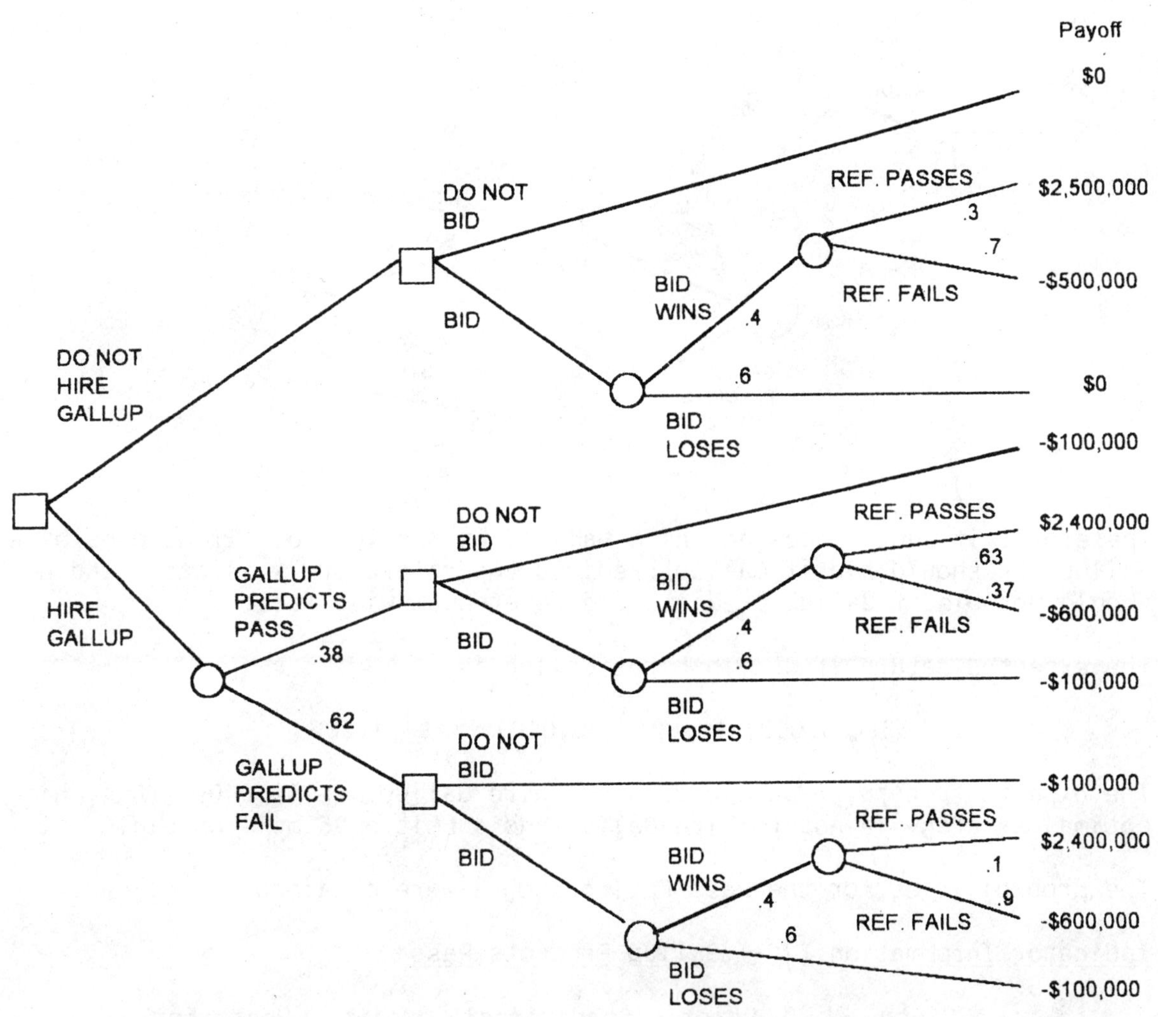

Beginning at the ends of the tree and working towards the root gives the expected returns on the following page:

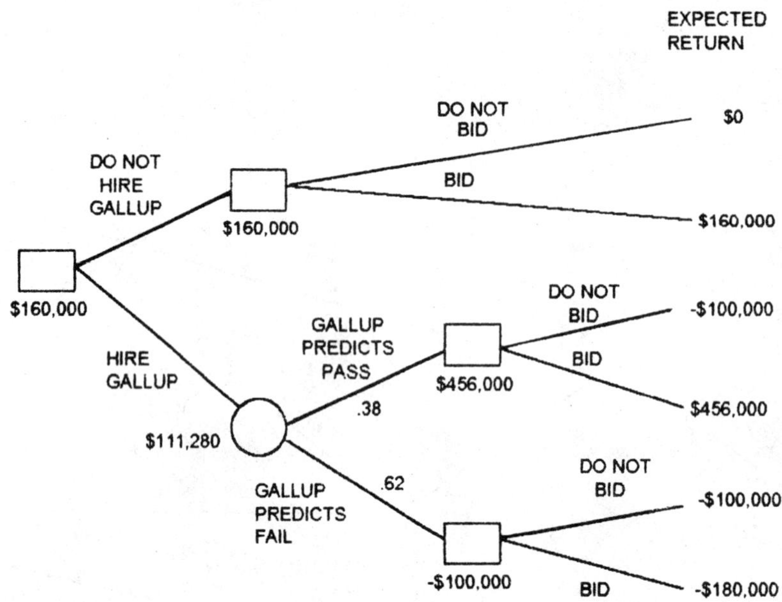

Therefore, if Justin does not hire Gallup, he should bid. If he does hire Gallup, he should bid if Gallup predicts the referendum will pass, and he should not bid if Gallup predicts the referendum will fail.

The expected return if Justin hires Gallup is:

$$.38(456,000) + .62(-100,000) = \$111,280$$

The expected return if Justin does not hire Gallup = $160,000. Thus, his optimal strategy is not to hire Gallup and submit a $5 million bid.

The probabilities for the Pass/Fail branches were obtained as follows:

<u>Indicator Information I_1 -- Gallup Predicts Pass</u>

State	Prior	Conditional	Joint	Posterior
Referendum Passes	.30	.80	.24	.63
Referendum Fails	.70	.20	.14	.37
		Total	.38	1.00

<u>Indicator Information I_2 -- Gallup Predicts Fail</u>

State	Prior	Conditional	Joint	Posterior
Referendum Passes	.30	.20	.06	.10
Referendum Fails	.70	.80	.56	.90
		Total	.62	1.00

PROBLEM 5

East West Distributing is in the process of trying to determine where they should schedule next year's production of a popular line of kitchen utensils which they distribute. Manufacturers in four different countries have submitted bids to East West. However, a pending trade bill in Congress will greatly affect the cost to East West due to proposed tariffs, favorable trading status, etc.

After careful analysis, East West has determined the following cost breakdown for the four manufacturers (in $1,000's) based on whether or not the trade bill passes:

	Bill Passes	Bill Fails
Country A	260	210
Country B	320	160
Country C	240	240
Country D	275	210

a) If East West estimates that there is a 40% chance of the bill passing, which country should they choose for manufacturing?

b) Over what range of values for the "bill passing" will the solution in part (a) remain optimal?

SOLUTION 5

a) Using the expected value approach, calculate the expected value for each country. Note that country D's costs are dominated by country A's costs (whether the bill passes or not, production is at least as expensive in country D as in country A) and therefore country D need not be considered. (Note that the probability that the bill will fail is $1 - .4 = .6$.)

$$EV(A) = .4(260) + .6(210) = 230$$
$$EV(B) = .4(320) + .6(160) = 224$$
$$EV(C) = .4(240) + .6(240) = 240$$

East West should choose the country with the lowest expected cost: country B.

b) To determine the range for the probability of the bill passing over which country B will be optimal, compare choosing country B versus country A, and then compare choosing country B versus country C. Now let,

p = the probability of the trade bill passing.

Country B would be preferred to country A as long as:

$$EV(B) \leq EV(A) \quad \text{or}$$

$$p(320) + (1-p)160 \leq p(260) + (1-p)(210)$$

$$160p + 160 \leq 50p + 210$$

$$110p \leq 50$$

$$p \leq .455$$

Similarly, Country B would be preferred to C as long as $EV(B) \leq EV(C)$. Using the same approach as above, this is equivalent to $p(320) + (1-p)160 \leq 240$. Solving, $p \leq .50$.

Thus as long as the probability of the bill passing is less than .455, then East West should choose Country B. The following graph illustrates the expected value of the decisions as a function of p:

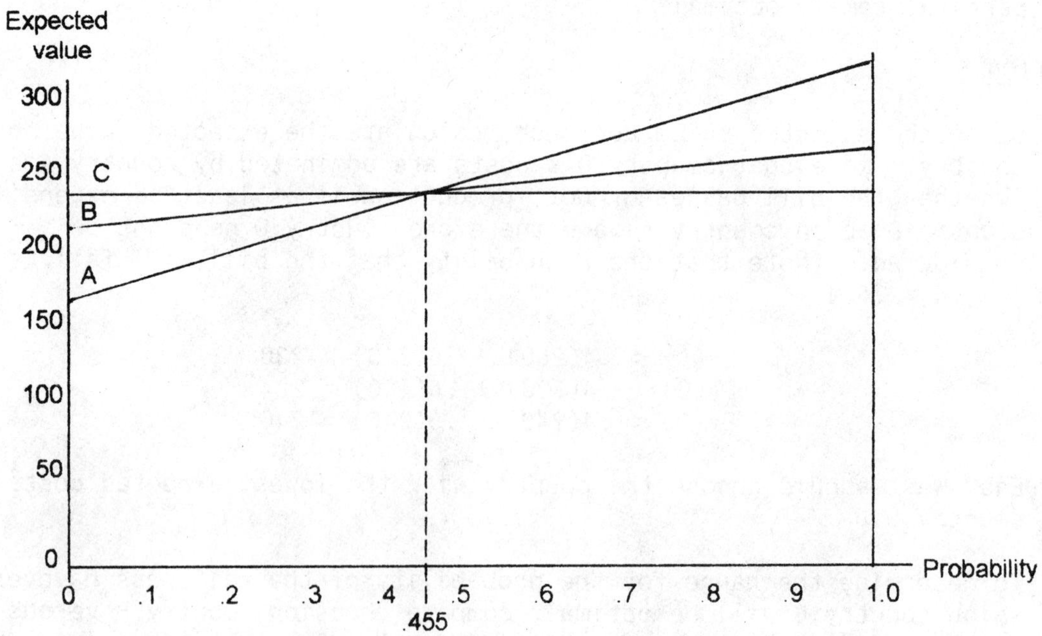

ANSWERED PROBLEMS

PROBLEM 6

Mark Investment Advisors has just completed an analysis on the returns of five utility stocks for next year. Mark hypothesizes that next year the economy will either be in a depression (s_1), a recession (s_2), an upward period (s_3), or a major expansionary period (s_4). The per dollar growth for the five stocks corresponding to each state of the economy are:

	s_1	s_2	s_3	s_4
Stock A	-.40	-.20	+.10	+.60
Stock B	-.30	-.10	0	+.30
Stock C	-.10	0	+.05	+.30
Stock D	0	+.05	+.10	+.15
Stock E	+.05	+.15	-.10	-.20

a) If you had a chance to purchase shares of Stock B or Stock C, which would you purchase? Why?

b) Find the best stock to purchase undereach approach: (1) optimistic; (2) minimax regret; (3) conservative.

c) Suppose Mark's financial outlook for next year is $P(s_1) = .2$; $P(s_2) = .4$; $P(s_3) = .2$; and $P(s_4) = .2$. Using the expected value approach, which stock would Mark recommend?

PROBLEM 7

Transrail is bidding on a project which it figures will cost $400,000 to perform. Using a 25% markup, it will charge $500,000, netting a profit of $100,000. However, it has been learned that another company, Rail Freight, is also considering bidding on the project. If Rail Freight does submit a bid, it figures to be a bid of about $470,000.

Transrail really wants this project and is considering a bid with only a 15% markup to $460,000 to ensure winning regardless of whether or not Rail Freight submits a bid.

a) Prepare a profit payoff table from Transrail's point of view.

b) What decision would be made if Transrail was conservative?

c) If Rail Freight is known to submit bids on only 25% of the projects it considers, what decision should Transrail make?

d) Given the information in (c), how much would a corporate spy be worth to Transrail to find out if Rail Freight will bid?

PROBLEM 8

The Super Cola Company must decide whether or not to introduce a new diet soft drink. Management feels that if it does introduce the diet soda it will yield a profit of $1 million if sales are around 100 million, a profit of $200,000 if sales are around 50 million, or it will lose $2 million if sales are only around 1 million bottles. If Super Cola does not market the new diet soda, it will suffer a loss of $400,000.

a) Construct a payoff table for this problem.

b) Construct a regret table for this problem.

c) Should Super Cola introduce the soda if the company: (1) is conservative; (2) is optimistic; (3) wants to minimize its maximum disappointment?

d) An internal marketing research study has found P(100 million in sales) = 1/3; P(50 million in sales) = 1/2; P(1 million in sales) = 1/6. Should Super Cola introduce the new diet soda?

e) A consulting firm can perform a more thorough study for $275,000. Should management have this study performed?

PROBLEM 9

Super Cola is also considering the introduction of a root beer drink. The company feels that the probability that the product will be a success is .6. The payoff table is as follows:

	Success (s_1)	Failure (s_2)
Produce (d_1)	$250,000	-$300,000
Do Not Produce (d_2)	-$ 50,000	-$ 20,000

The company has a choice of two research firms to obtain information for this product. Stanton Marketing claims that it has market indicators, I_1 and I_2 for which $P(I_1|s_1) = .7$ and $P(I_1|s_2) = .4$. New World Marketing has indicators J_1 and J_2 for which $P(J_1|s_1) = .6$ and $P(J_1|s_2) = .3$.

a) What is the optimal decision if neither firm is used? Over what probability of success range is this decision optimal?

b) What is the EVPI?

[more questions on next page]

c) Find the EVSIs and efficiencies for Stanton and New World.

d) If both firms charge $5,000, which firm should be hired?

e) If Stanton charges $10,000 and New World charges $4,000, which firm should Super Cola hire? Why?

PROBLEM 10

Metropolitan Cablevision is investigating the installation of a cable TV system in town. The engineering department estimates the cost of the system (in present worth dollars) to be $700,000. The sales department has investigated four pricing plans. For each pricing plan the marketing division has estimated the revenue per household in present worth dollars to be:

Plan	Revenue Per Household
I	$15
II	$18
III	$20
IV	$24

The sales department estimates the number of household subscribers would be approximately either 10,000, 20,000, 30,000, 40,000, 50,000 or 60,000.

a) Construct a payoff table for this problem.

b) What is the company's optimal decision under (1) the optimistic approach; (2) the conservative approach; and (3) the minimax regret approach?

c) Suppose the sales department has determined that the number of subscribers will be a function of the pricing plan. The probability distributions for the pricing plans are given below. Use decision tree analysis to determine which pricing plan is optimal under the expected value approach.

Number of Subscribers	Probability Under Pricing Plan I	II	III	IV
10,000	0	.05	.10	.20
20,000	.05	.10	.20	.25
30,000	.05	.20	.20	.25
40,000	.40	.30	.20	.15
50,000	.30	.20	.20	.10
60,000	.20	.15	.10	.05

PROBLEM 11

Dicom Corporation has developed a new high speed computer which it intends to sell for $150,000. Dicom's salesmen have scheduled demonstrations with four clients next month. For each client, Dicom estimates there is a 40% chance of his purchasing the computer.

Dicom plans to make at least one computer next month but could make as many as four. Production costs are $100,000 for producing one computer, $190,000 for two, $260,000 for three, and $310,000 for four.

Any unsold computers produced will be sold at $60,000. Also, if a client wants to purchase a computer, but all computers produced have been sold, the company estimates it loses $20,000.

a) Determine a payoff table for this problem.

b) What is the optimal strategy using the expected monetary value criterion? (HINT: Use the binomial distribution to determine the probabilities for the states of nature.)

c) Dicom can have a survey performed to indicate the market impression of the new computer -- favorable or unfavorable. The following probabilities are believed to hold:

$P(\text{favorable}\mid 0 \text{ sold}) = .1$ $P(\text{favorable}\mid 3 \text{ sold}) = .9$

$P(\text{favorable}\mid 1 \text{ sold}) = .2$ $P(\text{favorable}\mid 4 \text{ sold}) = 1.0$

$P(\text{favorable}\mid 2 \text{ sold}) = .6$

How much should Dicom pay for this survey and what is its efficiency?

PROBLEM 12

Dollar Department Stores has just acquired the chain of Wenthrope and Sons Custom Jewelers. Dollar has received an offer from Harris Diamonds to purchase the Wenthrope store on Grove Street for $120,000.

Dollar has determined probability estimates of the store's future profitability, based on economic outcomes, as: P($80,000) = .2, P($100,000) = .3, P($120,000) = .1, and P($140,000) = .4.

a) Should Dollar sell the store on Grove Street?

b) What is the EVPI?

c) Dollar can have an economic forecast performed, costing $10,000, that produces indicators I_1 and I_2, for which $P(I_1\mid 80{,}000) = .1$; $P(I_1\mid 100{,}000) = .2$; $P(I_1\mid 120{,}000) = .6$; $P(I_1\mid 140{,}000) = .3$. Should Dollar purchase the forecast?

PROBLEM 13

Cashman Co. will be leasing a new copier and is considering four plans.

Plan	Monthly Lease	Unit Copy Cost
I	$100	$.02 for the first 10,000; $.016 thereafter
II	$200	$.012 for all copies
III	$150	first 5,000 free; $.022 thereafter
IV	$300	$.005 for all copies

The company has determined it will make either 12,600, 14,400, 16,200, 18,000, 19,800, 21,600 copies per month with probabilities of .05, .10, .15, .25, .25, and .20 respectively.

a) Construct a monthly payoff table for Cashman in terms of costs.

b) What is the optimal plan if the company uses the (1) optimistic approach or (2) the conservative approach?

c) What is the optimal plan using the expected value approach?

PROBLEM 14

An appliance dealer must decide how many (if any) new microwave ovens to order for next month. The ovens cost $220 and sell for $300. Because the oven company is coming out with a new product line in two months, any ovens not sold next month will have to be sold at the dealer's half price clearance sale. Additionally, the appliance dealer feels he suffers a loss of $25 for every oven demanded when he is out of stock. On the basis of past months' sales data, the dealer estimates the probabilities of monthly demand (D) for 0, 1, 2, or 3 ovens to be .3, .4, .2, and .1, respectively.

The dealer is considering conducting a telephone survey on the customers' attitudes towards microwave ovens. The results of the survey will either be favorable (F), unfavorable (U) or no opinion (N). The dealer's probability estimates for the survey results based on the number of units demanded are:

$P(F|D = 0) = .1$ $P(F|D = 2)\ .3$ $P(U|D = 0) = .8$ $P(U|D = 2) = .1$

$P(F|D = 1) = .2$ $P(F|D = 3)\ .9$ $P(U|D = 1) = .3$ $P(U|D = 3) = .1$

a) What is the dealer's optimal decision without conducting the survey?

b) What is the EVPI?

c) Based on the survey results what is the optimal decision strategy for the dealer?

d) What is the maximum amount he should pay for this survey?

TRUE/FALSE

15. The expected value of sample information can never be less than the expected value of perfect information.

16. The expected value of perfect information must always be nonnegative.

17. The expected value of sample information is the difference between the expected value with perfect information and the expected value without perfect information.

18. Using the optimistic and conservative approaches will never give the same optimal decision.

19. The $P(I_k|s_j)$ must equal $P(s_j|I_k)$.

20. For each indicator, I_k, the joint probabilities must sum to 1.

21. Posterior probabilities are calculated by dividing each joint probability by the sum of the joint probabilities for that indicator.

22. The sum of $P(I_k|s_j)$ for all s_j is 1.0.

23. Sample information with an efficiency rating of 100% is perfect informaion.

24. Sensitivity analysis on state-of-nature probability estimates cannot be performed on problems with more than two states-of-nature.

25. If the expected value of sample information exceeds the cost of purchasing the sample information, one should not attempt to obtain the sample information.

26. The states of nature in a decision problem must be mutually exclusive and collectively exhaustive.

27. Maximizing the expected payoff and minimizing the expected opportunity loss result in the same recommended decision.

28. The expected value approach is more appropriate for a one-time decision than a repetitive decision.

29. $P(I_k|s_j)$ is a posterior probability.

Chapter 5
Utility and Decision Making

KEY CONCEPTS

CONCEPT	ILLUSTRATED PROBLEMS	ANSWERED PROBLEMS
Determining Utilities	3,4	7,8,10,11,12
Decision Making Using Utility	1,2,3	5,6,7,8,9,10
Attitudes Towards Risk	1,2	5,6,7,8,10,11

REVIEW

1. Utility is a measure of the total worth of a particular outcome, reflecting the decision maker's attitude towards a collection of factors. Some of these factors may be profit, loss, and risk. Utilities are used in decision making when the decision criteria must be based on more than just expected monetary values.

2. One common way to define a utility measure is the concept of a lottery. To use the lottery concept, define the utility of the best payoff to be 1 and the utility of the worst payoff to be 0. The decision maker is then asked to assign a probability, p, that would make him indifferent between choosing the payoff, or playing a lottery in which he will get the best payoff with probability p and the worst payoff with probability 1-p. These indifference probabilities define the utility function for the decision maker.

3. Once a utility function has been determined, the optimal decision can be chosen using the expected utility approach. Here, for each decision alternative, the utility corresponding to each state of nature is multiplied by the probability for that state of nature. The sum of these products for each decision alternative represents the expected utility for that alternative. The decision alternative with the highest expected utility is chosen.

4. Utility values are influenced by the attitude of the decision maker towards risk. A risk avoider will have a concave utility function when utility is measured on the vertical axis and monetary value is measured on the horizontal axis. Individuals purchasing insurance exhibit risk avoidance behavior.

5. Risk takers, such as gamblers, pay a premium to obtain risk. Their utility function is convex. This reflects the decision maker's increasing marginal value for money.

6. A risk neutral decision maker has a linear utility function. In this case, the expected value approach can be used.

7. Most individuals' risk avoidance or risk taking depends on the amount of money involved. For some relatively large amounts of money they are risk avoiders; for relatively small amounts of money they are risk takers. This explains why the same individual will both purchase insurance and also a lottery ticket.

8. While determining utility values is not an easy task, such an analysis should be performed in cases where payoffs can assume extremely high or extremely low values.

ILLUSTRATED PROBLEMS

PROBLEM 1

Consider a three-state, four-decision problem with the following payoff table (in $'s):

	s_1	s_2	s_3
d_1	100,000	+40,000	-60,000
d_2	50,000	+20,000	-30,000
d_3	20,000	+20,000	-10,000
d_4	40,000	+20,000	-60,000

The probabilities for the three states of nature are: $P(s_1) = .1$, $P(s_2) = .3$, and $P(s_3) = .6$.

a) If the decision maker is risk neutral, what is the optimal decision?

b) Graph the utility curves for the decision makers having the following utility values:

	Utility	
Amount	Decision Maker I	Decision Maker II
$100,000	100	100
$ 50,000	94	58
$ 40,000	90	50
$ 20,000	80	35
-$ 10,000	60	18
-$ 30,000	40	10
-$ 60,000	0	0

c) Classify each of the two decision makers as either a risk avoider, a risk taker, or risk neutral.

d) Find the optimal decision for each of the decision makers.

SOLUTION 1

a) If the decision maker is risk neutral the expected value approach is applicable.

$$EV(d_1) = .1(100{,}000) + .3(40{,}000) + .6(-60{,}000) = -\$14{,}000$$
$$EV(d_2) = .1(\ 50{,}000) + .3(20{,}000) + .6(-30{,}000) = -\$\ 7{,}000$$
$$EV(d_3) = .1(\ 20{,}000) + .3(20{,}000) + .6(-10{,}000) = +\$\ 2{,}000$$

Note the EV for d_4 need not be calculated as decision d_4 is dominated by decision d_2. The optimal decision is d_3.

b)

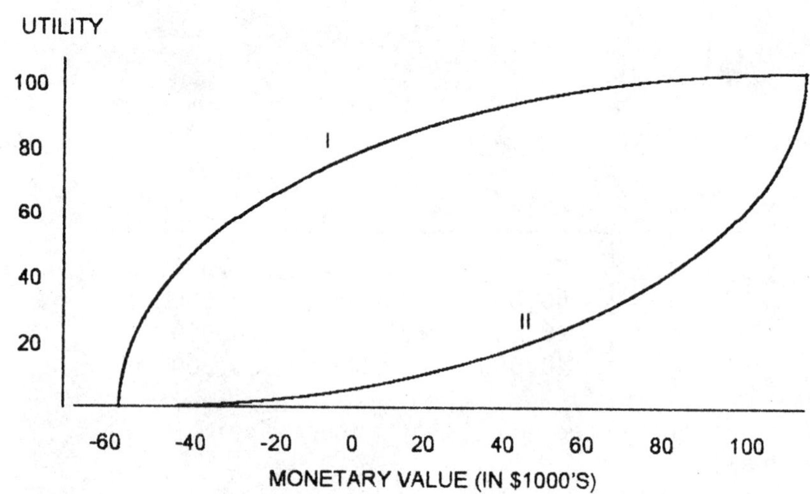

c) Decision Maker I has a concave utility function -- he is a risk avoider. Decision Maker II has a convex utility function -- he is a risk taker.

d) Note again that d_4 is dominated by d_2 and hence is not considered. For the remaining decisions, compute the expected utility for each decision maker using the probabilities given.

<u>Utility Table I</u>

	s_1	s_2	s_3	Expected Utility	
d_1	100	90	0	37.0	
d_2	94	80	40	57.4	
d_3	80	80	60	68.0	<===== best choice
Probability	.1	.3	.6		

<u>Utility Table II</u>

	s_1	s_2	s_3	Expected Utility	
best choice ====> d_1	100	50	0	25.0	<===== greatest expected utility
d_2	58	35	10	22.3	
d_3	35	35	18	24.8	
Probability	.1	.3	.6		

PROBLEM 2

In problem (1) suppose the probabilities for the three states of nature are changed to: $P(s_1) = .5$, $P(s_2) = .3$, and $P(s_3) = .2$.

a) Find the optimal decision for a risk neutral decision maker.

b) Find the optimal decision for Decision Makers I and II.

c) Approximately what is the value of this decision problem to Decision Maker I and Decision Maker II? What conclusion can you draw from this?

SOLUTION 2

a) Use the EV approach for a risk neutral decision maker:

$$EV(d_1) = .5(100{,}000) + .3(40{,}000) + .2(-60{,}000) = 50{,}000 \Longleftarrow$$
$$EV(d_2) = .5(\ 50{,}000) + .3(20{,}000) + .2(-30{,}000) = 25{,}000$$
$$EV(d_3) = .5(\ 20{,}000) + .3(20{,}000) + .2(-10{,}000) = 14{,}000$$

Hence, the risk neutral optimal decision (with the largest EV) is d_1.

b) Use the expected utility criterion for each decision maker:

Decision Maker I

$$EU(d_1) = .5(100) + .3(90) + .2(\ 0) = 77.0$$
$$EU(d_2) = .5(\ 94) + .3(80) + .2(40) = 79.0 \Longleftarrow d_2 \text{ best}$$
$$EU(d_3) = .5(\ 80) + .3(80) + .2(60) = 76.0$$

Decision Maker II

$$EU(d_1) = .5(100) + .3(50) + .2(\ 0) = 65.0 \Longleftarrow d_1 \text{ best}$$
$$EU(d_2) = .5(\ 58) + .3(35) + .2(10) = 41.5$$
$$EU(d_3) = .5(\ 35) + .3(35) + .2(18) = 31.6$$

c) To determine the value of the problem to a decision maker, find the amount that corresponds to the expected utility of the optimal decision.

For Decision Maker I, the optimal expected utility is 79. He assigned a utility of 80 to +$20,000, and a utility of 60 to -$10,000. Linearly interpolating in this range 1 point is worth $30,000/20 = $1,500. Thus a utility of 79 is worth about $20,000 - $1,500 = $18,500.

For Decision Maker II, the optimal expected utility is 65. He assigned a utility of 100 to 100,000, and a utility of 58 to $50,000. In this range, 1 point is worth $50,000/42 = $1190. Thus a utility of 65 is worth about $50,000 + 7($1190) = $58,330.

Thus, the decision problem is worth more to Decision Maker II.

PROBLEM 3

Each project manager at Rockford Research Corp. is given three development projects per year to supervise. The manager's salary is determined by the number of successfully completed projects.

Managers have a choice of three salary payment plans:

	Number Of Successfully Completed Projects			
	0	1	2	3
Plan 1	25,000	25,000	25,000	25,000
Plan 2	15,000	20,000	30,000	50,000
Plan 3	20,000	25,000	25,000	30,000

For a lottery having a payoff of \$50,000 with probability p and \$15,000 with probability (1-p), three managers expressed the following indifference probabilities:

	Indifference Probability (p)		
Amount	Manager 1	Manager 2	Manager 3
\$30,000	.5	.6	.8
\$25,000	.4	.4	.5
\$20,000	.3	.2	.1

If the probability of successfully completing a single project is .5, determine the best salary plan for each of the three managers.

SOLUTION 3

Using the binomial distribution with the probability of success = .5, determine the probabilities of the number of projects successfully completed to be P(0) = .125, P(1) = .375, P(2) = .375, P(3) = .125. For each manager construct the utility table corresponding to his indifference probabilities:

Manager 1

	Number of Projects Completed				Expected	
	0	1	2	3	Utility	
Plan 1	.4	.4	.4	.4	.4000	
Plan 2	0	.3	.5	1.0	.4250	⟸ Plan 2 best
Plan 3	.3	.4	.4	.5	.4000	
Probability	.125	.375	.375	.125		

Manager 2

	Number of Projects Completed 0	1	2	3	Expected Utility	
Plan 1	.4	.4	.4	.4	.4000	
Plan 2	0	.2	.6	1.0	.4125	⟸ Plan 2 best
Plan 3	.2	.4	.4	.6	.4000	
Probability	.125	.375	.375	.125		

Manager 3

	Number of Projects Completed 0	1	2	3	Expected Utility	
Plan 1	.5	.5	.5	.5	.5000	⟸ Plan 1 best
Plan 2	0	.1	.8	1.0	.4623	
Plan 3	.1	.5	.5	.8	.4875	
Probability	.125	.375	.375	.125		

PROBLEM 4

Mark Investment Advisors have analyzed the profit potential of five different investments. The probabilities of the gains on \$1000 are as follows:

	Gain			
Investment	\$0	\$200	\$500	\$1000
A	.9	0	0	.1
B	0	.8	.2	0
C	.05	.9	0	.05
D	0	.8	.1	.1
E	.6	0	.3	.1

One of Mark's investors informs Mark that he is indifferent between investments A, B, and C. On the basis of this information, would he prefer investment D to investment E? Why?

SOLUTION 4

Assign a utility of 10 to a \$1000 gain and a utility of 0 to a gain of \$0. Let x = the utility of a \$200 gain and y = the utility of a \$500 gain.

The expected utility on investment A is then .9(0) + .1(10) = 1.

Since the investor is indifferent between investments A and C, this must mean the expected utility of investment C = the expected utility of investment A = 1. But the expected utility of investment C = .05(0) +.90x + .05(10). Since this must equal 1, solving for x, gives x = 5/9.

Also since the investor is indifferent between A, B, and C, the expected utility of investment B must be 1. Thus, 0(0) + .8(5/9) + .2y + 0(10) = 1. Solving for y, gives y = 25/9. Thus the utility values for gains of 0, 200, 500, and 1000 are 0, 5/9, 25/9, and 10 respectively.

For investment D, EU(D) = 0(0) + .8(5/9) + .1(25/9) + .1(10) = 1.72. For investment E, EU(E) = .6(0) + 0(5/9) + .3(25/9) + .1(10) = 1.83.

Thus the investor should prefer investment E.

ANSWERED PROBLEMS

PROBLEM 5

Burger Prince Restaurant is considering the purchase of a $100,000 fire insurance policy. The fire statistics indicate that in a given year the probability of property damage in a fire is as follows:

Fire Damage	$0	$10,000	$25,000	$50,000	$75,000	$100,000
Probability	.980	.005	.003	.004	.002	.006

a) If Burger Prince was risk neutral, how much would they be willing to pay for fire insurance?

b) If Burger Prince has the utility values given below, approximately how much would they be willing to pay for fire insurance?

Loss Amount ($)	100,000	75,000	50,000	25,000	10,000	5,000	0
Utility	0	30	60	85	95	99	100

PROBLEM 6

Super Cola is considering the introduction of a new 8 oz. root beer. The probability that the root beer will be a success is believed to equal .6. The payoff table is as follows:

	Success (s_1)	Failure (s_2)
Produce	$250,000	-$300,000
Do Not Produce	-$ 50,000	-$ 20,000

Company management has determined the following utility values:

Payoff Amount ($)	250,000	-20,000	-50,000	-300,000
Utility	100	60	55	0

a) Is the company a risk taker, risk averse, or risk neutral?

b) What is Super Cola's optimal decision?

c) Stanton Marketing has market indicators, I_1 and I_2 for which $P(I_1"s_1)$ = .7 and $P(I_1"s_2)$ =.4. New World Marketing has market indicators J_1 and J_2 for which $P(J_1"s_1)$ = .6 and $P(J_1"s_2)$ = .3. If both indicators are available for free, which one should be selected?

PROBLEM 7

The president of Metropolitan Cablevision has asked two of his vice presidents for a recommendation concerning the offering of pay TV. Metropolitan has the choice of using one of three pay TV systems. Profits are believed to be a function of customer acceptance. The payoff to Metropolitan for the three systems is:

	System		
Acceptance Level	I	II	III
High	$150,000	$200,000	$200,000
Medium	$ 80,000	$ 20,000	$ 80,000
Low	$ 20,000	-$ 50,000	-$100,000

The probabilities of customer acceptance for each system are:

	System		
Acceptance Level	I	II	III
High	.4	.3	.3
Medium	.3	.4	.5
Low	.3	.3	.2

The first vice president believes that the indifference probabilities for Metropolitan should be:

Amount	Probability
$150,000	.90
$ 80,000	.70
$ 20,000	.50
-$ 50,000	.25

The second vice president believes Metropolitan should assign the following utility values:

Amount	Utility
$200,000	125
$150,000	95
$ 80,000	55
$ 20,000	30
-$ 50,000	10
-$100,000	0

a) Which vice president is a risk taker? Which one is risk averse?

b) Which system will each vice president recommend?

c) What system would a risk neutral vice president recommend?

PROBLEM 8

Chez Paul is contemplating either opening another restaurant or expanding its existing location. The payoff table for these two decisions is:

	s_1	s_2	s_3
New Restaurant	-\$80,000	\$20,000	\$160,000
Expand	-\$40,000	\$20,000	\$100,000

Paul has calculated the indifference probability for the lottery having a payoff of \$160,000 with probability p and -\$80,000 with probability (1-p) as follows:

Amount	Indifference Probability (p)
-\$ 40,000	.4
\$ 20,000	.7
\$100,000	.9

a) Is Paul a risk avoider, risk taker, or risk neutral?

b) Suppose Paul has defined the utility of -\$80,000 to be 0 and the utility of \$160,000 to be 80. What would be the utility values for -\$40,000, \$20,000, and \$100,000 based on the indifference probabilities?

c) Suppose the utility of -\$80,000 is defined to be -80 and the utility of \$160,000 is defined to be +160. Now what are the utility values for -\$40,000, \$20,000, and \$100,000?

d) Suppose $P(s_1) = .4$, $P(s_2) = .3$, and $P(s_3) = .3$. Which decision should Paul make? Compare with the decision using the Expected Value approach.

e) A competitor is willing to pay Paul \$20,000 not to open another restaurant or expand his existing restaurant, i.e. maintain the status quo. Should Paul accept the offer? Why?

PROBLEM 9

Dollar Department Stores has the opportunity of acquiring either 3, 5, or 10 leases from the bankrupt Granite Variety Store chain. Dollar estimates the profit potential of the leases depends on the state of the economy over the next five years. The payoff table is given on the next page (payoffs are in \$1,000,000's).

There are four possible states of the economy as modeled by Dollar Department Stores and its president estimates $P(s_1) = .4$, $P(s_2) = .3$, $P(s_3) = .1$, and $P(s_4) = .2$. The utility has also been estimated. Given the payoff and utility tables on the next page, which decision should Dollar make?

Payoffs (in $millions)

Decision	State Of The Economy Over The Next 5 Years			
	s_1	s_2	s_3	s_4
d_1 (buy 10 leases)	10	5	0	-20
d_2 (buy 5 leases)	5	0	-1	-10
d_3 (buy 3 leases)	2	1	0	- 1
d_4 (buy 0 leases)	0	0	0	0

Payoff (in $1,000,000's)	+10	+5	+2	0	-1	-10	-20
Utility	+10	+5	+2	0	-1	-20	-50

PROBLEM 10

Consider the following problem with four states of nature, three decision alternatives, and the following payoff table (in $'s):

	s_1	s_2	s_3	s_4
d_1	200	2600	-1400	200
d_2	0	200	- 200	200
d_3	-200	400	0	200

The indifference probabilities for three individuals are:

	Indifference Probabilities		
Payoff	Person 1	Person 2	Person 3
$2600	1.00	1.00	1.00
$ 400	.40	.45	.55
$ 200	.35	.40	.50
$ 0	.30	.35	.45
-$ 200	.25	.30	.40
-$1400	0	0	0

a) Plot the utility function for these three people.

b) Classify each person as a risk avoider, risk taker, or risk neutral.

c) For the payoff of $400, what is the premium the risk avoider will pay to avoid risk? What is the premium the risk taker will pay to have the opportunity of the high payoff?

d) Suppose each state is equally likely. What are the optimal decisions for each of these three people?

THE PROBLEMS ON THIS PAGE DEPEND ON YOUR PERSONAL ASSIGNMENT OF INDIFFERENCE PROBABILITIES.

PROBLEM 11

You can purchase a lottery ticket whose prize is $10,000.

a) What would be the minimum probability of winning that you would accept to buy the ticket if it cost $1; $5; $10; $100; $500; $1000?

b) Now you are given the option of receiving an amount, $x, or a ticket in a lottery which wins $10,000 with probability p and wins $0 with probability (1-p). Find the indifference probability for x equal to $1; $5; $10; $100; $500; $1000.

c) Using your answers to (a) and (b), plot your utility function.

d) Does this indicate you are risk neutral or a risk avoider or risk taker?

PROBLEM 12

Consider the following gambling situations:

a) You are offered an amount of money, $x, or a lottery ticket. The lottery ticket pays $10,000 with probability .5 and pays $0 with probability .5. What amount, $x, would make you indifferent to this lottery?

b) You are offered an amount of money, $y, or a lottery ticket. The lottery ticket pays $10,000 with probability .5 and pays $x (the amount in part (a)) with probability .5. What amount, $y, would make you indifferent to this lottery?

c) You are offered an amount of money, $z, or a lottery ticket. The lottery ticket pays $x (the amount in part (a)) with probability .5 and pays $0 with probability .5. What amount, $z, would make you indifferent to this lottery.

d) You are offered an amount of money, $d, or a lottery ticket. The lottery ticket pays $y (your answer to part (b)) with probability .5 and pays $z (your answer to part (c)) with probability .5 What amount, $d, would make you indifferent to this lottery?

e) If the utility of $10,000 is defined to be 100 and the utility of $0 is defined to be 0, find the utility of $x, $y, $z, and $d. Is the utility of $x greater than, less than, or equal to the utility of $d? Are your values for $d and $x consistent with their utilities?

TRUE/FALSE

13. If one outcome is preferred to another, it will have a higher utility value.

14. Given two decision makers, one risk neutral and the other a risk avoider, the risk avoider will always give a lower utility value for a given outcome.

15. A risk avoider will have a concave utility function.

16. A risk neutral decision maker will choose decisions identical to those chosen using the expected value approach.

17. If an outcome is certain, it is given a utility value of 1.

18. If a decision maker is indifferent between receiving $1,000 or playing a lottery in which he wins nothing with probability .8 and $10,000 with probability .2, then the decision maker could be characterized as risk averse.

19. Consider the decision maker in question 6. If he assigns a utility of 0 to the outcome of a $0 return and a utility of 10 to the $10,000 return, then he would assign a utility value of 1 to $1,000.

20. When using the expected utility approach, a risk avoider and a risk taker will never choose the same decision.

21. The utility function for a risk avoider typically shows a diminishing marginal return for money.

22. A risk neutral decision maker will have a linear utility function.

23. The decision to buy state lottery tickets has a negative expected monetary value.

24. Measuring a decision maker's utility is, at least in part, subjective.

25. In most cases, the decision to buy insurance for a house has a positive expected monetary value.

26. The expected monetary value approach and the expected utility approach to decision making usually result in the same decision choice unless extreme payoffs are involved.

27. It is rare to find a person who is both a risk taker and a risk avoider.

Chapter 6
Forecasting

KEY CONCEPTS

CONCEPT	ILLUSTRATED PROBLEMS	ANSWERED PROBLEMS
Smoothing Methods		
Moving Average	1	9
Weighted Moving Average	2	6
Exponential Smoothing	1	6,7
Linear Trend Projection	2	10,12
Multiplicative Time Series Model	3,4	8,11,13
Regression Analysis	5	14
Mean Squared Error	1	6,7,9

REVIEW

1. A time series is a set of observations measured at successive points in time or over successive periods of time. A time series is analyzed so that one may determine good forecasts or predictions of future values for the time series.

2. While a time series may consist of numerous components, a usual assumption is that four separate components combine to affect the values of a time series. These four components are: (1) a trend component; (2) a cyclical component; (3) a seasonal component; and, (4) irregular components.

3. The trend component accounts for the gradual shifting of the time series over a long period of time.

4. Any regular pattern of sequences of values above and below the trend line is attributable to the cyclical component of the series.

5. The seasonal component of the series accounts for regular patterns of variability within certain time periods, such as over a year.

6. The irregular component of the series is caused by short-term, unanticipated and non-recurring factors that affect the values of the time series. One cannot attempt to predict its impact on the time series in advance.

7. In cases in which the time series is fairly stable and has no significant trend, seasonal, or cyclical effects, one can use smoothing methods to average out the irregular components of the time series.

8. The moving average smoothing method consists of computing an average of the most recent n data values for the series and using this average for forecasting the value of the time series for the next period.

9. The centered moving average method consists of computing an average of n periods' data and associating it with the midpoint of the periods. For example, the average for periods 5, 6, and 7 is associated with period 6. This methodology is useful in the process of computing season indexes.

10. In the weighted moving average smoothing method for computing the average of the most recent n periods, the more recent observations are typically given more weight than older observations. (For convenience, the weights usually sum to 1.)

11. One difficulty of both the moving average and the weighted moving average methods is that n historical data points must be stored in order to compute the forecast for the next period. In <u>exponential smoothing</u> only two pieces of information are needed to compute the forecast: (1) the forecasted value for the current period, and (2) the actual value for the current period.

12. Using <u>exponential smoothing</u>, the forecast is calculated by:

    α[the actual value for the current period] +

    $(1-\alpha)$[the forecasted value for the current period],

    where the <u>smoothing constant</u>, α, is a number between 0 and 1.

13. Another way to view <u>exponential smoothing</u> is that the forecast for the next period is equal to the forecast for the current period plus a proportion (α) of the forecast error in the current period.

14. It is essential that forecasts be as accurate as possible. One measure of <u>forecast accuracy</u> is known as the <u>mean squared error</u>. In this measure the average of the squared forecast errors for the historical data is calculated. The forecasting method or parameter(s) which minimize this mean squared error is then selected.

15. An alternative measure for the performance of a forecasting technique is the <u>mean absolute deviation (MAD)</u>. In this measure, the mean of the absolute values of all forecast errors is calculated, and the forecasting method or parameter(s) which minimize this measure is selected. The mean absolute deviation measure is less sensitive to individual large forecast errors than the mean squared error measure.

16. If a time series exhibits a linear trend, the <u>method of least squares</u> may be used to determine a trend line (projection) for future forecasts. This statistical technique, also used in regression analysis, determines the unique trend line forecast which minimizes the mean square error between the trend line forecasts and the actual observed values for the time series.

17. Using the method of least squares, the formula for the <u>trend projection</u> is: $T_t = b_0 + b_1 t$.

    Here, T_t = the trend forecast for time period t
    b_1 = the slope of the trend line
    b_0 = the trend line projection for time 0

    Where $$b_1 = \frac{n\sum tY_t - \sum t \sum Y_t}{n\sum t^2 - (\sum t)^2} \qquad b_0 = \bar{Y} - b_1 \bar{t}$$

Here, Y_t = the observed value of the time series at time period t

$\bar{Y}$ = the average of the observed values for Y_t

$\bar{t}$ = the average time period for the n observations

18. In the case of nonlinear trend, a more advanced statistical technique might possibly be used to develop the forecasting curve.

19. The multiplicative time series model assumes that the actual time series value, Y_t, is equal to the product of the four time series components: (1) trend (T_t); (2) cyclical (C_t); (3) seasonal (S_t); and (4) irregular (I_t). Thus, $Y_t = T_t C_t S_t I_t$.

20. In situations in which no historical data is available or when historical data will not give an accurate picture of the future, nonquantitative techniques for forecasting may be used.

21. An example of a nonquantitative forecasting technique is the delphi approach. A panel of experts, each of whom is physically separated from the others and is anonymous, is asked to respond to a sequential series of questionnaires. After each questionnaire, the responses are tabulated and the information and opinions of the entire group are made known to each of the other panel members so that they may revise their previous forecast response. The process continues until some degree of consensus is achieved.

22. Another nonquantitative approach, scenario writing, consists of developing a conceptual scenario of the future based on a well defined set of assumptions. After several different scenarios have been developed, the decision maker determines which is most likely to occur in the future and makes decisions accordingly.

23. Subjective or interactive qualitative approaches, commonly known as "brainstorming sessions" are another way to perform a nonquantitative forecast. It is important in such sessions that any ideas or opinions be permitted to be presented without regard to its relevancy and without fear of criticism.

MULTIPLICATIVE TIME SERIES PROCEDURE

1. Calculate the centered moving averages (CMAs).
   The centered moving average represents the combined trend and cyclical components of the series. Calculate n-period moving averages (where n is the number of seasons, i.e. quarterly data would have four seasons whereas monthly data would have twelve seasons.)

2. Center the CMAs on integer-valued periods.
   Associate each moving average with the middle period of the n data points comprising the average. When n is an even number there is no distinct middle period. In this case, taking the average of two successive moving averages (one centered just above the period and one centered just below the period) gives the moving average associated with that period.

3. Determine the seasonal and irregular factors (S_tI_t).
   For each centered moving average found in step 2, divide this value into the observed value, Y_t. This quotient represents the seasonal and irregular factors.

4. Determine the average seasonal factors.
   For each season, average the corresponding quotients found in step 3 to smooth out the irregular component and isolate the seasonal factors.

5. Scale the seasonal factors (S_t).
   To ensure that the seasonal factors average to 1, adjust the seasonal factors by dividing each by the average seasonal factor value.

6. Determine the deseasonalized data.
   Divide each data value, Y_t, by its seasonal factor.

7. Determine a trend line of the deseasonalized data.
   Use the method of least squares on this data set to identify the trend line for the data.

8. Determine the deseasonalized predictions.
   Determine the trend forecast(s) associated with the future period(s) by using the trend line equation found in step 7.

9. Take into account the seasonality.
   Multiply each deseasonalized prediction by the appropriate seasonal factor.

FLOW CHART OF MULTIPLICATIVE TIME SERIES PROCEDURE

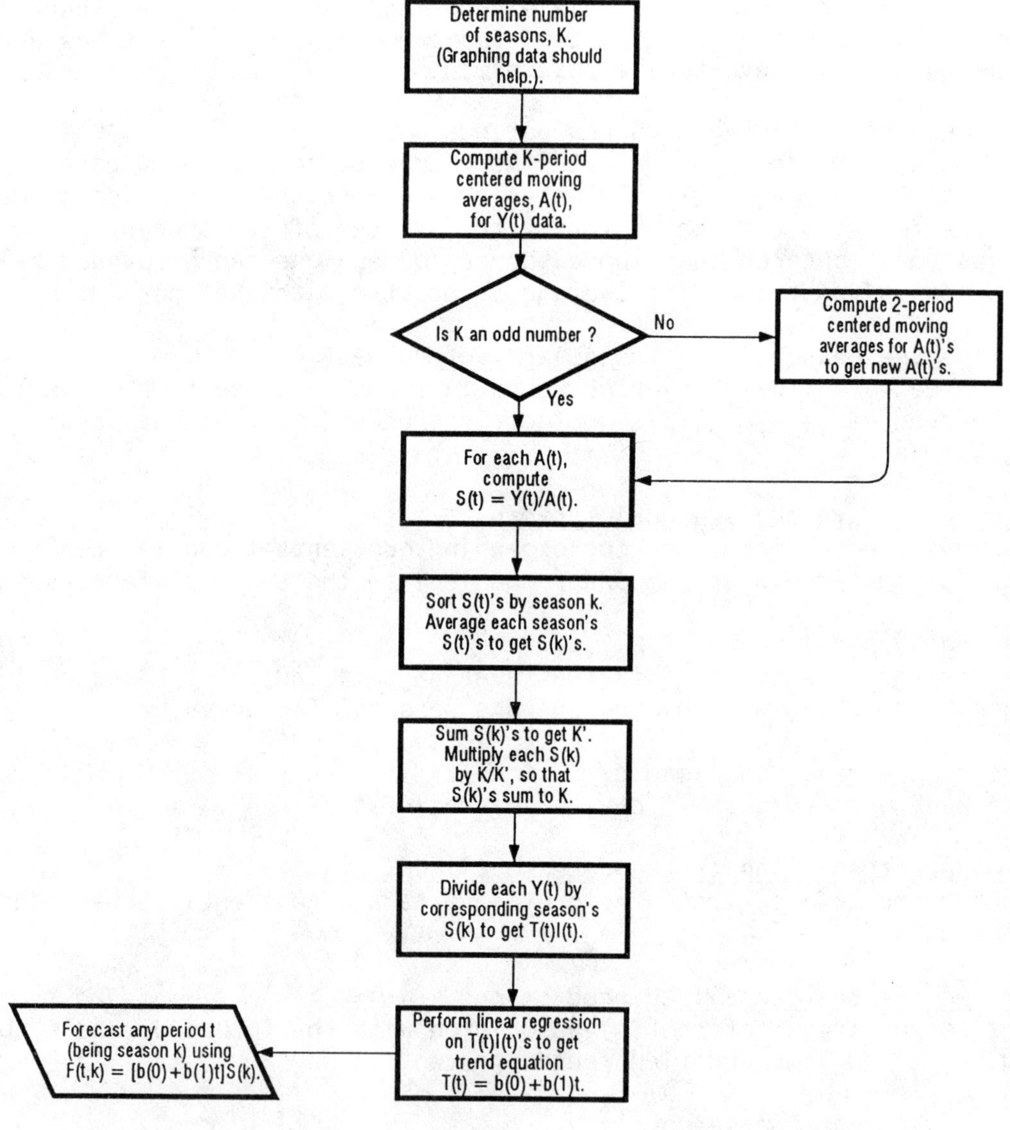
Determine number of seasons, K. (Graphing data should help.).
Compute K-period centered moving averages, A(t), for Y(t) data.
Is K an odd number ?
No
Yes
Compute 2-period centered moving averages for A(t)'s to get new A(t)'s.
For each A(t), compute S(t) = Y(t)/A(t).
Sort S(t)'s by season k. Average each season's S(t)'s to get S(k)'s.
Sum S(k)'s to get K'. Multiply each S(k) by K/K', so that S(k)'s sum to K.
Divide each Y(t) by corresponding season's S(k) to get T(t)I(t).
Perform linear regression on T(t)I(t)'s to get trend equation T(t) = b(0)+b(1)t.
Forecast any period t (being season k) using F(t,k) = [b(0)+b(1)t]S(k).

ILLUSTRATED PROBLEMS

PROBLEM 1

During the past ten weeks, sales of cases of Comfort brand headache medicine at Robert's Drugs have been as follows:

Week	Sales	Week	Sales
1	110	6	120
2	115	7	130
3	125	8	115
4	120	9	110
5	125	10	130

a) If Robert's uses exponential smoothing to forecast sales, which value for the smoothing constant α, $\alpha = .1$ or $\alpha = .8$, gives better forecasts?

b) Using your value for α in part (a) that gave better forecasts, forecast the sales for week 11.

c) Forecast sales in week 11 using a three week moving average.

SOLUTION 1

a) To evaluate the two smoothing constants, determine how the forecasted values would compare with the actual historical values in each case. Let

Y_t = actual sales in week t
F_t = forecasted sales in week t

For $\alpha = .1, \quad 1 - \alpha = .9$

$F_1 = Y_1 = 110$. For other weeks,

$F_{t+1} = .1Y_t + .9F_t$

$$
\begin{aligned}
F_1 & & &= 110 \\
F_2 &= .1Y_1 + .9F_1 &= .1(110) + .9(110) &= 110 \\
F_3 &= .1Y_2 + .9F_2 &= .1(115) + .9(110) &= 110.5 \\
F_4 &= .1Y_3 + .9F_3 &= .1(125) + .9(110.5) &= 111.95 \\
F_5 &= .1Y_4 + .9F_4 &= .1(120) + .9(111.95) &= 112.76 \\
F_6 &= .1Y_5 + .9F_5 &= .1(125) + .9(112.76) &= 113.98 \\
F_7 &= .1Y_6 + .9F_6 &= .1(120) + .9(113.98) &= 114.58 \\
F_8 &= .1Y_7 + .9F_7 &= .1(130) + .9(114.58) &= 116.12 \\
F_9 &= .1Y_8 + .9F_8 &= .1(115) + .9(116.12) &= 116.01 \\
F_{10} &= .1Y_9 + .9F_9 &= .1(110) + .9(116.01) &= 115.41
\end{aligned}
$$

For $\alpha = .8, \quad 1 - \alpha = .2$

$F_1 = 110$
$F_2 = .8(110) + .2(110) = 110$
$F_3 = .8(115) + .2(110) = 114$
$F_4 = .8(125) + .2(114) = 122.80$
$F_5 = .8(120) + .2(122.80) = 120.56$
$F_6 = .8(125) + .2(120.56) = 124.11$
$F_7 = .8(120) + .2(124.11) = 120.82$
$F_8 = .8(130) + .2(120.82) = 128.16$
$F_9 = .8(115) + .2(128.16) = 117.63$
$F_{10} = .8(110) + .2(117.63) = 111.53.$

In order to determine which smoothing constant gives the better performance, calculate, for each, the mean squared error for the nine weeks of forecasts, weeks 2 through 10 by:

$$[(Y_2-F_2)^2 + (Y_3-F_3)^2 + (Y_4-F_4)^2 + \ldots + (Y_{10}-F_{10})^2] / 9$$

		$\alpha = .1$		$\alpha = .8$	
Week	Y_t	F_t	$(Y_t - F_t)^2$	F_t	$(Y_t - F_t)^2$
1	110				
2	115	110.00	25.00	110.00	25.00
3	125	110.50	210.25	114.00	121.00
4	120	111.95	64.80	122.80	7.84
5	125	112.76	149.94	120.56	19.71
6	120	113.98	36.25	124.11	16.91
7	130	114.58	237.73	120.82	84.23
8	115	116.12	1.26	128.16	173.30
9	110	116.01	36.12	117.63	58.26
10	130	115.41	212.87	111.53	341.27
		Sum	974.22	Sum	847.52
	MSE	Sum/9	108.25	Sum/9	94.17

Hence, based on the mean squared error criterion, using $\alpha = .8$ gives a slightly better forecast than using $\alpha = .1$.

b) If $\alpha = .8$, then the forecast for week 11 will be $.8Y_{10} + .2F_{10} = .8(130) + .2(111.53) = 126.31$.

c) Using a three week moving average, the forecast for week 11 will be the average of the preceding three weeks: weeks 8, 9, and 10.
$F_{11} = (115 + 110 + 130)/3 = 118.33$

PROBLEM 2

The number of plumbing repair jobs performed by Auger's Plumbing Service in each of the last nine months are listed below.

Month	Jobs	Month	Jobs	Month	Jobs
March	353	June	374	September	399
April	387	July	396	October	412
May	342	August	409	November	408

a) Assuming a linear trend function, forecast the number of repair jobs Auger's will perform in December using the squares method.

b) What is your forecast for December using a three-period weighted moving average with weights of .6, .3, and .1? How does it compare with your forecast from part (a)?

SOLUTION 2

> **NOTE:** The method of least squares requires time periods to be numbered. If your periods are labeled with words (e.g. February or Thursday) or the number labels are large (e.g. 1983), simply assign the first period in your data set the number 1, etc. Determine the number of the time period you want to forecast accordingly. For example, if 1983 is period 1, then 1998 is period 16.

a) The trend line is $T_t = b_0 + b_1t$. The least squares method gives:

(month) t	Y_t	tY_t	t^2
(Mar.) 1	353	353	1
(Apr.) 2	387	774	4
(May) 3	342	1026	9
(June) 4	374	1496	16
(July) 5	396	1980	25
(Aug.) 6	409	2454	36
(Sep.) 7	399	2793	49
(Oct.) 8	412	3296	64
(Nov.) 9	408	3672	81
Sum 45	3480	17844	285

Thus, $\bar{t} = 5$ $\quad \bar{Y} = 386.667$

$$b_1 = \frac{n\Sigma tY_t - \Sigma t\Sigma Y_t}{n\Sigma t^2 - (\Sigma t)^2} = \frac{(9)(17844) - (45)(3480)}{(9)(285) - (45)^2} = 7.4$$

$$b_0 = \bar{Y} - b_1\bar{t} = 386.667 - 7.4(5) = 349.667$$

$$T_{10} = 349.667 + (7.4)(10) = 423.667$$

b) Using a three-month weighted moving average, the forecast for December will be the weighted average of the preceding three months: September, October, and November.

$$F_{10} = .1Y_{Sep.} + .3Y_{Oct.} + .6Y_{Nov.} = .1(399) + .3(412) + .6(408) = 408.3$$

Due to the positive trend component in the time series, the least squares method produced a forecast that is more in tune with the trend that exists. The weighted moving average, even with heavy (.6) placed on the current period, produced a forecast that is lagging behind the changing data.

PROBLEM 3

Quarterly revenues (in $1,000,000's) for a national restaurant chain for a five year period were as follows:

	Year				
Quarter	1	2	3	4	5
1	33	42	54	70	85
2	36	40	53	67	82
3	35	42	54	70	87
4	38	47	62	77	99

Forecast the revenues for the next four quarters.

SOLUTION 3

Assume the data values are a multiplicative function of the data's trend, cyclical, seasonal, and irregular factors, i.e.

$$Y_t = T_t * C_t * S_t * I_t$$

Step 1: Calculate the centered moving averages (CMAs).

First, use a moving average over the four quarters to mask the effects of the seasonal and irregular factors. For each four quarter period, calculate the moving average and associate it with the "middle period". For example, the first moving average is: (33+36+35+38)/4 = 35.5. The second equals = 37.75, etc.

Step 2: Center the CMAs on integer-valued periods.

When the number of quarters is even, there is no integer valued "middle period" (the middle of the first four quarters would be quarter 2.5).

In order to have the moving average "centered" at a particular quarter, average the half-period moving average preceding this quarter and the half-period moving average succeeding this quarter. For example, the moving averages of quarters 2.5 and 3.5 are 35.5 and 37.75, respectivetly. Thus the centered moving average for quarter 3 is (35.5 + 37.75)/2 = 36.625.

Year	Quarter	Revenues	Four Quarter Moving Average	Centered Moving Average
1	1	33		
	2	36		
	(2.5)		35.50	
	3	35		36.625
	(3.5)		37.75	
	4	38		38.250
	(4.5)		38.75	
2	1	42		39.625
	(1.5)		40.50	
	2	40		41.625
	(2.5)		42.75	
	3	42		44.250
	(3.5)		45.75	
	4	47		47.375
	(4.5)		49.00	
3	1	54		50.500
	(1.5)		52.00	
	2	53		53.875
	(2.5)		55.75	
	3	54		57.750
	(3.5)		59.75	
	4	62		61.500
	(4.5)		63.25	
4	1	70		65.250
	(1.5)		67.25	
	2	67		69.125
	(2.5)		71.00	
	3	70		72.875
	(3.5)		74.75	
	4	77		76.625
	(4.5)		78.50	
5	1	85		80.625
	(1.5)		82.75	
	2	82		85.500
	(2.5)		88.25	
	3	87		
	4	99		

Step 3: Determine the seasonal and irregular factors (S_tI_t).

The centered moving averages represent the combine effects of the trend and cyclical factors (T_tC_t). Since $Y_t = T_tC_tS_tI_t$, $S_tI_t = Y_t/(T_tC_t) = Y_t/$(centered moving average for period t). Hence, dividing each data point by its centered moving average gives an estimate of S_tI_t.

For example for period 3 (year 1, quarter 3), the data point, $Y_3 = 35$, and its centered moving average $T_3C_3 = 36.625$. Thus, for this period, $S_3I_3 = 35/36.625 = .956$

Continue this procedure for determining S_tI_t for all periods:

Year	Quarter	Revenues (Y_t)	Average (T_tC_t)	S_tI_t
1	3	35	36.625	.956
	4	38	38.250	.993
2	1	42	39.625	1.060
	2	40	41.625	.961
	3	42	44.250	.949
	4	47	47.375	.992
3	1	54	50.500	1.069
	2	53	53.875	.984
	3	54	57.750	.935
	4	62	61.500	1.008
4	1	70	65.250	1.073
	2	67	69.125	.969
	3	70	72.875	.961
	4	77	76.625	1.005
5	1	85	80.625	1.054
	2	82	85.500	.959

Step 4: Determine the average seasonal factors.

To eliminate the irregular effects, take the average of the S_tI_t over the four years. That is, to find the average of S_tI_t for quarter 1, average the quarter 1 values for years 2, 3, 4 and 5. Do the same for quarter 2. For quarters 3 and 4, the average would be over years 1, 2, 3, and 4. This gives:

$$S_1 = (1.060 + 1.069 + 1.073 + 1.054) / 4 = 1.064$$
$$S_2 = (.961 + .984 + .969 + .959) / 4 = .968$$
$$S_3 = (.956 + .949 + .935 + .961) / 4 = .950$$
$$S_4 = (.993 + .992 + 1.008 + 1.005) / 4 = 1.000$$

Step 5: Scale the seasonal factors (S_t).

Each seasonal average must be adjusted by the average of the seasonal factors, (1.064 + .968 + .950 + 1.000) / 4 = .9955, giving:

$$S_1 = 1.064/.9955 = 1.069$$
$$S_2 = .968/.9955 = .973$$
$$S_3 = .950/.9955 = .954$$
$$S_4 = 1.000/.9955 = 1.004$$

Step 6: Determine the deseasonalized data.

The seasonal factors (S_t) can now be removed from the data by dividing each data point by its seasonal factor. This gives deseasonalized data which will only be a function of trend, cyclical and irregular factors.

Year	Quarter	Y_t	Deseasonalized (Y_t/S_t)
1	1	33	33/1.069 = 30.87
	2	36	36/ .973 = 37.00
	3	35	35/ .954 = 36.69
	4	38	38/1.004 = 37.84
2	1	42	42/1.069 = 39.29
	2	40	40/ .973 = 41.11
	3	42	42/ .954 = 44.03
	4	47	47/1.004 = 46.44
3	1	54	54/1.069 = 50.51
	2	53	53/ .973 = 54.47
	3	54	54/ .954 = 56.60
	4	62	62/1.004 = 61.75
4	1	70	70/1.069 = 65.48
	2	67	67/ .973 = 68.86
	3	70	70/ .954 = 73.38
	4	77	77/1.004 = 76.69
5	1	85	85/1.069 = 79.51
	2	82	82/ .973 = 84.28
	3	87	87/ .954 = 91.19
	4	99	99/1.004 = 98.61

Step 7: Determine a trend line of the deseasonalized data.

Now, label the periods t = 1 through t = 20 and use the regression trend analysis (see problem 2) to determine the following trend line describing the seasonally adjusted data over the 20 quarters:

$$T_t = 23.436 + 3.361t$$

Step 8: Determine the deseasonalized predictions.

Use this trend line to determine the trend predictions for the four quarters of year 6.

Step 9: Take into account the seasonality.

Then adjust these quarterly predictions by multiplying each by its seasonal adjustment factor.

Quarter	Period t	Trend Prediction (T_t=23.436+3.361t)	Seasonally Adjusted Forecast (T_tS_t)
1	21	94.02	(94.02)(1.069) = 100.50
2	22	97.38	(97.38)(.973) = 94.72
3	23	100.74	(100.74)(.954) = 96.15
4	24	104.10	(104.10)(1.004) = 104.53

PROBLEM 4

Business at Terry's Tie Shop can be viewed as falling into three distinct seasons: (1) Christmas (November-December); (2) Father's Day (late May - mid-June); and (3) all other times. Average weekly sales (in $'s) during each of these three seasons during the past four years has been as follows:

	Year			
Season	1	2	3	4
1	1856	1995	2241	2280
2	2012	2168	2306	2408
3	985	1072	1105	1120

Determine a forecast for the average weekly sales in year 5 for each of the three seasons.

SOLUTION 4

The table on the next page summarizes the computations in steps 1-6.

Step 1: Calculate the centered moving averages.
There are three distinct seasons in each year. Hence, take a three season moving average to eliminate seasonal and irregular factors. For example the first moving average is: (1856 + 2012 + 985)/3 =1617.67.

Step 2: Center the CMAs on integer-valued periods.
The first moving average computed in step 1 (1617.67) will be centered on season 2 of year 1. Note that the moving averages from step 1 center themselves on integer-valued periods because n is an odd number.

Step 3: Determine the seasonal and irregular factors (S_t,I_t).
Isolate the trend and cyclical components. For each period t, this is given by Y_t/(Moving Average for period t).

Step 4: Determine the average seasonal factors.
Averaging all S_tI_t values corresponding to that season:

Season 1: (1.163 + 1.196 + 1.181) / 3 = 1.180
Season 2: (1.244 + 1.242 + 1.224 + 1.244) / 4 = 1.238
Season 3: (.592 + .587 + .582) / 3 = .587

Step 5: Scale the seasonal factors (S_t).
Divide each seasonal factor by the average of the seasonal factors. Then average the seasonal factors = (1.180 + 1.238 + .587)/3 = 1.002.

Season 1: 1.180/1.002 = 1.178
Season 2: 1.238/1.002 = 1.236
Season 3: .587/1.002 = .586

Step 6: Determine the deseasonalized data.

Divide the data point values, Y_t, by S_t.

Year	Season	Dollar Sales (Y_t)	Moving Average	S_tI_t	Scaled S_t	Y_t/S_t
1	1	1856			1.178	1576
	2	2012	1617.67	1.244	1.236	1628
	3	985	1664.00	.592	.586	1681
2	1	1995	1716.00	1.163	1.178	1694
	2	2168	1745.00	1.242	1.236	1754
	3	1072	1827.00	.587	.586	1829
3	1	2241	1873.00	1.196	1.178	1902
	2	2306	1884.00	1.224	1.236	1866
	3	1105	1897.00	.582	.586	1886
4	1	2280	1931.00	1.181	1.178	1935
	2	2408	1936.00	1.244	1.236	1948
	3	1120			.586	1911

Step 7: Determine a trend line of the deseasonalized data.

Use the linear regression method illustrated in problem 2. For $t = 1, 2, \ldots, 12$, this gives:

$$T_t = 1580.11 + 33.96t.$$

Step 8: Determine the deseasonalized predictions for quarters (13, 14, 15).

Substitute t = 13, 14, and 15 into the above equation:

$$T_{13} = 1580.11 + (33.96)(13) = 2022$$
$$T_{14} = 1580.11 + (33.96)(14) = 2056$$
$$T_{15} = 1580.11 + (33.96)(15) = 2090$$

Step 9: Take into account the seasonality.

Multiply each deseasonalized prediction by its seasonal factor to give the following forecasts for year 5:

Season 1: (1.178)(2022) = 2382
Season 2: (1.236)(2056) = 2541
Season 3: (.586)(2090) = 1225

PROBLEM 5

Connie Harris, in charge of office supplies at First Capital Mortgage Corp., would like to predict the quantity of paper used in the office photocopying machines per month. She believes that the number of loans originated in a month influence the volume of photocopying performed. She has compiled the following recent monthly data:

Number of Loans Originated in Month	Sheets of Photocopy Paper Used (000's)
25	16
25	13
35	18
40	25
40	21
45	22
50	24
60	25

a) Develop the least-squares estimated regression equation that relates sheets of photocopy paper used to loans originated.

b) Use the regression equation developed in part (a) to forecast the amount of paper used in a month when 65 loan originations are expected.

SOLUTION 5

a) The regression equation is $\hat{y} = b_0 + b_1x$. The least squares method gives:

Month (i)	y_i	x_i	x_iy_i	x_i^2
1	16	25	400	625
2	13	25	325	625
3	18	35	630	1225
4	25	40	1000	1600
5	21	40	840	1600
6	22	45	990	2025
7	24	50	1200	2500
8	25	60	1500	3600
Totals	164	320	6885	13800

$$b_1 = \frac{\Sigma x_iy_i - (\Sigma x_i \Sigma y_i)/n}{\Sigma x_i^2 - (\Sigma x_i)^2/n} = \frac{6885 - (320)(164)/8}{13800 - (320)^2/8} = \frac{325}{1000} = 0.325$$

$$b_0 = \bar{y} - b_1\bar{x} = \Sigma y_i/n - b_1(\Sigma x_i/n) = 164/8 - .325(320/8) = 20.5 - 13 = 7.5$$

Thus, the estimated regression equation is $\hat{y} = 7.5 + .325x$

b) The forecast is $\hat{y} = 7.5 + .325x = 7.5 + .325(65) = 28{,}625$ sheets.

ANSWERED PROBLEMS

PROBLEM 6

The monthly electricity bill at the Chez Paul Restaurant over the past 12 months has been as follows:

Month	Amount	Month	Amount
Jan	$271.90	Jul	$330.70
Feb	305.70	Aug	300.10
Mar	306.40	Sep	275.50
Apr	297.30	Oct	301.30
May	315.30	Nov	279.40
Jun	297.20	Dec	306.60

Paul is considering using exponential smoothing with $\alpha = .5$ or a four period weighted moving average with weights of .4, .3, .2, and .1 to forecast future electricity costs.

a) Which forecasting technique will give the smallest mean square error?

b) Give next January's forecast for each method.

PROBLEM 7

Sales (in thousands) of the new Thorton Model 506 convection oven over the eight week period since its introduction have been as follows:

Week	Sales
1	18.6
2	21.4
3	25.2
4	22.4
5	24.6
6	19.2
7	21.7
8	23.8

a) Which exponential smoothing model provides better forecasts, one using $\alpha = .6$ or $\alpha = .2$? Compare them using mean squared error.

b) Using the two forecast models in part (a), what are the forecasts for week 9?

PROBLEM 8

Forecast the sales of Jami Michelle skin cream for year 6 given the following quarterly sales (in thousands) over the past five years:

	Year				
Quarter	1	2	3	4	5
1	34	38	43	47	49
2	27	33	37	39	45
3	49	51	60	68	72
4	27	28	29	32	40

PROBLEM 9

Weekly sales of the Weber La Guillotine food processor for the past ten weeks have been:

Week	Sales	Week	Sales
1	980	6	990
2	1040	7	1030
3	1120	8	1260
4	1050	9	1240
5	960	10	1100

a) Determine whether a three period simple moving average model or a four period simple moving average model gives a better forecast for this problem. Evaluate on the basis of minimizing the mean square error.

b) For each model, forecast sales for week 11.

PROBLEM 10

Four months ago, the Bank Drug Company introduced Jeffrey William brand designer bandages. Advertised using the slogan, "What the best dressed cuts are wearing", weekly sales for this period (in 1000's) have been as follows:

Week	Sales	Week	Sales	Week	Sales
1	12.8	7	20.6	12	23.8
2	14.6	8	18.5	13	25.1
3	15.2	9	19.9	14	24.7
4	16.1	10	23.6	15	26.5
5	15.8	11	24.2	16	28.9
6	17.2				

a) Plot a graph of sales vs. weeks. Does linear trend appear reasonable?

b) Assuming linear trend, forecast sales for weeks 17, 18, 19, and 20.

PROBLEM 11

The number of haircuts performed each day at KwikKuts in the last four weeks are lissted below:

Week	Workday Monday	Tuesday	Wednesday	Thursday	Friday
1	122	122	103	133	98
2	127	130	106	137	97
3	126	131	111	151	104
4	135	135	110	146	107

a) Plot the sales data. Do you see both trend and seasonality components in the data?

b) Forecast the number of haircuts to be performed in each workday of week 6.

PROBLEM 12

At a local car dealership the following is a record of sales for the past 12 months:

Month	Sales	Month	Sales
Jan	36	Jul	25
Feb	34	Aug	22
Mar	28	Sep	26
Apr	30	Oct	22
May	27	Nov	21
Jun	24	Dec	19

a) Using the method of least squares, determine a trend line for forecasting future sales.

b) Using your model in part (a), determine how long it will be before zero sales are forecasted.

c) Consider your answer to part (b). What will be the forecasted sales for the month after that? Does this make sense? Comment on the validity of the model. What assumption about the model appears to be in error?

PROBLEM 13

A 24-hour coffee/donut shop makes donuts every eight hours. The manager must forecast donut demand so that the bakers have the fresh ingredients they need. Listed below is the actual number of glazed donuts (in dozens) sold in each of the preceding 13 eight-hour shifts.

Date	Shift	Demand (dozens)
June 3	Day	59
	Evening	47
June 4	Night	35
	Day	64
	Evening	43
June 5	Night	39
	Day	62
	Evening	46
June 6	Night	42
	Day	64
	Evening	50
June 7	Night	40
	Day	69

Forecast the demand for glazed donuts for the three shifts of June 8 and the three shifts of June 9.

PROBLEM 14

Scott Bell Builders would like to predict the total number of labor hours spent framing a house based on the square footage of the house. The following data has been compiled on ten houses recently built.

Square Footage (100's)	Framing Labor Hours	Square Footage (100's)	Framing Labor Hours
20	195	27	225
21	170	29	240
23	220	31	225
23	200	32	275
26	230	35	260

a) Develop the least-squares estimated regression equation that relates framing labor hours to house square footage.

b) Use the regression equation developed in part (a) to predict framing labor hours when the house size is 3350 square feet.

TRUE/FALSE

15. If a time series has a trend component, then one should not use a moving average to forecast.

16. In forecasting with trend and seasonal components using a multiplicative model, one computes moving averages in order to isolate the combined seasonal and irregular components.

17. If the random variability in a time series is great, a high α value should be used to exponentially smooth out the fluctuations.

18. In exponential smoothing, one typically chooses the smoothing constant as that value which minimizes the mean squared error.

19. Forecasting errors are always less using exponential smoothing than a weighted moving average.

20. A forecaster would choose trend projection using the least squares method over exponential smoothing if the data exhibited a trend component.

21. To forecast using the multiplicative model, one must adjust the trend component by the seasonal factor.

22. In a weighted moving average, the most recent occurrence is typically given the least weight.

23. In using the Delphi technique, one attempts to obtain a group consensus.

24. One advantage of exponential smoothing over moving averages is that fewer data points are used in the forecast.

25. An α equal to 0.2 will cause an exponential smoothing forecast to react more quickly to a sudden drop in demand than will an α equal to 0.4.

26. Exponential smoothing with $\alpha = .2$ and a moving average with $n = 5$ put the same weight on the actual value for the current period.

27. The sum of the seasonal indexes should be adjusted, if necessary, to equal 1.

28. With fewer periods in a moving average, it will take longer to adjust to a new level of demand.

29. A causal forecasting method is most effective when demand data exhibit fluctuations caused by seasonal influences.

Chapter 7
Linear Programming: The Graphical Method

KEY CONCEPTS

CONCEPT	ILLUSTRATED PROBLEMS	ANSWERED PROBLEMS
Formulation	7,8	15,16,18,19,20
Minimization	2,5	9,10,15,19
Standard Form	1	14
Slack/Surplus Variables	1	16
Equal-to Constraints	3,5	14
Redundant Constraints	5,7	12,13
Extreme Points	2,5	11,16
Alternative Optimal Solutions	7	10,11,15
Infeasibility	4	14
Unboundedness	4	11
Sensitivity Analysis Objective Function Changes Righthand Side Changes	6,8	17-20

REVIEW

1. A mathematical programming problem is one that seeks to maximize an objective function subject to constraints. If both the objective function and the constraints are linear, the problem is referred to as a linear programming problem.

2. Linear functions are functions in which each variable appears in a separate term raised to the first power and is multiplied by a constant (which could be 0).

3. Linear constraints are linear functions that are restricted to be "less than or equal to", "equal to", or "greater than or equal to" a constant.

4. The properties of linear programming models are:
   (1) proportionality -- the profit contribution and the amount of the resources used by a decision variable is directly proportional to its value;
   (2) additivity -- the value of the objective function and the amount of the resources used can be calculated by summing the individual contributions of the decision variables;
   (3) divisibility -- fractional values of the decision variables are permitted.

5. The maximization or minimization of some quantity is the objective in all linear programming problems.

6. A feasible solution satisfies all the problem's constraints.

7. A linear program which is overconstrained so that no point satisfies all the constraints is said to be infeasible. Changes to the objective function coefficients do not affect the feasibility of the problem.

8. An optimal solution is a feasible solution that results in the largest possible objective function value, Z, when maximizing or smallest possible Z when minimizing.

9. A graphical solution method can be used to solve a linear program with two variables.

10. If a linear program possesses an optimal solution, then an extreme point will be optimal.

11. If a constraint can be removed without affecting the shape of the feasible region, the constraint is redundant. If changes are anticipated to the linear programming model, constraints which were redundant in the original formulation may not be redundant in the revised formulation.

12. In the graphical method, if the objective function line is parallel to a boundary constraint in the direction of optimization, there are alternate optimal solutions, with all points on this line segment being optimal.

13. A feasible region may be unbounded and yet there may be optimal solutions. This is common in minimization problems and is possible in maximization problems.

14. The feasible region for a two-variable linear programming problem can be: a) nonexistent, b) a single point, c) a line, d) a polygon, or e) an unbounded area.

15. Any linear program either (a) is infeasible, (b) has a unique optimal solution or alternate optimal solutions, or (c) has an objective function that can be increased without bound.

16. A linear program in which all the variables are non-negative and all the constraints are equalities is said to be in standard form. Standard form is attained by adding slack variables to "less than or equal to" constraints, and by subtracting surplus variables from "greater than or equal to" constraints. They represent the difference between the left and right sides of the constraints.

17. Slack and surplus variables have objective function coefficients equal to 0. If, however, extra resources could be sold at a a profit, or if there were a penalty for surplus resources, the objective function coefficients would not be 0 and these variables would, in effect, become new decision variables.

18. Sensitivity analysis is used to determine effects on the optimal solution within specified ranges for the objective function coefficients, constraint coefficients, and right hand side values. This provides answers to certain what-if questions.

19. A range of optimality of an objective function coefficient is found by determining an interval for the objective function coefficient in which the original optimal solution remains optimal while keeping all other data of the problem constant. The value of the objective function may change in this range.

20. Graphically, the limits of a range of optimality are found by changing the slope of the objective function line within the limits of the slopes of the binding constraint lines. This would also apply to simultaneous changes in the objective coefficients. The slope of an objective function line, MAX $c_1x_1 + c_2x_2$, is $-c_1/c_2$, and the slope of a constraint i,

$$a_{i1}x_1 + a_{i2}x_2 = b_i, \text{ is } -a_{i1}/a_{i2}.$$

21. A <u>shadow price</u> for a right hand side value (or resource limit) is the amount the objective function will <u>change</u> per unit increase in the right hand side value of a constraint.

22. Graphically, a <u>shadow price</u> is determined by adding +1 to the right hand side value in question and then resolving for the optimal solution in terms of the same two binding constraints. The shadow price is equal to the difference in the objective functions values between the new and original problems.

23. A <u>dual price</u> for a right hand side value (or resource limit) is the amount the objective function will <u>improve</u> per unit increase in the right hand side value of a constraint. Thus, for maximization problems dual prices and shadow prices are the same, whereas for minimization problems, shadow prices are the negative of dual prices.

24. A <u>nonbinding constraint</u> has <u>positive slack</u> or <u>surplus</u> when evaluated at the optimal solution. The shadow price for a nonbinding constraint is 0.

25. The <u>range of feasibility</u> for a change in the right hand side value is the range of values for this coefficient for which the original <u>shadow price</u> remains constant.

26. Graphically, the <u>range of feasibility</u> is determined by finding the values of a right hand side coefficient such that the same two lines that determined the original optimal solution continue to determine the optimal solution for the problem.

GRAPHICAL SOLUTION PROCEDURE

1. Graph the constraints and shade in the feasible region, considering the feasible side of each constraint line.

2. Set the objective function equal to any arbitrary constant and graph it. If the line does not lie in the feasible region, move it (maintaining its slope) into the feasible region.

3. Move the objective function line parallel to itself in the direction that increases its value when maximizing (decreases its value when minimizing) until it touches the last point(s) of the feasible region.

4. If the optimal extreme point falls on an axis (say, X_2 axis), use the binding constraint equation to solve for the unknown X* (in this case X_2*, since X_1* is zero). Otherwise, solve the two equations (binding constraints) in two unknowns (X_1* and X_2*) that determine the optimal extreme point.

5. Find Z by substituting X_{1*} and X_{2*} in the objective function.

FLOW CHART OF GRAPHICAL SOLUTION PROCEDURE

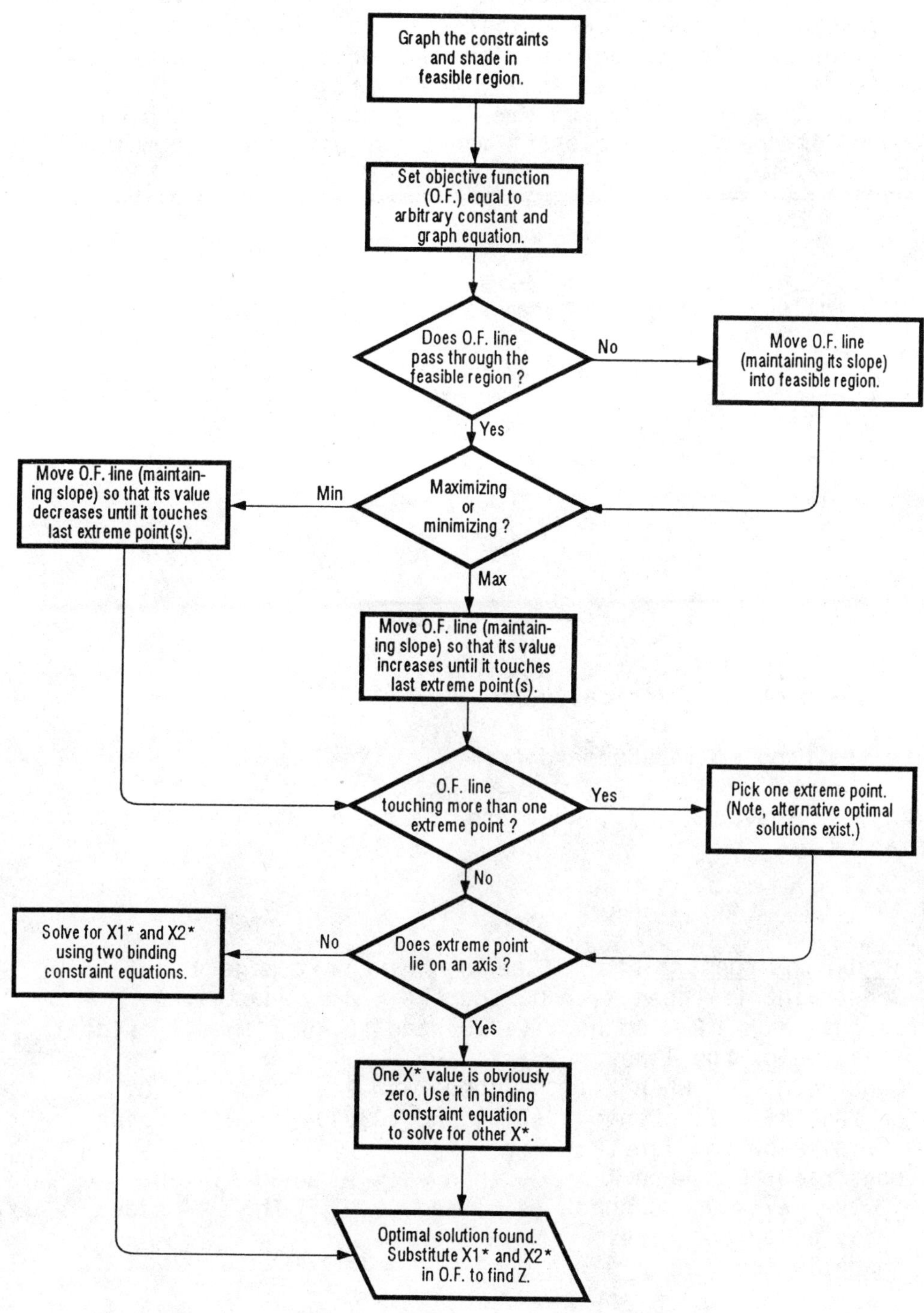
Graph the constraints and shade in feasible region.
Set objective function (O.F.) equal to arbitrary constant and graph equation.
Does O.F. line pass through the feasible region ?
No
Move O.F. line (maintaining its slope) into feasible region.
Yes
Maximizing or minimizing ?
Min
Move O.F. line (maintaining slope) so that its value decreases until it touches last extreme point(s).
Max
Move O.F. line (maintaining slope) so that its value increases until it touches last extreme point(s).
O.F. line touching more than one extreme point ?
Yes
Pick one extreme point. (Note, alternative optimal solutions exist.)
No
Does extreme point lie on an axis ?
No
Solve for X1* and X2* using two binding constraint equations.
Yes
One X* value is obviously zero. Use it in binding constraint equation to solve for other X*.
Optimal solution found. Substitute X1* and X2* in O.F. to find Z.

ILLUSTRATED PROBLEMS

> **NOTE:** Plotting an initial objective function line involves little more than reversing the objective coefficients for X_1 and X_2. Consider Problem 1 below. The objective line will cross the X_1 axis at 4 (X_2's coefficient) and the X_2 axis at 3 (X_1's coefficient). If the coefficients are too large (or small) for convenient graphing, scale them down (or up) in a consistent manner by dividing (or multiplying) both by, say, 10.

PROBLEM 1

Given the following linear program:

$$\text{MAX} \quad Z = 3X_1 + 4X_2$$

$$\text{S.T.} \quad 2X_1 + 3X_2 \leq 24$$

$$3X_1 + X_2 \leq 21$$

$$X_1 + X_2 \leq 9$$

$$X_1, X_2 \geq 0$$

a) Solve the problem graphically.

b) Write the problem in standard form.

c) Given your answer to (a), what are the optimal values of the slack variables.

SOLUTION 1

a) (1) Graph the constraints. (See graph on next page.)
Constraint 1: When $X_1 = 0$, then $X_2 = 8$; when $X_2 = 0$, then $X_1 = 12$. Connect (12,0) and (0,8). The "<" side is below the line.
Constraint 2: When $X_1 = 0$, then $X_2 = 21$; when $X_2 = 0$, then $X_1 = 7$. Connect (7,0) and (0,21). The "<" side is below the line.
Constraint 3: When $X_1 = 0$, then $X_2 = 9$; when $X_2 = 0$, then $X_1 = 9$. Connect (9,0) and (0,9). The "<" side is below the line.
Shade in the feasible region.

(2) <u>Graph the objective function</u> by setting the objective function equal to any arbitrary value (say 12) and graphing it. For $3X_1 + 4X_2 = 12$, when $X_2 = 0$, $X_1 = 4$; when $X_1 = 0$, $X_2 = 3$. Connect (4,0) and (0,3), the thick line on the graph.

(3) <u>Move the objective function line parallel to itself</u> in the direction that increases its value (upward) until it touches the last point of the feasible region. It is at the intersection of the first and third constraint lines.

(4) <u>Solve these two equations in two unknowns</u>:

$$\begin{array}{rcl} 2X_1 + 3X_2 = 24 & \text{======>} & 2X_1 + 3X_2 = 24 \\ X_1 + X_2 = 9 & \text{======>} & 2X_1 + 2X_2 = 18 \\ \hline & & X_2 = 6 \end{array}$$

Substituting into $X_1 + X_2 = 9$, then $X_1 = 3$.

(5) <u>Solve for Z</u>: $Z = 3X_1 + 4X_2 = 3(3) + 4(6) = 33$.
Thus the optimal solution is $X_1 = 3$, $X_2 = 6$, $Z = 33$.

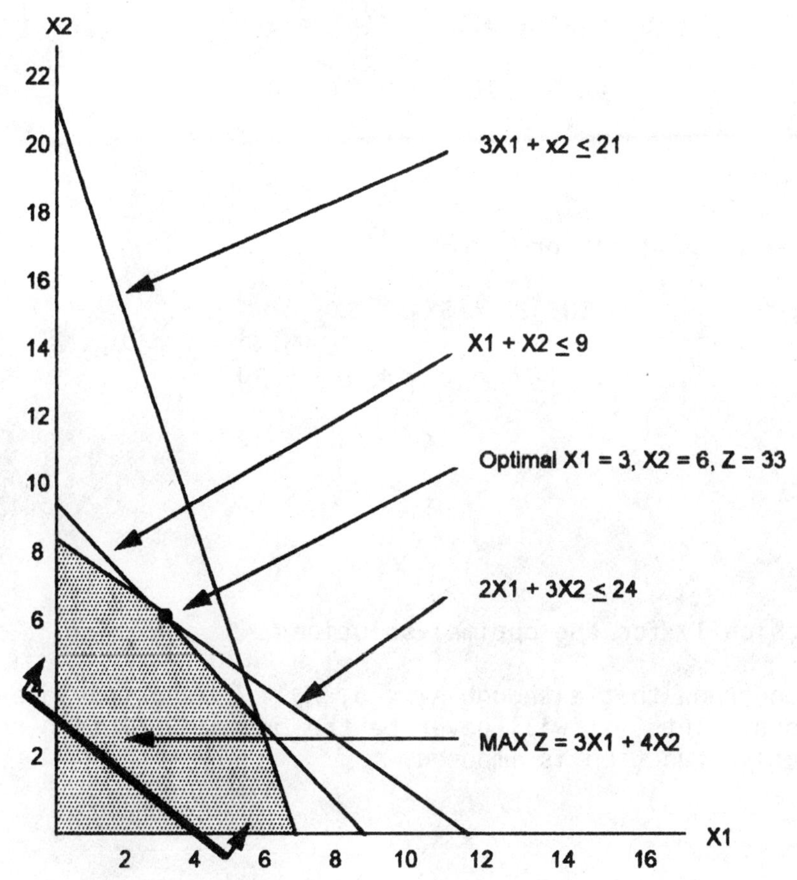

b) To write the problem in standard form, since each constraint is a "$\leq$" constraint, add a slack variable to each constraint.

$$\begin{aligned}
\text{MAX} \quad Z &= 3X_1 + 4X_2 + 0S_1 + 0S_2 + 0S_3 \\
\text{S.T.} \quad & 2X_1 + 3X_2 + S_1 = 24 \\
& 3X_1 + X_2 + S_2 = 21 \\
& X_1 + X_2 + S_3 = 9 \\
& X_j \geq 0 \quad j = 1,2 \\
& S_j \geq 0 \quad j = 1,2,3
\end{aligned}$$

c) Since the optimal solution was $X_1 = 3$, $X_2 = 6$, then substituting these values into the above equations gives:

$$S_1 = 24 - 2(3) - 3(6) = 0$$

$$S_2 = 21 - 3(3) - 1(6) = 6$$

$$S_3 = 9 - 1(3) - 1(6) = 0$$

PROBLEM 2

Given the following linear program:

$$\begin{aligned}
\text{MIN} \quad Z &= 5X_1 + 2X_2 \\
\text{S.T.} \quad & 2X_1 + 5X_2 \geq 10 \\
& 4X_1 - X_2 \geq 12 \\
& X_1 + X_2 \geq 4 \\
& X_1, X_2 \geq 0
\end{aligned}$$

a) Solve graphically for the optimal solution.

b) How does one know that although $X_1 = 5$, $X_2 = 3$ is a feasible solution for the constraints, it will never be the optimal solution no matter what objective function is imposed?

SOLUTION 2

a) (1) Graph the constraints. (See graph next page.)
Constraint 1: When $X_1 = 0$, then $X_2 = 2$; when $X_2 = 0$, then $X_1 = 5$. Connect (5,0) and (0,2). The ">" side is above this line.
Constraint 2: When $X_2 = 0$, then $X_1 = 3$. But setting X_1 to 0 will yield $X_2 = -12$, which is not on the graph. Thus, to get a second point on this line, set X_1 to any number larger than 3 and solve for X_2: when $X_1 = 5$, then $X_2 = 8$. Connect (3,0) and (5,8). The ">" side is to the right.
Constraint 3: When $X_1 = 0$, then $X_2 = 4$; when $X_2 = 0$, then $X_1 = 4$. Connect (4,0) and (0,4). The ">" side is above this line.
Shade in the feasible region.

(2) Graph the objective function by setting the objective function equal to an arbitrary constant (say 20) and graphing it.
For $5X_1 + 2X_2 = 20$, when $X_1 = 0$, then $X_2 = 10$; when $X_2 = 0$, then $X_1 = 4$. Connect (4,0) and (0,10).

(3) Move the objective function line in the direction which lowers its value (down) until it touches the last point of the feasible region, determined by the last two constraints.

(4) Solve these two equations in two unknowns.

$$4X_1 - X_2 = 12$$
$$X_1 + X_2 = 4$$

Adding these two equations gives: $5X_1 = 16$ or $X_1 = 16/5$.
Substituting this into $X_1 + X_2 = 4$ gives: $X_2 = 4/5$.

(5) Solve for $Z = 5X_1 + 2X_2 = 5(16/5) + 2(4/5) = 88/5$.
Thus the optimal solution is $X_1 = 16/5$; $X_2 = 4/5$; $Z = 88/5$.

b) Although (5,3) lies in the feasible region, it is not an extreme point (or on the boundary). Hence it can never be the last point touched by moving the objective function line, and thus, can never be optimal. This can be seen in the graph on the next page.

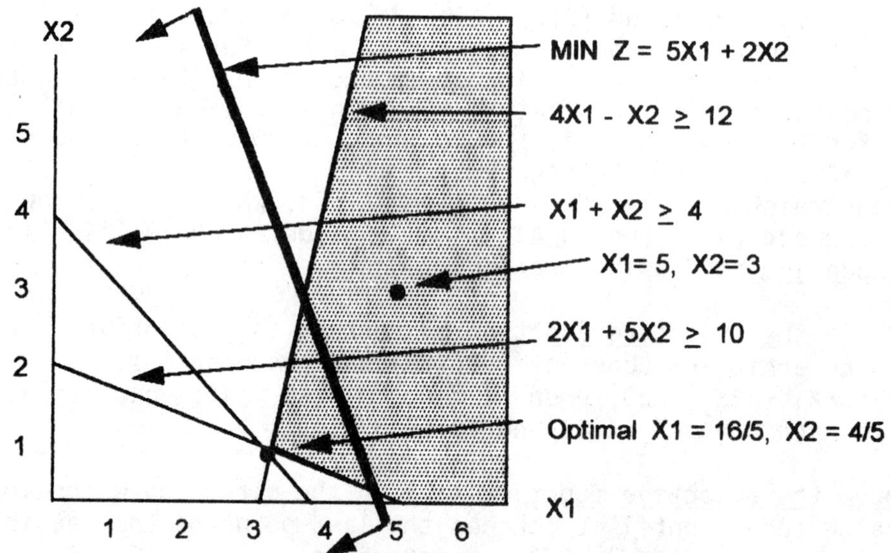
X2
MIN Z = 5X1 + 2X2
4X1 - X2 ≥ 12
X1 + X2 ≥ 4
X1= 5, X2= 3
2X1 + 5X2 ≥ 10
Optimal X1 = 16/5, X2 = 4/5
X1
1
2
3
4
5
6

PROBLEM 3

Given the following linear program:

$$\begin{aligned} \text{MAX} \quad & Z = 4X_1 + 5X_2 \\ \text{S.T.} \quad & X_1 + 3X_2 \leq 22 \\ & -X_1 + X_2 \leq 4 \\ & X_2 \leq 6 \\ & 2X_1 - 5X_2 \leq 0 \\ & X_1, X_2 \geq 0 \end{aligned}$$

a) Solve the problem by the graphical method.

b) What would be the optimal solution if the second constraint were $-X_1 + X_2 = 4$?

c) What would be the optimal solution if the first constraint were $X_1 + 3X_2 \geq 22$?

SOLUTION 3

a) (1) Graph the constraints. (See graph next page.)
Constraint 1: When $X_1 = 0$, $X_2 = 22/3$; when $X_2 = 0$, then $X_1 = 22$. Connect (22,0) and (0,22/3). The "<" side is below this line.
Constraint 2: When $X_1 = 0$, then $X_2 = 4$. Setting X_2 to 0 would give $X_1 = -4$, which is outside the graph. Set X_2 to a number greater than 4 and solve for X_1. When $X_2 = 6$, then $X_1 = 2$. Connect (0,4) and (2,6). (0,0) is on the "<" side.
Constraint 3: This is a horizontal line through $X_2 = 6$.
Constraint 4: When $X_2 = 0$, then $X_1 = 0$; Set X_1 to any positive constant and solve for X_2. When $X_1 = 5$, then $X_2 = 2$. Connect the points (0,0) and (5,2). To determine the "<" side select any arbitrary point on one side of the line and substitute into the inequality. Arbitrarily choosing (0,5), this gives $2(0) - 5(5) = -25$. Thus the side containing (0,5) is the "<" side.
Shade in the feasible region.

(2) Graph the objective function by setting it to an arbitrary value, say 20. For $4X_1 + 5X_2 = 20$, when $X_1 = 0$, then $X_2 = 4$; when $X_2 = 0$, then $X_1 = 5$. Connect with a broken line the points (5,0) and (0,4).

(3) <u>Move the objective function line parallel to itself</u> in the direction that increases its value until it touches the last point of the feasible region. This is at the intersection of the first and fourth constraints.

(4) <u>Solve these two equations in two unknowns</u>:

$$X_1 + 3X_2 = 22 \quad \text{========>} \quad 2X_1 + 6X_2 = 44$$
$$2X_1 - 5X_2 = 0 \quad \text{========>} \quad 2X_1 - 5X_2 = 0$$

Subtracting the second equation from the first yields: $11X_2 = 44$ or $X_2 = 4$. Substituting $X_2 = 4$ into the first equation gives $X_1 = 10$.

(5) <u>Substitute for Z</u> $= 4X_1 + 5X_2 = 4(10) + 5(4) = 60$. Thus the optimal solution is $X_1 = 10$; $X_2 = 4$; $Z = 60$.

b) The feasible region is now the line segment of $-X_1 + X_2 = 4$ between (0,4) and (2,6). (2,6) now gives the optimal solution.

c) The feasible region is now the triangular section between (4,6), (15,6), and (10,4). (15,6) is now the optimal solution.

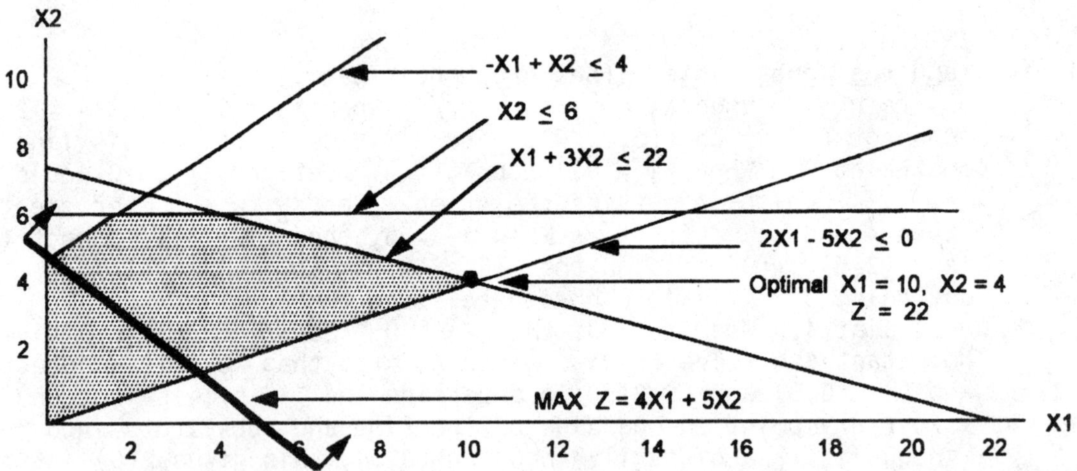

PROBLEM 4

Show graphically why the following two linear programs do not have optimal solutions and explain the difference between the two.

(a) MAX $Z = 2X_1 + 6X_2$

S.T. $4X_1 + 3X_2 \leq 12$

$2X_1 + X_2 \geq 8$

$X_1, X_2 \geq 0$

(b) MAX $Z = 3X_1 + 4X_2$

S.T. $X_1 + X_2 \geq 5$

$3X_1 + X_2 \geq 8$

$X_1, X_2 \geq 0$

SOLUTION 4

Refer to the graphs below. Note that (a) has no points that satisfy both constraints, hence has no feasible region, and no optimal solution. (a) is infeasible.

Note that in (b) the feasible region is unbounded and the objective function line can be moved parallel to itself without bound so that Z can be increased infinitely. (b) is unbounded.

(a)

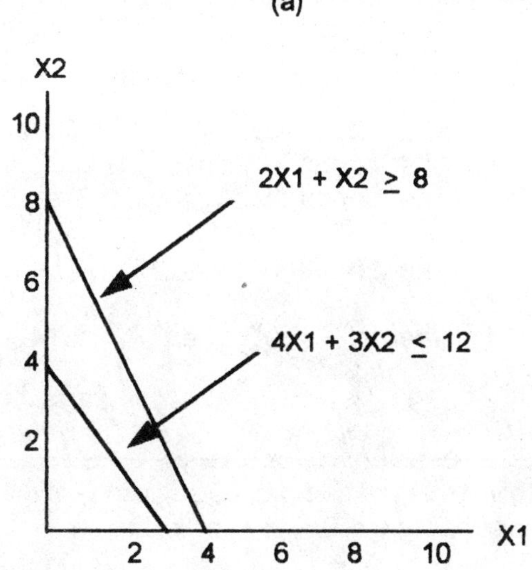

(b)

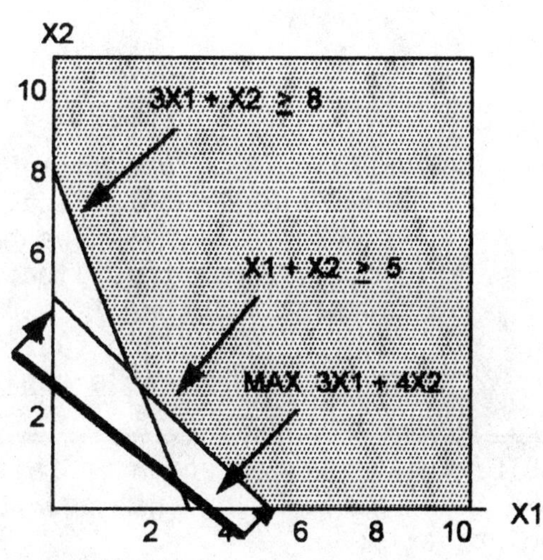

PROBLEM 5

Given the following linear program:

$$\text{MIN } Z = 150X_1 + 210X_2$$

$$\begin{aligned} \text{S.T.} \quad 3.8X_1 + 1.2X_2 &\geq 22.8 \\ X_2 &\geq 6 \\ X_2 &\leq 15 \\ 45X_1 + 30X_2 &= 630 \\ X_1, X_2 &\geq 0 \end{aligned}$$

a) Solve the problem graphically. How many extreme points exist?

b) What would be the optimal solution if the "=" in the fourth constraint was changed to "$\leq$"?

c) If the "=" in the fourth constraint was changed to "$\geq$", how would the problem be affected?

SOLUTION 5

a) (1) Graph the constraints.
Constraint 1: When $X_1 = 0$, $X_2 = 19$. When $X_2 = 0$, $X_1 = 6$. Connect (6,0) and (0,9). The ">" side is to the right of this line.
Constraint 2: This is a horizontal line through $X_2 = 6$. The ">" side is above this line.
Constraint 3: This is a horizontal line through $X_2 = 15$. The "<" side is above this line.
Constraint 4: When $X_1 = 0$, $X_2 = 21$; when $X_2 = 0$, then $X_1 = 14$. Connect (14,0) and (0,21).
Shade in the feasible region.

> **NOTE:** The feasible region in this problem is limited to a segment of the line representing the "equal to" constraint. Only two extreme points exist.

(2) Graph the objective function by setting the function equal to an arbitrary constant as previously demonstrated or by doing the following. Scale down the objective coefficients c_1 and c_2 (say, by dividing both by 10 to get 8 and 13, respectively). Now, use X_1's coefficient as a value to plot on the X_2 axis and use X_2's as a value to plot on the X_1 axis. Connect points (0,15) and (21,0).

(3) Move the objective function line in the direction that lowers its value until it touches the last point of the feasible region. The point is determined by the second and fourth constraints.

(4) Solve for the unknown X by substituting $X_2 = 6$ into $45X_1 + 30X_2 = 630$, yielding $X_1 = 10$.

(5) Solve for $Z = 150X_1 + 210X_2 = 150(10) + 210(6) = 2760$. Thus the optimal solution is $X_1 = 10$, $X_2 = 6$, and $Z = 2760$.

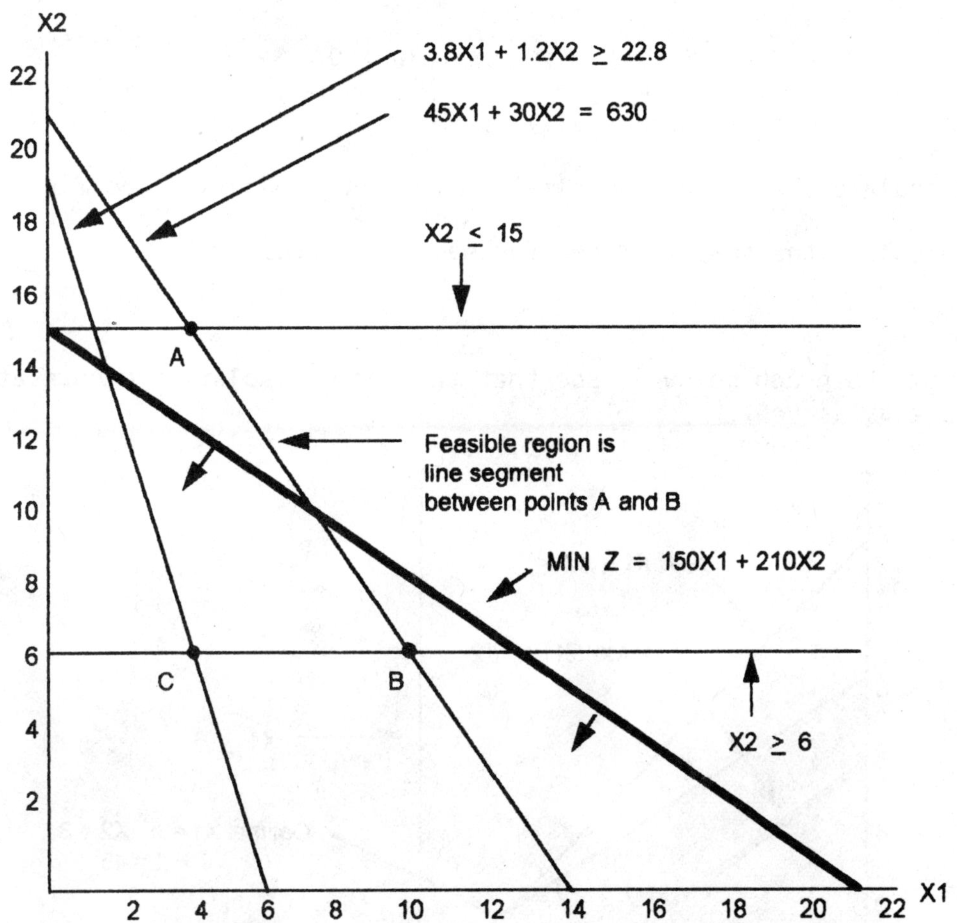

b) The feasible region is now shaped by all four constraints. The optimal extreme point is determined by the first and second constraints. Solving these two equations in two unknowns, the optimal solution is (4.105,6), point C on the graph.

c) The optimal solution is now (10,6), point B on the graph, and the first constraint is now redundant.

PROBLEM 6

Given the following linear program:

$$\text{MAX } Z = 5X_1 + 7X_2$$

$$\begin{aligned} \text{S.T.} \quad X_1 \quad\quad &\leq 6 \\ 2X_1 + 3X_2 &\leq 19 \\ X_1 + X_2 &\leq 8 \\ X_1, X_2 &\geq 0 \end{aligned}$$

a) Solve the problem graphically.

b) Calculate the range of optimality for each objective coefficient.

c) Calculate the shadow prices for each resource.

SOLUTION 6

a) From the graph below we see that the optimal solution occurs at $X_1 = 5$, $X_2 = 3$, $Z = 46$.

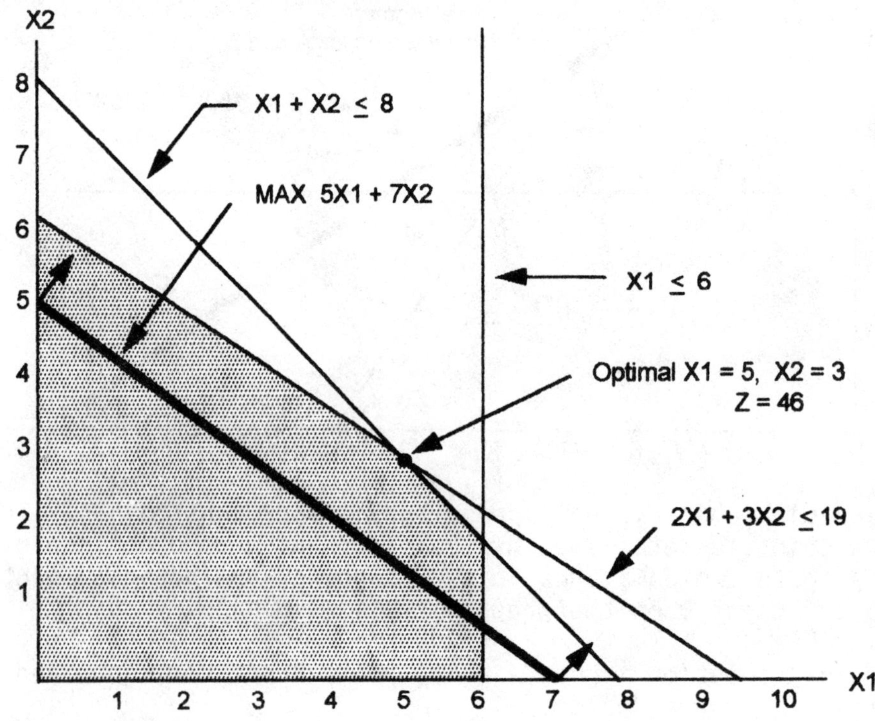

b) The slope of the objective function line is $-C_1/C_2$. The slope of the first binding constraint, $X_1 + X_2 = 8$, is -1 and the slope of the second binding constraint, $2X_1 + 3X_2 = 19$ is -2/3.

<u>Range of optimality for C_1:</u>
Find the range of values for C_1 (with C_2 staying 7) such that the objective function line slope lies between that of the two binding constraints:

$$-1 \leq -C_1/7 \leq -2/3.$$

Multiplying through by -7 (and reversing the inequalities):

$$14/3 \leq C_1 \leq 7.$$

<u>Range of optimality for C_2:</u>
Find the range of values for C_2 (with C_1 staying 5) such that the objective function line slope lies between that of the two binding constraints:

$$-1 \leq -5/C_2 \leq -2/3.$$

Multiplying by -1: $\quad 1 \geq 5/C_2 \geq 2/3.$

Inverting: $\quad 1 \leq C_2/5 \leq 3/2.$

Multiplying by 5: $\quad 5 \leq C_2 \leq 15/2.$

c) <u>Shadow prices:</u>
Constraint 1: Since $X_1 \leq 6$ is not a binding constraint, its shadow price is 0.
Constraint 2: Change the right hand side of the second constraint to 20 and resolve for the optimal point determined by the last two constraints: $2X_1 + 3X_2 = 20$ and $X_1 + X_2 = 8$. The solution is $X_1 = 4$, $X_2 = 4$, $Z = 48$. Hence, the shadow price = $Z_{new} - Z_{old} = 48 - 46 = 2$.
Constraint 3: Change the right hand side value of the third constraint to 9 and resolve for the optimal point determined by the last two constraints: $2X_1 + 3X_2 = 19$ and $X_1 + X_2 = 9$. The solution is: $X_1 = 8$, $X_2 = 1$, $Z = 47$. Hence, the shadow price is $Z_{new} - Z_{old} = 47 - 46 = 1$.

Summarizing, the shadow price for the first resource is 0, for the second resource is 2, and for the third is 1. Note that these shadow prices are only valid in the range of feasibility for each resource.

PROBLEM 7

A manager of a small fabrication plant must decide on a production schedule of two new products for the automobile industry. The profit on product 1 is $1(thousand) and on product 2 is $3(thousand).

The manufacture of these products depends largely on the availability of certain subassemblies the plant receives daily from a local distributor. It takes three of these subassemblies for each unit of product 1 and two for each unit of product 2. Twelve such subassemblies are delivered daily.

Further, it takes two hours to make a unit of product 1 and six hours to make a unit of product 2. The plant has assigned only three workers working 8-hour shifts for these new products.

Due to limited demand, the manager does not want more than seven units of product 2 produced daily.

a) Formulate this problem as a linear program.

b) Solve graphically for the optimal solution. Describe the set of all optimal solutions. Identify any redundant constraints.

c) Give an optimal daily production schedule that manufactures exactly one unit of product 1.

d) Discuss the applicability of linear programming for this problem.

SOLUTION 7

a) (1) Define variables: X_1 and X_2 = the amount of product 1 and product 2 produced daily.

(2) Define objective function:
Maximize total daily profits:
MAX $1X_1 + 3X_2$ (in thousands of dollars).

(3) Define constraints:
Subassemblies: Number used daily $\leq$ number available
$3X_1 + 2X_2 \leq 12$

Labor: Number of hours used daily $\leq$ (3 men)x(8 hrs./day)
$2X_1 + 6X_2 \leq 24$

Product 2: Quantity produced daily $\leq$ specified limit
$X_2 \leq 7$

Non-negativity of variables:
$X_1, X_2 \geq 0$

Summarizing,

$$\text{MAX} \quad Z = 1X_1 + 3X_2$$

$$\text{S.T.} \quad 3X_1 + 2X_2 \leq 12$$

$$2X_1 + 6X_2 \leq 24$$

$$X_2 \leq 7$$

$$X_1, X_2 \geq 0$$

b) Graphically,

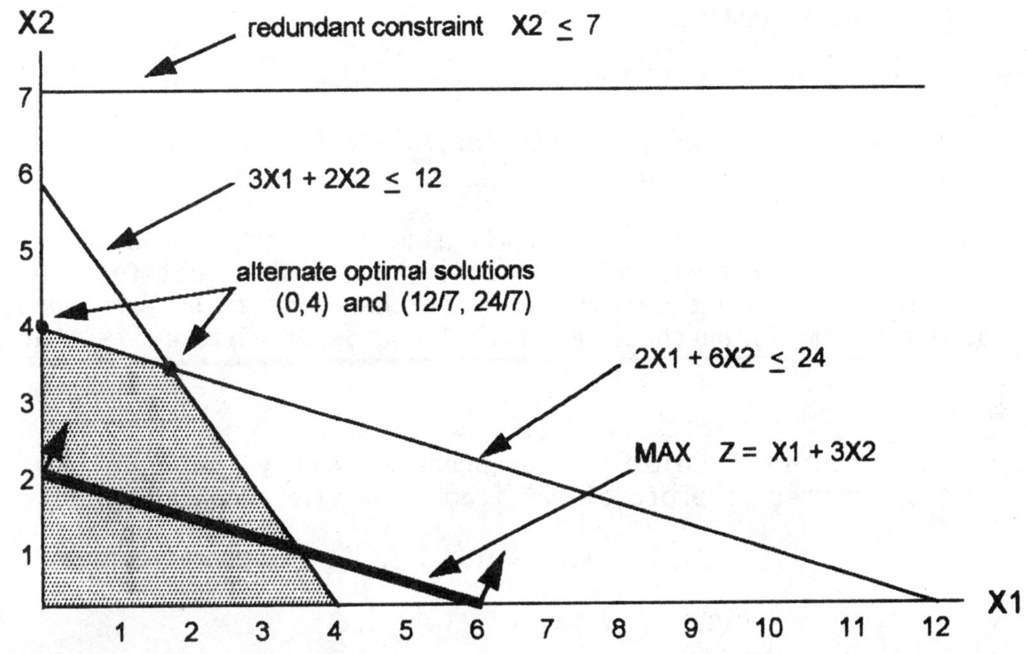

The optimal solution occurs at $X_1 = 0$, $X_2 = 4$ and at $X_1 = 12/7$, $X_2 = 24/7$, and at all points in between on the line $2X_1 + 6X_2 = 24$. At any point on this line, $Z = 12$ (thousand). The $X_2 \leq 7$ constraint does not help shape the feasible region and thus is redundant.

c) On the optimal solution line, $2X_1 + 6X_2 = 24$, when $X_1 = 1$, then $X_2 = 11/3$. Still, $Z = 1(1) + 3(11/3) = 12$ (thousand).

d) One must consider whether these variables can be allowed to assume values which are not integers. For continuous production, frequently a fractional value can be considered as "work in progress"; products not finished on one day are simply completed the next day. Thus, linear programming appears to be appropriate for this problem.

PROBLEM 8

A small company will be introducing a new line of lightweight bicycle frames to be made from special aluminum and steel alloys. The frames will be produced in two models, deluxe and professional. The anticipated unit profits are currently $10 for a deluxe frame and $15 for a professional frame. The number of pounds of each alloy needed per frame is summarized in the table below. A supplier delivers 100 pounds of the aluminum alloy and 80 pounds of the steel alloy weekly.

	Aluminum Alloy	Steel Alloy
Deluxe	2	3
Professional	4	2

a) What is the optimal weekly production schedule?

b) Within what limits must the unit profits lie for each of the frames for this solution to remain optimal?

c) Suppose the unit profits assumed all aluminum purchased would be used and hence the profit figures did not include a unit cost for the aluminum. Now extra aluminum can be purchased at $2.50 per pound. Should the company purchase additional pounds of aluminum at that price?

SOLUTION 8

a) Let: X_1 = number of deluxe frames produced weekly
X_2 = number of professional frames produced weekly

$$\text{MAX } Z = 10X_1 + 15X_2$$

$$\text{S.T.} \quad 2X_1 + 4X_2 \leq 100$$

$$3X_1 + 2X_2 \leq 80$$

$$X_1, X_2 \geq 0$$

Solving graphically (on the next page), observe that the optimal production schedule is to produce X_1 = 15 deluxe frames weekly and X_2 = 17.5 professional frames weekly for an optimal weekly profit of $412.50.

b) Note that the binding constraints are the aluminum and the steel constraints, with slopes -1/2 and -3/2 respectively.

Range of optimality for deluxe profits (C_1):

$$-3/2 \le -C_1/15 \le -1/2 \quad \text{OR} \quad 15/2 \le C_1 \le 45/2.$$

Range of optimality for professional profits (C_2):

$$-3/2 \le -10/C_2 \le -1/2 \quad \text{OR} \quad 20/3 \le C_2 \le 20.$$

c) The aluminum costs are then considered <u>sunk</u> costs and the shadow price for aluminum would yield the maximum worth for additional aluminum. Resolve the two equations and two unknown with the right hand side of the aluminum constraint changed to 101. This results in $X_1 = 59/4$, $X_2 = 143/8$, $Z = \$415.625$. Hence the shadow price for aluminum is \$415.625 - \$412.50 = \$3.125. Since this is greater than the selling price of \$2.50 per pound of aluminum, additional aluminum should be purchased at this price.

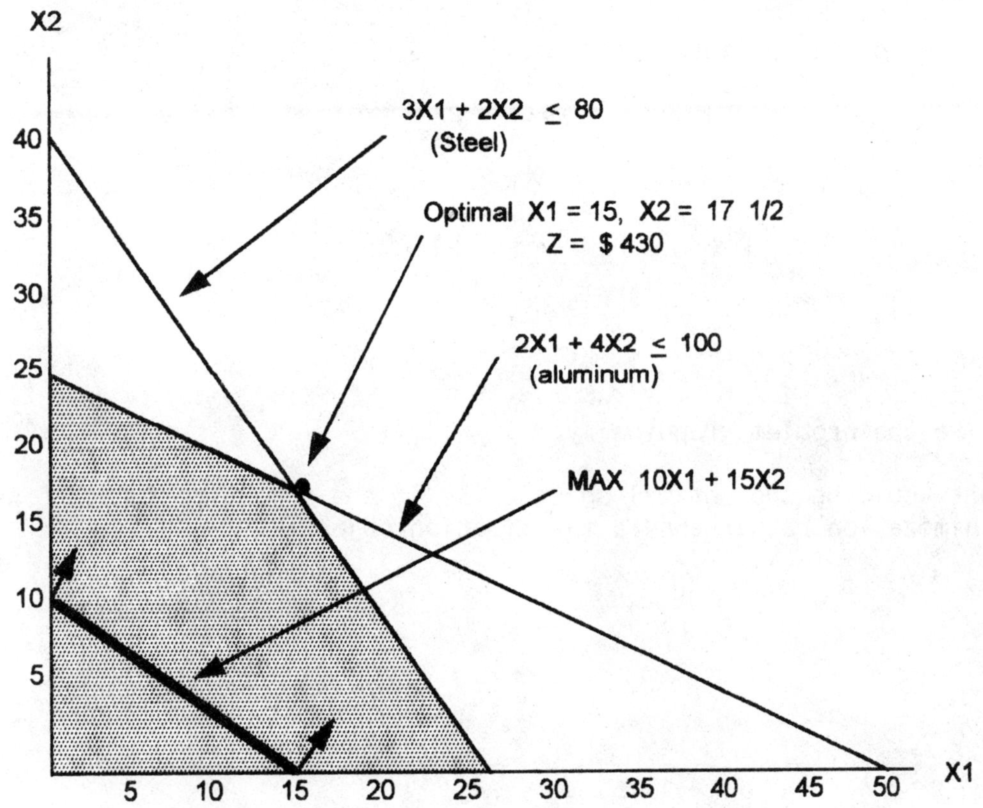

ANSWERED PROBLEMS

PROBLEM 9

Solve graphically for the optimal solution to the following linear program:

$$\begin{aligned} \text{MIN} \quad Z &= 16X_1 + 12X_2 \\ \text{S.T.} \quad 8X_1 + 4X_2 &\leq 36 \\ X_1 + X_2 &\leq 7 \\ 3X_1 + 12X_2 &\geq 24 \\ 4X_1 + 5X_2 &\geq 20 \\ X_1, X_2 &\geq 0 \end{aligned}$$

PROBLEM 10

Given the following linear program:

$$\begin{aligned} \text{MAX} \quad Z &= 4X_1 + 2X_2 \\ \text{S.T.} \quad X_1 &\leq 4 \\ 3X_1 + 8X_2 &\leq 24 \\ 2X_1 + X_2 &\geq 6 \\ X_1, X_2 &\geq 0 \end{aligned}$$

a) Solve the problem graphically.

b) What would be the optimal solution(s) if the objective function were a minimization rather than a maximization objective?

PROBLEM 11

Consider a linear programming problem with the following constraint set:

$$2X_1 + X_2 \geq 4$$

$$X_1 + 2X_2 \geq 5$$

$$X_1 - 2X_2 \leq 1$$

$$X_1, X_2 \geq 0$$

a) Graph the feasible region and note it is unbounded.

b) Identify all extreme points.

c) Solve the problem with each of the three following possible objective functions. Discuss the implications of the results.

(1) $\text{MAX } Z = 2X_1 - 5X_2$
(2) $\text{MAX } Z = 2X_1 - 4X_2$
(3) $\text{MAX } Z = 2X_1 - 3X_2$

> **NOTE:** This problem shows that an unbounded maximization problem does not always have an unbounded objective function value.

PROBLEM 12

Given the following linear programming problem:

$$\text{MAX } Z = 3X_1 + 5X_2$$

$$\text{S.T.} \quad 4X_1 + 3X_2 \geq 24$$

$$2X_1 + 3X_2 \leq 18$$

$$X_2 \geq 3$$

$$X_1, X_2 \geq 0$$

a) Solve the problem graphically.

> **NOTE:** The feasible region in this problem is limited to a single point. A common error is to mistake this situation for infeasibility.

b) Suppose the objective function were changed to: $\text{MAX } Z = 5X_1 + 4X_2$. What effect would this have on the model?

PROBLEM 13

Given the following linear programming problem:

$$\text{MAX } Z = 8X_1 + 10X_2$$

$$\text{S.T.} \quad X_1 + X_2 \leq 35$$

$$3X_1 + 2X_2 \leq 60$$

$$X_2 \leq 15$$

$$X_1, X_2 \geq 0$$

a) Solve for the optimal solution.

b) State why the first constraint is redundant.

c) Suppose the second constraint's right hand side is changed from 60 to 100. Solve for the new optimal solution and show that the first constraint is now binding and NOT redundant.

PROBLEM 14

Consider the following linear program:

$$\text{MAX } Z = 60X_1 + 43X_2$$

$$\text{S.T.} \quad X_1 + 3X_2 \geq 9$$

$$6X_1 - 2X_2 = 12$$

$$X_1 + 2X_2 \leq 10$$

$$X_1, X_2 \geq 0$$

a) Write the problem in standard form.

b) What is the feasible region for the problem?

c) Show that regardless of the values of the actual objective function coefficients, the optimal solution will occur at one of two points. Solve for these points and then determine which one maximizes the current objective function.

PROBLEM 15

A businessman is considering opening a small specialized trucking firm. To make the firm profitable, it is estimated that it must have a daily trucking capacity of at least 84,000 cu. ft. Two types of trucks are appropriate for the specialized operation. Their characteristics and costs are summarized in the table below. Note that truck 2 requires 3 drivers for long haul trips. There are 41 potential drivers available and there are facilities for at most 40 trucks.

The businessman's objective is to minimize the total cost outlay for trucks.

Truck	Cost	Capacity (Cu. ft.)	Drivers Needed
X_1	\$18,000	2,400	1
X_2	\$45,000	6,000	3

Solve the problem graphically and note there are alternate optimal solutions. Which optimal solution

a) uses only one type of truck?

b) utilizes the minimum total number of trucks?

c) uses the same number of truck X_1 as truck X_2?

PROBLEM 16

A baseball glove manufacturer has 1200 linear feet of cowhide and 800 linear feet of synthetic material. It makes two styles of baseball gloves: child's and adult's. Requirements and profit PER DOZEN are summarized below:

	COWHIDE	SYNTHETIC	PROFIT
CHILDS	4	4	\$60
ADULTS	12	6	\$95

a) Solve for the optimal number of dozen of each model to manufacture. What are the values of the slack variables?

b) Suppose the company could make \$1 on each unused linear foot of cowhide and \$.25 on each unused linear foot of synthetic material.
Reformulate the linear programming model. By the methods of Chapter 5, the new optimal solution is to make 200 dozen child models and no adult models and sell 400 linear feet of cowhide.
Locate this new point on your graph and show it is not the optimal extreme point of part (a).

PROBLEM 17

Given the following linear program:

$$\text{MAX} \quad Z = 6X_1 + 5X_2$$

$$\begin{aligned} \text{S. T.} \quad X_1 + X_2 &\leq 6 \\ 2X_1 + X_2 &\leq 8 \\ X_1 &\leq 3 \\ X_1, X_2 &\geq 0 \end{aligned}$$

a) Solve graphically for the optimal solution.

b) Calculate the range of optimality for both C_1 and C_2.

c) What is the new optimal point when C_2 slightly exceeds the upper limit determined in (a)?

d) Determine the shadow price for iron, the resource of the second constraint. Interpret.

e) For what values of zinc, the third resource, will its shadow price be 0?

PROBLEM 18

The Asia Import Company (AIC) has 600 cu. ft. of excess cargo space on its ships and has decided to import two new items: jade figurines and linen placemats. Each container of jade figurines is 4 cu. ft. and will net a profit of $80 per container. Each box of linen placemats is 2 cu. ft. and will realize a profit of $60 per container. AIC expects no more than 140 containers of jade figurines available on any trip.

Additionally, AIC wishes to use no more than 480 man-hours for loading, storing, and processing the items through customs. The normal estimate is that a container requires 2 man-hours. However, because of special agricultural restrictions, an extra 2 man-hours can be expected for the linen products.

a) Using the graphical method, determine the number of containers of each item that should be shipped.

b) What is the range of profit on jade containers for which the solution in (a) remains optimal?

c) Determine the value of: (1) an extra man-hour; (2) an extra cubic foot of cargo space; and, (3) the availability of an extra jade container.

PROBLEM 19

Tom manages Leisure Time Motors, a dealership selling minivans and large travel trailers. He is trying to decide how to allocate 90,000 square feet of outside display space to his two products. The products differ in terms of required display space, monthly upkeep, and generated monthly profit as summarized below on a per-unit basis:

	Space Requirement	Monthly Upkeep	Monthly Profit
Minivan	300 sq. ft.	2.0 man-hours	\$3200.
Trailer	500	3.2	4500.

Leisure Motors has three yard men, each working a 150-hour month, keeping the minivans and trailers clean. Tom feels he needs a minimum of 50 minivans on display. The manufacturer of his trailers requires that he display at least 75 trailers.

a) Graphically solve for the numbers of minivans and trailers on display that will maximize Leisure Time's profit.

b) Calculate the range of optimality for both C_1 and C_2.

c) Determine the shadow price for yard men, the resource of the second constraint. Interpret.

PROBLEM 20

Harvey owns a Harley (motorcycle) and a Hauler (pickup truck). The Harley gets an average of 45 miles per gallon (mpg) using 93 octane gasoline that sells for \$1.35 per gallon. The Hauler averages 26 mpg using 89 octane that sells for \$1.17 per gallon.

The Harley requires 15 hours of maintenance work per 5000 miles ridden. The Hauler requires 10 hours of maintenance per 5000 miles. Harvey does his own maintenance work, but he cannot devote more than 100 hours annually to the task.

Harvey predicts he will have to transport himself 45,000 miles in the upcoming year. He would like to ride his Harley a minimum of 5,000 miles annually in order to stay in practice.

a) How should Harvey divide his mileage among his Harley and Hauler so that his annual fuel expense is minimized?

b) What is the value of an additional hour of Harvey's time per year for maintenance?

c) By how much will Harvey's annual fuel expense increase for each mile that he travels in excess of 45,000?

TRUE/FALSE

21. A problem formulation that includes a term that is the product of two variables would not be a linear program.

22. A nonbinding constraint, like a binding constraint, helps form the shape (boundaries) of the feasible region.

23. If a linear program has an optimal solution, then an extreme point must be optimal.

24. All optimal solutions are extreme points.

25. A redundant constraint lies entirely within the feasible region.

26. It is possible to have exactly two optimal solutions to a linear programming problem.

27. A linear programming problem can be both unbounded and infeasible.

28. If a problem has a constraint which is parallel to the objective function, then there must be alternate optimal solutions.

29. An infeasible problem is one in which the objective function can be increased to infinity.

30. A slack variable is a variable that represents the difference between the amount of a resource that was available and the actual amount used by the solution.

31. In a feasible problem, an equal-to constraint cannot be redundant.

32. A variable in a linear programming problem must be allowed to assume fractional values.

33. Any change to an objective function coefficient of a variable that is positive in the optimal solution will change the optimal solution.

34. An unbounded feasible region might not result in an unbounded solution for a minimization or maximization problem.

35. Increasing the right-hand side of a nonbinding constraint will not cause a change in the optimal solution.

Chapter 8
Linear Programming: Formulation, Computer Solution, and Interpretation

KEY CONCEPTS

CONCEPT	ILLUSTRATED PROBLEMS	ANSWERED PROBLEMS
Changes to Objective Function Coefficients		
Reduced Costs	4	
Range of Optimality	1-4	5-9
Changes to Right Hand Side Values		
Shadow/Dual Prices	1-4	6-9
Range of Feasibility	1-3	6-9
Sunk/Relevant Costs	3	6
100% Rule	1-4	6-9

REVIEW

1. Sensitivity analysis is used to determine how the optimal solution is affected by changes, within specified ranges, in the objective function coefficients, the right-hand side (RHS) values, and the constraint coefficients.

2. Sensitivity analysis is important to the manager who must operate in a dynamic environment with imprecise estimates of the coefficients. Sensitivity analysis allows him to ask certain what-if questions about the problem.

3. A reduced cost for a decision variable whose value is 0 in the optimal solution is the amount the variable's objective coefficient would have to improve (increase for maximization problems, decrease for minimization problems) before this variable could assume a positive value. Thus, the reduced cost for a decision variable with a positive value is 0.

4. A range of optimality of an objective function coefficient is found by determining an interval for the objective function coefficient in which the original solution remains optimal while keeping all other data of the problem constant. The value of Z might change in this range.

5. The 100% rule states that simultaneous changes in objective function coefficients will not change the optimal solution as long as the sum of the percentages of the change divided by the corresponding maximum allowable change in the range of optimality for each coefficient does not exceed 100%.

6. A shadow price for a right-hand side value (or resource limit) is the amount the objective function value Z will change per unit increase in the right-hand side value of a constraint.

7. A Shadow price reflects the value of an additional unit of the resource if the resource cost is sunk. It represents the extra value over the normal cost of the resource when the resource cost is relevant.

8. A resource cost is relevant if the amount paid for it is dependent upon the amount of the resource used by the decision variables. Relevant costs are reflected in the objective function coefficients.

9. A resource cost is sunk if it must be paid regardless of the amount of the resource actually used by the decision variables. Sunk resource costs are not reflected in the objective function coefficients.

10. A dual price for a right-hand side (or resource limit) is the amount the objective function will improve per unit increase in the right-hand side value of a constraint. Thus, for maximization problems dual prices and shadow prices are the same, whereas for minimization problems, shadow prices are the negative of dual prices.

11. A nonbinding constraint is one in which there is positive slack or surplus when evaluated at the optimal solution. The shadow price for a nonbinding constraint is 0.

12. The range of feasibility for a change in a right-hand side value is the range of values for this parameter in which the original shadow price remains constant.

13. The 100% rule also states that simultaneous changes in right- hand sides will not change the shadow prices as long as the sum of the percentages of the changes divided by the corresponding maximum allowable change in the range of feasibility for each right-hand side does not exceed 100%.

14. Computer software packages (such as The Management Scientist or LINDO/PC) that solve linear programming problems all give five sections of relevant information about the optimal solution:

    1. The optimal value of the objective function;

    2. Information about the decision variables:
       (a) their values, (b) their reduced costs;

    3. Information about the constraints:
       (a) the amount of slack or surplus, (b) the dual prices;

    4. Objective function coefficient ranges (ranges of optimality):
       (a) lower limit, (b) upper limit; and

    5. Right-hand side ranges (ranges of feasibility):
       (a) lower limit, (b) upper limit.

ILLUSTRATED PROBLEMS

PROBLEM 1

Consider the following linear program:

$$\text{MAX } Z = 3X_1 + 4X_2 \quad (\$\text{ Profit})$$

$$\text{S.T.} \quad X_1 + 3X_2 \leq 12$$

$$2X_1 + X_2 \leq 8$$

$$X_1 \leq 3$$

$$X_1, X_2 \geq 0$$

This problem was solved by The Management Scientist giving the following output:

OBJECTIVE FUNCTION VALUE = 20.000

VARIABLE	VALUE	REDUCED COST
X1	2.400	0.000
X2	3.200	0.000

CONSTRAINT	SLACK/SURPLUS	DUAL PRICES
1	0.000	1.000
2	0.000	1.000
3	0.600	0.000

OBJECTIVE COEFFICIENT RANGES

VARIABLE	LOWER LIMIT	CURRENT VALUE	UPPER LIMIT
X1	1.333	3.000	8.000
X2	1.500	4.000	9.000

RIGHTHAND SIDE RANGES

CONSTRAINT	LOWER LIMIT	CURRENT VALUE	UPPER LIMIT
1	9.000	12.000	24.000
2	4.000	8.000	9.000
3	2.400	3.000	NO UPPER LIMIT

a) What is the optimal solution including the optimal value of the objective function?

b) Suppose the profit on X1 is increased to $7. Is the above solution still optimal? What is the value of the objective function when this unit profit is increased to $7?

c) If the unit profit on X2 was $10 instead of $4, would the optimal solution change?

d) If simultaneously the profit on X1 was raised to $5.5 and the profit on X2 was reduced to $3, would the current solution still remain optimal?

<u>SOLUTION 1</u>

a) According to the output X1 = 2.4 and X2 = 3.2, and the objective function value = $20.00.

b) The output states that the solution remains optimal as long as the objective function coefficient of X1 is between 1.333 and 8.0. Since 7 is within this range, the optimal solution will not change. However, the optimal profit will be affected: Z = 7X1 + 4X2 = 7(2.4) + 4(3.2) = $29.60.

c) The output states that the solution remains optimal as long as the objective function coefficient of X2 is between 1.5 and 9.0. Since 10 is outside this range, the optimal solution would change.

d) Use the 100% rule for simultaneous changes. If C1 = 5.5, the amount C1 changed is 5.5 - 3 = 2.5. The maximum allowable increase is 8 - 3 = 5, so this is a 2.5/5 = a 50% change. If C2 = 3, the amount that C2 changed is 4 - 3 = 1. The maximum allowable decrease is 4 - 1.5 = 2.5, so this is a 1/2.5 = a 40% change. The sum of the change percentages is 50% + 40% = 90%. Since this does not exceed 100% the optimal solution would not change.

NOTE: For the 100% rule, a reduction does not offset (or negate, cancel-out) an increase. For example, increasing C1 by 70% of its allowed maximum increase and <u>decreasing</u> C2 by 50% of its allowed maximum decrease does <u>not</u> result in a combined change of 20%. The combined change is 120%, which means the problem should be solved again because the simultaneous changes to C1 and C2 might have (probably) changed the optimal solution (X1 and X2's values).

PROBLEM 2

Consider the following linear program:

$$\text{MIN } Z = 6X_1 + 9X_2 \quad (\$ \text{ cost})$$

$$\text{S.T.} \quad X_1 + 2X_2 \leq 8$$

$$10X_1 + 7.5X_2 \geq 30$$

$$X_2 \geq 2$$

$$X_1, X_2 \geq 0$$

This problem was solved by The Management Scientist giving the following output:

```
===============================================================
OBJECTIVE FUNCTION VALUE =    27.000

     VARIABLE              VALUE           REDUCED COST
------------------  -----------------  -----------------
        X1                 1.500              0.000
        X2                 2.000              0.000

    CONSTRAINT          SLACK/SURPLUS        DUAL PRICES
------------------  -----------------  -----------------
         1                 2.500              0.000
         2                 0.000             -0.600
         3                 0.000             -4.500

OBJECTIVE COEFFICIENT RANGES

  VARIABLE      LOWER LIMIT     CURRENT VALUE     UPPER LIMIT
------------  -------------  ---------------  -------------
     X1            0.000            6.000           12.000
     X2            4.500            9.000       NO UPPER LIMIT

RIGHTHAND SIDE RANGES

 CONSTRAINT     LOWER LIMIT     CURRENT VALUE     UPPER LIMIT
------------  -------------  ---------------  -------------
      1            5.500            8.000       NO UPPER LIMIT
      2           15.000           30.000           55.000
      3            0.000            2.000            4.000
===============================================================
```

a) What is the optimal solution including the optimal value of the objective function?

b) Suppose the unit cost of X1 is decreased to $4. Is the above solution still optimal? What is the value of the objective function when this unit cost is decreased to $4?

c) How much can the unit cost of X2 be decreased without concern for the optimal solution changing?

d) If simultaneously the cost of X1 was raised to $7.5 and the cost of X2 was reduced to $6, would the current solution still remain optimal?

e) If the right-hand side of constraint 3 is increased by 1, what will be the effect on the optimal solution?

SOLUTION 2

a) According to the output X1 = 1.5 and X2 = 2.0, and the objective function value = 27.00.

b) The output states that the solution remains optimal as long as the objective function coefficient of X1 is between 0 and 12. Since 4 is within this range, the optimal solution will not change. However, the optimal total cost will be affected: Z = 6X1 + 9X2 = 4(1.5) + 9(2.0) = $24.00.

c) The output states that the solution remains optimal as long as the objective function coefficient of X2 does not fall below 4.5.

d) Use the 100% rule for simultaneous changes. If C1 = 7.5, the amount C1 changed is 7.5 - 6 = 1.5. The maximum allowable increase is 12 - 6 = 6, so this is a 1.5/6 = 25% change. If C2 = 6, the amount that C2 changed is 9 - 6 = 3. The maximum allowable decrease is 9 - 4.5 = 4.5, so this is a 3/4.5 = 66.7% change. The sum of the change percentages is 25% + 66.7% = 91.7%. Since this does not exceed 100% the optimal solution would not change.

e) A dual price represents the improvement in the objective function value per unit increase in the right-hand side. A negative dual price indicates a deterioration (negative improvement) in the objective, which in this problem means an increase in total cost because we're minimizing. Since the right-hand side remains within the range of feasibility, there is no change in the optimal solution. However, the objective function value increases by $4.50.

PROBLEM 3

A small company will be introducing a new line of lightweight bicycle frames to be made from special aluminum and steel alloys. The frames will be produced in two models, deluxe and professional. The anticipated unit profits are currently $10 for a deluxe frame and $15 for a professional frame.

The number of pounds of each alloy needed per frame is summarized in the table below. A supplier delivers 100 pounds of the aluminum alloy and 80 pounds of the steel alloy weekly.

	Aluminum Alloy	Steel Alloy
Deluxe	2	3
Professional	4	2

The Management Scientist provided the following solution output:

```
=================================================================
Objective Function Value = 412.500

     VARIABLE                 VALUE               REDUCED COST
------------------      -----------------      -----------------
        X1                   15.000                  0.000
        X2                   17.500                  0.000

    CONSTRAINT            SLACK/SURPLUS           DUAL PRICES
------------------      -----------------      -----------------
         1                    0.000                  3.125
         2                    0.000                  1.250

OBJECTIVE FUNCTION RANGES

  VARIABLE       LOWER LIMIT      CURRENT VALUE      UPPER LIMIT
------------   -------------   ---------------   -------------
     X1             7.500           10.000             22.500
     X2             6.667           15.000             20.000

RIGHTHAND SIDE RANGES

 CONSTRAINT      LOWER LIMIT      CURRENT VALUE      UPPER LIMIT
------------   -------------   ---------------   -------------
     1             53.333          100.000            160.000
     2             50.000           80.000            150.000
=================================================================
```

a) What is the optimal solution including the optimal value of the objective function?

b) Suppose the profit on deluxe frames is increased to $20. Is the above solution still optimal? What is the value of the objective function when this unit profit is increased to $20?

c) If the unit profit on deluxe frames were $6 instead of $10 would the optimal solution change?

d) If simultaneously the profit on deluxe frames were raised to $16 and the profit on professional frames were raised to $17, would the current solution still remain optimal?

e) Given that aluminum is a sunk cost, what is the maximum amount the company should pay for 50 extra pounds of aluminum? (Constraint 1 pertains to aluminum availability.)

f) How would your answer to (e) change if aluminum were a relevant cost?

<u>SOLUTION 3</u>

a) According to the output X1 (deluxe frames) = 15, and X2 (professional frames) = 17.5, and the objective function value = $412.50.

b) The output states that the solution remains optimal as long as the objective function coefficient of X1 is between 7.5 and 22.5. Since 20 is within this range, the optimal solution will not change. However the optimal profit will be affected: Z = 20X1 + 15X2 = 20(15) + 15(17.5) = $562.50.

c) The output states that the solution remains optimal as long as the objective function coefficient of X1 is between 7.5 and 22.5. Since 6 is outside this range, the optimal solution would change.

d) Use the 100% rule for simultaneous changes. If C1 = 16, the amount C1 changed is 16 - 10 = 6 . The maximum allowable increase is 22.5 - 10 = 12.5, so this is a 6/12.5 = 48% change. If C2 = 17, the amount that C2 changed is 17 - 15 = 2. The maximum allowable increase is 20 - 15 = 5 so this is a 2/5 = 40% change. The sum of the change percentages is 88%. This is less than 100%, so the optimal solution would not change.

e) Since the cost for aluminum is a sunk cost, the shadow price provides the value of extra aluminum. The shadow price for aluminum is the same as its dual price (for a maximization problem). The shadow price for aluminum is $3.125 per pound. Thus, the value of 50 additional pounds is = $156.25. 54

This analysis is valid only if the change is within the range of feasibility for aluminum. From the output we can see that the maximum allowable increase for aluminum is 60. Since 50 is in this range, then the $156.25 is valid.

f) If aluminum were a relevant cost, the shadow price would be the amount above the normal price of aluminum the company would be willing to pay. Thus if initially aluminum cost \$4 per pound, then additional units in the range of feasibility would be worth \$4 + \$3.125 = \$7.125 per pound.

PROBLEM 4

Comfort Plus Inc. (CPI) manufactures a standard dining chair used in restaurants. The demand forecasts for quarter 1 (January-March) and quarter 2 (April-June) are 3700 chairs and 4200 chairs, respectively. CPI has a policy of satisfying all demand in the quarter in which it occurs.

The chair contains an upholstered seat that can be produced by CPI or purchased from DAP, a subcontractor. DAP currently charges \$12.50 per seat, but has announced a new price of \$13.75 effective April 1. CPI can produce the seat at a cost of \$10.25.

Seats that are produced or purchased in quarter 1 and used to satisfy demand in quarter 2 cost CPI \$1.50 each to hold in inventory, but maximum inventory cannot exceed 300 seats.

The problem was formulated as follows:

X_1 = number of seats produced by CPI in quarter 1,
X_2 = number of seats purchased from DAP in quarter 1,
X_3 = number of seats carried in inventory from quarters 1 to 2,
X_4 = number of seats produced by CPI in quarter 2, and
X_5 = number of seats purchased from DAP in quarter 2.

$$\text{MIN } Z = 10.25X_1 + 12.5X_2 + 1.5X_3 + 10.25X_4 + 13.75X_5 \quad \text{(costs)}$$

S.T.

$$X_1 + X_2 - X_3 \geq 3700 \quad \text{(quarter 1 demand)}$$

$$X_3 + X_4 + X_5 \geq 4200 \quad \text{(quarter 2 demand)}$$

$$X_1 \leq 3800$$

$$X_4 \leq 3800$$

(CPI's production capacity in quarters 1 and 2)

$$X_3 \leq 300 \quad \text{(inventory capacity)}$$

$$X_1, X_2\ X_3, X_4, X_5 \geq 0$$

This problem was solved by The Management Scientist giving the following output:

OBJECTIVE FUNCTION VALUE = 82175.000

VARIABLE	VALUE	REDUCED COST
X1	3800.000	0.000
X2	0.000	0.250
X3	100.000	0.000
X4	3800.000	0.000
X5	300.000	0.000

CONSTRAINT	SLACK/SURPLUS	DUAL PRICES
1	0.000	-12.250
2	0.000	-13.750
3	0.000	2.000
4	0.000	3.500
5	200.000	0.000

OBJECTIVE COEFFICIENT RANGES

VARIABLE	LOWER LIMIT	CURRENT VALUE	UPPER LIMIT
X1	NO LOWER LIMIT	10.250	12.250
X2	12.250	12.500	NO UPPER LIMIT
X3	1.250	1.500	3.500
X4	NO LOWER LIMIT	10.250	13.750
X5	11.750	13.750	14.000

RIGHTHAND SIDE RANGES

CONSTRAINT	LOWER LIMIT	CURRENT VALUE	UPPER LIMIT
1	3500.000	3700.000	3800.000
2	3900.000	4200.000	NO UPPER LIMIT
3	3700.000	3800.000	4000.000
4	0.000	3800.000	4100.000
5	100.000	300.000	NO UPPER LIMIT

a) What is the optimal solution including the optimal value of the objective function?

b) If the per-unit inventory cost increased from \$1.50 to \$2.50, would the optimal solution change? Would the optimal value of the objective function change?

c) If in quarter 2 CPI's per-seat production cost increased by \$1.25 and DAP changed its mind about the announced price increase (thus leaving it at \$12.50 per seat), would the optimal solution change?

d) If DAP reduced its per-seat selling price in quarter 1 from $12.50 to $12.25, should CPI purchase any seats in quarter 1?

e) How much is it worth to CPI to increase its inventory capacity from 300 seats to 400?

f) If CPI increased its production capacity by 100 seats in both quarters 1 and 2, what would be the savings for CPI (ignoring the capacity-expansion expense)?

SOLUTION 4

a) CPI will produce 3800 seats in quarter 1 and another 3800 in quarter 2. 100 seats will be carried in inventory from quarter 1 to quarter 2. 300 seats will be purchased from DAP in quarter 2. Total cost for this plan is $82,175.

b) The optimal solution will not change as a result of a change in the per-unit inventory cost as long as the cost remains in the range of $1.25 to $3.50. The objective function value will change; it will increase by $100 to $82,275.

c) Use the 100% rule for simultaneous changes. The amount C4 changed is 1.25. The maximum allowable increase is 13.75 - 10.25 = 3.50, so this is a 1.25/3.50 = 35.7% change. If C5 = 12.50, the amount that C5 changed is 13.75 - 12.50 = 1.25. The maximum allowable decrease is 13.75 - 11.75 = 2.00, so this is a 1.25/2.00 = 62.5% change. The sum of the change percentages is 98.2%; the optimal solution would not change.

d) X2 is the number of seats purchased from DAP in quarter 1 and its current value is 0. Its reduced cost value is 0.25, indicating that if C2 improved (decreased in this case) by 0.25 or more, X2 would have a positive value in the new optimal solution. C2 = $12.25 represents an improvement of exactly 0.25, so the answer is yes.

e) Increasing the inventory capacity (without other changes) will not benefit CPI. Actually, a decrease as great as 200 seats will not change the optimal solution. This is indicated by the slack value of 200 for constraint 5.

f) Based on the dual prices for constraints 3 and 4, the objective function value (total cost) will decrease (remember, we're minimizing) by $5.50 (2.00 + 3.50) for each unit increase in CPI's production capacity in quarters 1 and 2. We can conclude that a 100-unit capacity increase will reduce the total cost by $550 if the 100% rule has not been violated. It has not. (For constraint 3 the percent of allowed increase is 50% (100/200) and for constraint 4 the percent of allowed increase is 33%, for a total of 83%.)

ANSWERED PROBLEMS

PROBLEM 5

Regal Investments has just received instructions from a client to invest in two stocks, one an airline stock, the other an insurance stock. The total maximum appreciation in stock value over the next year is to be maximized subject to the following restrictions:

(1) The total investment shall not exceed $100,000.
(2) At most $40,000 is to be invested in the insurance stock.
(3) Quarterly dividends must total at least $2,600.

The airline stock is currently selling for $40 per share and its quarterly dividend is $1 per share. The insurance stock is currently selling for $50 per share and the quarterly dividend is $1.50 per share.

Regal's analysts predict that over the next year the airline stock will increase $2 per share and the insurance stock will increase $3 per share.

The Management Scientist provided the following solution output:

```
==============================================================
OBJECTIVE FUNCTION VALUE =   5400.000

     VARIABLE               VALUE              REDUCED COST
 -----------------     ----------------     ----------------
        X1                 1500.000              0.000
        X2                  800.000              0.000

    CONSTRAINT          SLACK/SURPLUS          DUAL PRICES
 -----------------     ----------------     ----------------
         1                   0.000               0.050
         2                   0.000               0.010
         3                 100.000               0.000

OBJECTIVE COEFFICIENT RANGES

   VARIABLE      LOWER LIMIT      CURRENT VALUE      UPPER LIMIT
 -----------    ------------    ---------------    ------------
      X1            0.000            2.000              2.400
      X2            2.500            3.000         NO UPPER LIMIT

RIGHTHAND SIDE RANGES

  CONSTRAINT     LOWER LIMIT      CURRENT VALUE      UPPER LIMIT
 -----------    ------------    ---------------    ------------
      1          96000.000        100000.000       NO UPPER LIMIT
      2          20000.000         40000.000        100000.000
      3        NO LOWER LIMIT       2600.000          2700.000
==============================================================
```

a) How should the client's money be invested to satisfy his restrictions?

b) Suppose Regal's estimate of the airline stock's appreciation is in error. Within what limits must the actual appreciation lie for the answer in (a) to remain optimal?

PROBLEM 6

A company produces two products made from aluminum and copper. The table below gives the unit requirements, the unit production man-hours required, the unit profit and the availability of the resources (in tons).

	Aluminum	Copper	Man-hours	Unit Profit
Product 1	1	0	2	50
Product 2	1	1	3	60
Available	10	6	24	

The Management Scientist provided the following solution output:

```
=================================================================
OBJECTIVE FUNCTION VALUE  =    540.000

     VARIABLE                VALUE               REDUCED COST
------------------   -----------------    -----------------
        X1                  6.000                  0.000
        X2                  4.000                  0.000

    CONSTRAINT           SLACK/SURPLUS          DUAL PRICES
------------------   -----------------    -----------------
         1                  0.000                 30.000
         2                  2.000                  0.000
         3                  0.000                 10.000

OBJECTIVE COEFFICIENT RANGES

  VARIABLE      LOWER LIMIT      CURRENT VALUE      UPPER LIMIT
------------   -------------   ---------------   -------------
    X1             40.000            50.000            60.000
    X2             50.000            60.000            75.000

RIGHTHAND SIDE RANGES

 CONSTRAINT     LOWER LIMIT      CURRENT VALUE      UPPER LIMIT
------------   -------------   ---------------   -------------
     1              9.000            10.000            12.000
     2              4.000             6.000       NO UPPER LIMIT
     3             20.000            24.000            26.000
=================================================================
```

a) What is the optimal production schedule?

b) Within what range for the profit on product 2 will the solution in (a) remain optimal? What is the optimal profit when C_2 = 70?

c) Suppose that simultaneously the unit profits on X1 and X2 changed from 50 to 55 and 60 to 65 respectively. Would the optimal solution change?

d) Explain the meaning of the "DUAL PRICES" column. Given the optimal solution, why should the dual price for copper be 0?

e) What is the increase in the value of the objective function for an extra unit of aluminum?

f) Man-hours were not figured into the unit profit as it must pay three workers for eight hours of work regardless of the number of man-hours used. What is the shadow price for man-hours? Interpret.

g) On the other hand, aluminum and copper are resources that are ordered as needed. The unit profit coefficients were determined by: (selling price per unit) - (cost of the resources per unit). The 10 units of aluminum cost the company $100. What is the most the company should be willing to pay for extra aluminum?

PROBLEM 7

A small company produces only two sizes of frames for stereo receivers: standard size and slim-line. The accounting department has provided the following analysis of the unit profit:

	Standard	Slim-Line
Selling Price	$6.00	$4.25
Raw Materials	$0.75 (1.5 units @ .50/unit)	$0.50 (1 unit @ .50/unit)
Packaging	$0.25	$0.25
Labor*	0.40 hours	0.25 hours
Profit (excluding labor costs)	$5.00	$3.50

* Labor is considered a fixed cost as it is performed by salaried workers at the plant.

There are 350 units of the raw material and 300 packing boxes available daily. (Both products utilize the same packing boxes.) At most 10 workers (at 8 hrs./day) will be assigned to this project.

This problem was solved by The Management Scientist with output below:

OBJECTIVE FUNCTION VALUE = 1100.000

VARIABLE	VALUE	REDUCED COST
X1	33.333	0.000
X2	266.667	0.000

CONSTRAINT	SLACK/SURPLUS	DUAL PRICES
1	33.333	0.000
2	0.000	1.000
3	0.000	10.000

OBJECTIVE COEFFICIENT RANGES

VARIABLE	LOWER LIMIT	CURRENT VALUE	UPPER LIMIT
X1	3.500	5.000	5.600
X2	3.125	3.500	5.000

RIGHTHAND SIDE RANGES

CONSTRAINT	LOWER LIMIT	CURRENT VALUE	UPPER LIMIT
1	316.667	350.000	NO UPPER LIMIT
2	200.000	300.000	320.000
3	75.000	80.000	90.000

a) What is the optimal daily production plan?

b) What is the maximum selling price for standard models that will keep the same optimal solution as (a)?

c) What is the new optimal solution and optimal profit if an additional worker (8 additional hours) is assigned to the project? (Hint: The output states the current values for the right-hand sides of the constraints. Compare them with the resource data provided in the problem description to determine the constraint that corresponds with each resource.)

PROBLEM 8

Consider Problem 7 further.

a) Suppose C_1 was changed from 5 to 5.5. Would the optimal solution change?

b) Suppose C_2 was changed from 3.5 to 4. Would the optimal solution change?

c) Suppose simultaneously C_1 changed to 5.5 and C_2 changed to 4. Would the optimal solution change?

d) What is the shadow price for man-hours? Interpret.

e) What is the shadow price for the packaging? Interpret.

f) Suppose simultaneously the amount of material available increased from 350 to 500, the number of boxes available increased from 300 to 310 and the number of man-hours increased from 80 to 84. What conclusion can be drawn regarding the shadow prices?

PROBLEM 9

A client of an investment firm has $10,000 available for investment. He has instructed that his money be invested in three stocks so that no more than $5,000 is invested in any one stock but at least $1,000 is invested in each stock. He has further instructed the firm to use its current data and invest in a manner that maximizes his expected overall gain during a one-year period.

The stocks, the current price per share, and the firm's projected stock price a year from now are summarized in the following table.

Stock	Current Price	Projected Price 1 Year Hence
James Industries	$25	$35
QM Inc.	$50	$60
Delicious Candy Co.	$100	$125

This problem was formulated as follows:

X_1 = number of shares of James Industries to purchase,
X_2 = number of shares of QM Inc. to purchase, and
X_3 = number of shares of Delicious Candy Co. to purchase.

$$\text{MAX } Z = 10X_1 + 10X_2 + 25X_3$$

$$\begin{aligned} \text{S.T.} \quad 25X_1 + 50X_2 + 100X_3 &\leq 10000 \quad (\$\text{ available}) \\ 25X_1 &\leq 5000 \quad (\text{max. } \$\text{ stock 1}) \\ 50X_2 &\leq 5000 \quad (\text{max. } \$\text{ stock 2}) \\ 100X_3 &\leq 5000 \quad (\text{max. } \$\text{ stock 3}) \\ 25X_1 &\geq 1000 \quad (\text{min. } \$\text{ stock 1}) \\ 50X_2 &\geq 1000 \quad (\text{min. } \$\text{ stock 2}) \\ 100X_3 &\geq 1000 \quad (\text{min. } \$\text{ stock 3}) \end{aligned}$$

$$X_1, X_2, X_3 \geq 0$$

This problem was solved by The Management Scientist giving the following output:

```
==============================================================
OBJECTIVE FUNCTION VALUE = 3200.000

      VARIABLE              VALUE              REDUCED COST
------------------    ----------------    -----------------
        X1               200.000               0.000
        X2                20.000               0.000
        X3                40.000               0.000

     CONSTRAINT          SLACK/SURPLUS         DUAL PRICES
------------------    ----------------    -----------------
         1                 0.000               0.250
         2                 0.000               0.150
         3              4000.000               0.000
         4              1000.000               0.000
         5              4000.000               0.000
         6                 0.000              -0.050
         7              3000.000               0.000
```

OBJECTIVE COEFFICIENT RANGES

VARIABLE	LOWER LIMIT	CURRENT VALUE	UPPER LIMIT
X1	6.250	10.000	NO UPPER LIMIT
X2	NO LOWER LIMIT	10.000	12.500
X3	20.000	25.000	40.000

RIGHTHAND SIDE RANGES

CONSTRAINT	LOWER LIMIT	CURRENT VALUE	UPPER LIMIT
1	7000.000	10000.000	11000.000
2	4000.000	5000.000	8000.000
3	1000.000	5000.000	NO UPPER LIMIT
4	4000.000	5000.000	NO UPPER LIMIT
5	NO LOWER LIMIT	1000.000	5000.000
6	0.000	1000.000	4000.000
7	NO LOWER LIMIT	1000.000	4000.000

a) What is the optimal solution including the optimal value of the objective function?

b) How should the dual price for constraint 6 be interpreted?

c) If the client had an additional $1000 available for investing how much would the expected overall one-year gain increase?

d) If the client increased the allowed maximum investment amount to $6000 for just one stock, should it be Delicious Candy (the stock with the greatest gain)? Why?

e) Based on your stock choice in (d) above, how much would the objective function increase?

f) For your stock choice in (d) above, how much could the allowed maximum investment amount be raised before the optimal investment mix might change?

g) If the expected one-year gains on James Industries and QM Inc. each increased by $1.00, would the optimal investment mix change?

Note: If the range of optimality for an objective function coefficient (or the range of feasibility for a right-hand side) involved in a simultaneous change is unlimited in the direction of the change, the change to this coefficient (or constant) is of no concern.

TRUE/FALSE

10. Any change to an objective function coefficient of a variable which is positive in the optimal solution will change the optimal value of the objective function.

11. The shadow price for labor hours is $25. The profit coefficients c_1 and c_2 take into account a $10 per hour labor cost. Then the maximum value of an overtime hour is $35.

12. Ranges of optimality or feasibility are calculated for a single change only, and they assume no other coefficients in the problem have been changed.

13. Regarding the 100 percent rule, it is possible for the optimal solution to not change even though changes in the objective function coefficients exceed 100 percent.

14. If the range of feasibility for b_1 is between 16 and 37, then if $b_1 = 22$, the optimal solution will not change from the original optimal solution.

15. The 100 percent rule can be applied to changes in both objective function coefficients and right-hand sides at the same time.

16. Relevant costs should be reflected in the objective function, but sunk costs should not.

17. Dual price and shadow price are equivalent for maximization problems and are negative of each other for minimization problems.

18. For any constraint, either its slack/surplus value must be zero or its dual price must be zero.

19. For any decision variable, either its value must be zero or its reduced cost must be zero.

20. If the dual price for the right-hand side of a $\leq$ constraint is zero, there is no upper limit on its range of feasibility.

21. A $\leq$ constraint cannot have a negative dual price, regardless of whether it is a maximization or minimization problem.

22. Slack corresponds to $\leq$ constraints.

23. The Management Scientist can only be used to solve linear programs in two variables.

24. Shadow prices are only valid within the range of feasibility.

Chapter 9
Linear Programming Applications

KEY CONCEPTS

CONCEPT	ILLUSTRATED PROBLEMS	ANSWERED PROBLEMS
Programming Applications:		
Blending	1,4	14
Equipment Acquisition	2	10,15
Multiperiod Planning	3	11
Product Mix	4	12,13,14
Staff Scheduling	5	20
Portfolio Selection	6	16
Data Envelopment Analysis	7	19
Media Selection	8	17
Transportation	9	18
Computer Solutions	1,3,5,7,9	13,15,17,18,19

REVIEW

1. Linear programming applications include problems in production, marketing, finance, and numerous other business-related areas.

2. To develop a good formulation, one should strive to understand the problem thoroughly. Then one should: (1) define the decision variables (the inputs over which you have direct control); (2) define the objective (the goal that you wish to maximize or minimize); and, (3) define the constraints (the restrictions that deter you from even better values for the objective function.) Frequently it is advisable to write the objective function and constraints in English first before translating them into mathematical notation.

3. Computer packages, such as The Management Scientist may be used to solve linear programming problems giving the optimal solution and appropriate sensitivity analyses.

4. Data Envelopment Analysis (DEA) is an application of linear programming used to determine the relative operating efficiency of units with the same goals and objectives (e.g. banks, schools, company divisions, etc.)

5. DEA creates a fictitious composite unit made up of an optimal weighted average (W_1, W_2, etc.) of existing units. Then an individual unit, k, can be compared by determining E, the fraction of this unit's input resources required by the "optimal" composite unit.

6. The DEA model is given by:

   MIN E
   S.T. Weighted outputs $\geq$ Unit k's output for each measured output
   Weighted inputs $\leq$ E(Unit k's input) for each measured input
   The sum of the weights = 1
   E, weights $\geq$ 0

7. In DEA, if the optimal value of E is less than 1, unit k is less efficient than the composite unit and can be judged relatively inefficient. If E = 1, there is no evidence that unit k is inefficient, but one cannot conclude that unit k is absolutely efficient.

ILLUSTRATED PROBLEMS

NOTE: Students often confuse a constraint for the objective in a problem. If there is a limit imposed on an entity, it probably represents a constraint. (We are solving for the objective function's limit!)

NOTE: A common dilemma is whether to use "=" or an inequality sign ($\leq$ or $\geq$) in a constraint. There is no simple, definitive answer; the correct answer is problem specific. The use of "=" when not necessary might result in an infeasible problem. Quite often, if you are choosing between "$\leq$" and "=", "$\leq$" will do no harm if you are maximizing ("$\geq$" if you are minimizing); equality is likely to be achieved if it is possible. Of course, using "$\leq$" when you should be using "$\geq$" is very harmful!

PROBLEM 1

Frederick's Feed Company receives four raw grains from which it blends its dry pet food. The pet food advertises that each 8-ounce can meets the minimum daily requirements for vitamin C, protein and iron. The cost of each raw grain as well as the vitamin C, protein, and iron units per pound of each grain are summarized below.

Grain	Vitamin C Units/lb	Protein Units/lb	Iron Units/lb	Cost/lb
1	9	12	0	.75
2	16	10	14	.90
3	8	10	15	.80
4	10	8	7	.70

Frederick's is interested in producing the 8-ounce mixture at minimum cost while meeting the minimum daily requirements of 6 units of vitamin C, 5 units of protein, and 5 units of iron.

a) Formulate this problem as a linear program.

b) Solve for the optimal solution using a program such as The Management Scientist.

c) If the mixture costs 5.4 cents to can and Frederick's puts a 50% markup on the package to its retailers, how much will it charge its retailers for an 8-ounce can?

SOLUTION 1

a) Define the decision variables

X_j = the pounds of grain j (j = 1,2,3,4) used in the 8-ounce mixture

Define the objective

Minimize the total cost for an 8-ounce mixture:
MIN $.75X_1 + .90X_2 + .80X_3 + .70X_4$

Define the constraints

The total weight of the mixture ($X_1 + X_2 + X_3 + X_4$) is 8-ounces (.5 pounds):
(1) $X_1 + X_2 + X_3 + X_4 = .5$

Total amount of Vitamin C in the mixture is at least 6 units:
(2) $9X_1 + 16X_2 + 8X_3 + 10X_4 \geq 6$

Total amount of protein in the mixture is at least 5 units:
(3) $12X_1 + 10X_2 + 10X_3 + 8X_4 \geq 5$

Total amount of iron in the mixture is at least 5 units:
(4) $14X_2 + 15X_3 + 7X_4 \geq 5$

Nonnegativity of variables: $X_j \geq 0$ for all j

b) When solved by the Management Scientist the following output was generated:

OBJECTIVE FUNCTION VALUE = 0.406

VARIABLE	VALUE	REDUCED COSTS
X1	0.099	0.000
X2	0.213	0.000
X3	0.088	0.000
X4	0.099	0.000

Thus, the optimal blend is about .10 lb. of grain 1, .21 lb. of grain 2, .09 lb. of grain 3, and .10 lb. of grain 4.

c) The mixture costs Frederick's 40.6 cents. With 5.4 cents for packaging, this brings their costs to 46 cents. A 50% markup would mean it would charge retailers 1.5(46) = 69 cents per can.

PROBLEM 2

Floataway Tours has $400,000 that may be used to purchase new rental boats for hire during the summer. The boats can be purchased from two different manufacturers. Pertinent data concerning the boats are summarized below:

Boat	Manufacturer	Cost	Maximum Seating	Expected Daily Profit
Speedhawk	Sleekboat	$6000	3	$ 70
Silverbird	Sleekboat	$7000	5	$ 80
Catman	Racer	$5000	2	$ 50
Classy	Racer	$9000	6	$110

Floataway Tours would like to purchase at least 50 boats and would like to purchase the same number from Sleekboat as from Racer to maintain goodwill. At the same time, Floataway Tours wishes to have a total seating capacity of at least 200. Formulate this problem as a linear program.

SOLUTION 2

Define the decision variables

X_1 = the number of Speedhawks ordered
X_2 = the number of Silverbirds ordered
X_3 = the number of Catmans ordered
X_4 = the number of Classys ordered

Define the objective function

Maximize total expected daily profit:
MAX (Expected daily profit per unit)(Number of units)
MAX $70X_1 + 80X_2 + 50X_3 + 110X_4$

Define the constraints

Spend no more than $400,000:
(1) $6000X_1 + 7000X_2 + 5000X_3 + 9000X_4 \leq 400{,}000$

Purchase at least 50 boats:
(2) $X_1 + X_2 + X_3 + X_4 \geq 50$

Number of boats from Sleekboat equals number of boats from Racer:
(3) $X_1 + X_2 = X_3 + X_4$ or $X_1 + X_2 - X_3 - X_4 = 0$

Capacity at least 200:
(4) $3X_1 + 5X_2 + 2X_3 + 6X_4 \geq 200$

Nonnegativity of variables: $X_j \geq 0$, for j = 1,2,3,4

PROBLEM 3

Burt Wheeler is the production manager of Wheeler Wheels, Inc. Burt has just received orders for 1,000 standard wheels and 1,250 deluxe wheels next month and for 800 standard and 1,500 deluxe wheels the following month. All orders are to be filled.

The cost of producing standard wheels is $10 and deluxe wheels is $16. Overtime rates are 50% higher. There are 1,000 hours of regular time and 500 hours of overtime available each month. The cost of storing one wheel from one month to the next is $2.

Develop a two-month production schedule for Burt of standard and deluxe wheel production if it takes .5 hour to make a standard wheel and .6 hour to make a deluxe wheel and solve using a program such as the Management Scientist.

SOLUTION 3

Define the decision variables

We must determine how many of each type of wheel to make each month during regular time and overtime; also we must determine the number of each wheel stored from one month to the next. Thus we want to determine the production levels, X_j, as follows:

	Month 1		Month 2	
	Reg. Time	Overtime	Reg. Time	Overtime
Standard	X_1	X_2	X_5	X_6
Deluxe	X_3	X_4	X_7	X_8

Also let,

Y_1 = number of standard wheels stored from month 1 to month 2

Y_2 = number of deluxe wheels stored from month 1 to month 2.

Define the objective function

Minimize total production and storage costs:

MIN (cost per wheel)(number of wheels produced) + $2Y_1 + 2Y_2$

MIN $10X_1 + 15X_2 + 16X_3 + 24X_4 + 10X_5 + 15X_6 + 16X_7 + 24X_8$
$+ 2Y_1 + 2Y_2$

Define the constraints

Standard Wheel Product. Month 1 = (Requirements)+(Amount Stored)

(1) $X_1 + X_2 = 1{,}000 + Y_1$ or $X_1 + X_2 - Y_1 = 1{,}000$

Deluxe Wheel Production Month 1 = (Requirements)+(Amount Stored)

(2) $X_3 + X_4 = 1{,}250 + Y_2$ or $X_3 + X_4 - Y_2 = 1{,}250$

Standard Wheel Product. Month 2 = (Requirements)-(Amount Stored)
(3) $X_5 + X_6 = 800 - Y_1$ or $X_5 + X_6 + Y_1 = 800$

Deluxe Wheel Production Month 2 = (Requirements)-(Amount Stored)
(4) $X_7 + X_8 = 1{,}500 - Y_2$ or $X_7 + X_8 + Y_2 = 1{,}500$

Regular Hours Used Month 1 $\leq$ Regular Hours Available Month 1:
(5) $.5X_1 + .6X_3 \leq 1000$

Overtime Hours Used Month 1 $\leq$ Overtime Hours Available Month 1:
(6) $.5X_2 + .6X_4 \leq 500$

Regular Hours Used Month 2 $\leq$ Regular Hours Available Month 2:
(7) $.5X_5 + .6X_7 \leq 1000$

Overtime Hours Used Month 2 $\leq$ Overtime Hours Available Month 2:
(8) $.5X_6 + .6X_8 \leq 500$

Nonnegativity of variables:
$X_j \geq 0$, $j = 1,,8$ and $Y_j \geq 0$ $j = 1,2$

The Management Scientist provided the following solution:

OBJECTIVE FUNCTION VALUE = 67500.000

VARIABLE	VALUE	REDUCED COSTS
X1	500.000	0.000
X2	500.000	0.000
X3	1250.000	0.000
X4	0.000	2.000
X5	200.000	0.000
X6	600.000	0.000
X7	1500.000	0.000
X8	0.000	2.000
Y1	0.000	2.000
Y2	0.000	2.000

Thus, the following production schedule is recommended:

	Month 1		Month 2	
	Reg. Time	Overtime	Reg. Time	Overtime
Standard	500	500	200	600
Deluxe	1250	0	1500	0

No wheels are stored and the minimum total cost is $67,500.

PROBLEM 4

Target Shirt Company makes three varieties of shirts: Collegiate, Traditional and European. These shirts are made from different combinations of cotton and polyester.

The cost per yard of unblended cotton is $5 and for unblended polyester is $4. Target can receive up to 4,000 yards of raw cotton and 3,000 yards of raw polyester fabric weekly.

The table below pertinent data concerning the manufacture of the shirts.

Shirt	Total Yards	Fabric Requirements	Weekly Contracts	Weekly Demand	Selling Price
Collegiate	1.00	At least 50% cotton	500	600	$14.00
Traditional	1.20	No more than 20% polyester	650	850	$15.00
European	.90	As much as 80% polyester	280	675	$18.00

Formulate a linear program that would give a manufacturing policy for Target Shirt Company.

SOLUTION 4

Define the decision variables

Not only must we decide how many shirts to make and how much fabric to purchase, we also need to decide how much of each fabric is blended into each shirt.

Let, S_j = the total number of shirt style j produced
F_i = the number of yards of material i purchased
X_{ij} = yards of fabric i blended into shirt style j

where i = 1 (cotton) or 2 (polyester) and
j = 1 (collegiate), 2(traditional), or 3 (European)

Define the objective function

Maximize the overall profit.

To determine the profit function, subtract the cost of purchasing the fabric from the shirt sales revenue. Thus the objective function is:

$$\text{MAX } 14S_1 + 15S_2 + 18S_3 - 5F_1 - 4F_2$$

Define the constraints

Definition of Total Number of Shirts of Each Style

Total Number of each style =
(Total Yardage used in making the style) / (Yardage/Shirt)

(1) Collegiate: $S_1 = (X_{11} + X_{21}) / 1$
(2) Traditional: $S_2 = (X_{12} + X_{22}) / 1.2$
(3) European: $S_3 = (X_{13} + X_{23}) / .9$

Definition of Total Yardage of Materials

(4) Cotton: $F_1 = X_{11} + X_{12} + X_{13}$
(5) Polyester: $F_2 = X_{21} + X_{22} + X_{23}$

Weekly Availability of the Resources

(6) Cotton: $F_1 \leq 4000$
(7) Polyester: $F_2 \leq 3000$

Meet Weekly Contracts

(8) Collegiate: $S_1 \geq 500$
(9) Traditional: $S_2 \geq 650$
(10) European: $S_3 \geq 280$

Do Not Exceed Weekly Demand

(11) Collegiate: $S_1 \leq 600$
(12) Traditional: $S_2 \leq 850$
(13) European: $S_3 \leq 675$

Fabric Requirements

Collegiate At Least 50% Cotton:
(Total yds. of Cotton Used in Collegiate Shirts) $\geq$
[(.5(1.00) yds./shirt)(number of collegiate shirts)]
(14) $X_{11} \geq .5S_1$

Traditional At Most 20% Polyester:
(Total yds. Polyester Used in Traditional Shirts) $\leq$
[.2(1.20) yds./shirt)(number of traditional shirts)]
(15) $X_{22} \leq .24S_2$

European At Most 80% Polyester:
(Total yds. Polyester Used in European Shirts) $\leq$
[.8(.90) yds./shirt)(number of European shirts)]
(16) $X_{32} \leq .72S_3$

Nonnegativity of variables

$S_j, F_i, X_{ij} \geq 0$ for i = 1,2 and j = 1,2,3.

PROBLEM 5

The Accounting Department at Lenny's Restaurant requires information on the total number of employees it will be hiring for its new restaurant located across the street from a major university. Lenny's has broken down its requirements into 4-hour periods.

Time Period	Employees Required
7am-11am	12
11am- 3pm	20
3pm- 7pm	18
7pm-11pm	22
11pm- 7am	Closed

Staffing is done by hiring personnel for eight-hour shifts commencing at 7am, 11am, and 3pm. Also, there are enough students willing to work the before and after school eight-hour shift covering 7am-11am and 7pm-11pm.

a) Formulate and solve for the minimum number of personnel the Accounting Department at Lenny's should expect for this new restaurant.

b) Based on the solution in part (a), determine the timing and amount of overstaffing that will occur.

SOLUTION 5

a) Define the decision variables

X_1 = number of workers hired for 7am-3pm shift
X_2 = number of workers hired for 11am-7pm shift
X_3 = number of workers hired for 3pm-11pm shift
X_4 = number of workers hired for 7am-11am and 7pm-11pm shift

Define the objective function

Minimize the total number of personnel hired:
MIN $X_1 + X_2 + X_3 + X_4$

Define the constraints

Total personnel working during each 4-hour period must be greater than or equal to the number of employees required:
(1) $X_1 + X_4 \geq 12$
(2) $X_1 + X_2 \geq 20$
(3) $X_2 + X_3 \geq 18$
(4) $X_3 + X_4 \geq 22$

Nonnegativity of variables: $X_j \geq 0$ for j = 1,2,3,4

The Management Scientist provided the following solution:

OBJECTIVE FUNCTION VALUE = 42.000

VARIABLE	VALUE	REDUCED COSTS
X1	20.000	0.000
X2	0.000	0.000
X3	18.000	0.000
X4	4.000	0.000

CONSTRAINT	SLACK/SURPLUS	DUAL PRICES
1	12.000	0.000
2	0.000	-1.000
3	0.000	0.000
4	0.000	-1.000

(There are alternate optimal solutions, one of which is: $X_1 = 12$, $X_2 = 8$, $X_3 = 22$, and $X_4 = 0$.)

b) The timing and amount of overstaffing corresponds to the constraint surplus values shown in the computer output. The only four-hour period that is overstaffed is 7am–11am. It is overstaffed by 12 workers. Thus, the total man-hours of overstaffing is 4(12) = 48.

PROBLEM 6

Winslow Savings has $20 million available for investment. It wishes to invest over the next four months in such a way that it will maximize the total interest earned over the four month period as well as have at least $10 million available at the start of the fifth month for a high rise building venture in which it will be participating.

For the time being, Winslow wishes to invest only in 2-month government bonds (earning 2% over the 2-month period) and 3-month construction loans (earning 6% over the 3-month period). Each of these is available each month for investment. Funds not invested in these two investments are liquid and earn 3/4 of 1% per month when invested locally.

Formulate a linear program that will help Winslow Savings determine how to invest over the next four months if at no time does it wish to have more than $8 million in either government bonds or construction loans.

SOLUTION 6

Define the decision variables

G_j = amount of new investment in government bonds in month j
C_j = amount of new investment in construction loans in month j
L_j = amount invested locally in month j, where j = 1,2,3,4

Define the objective

Maximize the total interest earned over the four-month period:
MAX (interest rate on investment)(amount invested)

$$\text{MAX } .02G_1 + .02G_2 + .02G_3 + .02G_4 + .06C_1 + .06C_2 + .06C_3 + .06C_4 + .0075L_1 + .0075L_2 + .0075L_3 + .0075L_4$$

Define the constraints

Month 1's total investment amount limited to $20 million:
(1) $G_1 + C_1 + L_1 = 20{,}000{,}000$

Month 2's total investment amount limited to amount (principle and interest) invested locally in Month 1:
(2) $G_2 + C_2 + L_2 = 1.0075L_1$ or $G_2 + C_2 - 1.0075L_1 + L_2 = 0$

Month 3's total investment amount limited to (principle and interest) invested in government bonds in Month 1 and locally invested in Month 2:
(3) $G_3 + C_3 + L_3 = 1.02G_1 + 1.0075L_2$
or $-1.02G_1 + G_3 + C_3 - 1.0075L_2 + L_3 = 0$

Month 4's total investment amount limited to amounts (principle and interest) invested in construction loans in Month 1, in goverment bonds in Month 2, and locally invested in Month 3:
(4) $G_4 + C_4 + L_4 = 1.06C_1 + 1.02G_2 + 1.0075L_3$
or $-1.02G_2 + G_4 - 1.06C_1 + C_4 - 1.0075L_3 + L_4 = 0$

$10 million must be available at start of Month 5:
(5) $1.06C_2 + 1.02G_3 + 1.0075L_4 \geq 10{,}000{,}000$

No more than $8 million in government bonds at any time:
(6) $G_1 \leq 8{,}000{,}000$
(7) $G_1 + G_2 \leq 8{,}000{,}000$
(8) $G_2 + G_3 \leq 8{,}000{,}000$
(9) $G_3 + G_4 \leq 8{,}000{,}000$

No more than $8 million in construction loans at any time:
(10) $C_1 \leq 8{,}000{,}000$
(11) $C_1 + C_2 \leq 8{,}000{,}000$
(12) $C_1 + C_2 + C_3 \leq 8{,}000{,}000$
(13) $C_2 + C_3 + C_4 \leq 8{,}000{,}000$

Nonnegativity: $G_j, C_j, L_j \geq 0$ for j = 1,2,3,4

PROBLEM 7

The Langley County School District is trying to determine the relative efficiency of its three high schools. In particular, it wants to evaluate Roosevelt High School.

The district is evaluating performances on SAT scores, the number of seniors finishing high school, and the number of students who enter college as a function of the number of teachers teaching senior classes, the prorated budget for senior instruction, and the number of students in the senior class.

Input	Roosevelt	Linclon	Washington
Senior Faculty	37	25	23
Budget ($100,000's)	6.4	5.0	4.7
Senior Enrollments	850	700	600

Output	Roosevelt	Linclon	Washington
Average SAT Score	800	830	900
High School Graduates	450	500	400
College Admissions	140	250	370

a) Use data envelopment analysis to develop a linear program to determine the relative efficiency of Roosevelt High School.

b) Solve the linear program using the Management Scientist. Comment on the relative efficiency of Roosevelt High School for each of the output measures.

SOLUTION 7

a) The goal of data envelopment analysis is to compare Roosevelt High School to a fictitious composite high school developed by determining an optimal set of weights of all high schools in the Langley School District.

This set of weights minimizes the fraction, E, of Roosevelt High School's input resources required by the composite school.

If E = 1, the composite high school requires the same input resources as Roosevelt's and there would be no evidence that Roosevelt High School is inefficient. If E < 1, Roosevelt High School is operating inefficiently with its given inputs and further study of Roosevelt should be made to determine the reasons for this inefficiency.

Define the decision variables

E = Fraction of Roosevelt High School's input resources required by the composite high school
W_1 = Weight applied to Roosevelt High School's input/output resources by the composite high school
W_2 = Weight applied to Lincoln High School's input/output resources by the composite high school
W_3 = Weight applied to Washington High School's input/output resources by the composite high school

Define the objective

Minimize the fraction of Roosevelt High School's input resources required by the composite high school:
MIN E

Define the constraints

Sum of the Weights is 1:
(1) $W_1 + W_2 + W_3 = 1$

Output Constraints:
Since $W_1 = 1$ is possible, each output of the composite school must be at least as great as that of Roosevelt:
(2) $800W_1 + 830W_2 + 900W_3 \geq 800$ (SAT Scores)
(3) $450W_1 + 500W_2 + 400W_3 \geq 450$ (Graduates)
(4) $140W_1 + 250W_2 + 370W_3 \geq 140$ (College Admissions)

Input Constraints:
The input resources available to the composite school is a fractional multiple, E, of the resources available to Roosevelt. Since the composite high school cannot use more input than that available to it, the input constraints are:
(5) $37W_1 + 25W_2 + 23W_3 \leq 37E$ (Faculty)
(6) $6.4W_1 + 5.0W_2 + 4.7W_3 \leq 6.4E$ (Budget)
(7) $850W_1 + 700W_2 + 600W_3 \leq 850E$ (Seniors)

Nonnegativity of variables:
$E, W_1, W_2, W_3 \geq 0$

b) The problem was solved by the Management Scientist and the output is on the next page.

The output shows that the composite high school is made up of equal weights of Lincoln High School and Washington High School. Roosevelt High School is 76.5% efficient compared to this composite high school when measured by college admissions (because of the 0 slack on this constraint (#4)).

It is less than 76.5% efficient when using measures of SAT scores and high school graduates (there is positive slack in constraints 2 and 3.)

OBJECTIVE FUNCTION VALUE = 0.765

VARIABLE	VALUE	REDUCED COSTS
E	0.765	0.000
W1	0.000	0.235
W2	0.500	0.000
W3	0.500	0.000

CONSTRAINT	SLACK/SURPLUS	DUAL PRICES
1	0.000	-0.235
2	65.000	0.000
3	0.000	-0.001
4	170.000	0.000
5	4.294	0.000
6	0.044	0.000
7	0.000	0.001

PROBLEM 8

The SMM Company, which is manufacturing a new instant salad machine, has $350,000 to spend on advertising. The product is only to be test marketed initially in the Dallas area. The money is to be spent on an advertising blitz during one weekend (Friday, Saturday, and Sunday) in January, and SMM is limited to television advertising.

The company has three options available: day time advertising, evening news advertising and the Super Bowl. Even though the Super Bowl is a national telecast, the Dallas Cowboys will be playing in it, and hence, the viewing audience will be especially large in the Dallas area. A mixture of one-minute TV spots is desired. The table below gives pertinent data:

	Cost Per Ad	Estimated New Audience Reached With Each Ad
Day Time	$5,000	3000
Evening News	$7,000	4000
Super Bowl	$100,000	75,000

SMM has decided to take out at least one ad in each option. Further, there are only two Super Bowl ad spots available. There are 10 day time spots and 6 evening news spots available daily. If SMM wants to have at least 5 ads per day, but spend no more than $50,000 on Friday and no more than $75,000 on Saturday, formulate a linear program to help SMM decide how the company should advertise over the weekend.

SOLUTION 8

Define the decision variables

X_1 = the number of day ads on Friday
X_2 = the number of day ads on Saturday
X_3 = the number of day ads on Sunday
X_4 = the number of evening ads on Friday
X_5 = the number of evening ads on Saturday
X_6 = the number of evening ads on Sunday
X_7 = the number of Super Bowl ads

Define the objective function

Maximize the estimated total new audience reached:
MAX (new audience reached per ad of each type)(number of ads of each type)
MAX $3000X_1 + 3000X_2 + 3000X_3 + 4000X_4 + 4000X_5 + 4000X_6 + 75000X_7$

Define the constraints

Take out at least one ad of each type:
(1) $X_1 + X_2 + X_3 \geq 1$
(2) $X_4 + X_5 + X_6 \geq 1$
(3) $X_7 \geq 1$
10 daytime spots available:
(4) $X_1 \leq 10$
(5) $X_2 \leq 10$
(6) $X_3 \leq 10$
6 evening news spots available:
(7) $X_4 \leq 6$
(8) $X_5 \leq 6$
(9) $X_6 \leq 6$
Only two Super Bowl ad spots available:
(10) $X_7 \leq 2$
At least 5 ads per day:
(11) $X_1 + X_4 \geq 5$
(12) $X_2 + X_5 \geq 5$
(13) $X_3 + X_6 + X_7 \geq 5$
Spend no more than $50,000 on Friday:
(14) $5000X_1 + 7000X_4 \leq 50000$
Spend no more than $75,000 on Saturday:
(15) $5000X_2 + 7000X_5 \leq 75000$
Spend no more than $350,000 in total:
(16) $5000X_1 + 5000X_2 + 5000X_3 + 7000X_4 + 7000X_5 + 7000X_6 + 100000X_7 \leq 350000$
Nonnegativity:
$X_j \geq 0 \quad j = 1,\ldots,7$

PROBLEM 9

The Navy has 9,000 pounds of material in Albany, Georgia which it wishes to ship to three installations: San Diego, Norfolk, and Pensacola. They require 4,000, 2,500, and 2,500 pounds respectively. The following gives the shipping costs per pound for truck, railroad, and airplane transit.

	Destination		
Mode	San Diego	Norfolk	Pensacola
Truck	$12	$ 6	$ 5
Railroad	20	11	9
Airplane	30	26	28

Government regulations require equal distribution of shipping among the three carriers. Formulate and solve a linear program to determine the shipping arrangements (mode, destination, and quantity) that will minimize the total shipping cost.

SOLUTION 9

Define the decision variables

We want to determine the pounds of material, X_{ij}, to be shipped by mode i to destination j. The following table summarizes the decision variables:

	Destination		
Mode	San Diego	Norfolk	Pensacola
Truck	X_{11}	X_{12}	X_{13}
Railroad	X_{21}	X_{22}	X_{23}
Airplane	X_{31}	X_{32}	X_{33}

Define the objective function

Minimize the total shipping cost.
MIN (shipping cost per pound for each mode/destination pairing)
X (number of pounds shipped by mode/destination pairing):
MIN $12X_{11} + 6X_{12} + 5X_{13} + 20X_{21} + 11X_{22} + 9X_{23} + 30X_{31} + 26X_{32} + 28X_{33}$

Define the constraints

Equal use of transportation modes:
(1) $X_{11} + X_{12} + X_{13} = 3000$
(2) $X_{21} + X_{22} + X_{23} = 3000$
(3) $X_{31} + X_{32} + X_{33} = 3000$

Destination material requirements:
(4) $X_{11} + X_{21} + X_{31} = 4000$
(5) $X_{12} + X_{22} + X_{32} = 2500$
(6) $X_{13} + X_{23} + X_{33} = 2500$

Nonnegativity of variables:
$X_{ij} \geq 0, \quad i = 1,2,3 \quad \text{and} \quad j = 1,2,3$

The Management Scientist provided the following solution:

OBJECTIVE FUNCTION VALUE = 142000.000

VARIABLE	VALUE	REDUCED COSTS
X11	1000.000	0.000
X12	2000.000	0.000
X13	0.000	1.000
X21	0.000	3.000
X22	500.000	0.000
X23	2500.000	0.000
X31	3000.000	0.000
X32	0.000	2.000
X33	0.000	6.000

To summarize: San Diego will receive 1000 lbs. by truck and 3000 lbs. by airplane; Norfolk will receive 2000 lbs. by truck and 500 lbs. by railroad; Pensacola will receive 2500 lbs. by railroad. The total shipping cost will be $142,000.

NOTE: This problem is referred to as a transportation problem. Transportation problems have a mathematical structure that has enabled management scientists to develop efficient, specialized procedures for solving them. These procedures are covered in Chapter 7.

ANSWERED PROBLEMS

PROBLEM 10

Fullerton Trucking has $500,000 allocated to purchase at least 40 trucks. It will buy both Japanese and American-built trucks, but keeping with its "BUY-AMERICAN" image, it wishes to purchase at least twice as many American as Japanese-built trucks. Fullerton has narrowed its choices to three American and three Japanese models. It wishes to purchase at least 20 two-seat models. The following table summarizes the data for each model:

Truck	Country	Cost	Capacity	Seats
Hauler	U.S.	$20,000	1.50 tons	2
Mauler	U.S.	$18,000	1.00	2
Bruiser	U.S.	$13,000	.75	1
Econotruck	Japan	$ 7,000	.50	1
T-150	Japan	$12,000	.75	2
Maxitruck	Japan	$15,000	1.00	2

a) Formulate this problem as a linear program with the objective of maximizing the overall trucking capacity.

b) Why is linear programming not the technically correct procedure to use to solve this problem?

PROBLEM 11

National Wing Company (NWC) is gearing up for the new B-48 contract. Currently NWC has 100 equally qualified workers. Over the next three months NWC has made the following commitments for wing production:

Month	Contract
May	20
June	24
July	30

Each worker can either be placed in production or can train new recruits. A new recruit can be trained to be an apprentice in one month. The next month, he, himself, becomes a qualified worker (after two months from the start of training). Each trainer can train two recruits. The production rate and salary per employee is estimated below.

Employee	Production Rate (Wings/Month)	Salary Per Month
Production	.6	\$3,000
Trainer	.3	\$3,300
Apprentice	.4	\$2,600
Recruit	.05	\$2,200

At the end of July, NWC wishes to have no recruits or apprentices but have at least 140 full-time workers.

Formulate a linear program for NWC to accomplish this at minimum total cost.

PROBLEM 12

Triumph Trumpet Company makes two styles each of both trumpets and cornets: deluxe and professional models. Its unit profit on deluxe trumpets is \$80 and on deluxe cornets is \$60. The professional models realize twice the profit of the deluxe models.

Trumpets and cornets are made basically from two mixtures of two different brass alloys. The amount of each alloy (in pounds) required to produce each type of horn is summarized in the following table along with the monthly availability to Triumph of the alloys.

	Trumpets		Cornets		
	Deluxe	Pro.	Deluxe	Pro.	Monthly Availability
Alloy 1	2	1.5	1.5	1	2000
Alloy 2	1	1.5	1	1.5	1800

Triumph must fulfill contracts calling for at least 500 deluxe trumpets and 300 deluxe cornets monthly. Monthly demand for professional trumpets is not expected to exceed 150 and for professional cornets is not expected to exceed 100. Production set-ups are such that the company will produce exactly twice as many trumpets as cornets.

Formulate this problem as a linear program.

PROBLEM 13

Millard Construction is contemplating building a planned community with the help of federal funds. These funds are to be distributed only if Millard meets federal standards for low cost housing. There are three types of units -- houses, town-houses, and high rise condominiums. There are three styles each of the houses and town-houses -- low cost, standard, and deluxe. The high rise condominiums will have only standard and deluxe models.

The amount of total ground space (including allowances for parking and green belts) is given in the following table:

	Ground Area (Sq. Ft.)		
	Low Cost	Standard	Deluxe
Houses	1800	2200	3000
Town-Houses	740	1600	2230
Condominiums	X	1000	1500

The profit to Millard per unit is summarized in the following table:

	Profit ($1000's)		
	Low Cost	Standard	Deluxe
Town-Houses	4	10	18
Condominiums	X	9	16

Millard has 300,000 square feet for construction. To make the project "work", Millard wants houses and town-houses each to occupy between 25% and 40% of the total area while condominiums only need to occupy 10% to 25% of the total area.

The federal government requires that at least 25% of the total units built in the complex be low cost units.

a) Formulate this problem as a linear program.

b) Solve for the optimal solution using a computer package such as The Management Scientist.

c) Why is linear programming not the technically correct formulation procedure for this problem?

PROBLEM 14

Delicious Candy Company manufactures three types of candy bars-- Chompers, Smerks, and Delicious Chocolate. All three candies come in a one-ounce size while Delicious Chocolate also comes in a one-pound mini-bar bag.

The basic ingredients used are chocolate, peanuts, and caramel. Delicious Chocolate is all chocolate, while Chompers consists of chocolate and carmel, and Smerks consists of chocolate, caramel and peanuts. Chompers' recipe allows for the amount of caramel to be anywhere between 18% and 28% of the candy bar's weight with chocolate making up the rest. Smerks' recipe calls for an equal amount of caramel and peanuts, with chocolate making up between 20% and 40% of the bar's weight.

For each one-ounce bar, labor and packaging costs $.012, while labor and packaging for the one-pound bag costs $.039. The company has production facilities for making up to 20,000 one-ounce bars and up to 1000 one-pound bags daily.

Delicious has contracts to produce at least 3000 one-ounce bars of each type of candy daily. Also, the difference between the number of Chompers and the number of Smerks produced must be less than 10% of the total number of Chompers and Smerks made. The present prices for chocolate, caramel, and peanuts are $1.60, $.95, and $1.40 per pound respectively. The company has contracts which will supply it with at least 1,000 pounds of chocolate, exactly 350 pounds of caramel, and at most 500 pounds of peanuts daily.

The company currently sells Chompers one-ounce bars for $.14, Smerks one-ounce bars for $.16, Delicious Chocolate one- ounce bars for $.15, and Delicious Chocolate one-pound bags for $2.30. Formulate a linear program that would determine the optimal daily production schedule and ingredients required. (HINT: Variables must be established for each product type and the amount of each ingredient in each product.)

PROBLEM 15

WeBuild Construction must decide how many small bulldozers to purchase or lease for the coming year. Bulldozers may be purchased for $40,000 each and their salvage value at the end of a year is $20,000. WeBuild can also lease bulldozers for $8,000 per year payable in advance.

WeBuild has $1,000,000 available in its budget for purchase and/or lease of bulldozers. Any monies not invested in purchasing or leasing bulldozers will be invested at 8%.

There are 60 projects each requiring four bulldozers throughout the year. Because of timing and reliability, each new bulldozer will be available for eight projects, whereas each leased bulldozer will be available for five projects.

Formulate and solve for the number of bulldozers WeBuild should purchase and lease to minimize its total annual cost.

PROBLEM 16

John Sweeney is an investment advisor who is attempting to construct an "optimal portfolio" for a client who has $400,000 cash to invest. There are ten different investments, falling into four broad categories that John and his client have identified as potential candidates for this portfolio.

The following table lists the investments and their important characteristics. Note that Unidyde Equities and Unidyde Debt are two separate investments, whereas First General REIT is a single investment that is considered both an equities and a real estate investment.

Category	Investment	Expected Annual After Tax Return	Liquidity Factor	Risk Factor
Equities	Unidyde Corporation	15.0%	100	60
	Col. Must. Restaurants	17.0%	100	70
	First General REIT	17.5%	100	75
Debt	Metropolitan Electric	11.8%	95	20
	Unidyde Corporation	12.2%	92	30
	Lemonville Transit	12.0%	79	22
Real Estate	Fairview Apartment Partnership	22.0%	0	50
	First General REIT		(See above)	
Money	T-Bill Account	9.6%	80	0
	Money Market Fund	10.5%	100	10
	All Saver's Certificate	12.6%	0	0

Formulate a linear program to accomplish John's objective as an investment advisor which is to construct a portfolio that maximizes his client's total expected after-tax return over the next year, subject to a number of constraints placed upon him by the client for the portfolio:

1. Its (weighted) average liquidity factor must be at least 65.
2. The (weighted) average risk factor must be no greater than 55.
3. At most, $60,000 is to be invested in Unidyde Stocks or bonds.
4. No more than 40% of the investment can be in any one category except the money category.
5. No more than 20% of the investment can be in any one investment except the money market fund.
6. At least $1,000 must be invested in the money market fund.
7. The maximum investment in All Saver's Certificates is $15,000.
8. The minimum investment desired for debt is $90,000.
9. At least $10,000 must be placed in a T-Bill account.

PROBLEM 17

BP Cola must decide how much money to allocate for new soda and traditional soda advertising over the coming year. The advertising budget is $10,000,000.

Because BP wants to push its new sodas, at least one-half of the advertising budget is to be devoted to new soda advertising. However, at least $2,000,000 is to be spent on its traditional sodas. BP estimates that each dollar spent on traditional sodas will translate into 100 cans sold, whereas, because of the harder sell needed for new products, each dollar spent on new sodas will translate into 50 cans sold. To attract new customers BP has lowered its profit margin on new sodas to 2 cents per can as compared to 4 cents per can for traditional sodas.

How should BP allocate its advertising budget if it wants to maximize its profits while selling at least 750 million cans?

PROBLEM 18

Maybury Public School System has three high schools to serve a territory divided into five districts. The capacity of each high school, the student population in each district, and the distance (in miles) between each school and the center of each district are listed in the table below:

	High School			
District	McHale	McCallum	McBride	Student Population
Northeast	1.5	2.5	0.5	700
Southeast	4	1.5	3	1100
Southwest	2.5	3	3.5	900
Northwest	0.5	4	1.5	600
Central	1	2	1	800
Capacity	1500	1800	1100	

Formulate and solve a linear program to determine the school-student assignment that minimizes the total student-miles traveled per day.

PROBLEM 19

The June Company is a department store chain serving three states in the South: Georgia, Alabama, and Mississippi. Recently management has been concerned about the relative efficiency of its Alabama store.

The June Company tabulates the monthly gross sales of home appliances, clothing, home entertainment, and all other divisions and measures these outputs against inputs of store size, number of sales personnel for the store, and the population service area for each store (defined as the number of adults over 16 living within a 35 mile radius of the store.)

The tables below give the average monthly values for each of the inputs and outputs based on last year's data.

Inputs	Georgia	Alabama	Mississippi
Store Size (1000's sq. ft.)	25	24	18
Sales Personnel	250	210	180
Service Area Population (1000's)	600	750	375

Outputs: Average Monthly Sales ($mil.)	Georgia	Alabama	Mississippi
Appliances	1.2	0.8	0.6
Clothing	2.2	1.4	1.5
Home Entertainment	1.6	1.5	1.6
All Others	2.7	2.0	2.1

Based on last year's data, use data envelopment analysis to formulate and solve a linear program to help June Company determine the relative efficiency of its Alabama store.

PROBLEM 20

Niteton Power and Light Company (NPLC) wants to develop an efficient work schedule for its full- and part-time customer service clerks. The number of clerks needed to provide adequate service during each hour the office is open on a weekday is given below:

Hour	AM 8-9	9-10	10-11	11-12	PM 12-1	1-2	2-3	3-4	4-5	5-6
Clerks	5	4	6	8	10	9	7	4	7	5

A full-time clerk works 3 hours, has a 1-hour break, and then works another 3 hours. Part-time clerks work 4 consecutive hours. Full-timers get paid for their break. All clerks start work on the hour.

NPLC's office manager insists that at least one full-time clerk be on duty during all open hours and that a minimum of four full-time clerks are on the payroll. A full-time clerk costs NPLC $9.00 per hour, and a part-timer costs $6.50 per hour.

Formulate a linear program that will provide a schedule that will meet NPLC's customer service needs at a minimum labor cost. (Hint: there are 4 different full-time shifts and 7 different part-time shifts.)

TRUE/FALSE

21. Sunk costs should be viewed as relevant costs when developing the objective function for a linear programming model.

22. Double-subscript notation for decision variables should be avoided unless the number of decision variables exceeds nine.

23. Generating the data for large-scale LP models can be more time consuming than either the formulation of the model or the development of the computer solution.

24. Using minutes as the unit of measurement on the left-hand side of a constraint and using hours on the right-hand side is acceptable since both are a measure of time.

25. No real-world problem, when correctly formulated, has an unbounded solution.

26. A company makes two products from steel; one requires 2 tons of steel and the other requires 3 tons. There are 100 tons of steel available daily. A constraint on daily production could be written as: $2X_1 + 3X_2 \leq 100$.

27. Compared to the problems in the textbook, real-world problems generally require more variables and constraints.

28. For the multiperiod production scheduling problem in the textbook, period n-1's ending inventory variable was also used as period n's beginning inventory variable.

29. To reliably answer "what-if" questions about the effects of changes in the parameters used in an LP formulation, one should always resolve the problem.

30. If a real-world problem is correctly formulated, it is impossible to have alternative optimal solutions.

31. A company makes two products, A and B. A sells for $100 and B sells for $90. The variable production costs are $30 per unit for A and $25 for B. The company's objective could be written as: MAX $190X_1 - 55X_2$.

32. The primary limitation of linear programming's applicability is the requirement that all decision variables be nonnegative.

33. If an LP problem is not correctly formulated, the computer will indicate it is infeasible when trying to solve it.

34. The wide-spread use of linear programming is due largely to the fact that the nature of most business functions is linear.

35. A decision maker would be wise to not deviate from the optimal solution found by an LP model because it is the best solution.

Chapter 10
Linear Programming: The Simplex Method

KEY CONCEPTS

CONCEPT	ILLUSTRATED PROBLEMS	ANSWERED PROBLEMS
Problem Formulation	7	14
Standard Form	1,2,4,5,7	8,9,10,14,15
Tableau Form	1,2,4,5,7	8,9,10,14,15
Artificial Variables	4,5,7	,10,11,15
Minimization Problems	2,4	8,10
Infeasibility	5	11
Unboundedness	5	11
Alternate Optimal Solutions	6	14
Degeneracy		13

REVIEW

1. The simplex method is an algebraic method for solving linear programs. (See description of algorithm on the next page.) The more recently developed Karmarkar method holds promise of solving large linear programs even more quickly than the simplex method.

2. The steps leading to the simplex method are as follows:

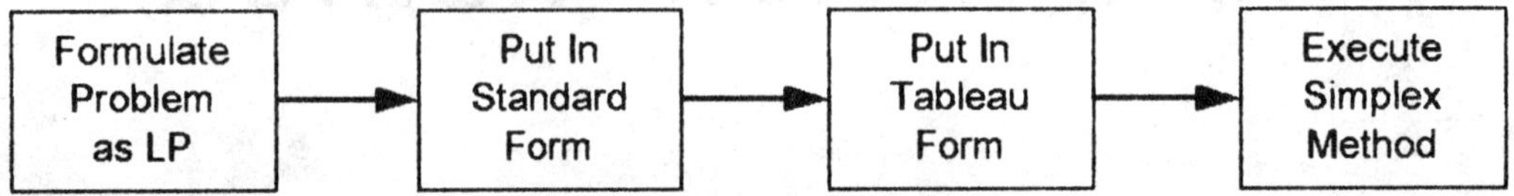
Formulate Problem as LP
Put In Standard Form
Put In Tableau Form
Execute Simplex Method

3. Putting an LP formulation into standard form involves adding slack and/or subtracting surplus variables, as discussed in Chapter 2.

4. The simplex tableau is a convenient means for performing the calculations required by the simplex method.

5. A set of equations is in tableau form if for each equation: (1) its right hand side (RHS) is non-negative and, (2) there is a basic variable. A basic variable for an equation is a variable whose coefficient in the equation is +1 and whose coefficient in all other equations of the problem is 0.

6. If a constraint is formulated with a negative right-hand side, multiply it by -1 before adding slack, surplus, or artificial variables.

7. To generate an initial tableau form, artificial variables must be added to all constraints which do not have a basic variable. These normally include "greater than or equal to" constraints and "equal to" constraints.

8. Artificial variables are given an objective function coefficient of -M in maximization problems (+M in minimization problems), where M is an extremely large number. Once an artificial variable becomes non-basic, it may be eliminated from further consideration by dropping its column.

9. If the problem has a minimization objective, multiply the objective function by -1 before using the simplex method.

10. A basic feasible solution for a problem in tableau form is found by setting the basic variables equal to the right hand side values of the equations and the other variables (the non-basic variables) to 0.

11. Basic feasible solutions are equivalent to <u>extreme points</u>, and for a linear program with an optimal solution, a basic feasible solution must be optimal.

12. The $c_j - z_j$ row of a simplex tableau represents the amount the objective function will increase per unit increase in the corresponding column variable. For a maximization problem, the most positive entry in this row determines the <u>entering variable</u>.

13. A <u>tableau's right-hand side</u> gives the values of the current basic variables.

14. The minimizing ratio between the right hand side values and positive numbers in the column of the entering variable determines which current basic variable will reach zero first as the entering variable is increased. This variable is called the <u>leaving variable</u>.

15. <u>Infeasibility</u> is detected in the simplex method when an artificial variable remains positive in the final tableau.

16. A linear program has an <u>unbounded solution</u> if all entries in an entering column are non-positive.

17. A linear program has <u>alternate optimal solutions</u> if the final tableau has a $C_j - Z_j$ value equal to 0 for a non-basic variable.

18. A <u>degenerate solution</u> to a linear program is one in which at least one of the basic variables equals 0. This can occur at formulation or if there is a tie for the minimizing value in the ratio test to determine the leaving variable.

SETTING UP INITIAL SIMPLEX TABLEAU

Step 1: If the problem is a minimization problem, multiply the objective function by -1.

Step 2: If the problem formulation contains any constraints with negative right-hand sides, multiply each constraint by -1.

Step 3: Add a slack variable to each $\leq$ constraint.

Step 4: Subtract a surplus variable and add an artificial variable to each $\geq$ constraint.

Step 5: Add an artificial variable to each = constraint.

Step 6: Set each slack and surplus variable's coefficient in the objective function equal to zero.

Step 7: Set each artificial variable's coefficient in the objective function equal to -M, where M is a very large number.

Step 8: Each slack and artificial variable becomes one of the basic variables in the initial basic feasible solution.

FLOW CHART FOR
SETTING UP INITIAL SIMPLEX TABLEAU

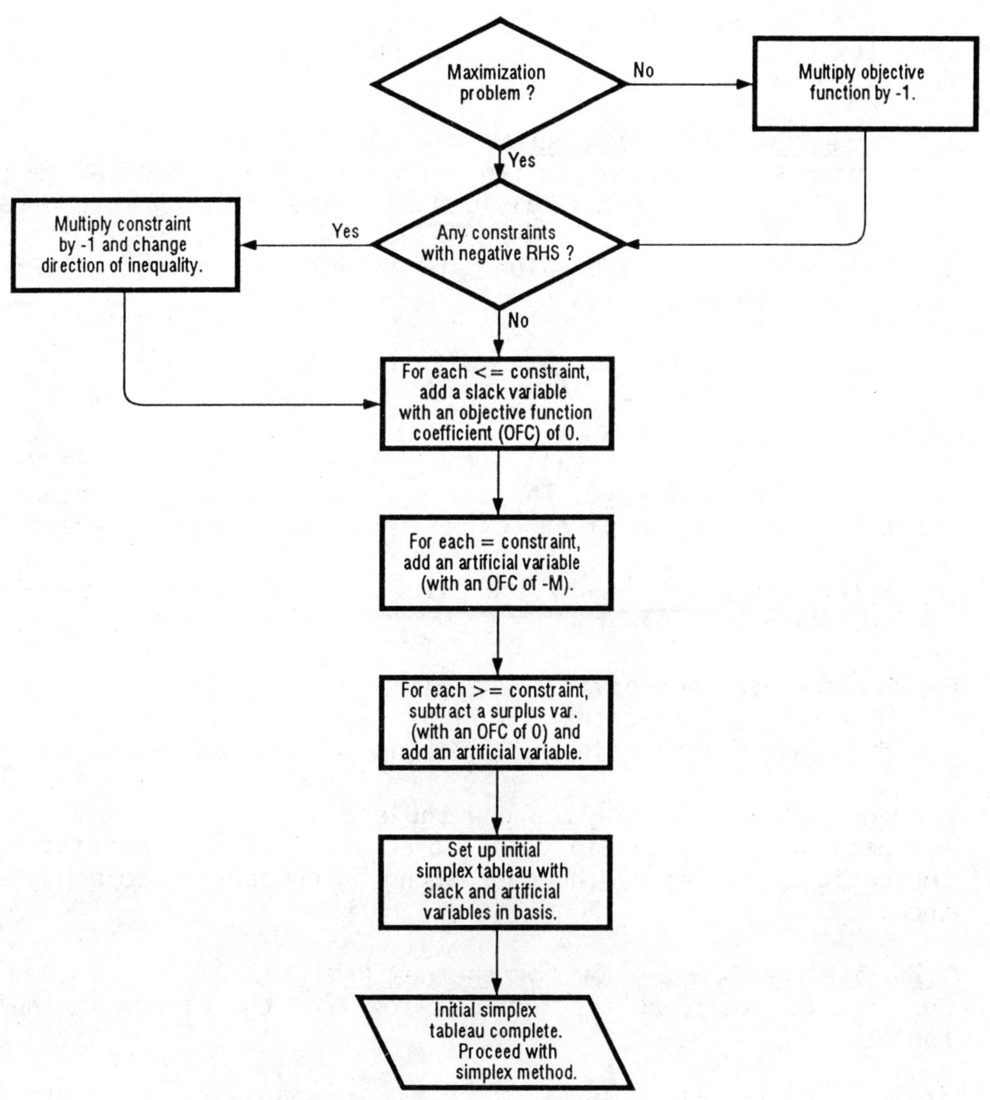
Maximization problem ?
No
Multiply objective function by -1.
Yes
Multiply constraint by -1 and change direction of inequality.
Yes
Any constraints with negative RHS ?
No
For each <= constraint, add a slack variable with an objective function coefficient (OFC) of 0.
For each = constraint, add an artificial variable (with an OFC of -M).
For each >= constraint, subtract a surplus var. (with an OFC of 0) and add an artificial variable.
Set up initial simplex tableau with slack and artificial variables in basis.
Initial simplex tableau complete. Proceed with simplex method.

SIMPLEX METHOD

Starting with the initial simplex tableau:

Step 1: Determine the entering variable.
Identify the variable with the most positive value in the $C_j - Z_j$ row.

Step 2: Determine the leaving variable.
For each positive number in the entering column, compute the ratio of the right-hand side values divided by these entering column values.

If there are no positive values in the entering column, STOP; the problem is unbounded.

Otherwise, select the variable with the minimal ratio.

Step 3: Generate the next tableau.
(The entering column is called the pivot column and the leaving row is called the pivot row. The entry which is at the intersection of the pivot row and the pivot column is called the pivot element.)

(a) Divide the pivot row by the pivot element to get a new row. We designate this new row as (row *).

(b) Replace each non-pivot row i with:
[new row i] = [current row i] - [(a_{ij}) x (row *)],
where a_{ij} is the value in entering column j of row i

Step 4: Calculate the Z_j row for the new tableau.
For each column j, multiply the objective function coefficients of the basic variables by the corresponding numbers in column j and sum them.

Step 5: Calculate the $C_j - Z_j$ row for the new tableau.
For each column j, subtract the Z_j row from the C_j row in the tableau.

If none of the values in the $C_j - Z_j$ row are positive, GO TO STEP 1.

If there is an artificial variable in the basis with a positive value, the problem is infeasible. STOP.

Otherwise, an optimal solution has been found. The current values of the basic variables are optimal. The optimal values of the non-basic variables are all zero. If any non-basic variable's $C_j - Z_j$ value is 0, alternate optimal solutions might exist. STOP.

FLOW CHART OF SIMPLEX METHOD

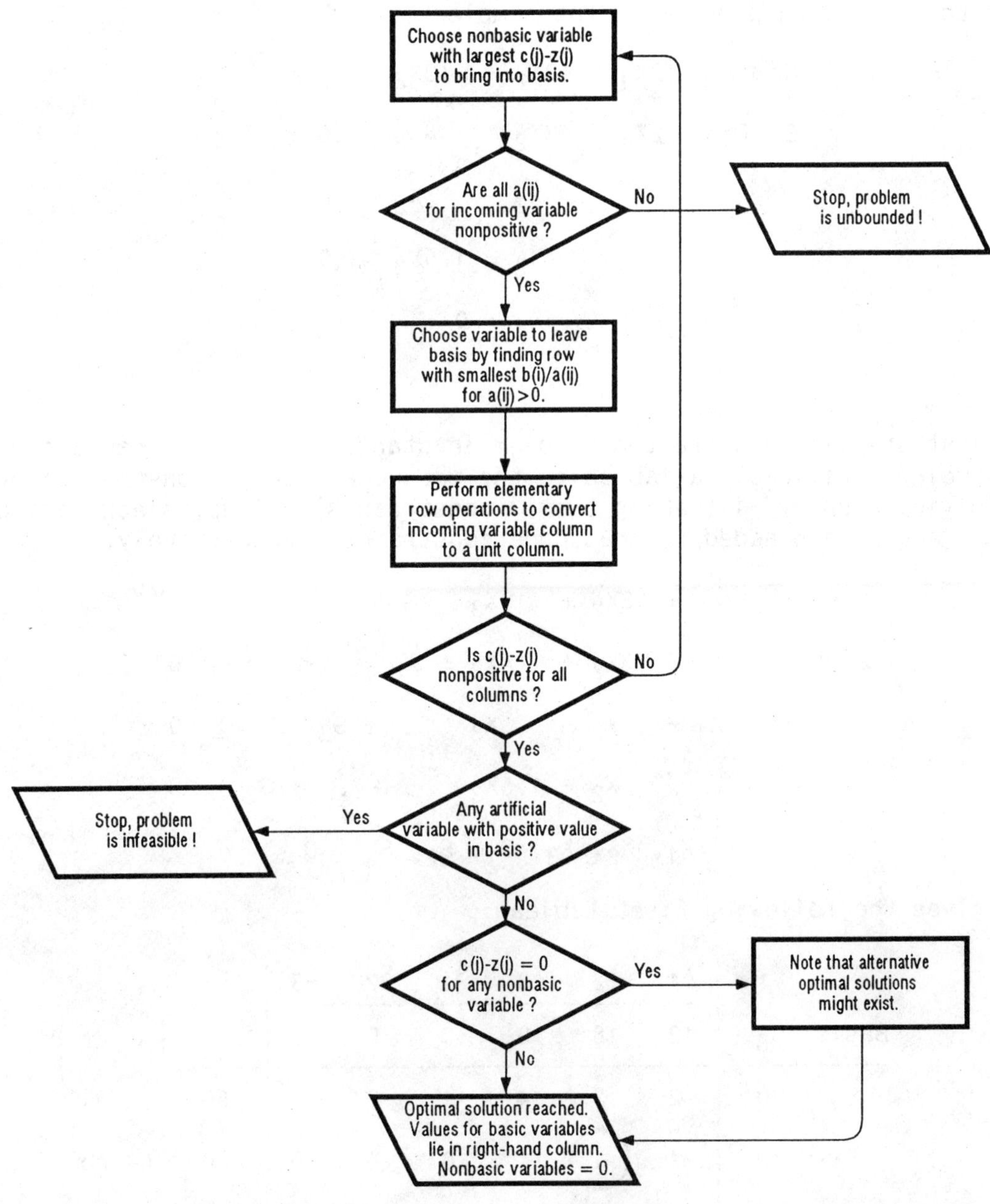
Choose nonbasic variable with largest c(j)-z(j) to bring into basis.
Are all a(ij) for incoming variable nonpositive ?
No
Stop, problem is unbounded !
Yes
Choose variable to leave basis by finding row with smallest b(i)/a(ij) for a(ij) > 0.
Perform elementary row operations to convert incoming variable column to a unit column.
Is c(j)-z(j) nonpositive for all columns ?
No
Yes
Any artificial variable with positive value in basis ?
Yes
Stop, problem is infeasible !
No
c(j)-z(j) = 0 for any nonbasic variable ?
Yes
Note that alternative optimal solutions might exist.
No
Optimal solution reached. Values for basic variables lie in right-hand column. Nonbasic variables = 0.

ILLUSTRATED PROBLEMS

PROBLEM 1

Solve the following problem by the simplex method:

$$\begin{aligned} \text{MAX } Z &= 12X_1 + 18X_2 + 10X_3 \\ \text{S. T.} \quad & 2X_1 + 3X_2 + 4X_3 \leq 50 \\ & X_1 - X_2 - X_3 \geq 0 \\ & X_2 - 1.5X_3 \geq 0 \\ & X_1, X_2, X_3 \geq 0 \end{aligned}$$

SOLUTION 1

The first step is to write the problem in standard form. We can avoid introducing artificial variables to the second and third constraints by multiplying each by -1 (making them $\leq$ constraints). Thus, slack variables S_1, S_2, and S_3 are added to the three constraints, respectively.

$$\begin{aligned} \text{MAX } Z &= 12X_1 + 18X_2 + 10X_3 \\ \text{S. T.} \quad & 2X_1 + 3X_2 + 4X_3 + S_1 \leq 50 \\ & X_1 - X_2 - X_3 + S_2 \geq 0 \\ & X_2 - 1.5X_3 + S_3 \geq 0 \\ & X_1, X_2, X_3, S_1, S_2, S_3 \geq 0 \end{aligned}$$

This gives the following first tableau:

		X_1	X_2	X_3	S_1	S_2	S_3		
Basis	C_B	12	18	10	0	0	0		
S_1	0	2	3	4	1	0	0	50	
S_2	0	-1	(1)	1	0	1	0	0	(* row)
S_3	0	0	-1	1.5	0	0	1	0	
Z_j		0	0	0	0	0	0	0	
$C_j - Z_j$		12	18	10	0	0	0		

Iteration 1

(Step 1) The most positive $C_j - Z_j = 18$. Thus X_2 is the entering variable.

(Step 2) Take the ratio between the right hand side and positive numbers in the X_2 column:

$$50/3 = 16\ 2/3$$
$$0/1 = 0 \quad \text{<==== minimum}$$

S_2 is the leaving variable and the 1 is the pivot element.

(Step 3) Divide the second row by 1, the pivot element. Call the "new" (in this case, unchanged) row the "* row".
Subtract 3 x (* row) from row 1.
Subtract -1 x (* row) from row 3.
New rows 1, 2, and 3 are shown in the tableau below.

(Step 4) The new Z_j row values are obtained by multiplying the C_B column by each column, element by element and summing. For example, $Z_1 = 5(0) + -1(18) + -1(0) = -18$.

(Step 5) The new $C_j - Z_j$ row values are obtained by subtracting Z_j value in a column from the C_j value in the same column. For example, $C_1 - Z_1 = 12 - (-18) = 30$.

Thus, the following tableau is derived with X_2 replacing S_2 as a basic variable.

		X_1	X_2	X_3	S_1	S_2	S_3		
Basis	C_B	12	18	10	0	0	0		
S_1	0	(5)	0	1	1	-3	0	50	(* row)
X_2	18	-1	1	1	0	1	0	0	
S_3	0	-1	0	2.5	0	1	1	0	
Z_j		-18	18	18	0	18	0	0	
$C_j - Z_j$		30	0	-8	0	-18	0		

Iteration 2

(Step 1) The most positive $C_j - Z_j = 30$. X_1 is the entering variable.

(Step 2) Take the ratio between the right hand side and positive numbers in the X_1 column:

$$10/5 = 2 \Longleftarrow \text{minimum}$$

There are no ratios for the second and third rows because their column elements (-1) are negative. Thus, S_1 (corresponding to row 1) is the leaving variable and 5 is the pivot element.

(Step 3) Divide row 1 by 5, the pivot element. (Call this new row 1 the "* row").
Subtract (-1) x (* row) from the second row.
Subtract (-1) x (* row) from the third row.
New rows 1, 2, and 3 are shown in the tableau below.

(Step 4) The new Z_j row values are obtained by multiplying the C_B column by each column, element by element and summing.
For example, $Z_3 = .2(12) + 1.2(18) + .2(0) = 24$.

(Step 5) The new C_j-Z_j row values are obtained by subtracting Z_j value in a column from the C_j value in the same column.
For example, C_3-Z_3 = 10 - (24) = -14.

Thus, the following tableau is derived with X_1 replacing S_1 as a basic variable.

		X_1	X_2	X_3	S_1	S_2	S_3	
Basis	C_B	12	18	10	0	0	0	
X_1	12	1	0	.2	.2	-.6	0	10
X_2	18	0	1	1.2	.2	.4	0	10
S_3	0	0	0	2.7	.2	.4	1	10
Z_j		12	18	24	6	0	0	300
$C_j - Z_j$		0	0	-14	-6	0	0	

Since there are no positive numbers in the $C_j - Z_j$ row, this tableau is optimal. The optimal solution is: $X_1 = 10$; $X_2 = 10$; $X_3 = 0$; $S_1 = 0$; $S_2 = 0$ $S_3 = 10$, and the optimal value of the objective function, $Z = 300$.

PROBLEM 2

Solve the following problem by the simplex method:

$$\text{MIN } Z = 8X_1 + 5X_2 + 4X_3$$

$$\begin{aligned} \text{S. T.} \quad X_1 + X_2 & \geq 10 \\ X_2 + X_3 & \geq 15 \\ X_1 + X_3 & \geq 12 \\ 20X_1 + 10X_2 + 15X_3 & \leq 300 \\ X_1, X_2, X_3 & \geq 0 \end{aligned}$$

SOLUTION 2

First, write the problem in standard form. Constraints 1, 2, and 3 each require a surplus variable. Constraint 4 requires a slack variable.

$$\text{MIN } Z = 8X_1 + 5X_2 + 4X_3$$

$$\begin{aligned} \text{S. T.} \quad X_1 + X_2 - S_1 & \geq 10 \\ X_2 + X_3 - S_2 & \geq 15 \\ X_1 + X_3 - S_3 & \geq 12 \\ 20X_1 + 10X_2 + 15X_3 + S_4 & \leq 300 \\ X_1, X_2, X_3, S_1, S_2, S_3, S_4 & \geq 0 \end{aligned}$$

To put in tableau form, add artificial variables A_1, A_2, and A_3 to the constraints 1, 2, and 3, respectively. Since this is a minimization problem, the A's have objective coefficients of +M.

$$\text{MIN } Z = 8X_1 + 5X_2 + 4X_3 + MA_1 + MA_2 + MA_3$$

$$\begin{aligned} \text{S. T.} \quad X_1 + X_2 - S_1 & \geq 10 \\ X_2 + X_3 - S_2 & \geq 15 \\ X_1 + X_3 - S_3 & \geq 12 \\ 20X_1 + 10X_2 + 15X_3 + S_4 & \leq 300 \\ X_1, X_2, X_3, S_1, S_2, S_3, S_4, A_1, A_2, A_3 & \geq 0 \end{aligned}$$

Before beginning the simplex method, the objective function is converted to maximization by multiplying it by -1.

Iteration 1

Basis	C_B	X_1	X_2	X_3	S_1	S_2	S_3	S_4	A_1	A_2	A_3	
		-8	-5	-4	0	0	0	0	-M	-M	-M	
A_1	-M	1	1	0	-1	0	0	0	1	0	0	10
A_2	-M	0	1	1	0	-1	0	0	0	1	0	15
A_3	-M	1	0	(1)	0	0	-1	0	0	0	1	12
S_4	0	20	10	15	0	0	0	1	0	0	0	300
Z_j		-2M	-2M	-2M	M	M	M	0	-M	-M	-M	-37M
$C_j - Z_j$		2M-8	2M-5	2M-4	-M	-M	-M	0	0	0	0	

Iteration 2 (Drop the A_3 column)

Basis	C_B	X_1	X_2	X_3	S_1	S_2	S_3	S_4	A_1	A_2	
		-8	-5	-4	0	0	0	0	-M	-M	
A_1	-M	1	1	0	-1	0	0	0	1	0	10
A_2	-M	-1	(1)	0	0	-1	1	0	0	1	3
X_3	-4	1	0	1	0	0	-1	0	0	0	12
S_4	0	5	10	0	0	0	15	1	0	0	120
Z_j		-4	-2M	-4	M	M	-M+4	0	-M	-M	-13M -48
$C_j - Z_j$		-4	2M-5	0	-M	-M	M-4	0	0	0	

Iteration 3 (Drop the A_2 column)

Basis	C_B	X_1	X_2	X_3	S_1	S_2	S_3	S_4	A_1	
		-8	-5	-4	0	0	0	0	-M	
A_1	-M	(2)	0	0	-1	1	-1	0	1	7
X_2	-5	-1	1	0	0	-1	1	0	0	3
X_3	-4	1	0	1	0	0	-1	0	0	12
S_4	0	15	0	0	0	10	5	1	0	90
Z_j		-2M+1	-5	-4	M	-M+5	M-1	0	-M	-7M-63
$C_j - Z_j$		2M-9	0	0	-M	M-5	-M+1	0	0	

Iteration 4 (Drop the A_1 column)

Basis	C_B	X_1	X_2	X_3	S_1	S_2	S_3	S_4	
		-8	-5	-4	0	0	0	0	
X_1	-8	1	0	0	-1/2	1/2	-1/2	0	7/2
X_2	-5	0	1	0	-1/2	-1/2	1/2	0	13/2
X_3	-4	0	0	1	1/2	-1/2	-1/2	0	17/2
S_4	0	0	0	0	15/2	5/2	25/2	1	75/2
Z_j		-8	-5	-4	9/2	1/2	7/2	0	-189/2
$C_j - Z_j$		0	0	0	-9/2	-1/2	-7/2	0	

This is the optimal tableau. Thus the optimal solution is:

$X_1 = 7/2$ $S_1 = 0$
$X_2 = 13/2$ $S_2 = 0$
$X_3 = 17/2$ $S_3 = 0$
$S_4 = 75/2$

Because we multiplied the objective function by -1, the optimal maximization value of Z is 189/2 or 94.5.

PROBLEM 3

At some iteration of the simplex method, the tableau is the following:

Basis	C_B	X_1	X_2	S_1	S_2	S_3	S_4	
		10	6	0	0	0	0	
X_2	6	0	1	3	0	-2	0	7
S_2	0	0	0	4	1	3	0	8
X_1	10	1	0	-2	0	2	0	16
S_4	0	0	0	0	0	4	1	10
Z_j		10	6	-2	0	8	0	202
$C_j - Z_j$		0	0	2	0	-8	0	

a) Explain the meaning of each number in the tableau.

b) Note S_1 will be the entering variable. Explain why the ratio test is performed only on positive numbers in the S_1 column.

c) Use the simplex method to solve for the optimal solution.

SOLUTION 3

a) The C_j row gives the gross increase in Z per unit increase in the corresponding variable. The Z_j row gives the gross decrease in Z per unit increase in the corresponding variable. Thus, the $C_j - Z_j$ row gives the "net increase" in Z per unit increase in the corresponding variable.

The large matrix (the a_{ij}'s) give the amount the basic variable associated with row i will decrease per unit increase in the corresponding variable of column j.

The C_B column gives the objective function coefficients for the basic variables. The numbers on the right hand side give the current values of the basic variables, i.e. $X_2 = 7$, $S_2 = 8$, $X_1 = 16$, $S_4 = 10$. The bottom right number gives the value of $Z = 202$.

b) As noted in (a), the a_{ij}'s are the amount of decrease in the basic variable of row i per unit increase in the corresponding variable of column j. Hence, as for every unit S_1 is increased, X_2 decreases by 3, S_2 decreases by 4, and X_1 increases by 2. S_4 will not change as S_1 is increased. From one iteration to the next the variables must stay non-negative. Thus S_1 can increase to 7/3 before X_2 goes to 0 and to 2 (=8/4) before S_2 goes to 0. These are the only limiting factors.

c) (Step 1) The most positive $C_j - Z_j$ is 2. S_1 enters.

(Step 2) The ratio test on positive numbers in the S_1 column gives:

7/3 = 7/3
8/4 = 2 ⟸ minimum

S_2 leaves.

(Step 3) Divide row 2 by 4 to give a new (* row).
Subtract 3 x (* row) from row 1.
Subtract -2 x (* row) from row 3.
Leave row 4 as it is.

(Steps 4 and 5 are reflected in the tableau below.)

		X_1	X_2	S_1	S_2	S_3	S_4		
Basis	C_B	10	6	0	0	0	0		
X_2	6	0	1	0	-3/4	-17/4	0	1	
S_1	0	0	0	1	1/4	3/4	0	2	(* row)
X_1	10	1	0	0	1/2	7/2	0	20	
S_4	0	0	0	0	0	4	1	10	
Z_j		10	6	0	1/2	19/2	0	206	
$C_j - Z_j$		0	0	0	-1/2	-19/2	0		

Since the $C_j - Z_j$ row has no positive numbers, this is the optimal tableau and the optimal solution: $X_1 = 20$, $X_2 = 1$, $S_1 = 2$, $S_2 = 0$, $S_3 = 0$, $S_4 = 10$, and $Z = 206$.

PROBLEM 4

Given the following minimization problem:

$$\text{MIN } Z = 2X_1 - 3X_2 - 4X_3$$

$$\begin{aligned} \text{S.T.} \quad X_1 + X_2 + X_3 &\le 30 \\ 2X_1 + X_2 + 3X_3 &\ge 60 \\ X_1 - X_2 + 2X_3 &= 20 \\ X_j \ge 0 \quad j &= 1,2,3 \end{aligned}$$

a) Write the problem in standard form. Explain why this is not tableau form.

b) Add artificial variables and amend the objective function appropriately to obtain the first tableau form.

c) Solve the problem by the simplex method.

SOLUTION 4

a)

$$\text{MIN } Z = 2X_1 - 3X_2 - 4X_3$$

$$\begin{aligned} \text{S.T.} \quad X_1 + X_2 + X_3 + S_1 \qquad &= 30 \\ 2X_1 + X_2 + 3X_3 \qquad -S_2 &= 60 \\ X_1 - X_2 + 2X_3 \qquad &= 20 \\ X_j \ge 0 \quad j = 1,2,3; \quad S_j \ge 0 \quad j &= 1,2 \end{aligned}$$

This is not tableau form because the second and third constraints do not have basic variables, i.e. variables whose coefficient in that constraint is +1, and whose coefficient in the other constraints is 0.

b) Add artificial variables A_2 and A_3 to the second and third constraints, respectively. Since this is a minimization problem, the A's objective function coefficients are +M.

$$\text{MIN } Z = 2X_1 - 3X_2 - 4X_3 + MA_2 + MA_3$$

$$\begin{aligned} \text{S.T.}\quad & X_1 + X_2 + X_3 + S_1 = 30 \\ & 2X_1 + X_2 + 3X_3 - S_2 + A_2 = 60 \\ & X_1 - X_2 + 2X_3 + A_3 = 20 \\ & X_j \geq 0 \quad j = 1,2,3; \quad S_j,\ A_j \geq 0 \quad j = 1,2 \end{aligned}$$

c) Before beginning the simplex method, the objective function is multiplied by -1, so that the maximization algorithm may be used.

<u>Iteration 1</u>

Basis	C_B	X_1	X_2	X_3	S_1	S_2	A_2	A_3	
		-2	3	4	0	0	-M	-M	
S_1	0	1	1	1	1	0	0	0	30
A_2	-M	2	1	3	0	-1	1	0	60
A_3	-M	1	-1	(2)	0	0	0	1	20
Z_j		-3M	0	-5M	0	M	-M	-M	-80M
$C_j - Z_j$		3M-2	3	5M+4	0	-M	0	0	

<u>Iteration 2</u> (Drop the A_3 column)

Basis	C_B	X_1	X_2	X_3	S_1	S_2	A_2	
		-2	3	4	0	0	-M	
S_1	0	1/2	3/2	0	1	0	0	20
A_2	-M	1/2	(5/2)	0	0	-1	1	30
X_3	4	1/2	-1/2	1	0	0	0	10
Z_j		-(1/2M) +2	-(5/2)M -2	4	0	M	-M	-30M +40
$C_j - Z_j$		(1/2)M -4	(5/2)M +5	0	0	-M	0	

<u>Iteration 3</u> (Drop the A_2 column)

Basis	C_B	X_1	X_2	X_3	S_1	S_2	
		-2	3	4	0	0	
S_1	0	1/5	0	0	1	(3/5)	2
X_2	3	1/5	1	0	0	-2/5	12
X_3	4	3/5	0	1	0	-1/5	16
Z_j		3	3	4	0	-2	100
$C_j - Z_j$		-5	0	0	0	2	

<u>Iteration 4</u>

Basis	C_B	X_1	X_2	X_3	S_1	S_2	
		-2	3	4	0	0	
S_2	0	1/3	0	0	5/3	1	10/3
X_2	3	1/3	1	0	2/3	0	40/3
X_3	4	2/3	0	1	1/3	0	50/3
Z_j		11/3	3	4	10/3	0	320/3
$C_j - Z_j$		-17/3	0	0	-10/3	0	

This is the optimal tableau. Thus the optimal solution is:

$$X_1 = 0$$
$$X_2 = 40/3$$
$$X_3 = 50/3$$
$$S_1 = 0$$
$$S_2 = 10/3$$

Because we multiplied the objective function by -1, the optimal minimization value of $Z = -320/3$.

PROBLEM 5

Solve problem #4 of Chapter 7 by the simplex method.

SOLUTION 5

For the first problem, the standard form is:

$$\text{MAX } Z = 2X_1 + 6X_2$$

$$\text{S.T.} \quad 4X_1 + 3X_2 + S_1 = 12$$

$$2X_1 + X_2 - S_2 = 8$$

$$X_1, X_2, S_1, S_2 \geq 0$$

Artificial variable A_2 is added to the second constraint to obtain the first tableau form. (A_2 has an objective function coefficient of -M.)

Iteration 1

		X_1	X_2	S_1	S_2	A_2	
Basis	C_B	2	6	0	0	-M	
S_1	0	(4)	3	1	0	0	12
A_2	-M	2	1	0	-1	1	8
Z_j		-2M	-M	0	M	-M	-8M
$C_j - Z_j$		2M+2	6+M	0	-M	0	

Iteration 2

		X_1	X_2	S_1	S_2	A_2	
Basis	C_B	2	6	0	0	-M	
X_1	2	1	3/4	1/4	0	0	3
A_2	-M	0	-1/2	-1/2	-1	1	2
Z_j		2	(1/2)M+3/2	(1/2)M+1/2	M	-M	-2M+6
$C_j - Z_j$		0	-(1/2)M+9/2	-(1/2)M-1/2	-M	0	

This is the last tableau since all $C_j - Z_j \leq 0$. But since an artificial variable is still positive, this indicates the problem is infeasible.

For the second problem the standard form is:

$$\text{MAX } Z = 3X_1 + 4X_2$$

$$\text{S.T.} \quad X_1 + X_2 - S_1 = 5$$

$$3X_1 + X_2 - S_2 = 8$$

$$X_1, X_2, S_1, S_2 \geq 0$$

Artificial variables are added to both constraints to obtain the initial tableau form.

Iteration 1

		X_1	X_2	S_1	S_2	A_1	A_2	
Basis	C_B	3	4	0	0	-M	-M	
A_1	-M	1	1	-1	0	1	0	5
A_2	-M	(3)	1	0	-1	0	1	8
Z_j		-4M	-2M	M	M	-M	-M	-13M
$C_j - Z_j$		4M+3	2M+4	-M	-M	0	0	

Iteration 2 (Drop A_2)

		X_1	X_2	S_1	S_2	A_1	
Basis	C_B	3	4	0	0	-M	
A_1	-M	0	(2/3)	-1	1/3	1	7/3
X_1	3	1	1/3	0	-1/3	0	8/3
Z_j		3	-(2/3)M+1	M	-(1/3)M-1	-M	-(7/3)M+8
$C_j - Z_j$		0	(2/3)M+3	-M	(1/3)M+1	0	

Iteration 3 (Drop A_1)

Basis	C_B	X_1	X_2	S_1	S_2	
		3	4	0	0	
X_2	4	0	1	-3/2	1/2	7/2
X_1	3	1	0	(1/2)	-1/2	3/2
Z_j		3	4	-9/2	1/2	37/2
$C_j - Z_j$		0	0	9/2	-1/2	

Iteration 4

Basis	C_B	X_1	X_2	S_1	S_2	
		3	4	0	0	
X_2	4	3	1	0	-1	8
S_1	0	2	0	1	-1	3
Z_j		12	4	0	-4	32
$C_j - Z_j$		-9	0	0	4	

Note that $C_4 - Z_4 = 4$ (positive) but its column is all non- positive. This indicates that the problem is unbounded.

PROBLEM 6

Given the following optimal tableau for a linear programming problem:

		X_1	X_2	X_3	S_1	S_2	S_3	S_4	
Basis	C_B	2	4	6	0	0	0	0	
S_3	0	0	0	2	4	-2	1	0	8
X_2	4	0	1	2	2	-1	0	0	6
X_1	2	1	0	-1	1	2	0	0	4
S_4	0	0	0	1	3	2	0	1	12
Z_j		2	4	6	10	0	0	0	32
$C_j - Z_j$		0	0	0	-10	0	0	0	

a) Give the optimal solution associated with this tableau.

b) Give an optimal solution with X_3 replacing X_2 in the tableau.

c) Give an optimal solution with S_2 replacing X_1 in the tableau in part a).

d) Take an arbitrary weighted average of the extreme points found in (a), (b), and (c), say .5, .3, .2 respectively. Show that this point is feasible by substituting into the equations defined by the above tableau, and demonstrate that it is optimal by showing its objective function value is 32. CONCLUSION: A weighted average of optimal solutions is also optimal.

SOLUTION 6

a) $X_1 = 4$ $\quad S_1 = 0$ $\quad Z = 32$

$X_2 = 6$ $\quad S_2 = 0$

$X_3 = 0$ $\quad S_3 = 8$

$S_4 = 12$

b) X_3 is non-basic and its $C_3 - Z_3 = 0$. This indicates that there are alternate optimal solutions. This 0 indicates that if X_3 were increased, the value of the objective function would not change.
Thus, another optimal solution may be found by choosing X_3 as the entering variable and performing one iteration of the simplex method. This gives the following tableau:

		X_1	X_2	X_3	S_1	S_2	S_3	S_4	
Basis	C_B	2	4	6	0	0	0	0	
S_3	0	0	-1	0	2	-1	1	0	2
X_3	6	0	1/2	1	1	-1/2	0	0	3
X_1	2	1	1/2	0	2	3/2	0	0	7
S_4	0	0	-1/2	0	2	5/2	0	1	9
Z_j		2	4	6	10	0	0	0	32
$C_j - Z_j$		0	0	0	-10	0	0	0	

$X_1 = 7$ $S_1 = 0$ $Z = 32$
$X_2 = 0$ $S_2 = 0$
$X_3 = 3$ $S_3 = 2$
$S_4 = 9$

c) Similarly doing an iteration of the simplex iteration using S_2 as the entering variable in the given tableau yields:

		X_1	X_2	X_3	S_1	S_2	S_3	S_4	
Basis	C_B	2	4	6	0	0	0	0	
S_3	0	1	0	1	5	0	1	0	12
X_2	4	1/2	1	3/2	5/2	0	0	0	8
S_2	0	1/2	0	-1/2	1/2	1	0	0	2
S_4	0	-1	0	2	2	0	0	1	8
Z_j		2	4	6	10	0	0	0	32
$C_j - Z_j$		0	0	0	-10	0	0	0	

This gives an optimal solution of:

$X_1 = 0 \quad S_1 = 0 \quad Z = 32$
$X_2 = 8 \quad S_2 = 2$
$X_3 = 0 \quad S_3 = 12$
$S_4 = 8$

d) Take: .5 x (Values in part (a))
+ .3 x (Values in part (b))
+ .2 x (Values in part (c)).

This gives:

$X_1 = .5(4) + .3(7) + .2(0) = 4.1$
$X_2 = .5(6) + .3(0) + .2(8) = 4.6$
$X_3 = .5(0) + .3(3) + .2(0) = .9$
$S_1 = .5(0) + .3(0) + .2(0) = 0$
$S_2 = .5(0) + .3(0) + .2(2) = .4$
$S_3 = .5(8) + .3(2) + .2(12) = 7.0$
$S_4 = .5(12) + .3(9) + .2(8) = 10.3$

Feasibility:

The first equation is: $2X_3 + 4S_1 - 2S_2 + S_3 = 8$
Substituting, $2(.9) + 4(0) - 2(.4) + 7 = 8$

The second equation is: $X_2 + 2X_3 + 2S_1 - S_2 = 6$
Substituting, $4.6 + 2(.9) + 2(0) - .4 = 6$

The third equation is: $X_1 - X_3 + S_1 + 2S_2 = 4$
Substituting, $4.1 - .9 + 0 + 2(.4) = 4$

The fourth equation is: $X_3 + 3S_1 + 2S_2 + S_4 = 12$
Substituting, $.9 + 3(0) + 2(.4) + 10.3 = 12.$

Therefore this solution is feasible.

Optimality:

$Z = 2X_1 + 4X_2 + 6X_3 = 2(4.1) + 4(4.6) + 6(.9) = 32.$

Thus, this is also an optimal solution.

PROBLEM 7

The Hondasaki Motorbike Company has the capability of making three kinds of motorbikes -- the C-90, the C-250, and the C-700.

Although this is a small company, only three materials (denoted A, B, C) are in short enough supply to limit production. Daily supplies of materials A, B, and C are 400 lbs., 200 lbs., and 300 lbs., respectively. Whereas Hondasaki may have unused material B and C, all material A must be used daily for safety reasons.

The profit per motorbike and the amount of material needed to make each motorbike are given in the following table.

Motorbike	Profit	Material A	Material B	Material C
C-90	\$140	2	1	1
C-250	\$300	8	1	0
C-700	\$400	2	4	1

a) Solve for the optimal daily production of motorbikes.

b) How much of each of the materials A, B, and C are used daily?

SOLUTION 7

a) This problem can be formulated as follows:
X_1 = number of C-90's produced daily
X_2 = number of C-250's produced daily
X_3 = number of C-700's produced daily

$$\text{MAX } Z = 140X_1 + 300X_2 + 400X_3$$

$$\begin{aligned} \text{S.T.} \quad 2X_1 + 8X_2 + 2X_3 &= 400 \\ X_1 + X_2 + 4X_3 &\leq 200 \\ X_1 + X_3 &\leq 300 \\ X_1, X_2, X_3 &\geq 0 \end{aligned}$$

First add slack variables, S_2 and S_3, to the second and third constraints, respectively. Then add an artificial variable, A_1, to the first constraint. This gives the initial tableau (on the next page).

Using the simplex method, the optimal solution is to produce 40 C-250's and 40 C-700's daily for an optimal daily profit of \$28,000. Note that because $C_1 - Z_1$ is zero, there are alternate optimal solutions.

b) From the optimal tableau, $S_2 = 0$, $S_3 = 260$. All of material Aand B is used and 40 (= 300 - 260) of material C is used.

Iteration 1

Basis	C_B	X_1 140	X_2 300	X_3 400	S_2 0	S_3 0	A_1 -M	
A_1	-M	2	(8)	2	0	0	1	400
S_2	0	1	1	4	1	0	0	200
S_3	0	1	0	1	0	1	0	300
Z_j		-2M	-8M	-2M	0	0	-M	-400M
$C_j - Z_j$		2M+140	8M+300	2M+400	0	0	0	

Iteration 2 (Drop A_1)

Basis	C_B	X_1 140	X_2 300	X_3 400	S_2 0	S_3 0	
X_2	300	1/4	1	1/4	0	0	50
S_2	0	3/4	0	(15/4)	1	0	150
S_3	0	1	0	1	0	1	300
Z_j		75	300	75	0	0	15,000
$C_j - Z_j$		65	0	325	0	0	

Iteration 3 (This is the optimal tableau)

Basis	C_B	X_1 140	X_2 300	X_3 400	S_2 0	S_3 0	
X_2	300	1/5	1	0	-1/15	0	40
X_3	400	1/5	0	1	4/15	0	40
S_3	0	4/5	0	0	-4/15	1	260
Z_j		140	300	400	260/3	0	28,000
$C_j - Z_j$		0	0	0	-260/3	0	

ANSWERED PROBLEMS

PROBLEM 8

Consider the following linear program:

$$MIN\ Z = 2X_1 + 3X_2 + 8X_3$$

$$\begin{aligned} S.T.\quad 4X_1 + 2X_2 + X_3 &\geq 15 \\ 2X_1 + X_2 + 6X_3 &\geq 30 \\ X_1, X_2, X_3 &\geq 0 \end{aligned}$$

a) Write the problem in standard form.

b) Why can you not multiply the equations in (a) by -1 to obtain a first tableau to begin the simplex method?

c) Solve the problem by the simplex method.

PROBLEM 9

Solve the following problem by the simplex method:

$$MAX\ Z = X_1 + 2X_2 - 3X_3$$

$$\begin{aligned} S.T.\quad X_1 &\geq 5 \\ 2X_1 + 3X_2 + 4X_3 &\leq 24 \\ 3X_1 + 2X_2 + X_3 &= 18 \\ X_1, X_2, X_3 &\geq 0 \end{aligned}$$

PROBLEM 10

Solve the following problem by the simplex method.

$$MIN\ Z = 3X_1 + 5X_2 + 1X_3$$

$$\begin{aligned} S.T.\quad 2X_1 + 4X_2 + 3X_3 &\geq 20 \\ 5X_1 + 4X_2 + 6X_3 &\leq 45 \\ X_2 - .5X_3 &\leq 0 \\ X_1 &\geq 3 \\ X_1, X_2, X_3 &\geq 0 \end{aligned}$$

PROBLEM 11

Consider the following tableaus which have been generated at various times in different maximization linear programs. Give each tableau one of the following characterizations and perform the indicated operation consistent with the choice you have made.

Characterization	Operation
1. Tableau is optimal.	Give the optimal solution.
2. Tableau is feasible but not yet optimal.	Do one complete iteration of the simplex method.
3. Tableau indicates the entire problem is infeasible.	State why.
4. Tableau is infeasible, but cannot yet state whether or not the problem is feasible.	Do one complete iteration of the simplex method.
5. Tableau indicates the problem is unbounded.	State why.

a)

		X_1	X_2	X_3	S_1	S_2	S_3	A_2	
Basis	C_B	10	8	6	0	0	0	-M	
S_1	0	2	3	4	1	0	0	0	24
A_2	-M	0	1	2	0	-1	0	1	16
S_3	0	1	1	2	0	0	1	0	10
Z_j		0	-M	-2M	0	M	0	-M	-16M
$C_j - Z_j$		10	M+8	2M+6	0	-M	0	0	

b)

		X_1	X_2	X_3	S_1	S_2	
Basis	C_B	4	6	10	0	0	
S_1	0	3	0	6	1	-1	18
X_2	6	1	1	2	0	2	14
Z_j		6	6	12	0	12	84
$C_j - Z_j$		-2	0	-2	0	-12	

c)

Basis	C_B	X_1 5	X_2 6	X_3 7	S_1 0	S_2 0	
X_1	5	1	0	0	4	0	6
S_2	0	0	0	-2	-2	1	16
X_2	6	0	1	-1	2	0	26
Z_j		5	6	-6	32	0	186
$C_j - Z_j$		0	0	13	-32	0	

d)

Basis	C_B	X_1 10	X_2 8	X_3 4	S_1 0	S_3 0	A_2 -M	
X_1	10	1	2	0	1	0	0	6
A_2	-M	0	-2	0	-1	-1	1	4
X_3	4	0	6	1	1	2	0	2
Z_j		10	2M+44	4	M+14	M+8	-M	-4M+68
$C_j - Z_j$		0	-2M-36	0	-M-14	-M-8	0	

e)

Basis	C_B	X_1 4	X_2 5	X_3 7	S_1 0	S_2 0	
X_3	7	0	0	1	0	0	12
S_2	0	0	2	0	0	1	14
S_1	0	0	3	0	1	0	18
X_1	4	1	-1	0	0	0	20
Z_j		4	-4	7	0	0	164
$C_j - Z_j$		0	9	0	0	0	

PROBLEM 12

Consider the following tableau at a particular iteration of the simplex method:

Basis	C_B	X_1	X_2	X_3	S_1	S_2	S_3	
		4	2	-1	0	0	0	
		0	1	-1	6	0	1	10
		0	0	4	2	1	1	20
		1	0	0	-3	0	1	30
z_j								
$c_j - z_j$								

a) Complete the tableau.

b) What is the current basic solution?

c) What would be the change in the objective function for each of the following cases:
 (1) X_3 were increased by 1
 (2) X_3 were increased by 3
 (3) S_1 were increased by 1.5
 (4) S_3 were increased by 2

d) What is the entering variable? Write the equations corresponding to the above tableau. Now, delete all the non-basic variables (since they are set to 0 anyway) except for the entering variable. Use this remaining set of three equations in four unknowns to justify why the ratio test is only performed on positive numbers in the entering column.

e) Explain why the entering variable could not be increased to 10 at this iteration.

f) To what value will the entering variable increase?

g) Use (d) and (f) to determine by how much the objective function will be increased in the next tableau. Use your equations in (d) to determine the values of the other basic variables in the next tableau.

h) Do one iteration of the simplex method to justify your answer in (g).

PROBLEM 13

Consider the following linear programming tableau:

		X_1	X_2	X_3	S_1	S_2	S_3	
Basis	C_B	5	2	1	0	0	0	
X_3	1	2	0	1	-6	1	0	8
X_2	2	1	1	0	4	0	0	4
S_3	0	4	0	0	3	-3	1	20
Z_j		4	2	1	2	1	0	16
$C_j - Z_j$		1	0	0	-2	-1	0	

a) Do one iteration of the simplex method by choosing the first row as the leaving row. What is the new basic solution? Based on the new $C_j - Z_j$ row, is this solution optimal?

b) Repeat (a), but this time choose the second row as the leaving row. What is the new basic solution? Does the new $C_j - Z_j$ row indicate that the solution is optimal?

c) Interpret the results of (a) and (b) by stating a conclusion concerning optimality when degeneracy occurs.

PROBLEM 14

The Doorco Company can produce three kinds of closet doors. Each door must go through two operations: production and finishing. There are 1,000 man-hours available in the production area weekly and 600 man-hours available in the finishing area weekly. Below is a chart which summarizes the number of hours each door must spend in each area as well as the unit profit per door.

Door	Production	Finishing	Profit
Basic	2	2	\$3
Standard	3	2	\$6
Deluxe	4	2	\$8

a) Using the simplex method, show there is an optimal solution in which only one type of door is produced.

b) Using your resulting optimal tableau in (a), give another optimal solution in which two types of doors are produced.

PROBLEM 15

Given the following maximization problem:

$$\begin{aligned} \text{MAX } Z = 2X_1 + 5X_2 + 5X_3 + 3X_4 \\ \text{S.T.} \quad 10X_1 + 12X_2 + 10X_3 + 9X_4 \leq 150 \\ X_1 + X_2 + X_3 \geq 12 \\ -X_1 + X_2 + X_3 - X_4 \leq 0 \\ X_j \geq 0 \quad j = 1,2,3,4 \end{aligned}$$

a) Write the problem in standard form.

b) Set up the initial simplex tableau.

c) Solve the problem by the simplex method.

TRUE/FALSE

16. Once an artificial variable becomes non-basic, it can be dropped from the simplex tableau.

17. If the same slack variable enters the basis more than once, degeneracy exists.

18. Any tableau with a positive value for an artificial variable is infeasible.

19. Suppose X_4 is a non-basic variable in the optimal tableau in which all right-hand values are positive, but $C_4 - Z_4 = 0$. Then there exist optimal solutions with X_4 equal to 0 and also optimal solutions with X_4 positive.

20. One optimal solution to a linear program must be a basic feasible solution.

21. If X_4 is the entering variable and its corresponding column contains all non-positive entries, the problem is infeasible.

22. All elements in the C_j-Z_j row of a simplex tableau must be ≤ 0 for the current solution to be optimal.

23. A problem with degenerate basic feasible solutions could theoretically cycle between non-optimal solutions without reaching the optimal solution.

24. The ratio test determines which current basic variable reaches zero first as the entering variable is increased from zero.

25. A basic solution can be either feasible or infeasible.

26. Writing an LP problem in standard form sometimes requires the introduction of one or more artificial variables.

27. The C_j row determines the "gross" increase, and the Z_j row determines the "gross" decrease, in the objective function per unit increase in the variables. Hence, the $C_j - Z_j$ row gives the "net" increase in the objective function per unit increase in the variables.

28. Degeneracy results from there being alternate optimal solutions to a problem.

29. If there are any slack or surplus variables in the basis, the solution is infeasible for the real-world problem.

30. The simplex method is applicable to maximization problems only.

Chapter 11
Transportation, Assignment, and Transshipment Problems

KEY CONCEPTS

CONCEPT	ILLUSTRATED PROBLEMS	ANSWERED PROBLEMS
Transportation Problems		
Network Representation	1	8
Minimum-Cost Starting Solution	1-3	8-11
MODI/Stepping Stone Solution	1-3	8-11
Dummy Rows/Columns	2,3	10
Maximization Problems	3	11
Unacceptable Routes	3	11
Degeneracy	3	9
Assignment Problem		
Network Representation	4	13
Hungarian Solution Procedure	4,5	12,13,14
Dummy Rows/Columns	4	13
Maximization Problems	5	12,14
Unacceptable Assignments	5	14
Transshipment Problem		
Network Representation	6,7	15
LP Formulation	6	15

REVIEW

1. A network model is one which can be represented by a set of nodes, a set of arcs, and functions (e.g. costs, supplies, demands, etc.) associated with the arcs and/or nodes.

2. Transportation, assignment, and transshipment problems of this chapter, as well as the shortest route, minimal spanning tree, and maximal flow problems (Chapter 9) and PERT/CPM problems (Chapter 10) are all examples of network problems.

3. Each of the three models of this chapter (transportation, assignment, and transshipment models) can be formulated as linear programs and solved by general purpose linear programming codes. However, there are many computer packages (including The Management Scientist) which contain separate computer codes for these models which take advantage of their network structure. This radically enhances the speed of solving particularly large problems.

4. For each of the three models in this chapter, if the right-hand side of the linear programming formulations are all integers, the optimal solution will be in terms of integer values for the decision variables.

TRANSPORTATION PROBLEM

1. The <u>transportation problem</u> seeks to minimize the total shipping costs of transporting goods from m origins (each with a supply s_i) to n destinations (each with a demand d_j), when the unit shipping cost from an origin, i, to a destination, j, is c_{ij}.

2. The <u>network representation</u> for a transportation problem with two sources and three destinations is given below:

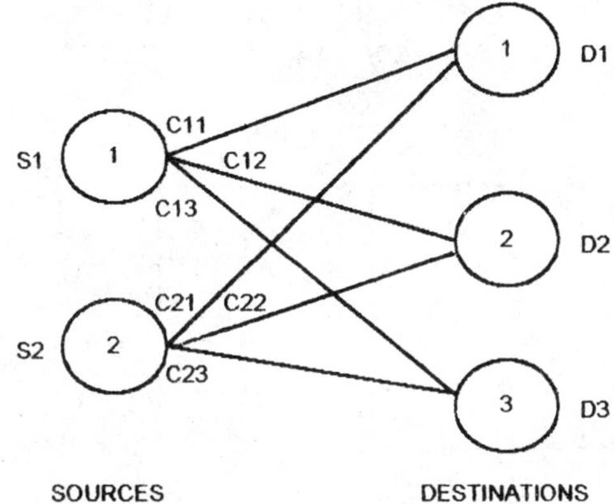

3. Transportation problems are special cases of linear programs. The <u>linear programming formulation</u> in terms of the amounts shipped from the origins to the destinations, x_{ij}, can be written as:

$$\text{MIN} \quad \sum_i \sum_j c_{ij} x_{ij}$$

$$\text{S.T.} \quad \sum_j x_{ij} \leq s_i \quad \text{for each origin } i$$

$$\sum_i x_{ij} = d_j \quad \text{for each destination } j$$

$$x_{ij} \geq 0 \text{ for all } i \text{ and } j.$$

4. The following <u>special-case modifications</u> to the linear programming formulation can be made:
   (a) Minimum shipping guarantees from i to j: $x_{ij} \geq L_{ij}$
   (b) Maximum route capacity from i to j: $x_{ij} \leq L_{ij}$
   (c) Unacceptable routes: delete the variable

5. To solve the transportation problem by its special <u>purpose algorithm</u>, it is required that the sum of the supplies at the origins equal the sum of the demands at the destinations. If the total supply is greater than the total demand, a <u>dummy destination</u> is added with demand equal to the excess supply, and shipping costs from all origins are zero. Similarly, if total supply is less than total demand, a <u>dummy origin</u> is added.

6. When solving a transportation problem by its special purpose algorithm, unacceptable shipping routes are given a <u>cost of +M</u> (a large number).

7. A <u>transportation tableau</u> giving a feasible solution and reduced costs is given below. Each <u>cell</u> represents a shipping route (which is an arc on the network and a decision variable in the LP formulation), and the unit shipping costs are given in an upper right hand box in the cell. If an arc is being used in the current solution, the cell is said to be <u>occupied</u> and the number in it represents its current value. If the arc is NOT being used the cell is <u>unoccupied</u>, its value is 0, and the circled number in the cell represents its reduced cost (the amount the objective function will change per unit increase in this variable).

	D1	D2	D3
O1	8 [4]	2 [4]	(-5) [2]
O2	(3) [7]	4 [3]	11 [6]

The above tableau is equivalent to the following:

Shipping Route	Decision Variable	Value	Total Cost	Reduced Cost
O1-D1	X11	8	8x5 = 40	0
O1-D2	X12	2	2x4 = 8	0
O1-D3	X13	0	0x2 = 0	-5
O2-D1	X21	0	0x7 = 0	3
O2-D2	X22	4	4x3 = 12	0
O2-D3	X23	11	11x6 = 66	0

		Total Cost	= 126	

8. The transportation problem is solved in <u>two phases</u>:
   Phase I -- Obtaining an initial feasible solution
   Phase II -- Moving toward optimality

9. In Phase I, the <u>Minimum-Cost Procedure</u> can be used to establish an initial basic feasible solution without doing numerous iterations of the simplex method. (See algorithm).

10. In Phase II, the <u>Stepping Stone Method</u>, using the MODI method for evaluating the reduced costs may be used to move from the initial feasible solution to the optimal one. (See algorithm).

TRANSPORTATION ALGORITHM

It is assumed that the problem is a minimization problem and that dummy origins and destinations have been added so that the sum of the total supply equals the sum of the total demand. (An equivalent greatest cost method is used for maximization.)

Phase I - Minimum-Cost Method

1. Select the cell with the least cost. Assign to this cell the minimum of its remaining row supply or remaining column demand.

2. Decrease the row and column availabilities by this amount and remove from consideration all other cells in the row or column with zero availability or demand. (If both are simultaneously reduced to 0, assign an allocation of 0 to any other unoccupied cell in the row or column before deleting both.) GO TO STEP 1.

Phase II - Stepping Stone Method

1. For each unoccupied cell, calculate the reduced cost by the MODI method described below. Select the unoccupied cell with the most negative reduced cost. (For maximization problems select the unoccupied cell with the largest reduced cost.) If none, STOP.

2. For this unoccupied cell generate a stepping stone path by forming a closed loop with this cell and occupied cells by drawing connecting alternating horizontal and vertical lines between them. (Note that lines may cross and may go through other occupied or unoccupied cells.) Determine the minimum allocation where a subtraction is to be made along this path.

3. Add this allocation to all cells where additions are to be made, and subtract this allocation to all cells where subtractions are to be made along the stepping stone path. (Note: An occupied cell on the stepping stone path now becomes 0 (unoccupied). If more than one cell becomes 0, make one unoccupied; make the others occupied with 0's.) GO TO STEP 1.

MODI Method (for obtaining reduced costs)

Associate a number, u_i, with each row and v_j with each column.

1. Set $u_1 = 0$.

2. Calculate the remaining u_i's and v_j's by solving the relationship $c_{ij} = u_i + v_j$ for occupied cells.

3. For unoccupied cells (i,j), the reduced cost $= c_{ij} - u_i - v_j$.

FLOW CHART OF TRANSPORTATION ALGORITHM, PHASE I (MINIMUM COST METHOD)

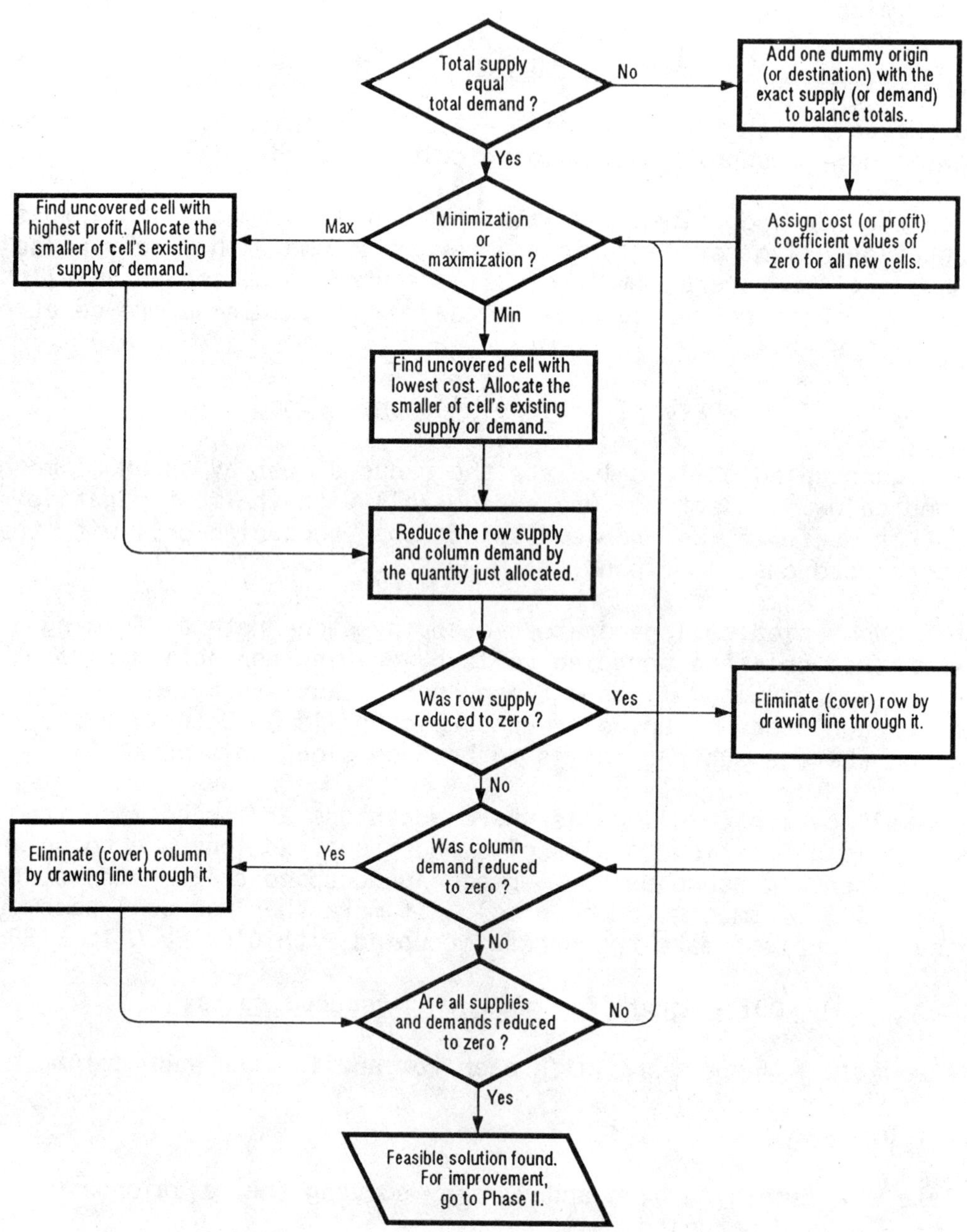
Total supply equal total demand ?
No
Add one dummy origin (or destination) with the exact supply (or demand) to balance totals.
Yes
Assign cost (or profit) coefficient values of zero for all new cells.
Minimization or maximization ?
Max
Find uncovered cell with highest profit. Allocate the smaller of cell's existing supply or demand.
Min
Find uncovered cell with lowest cost. Allocate the smaller of cell's existing supply or demand.
Reduce the row supply and column demand by the quantity just allocated.
Was row supply reduced to zero ?
Yes
Eliminate (cover) row by drawing line through it.
No
Was column demand reduced to zero ?
Yes
Eliminate (cover) column by drawing line through it.
No
Are all supplies and demands reduced to zero ?
No
Yes
Feasible solution found. For improvement, go to Phase II.

FLOW CHART OF TRANSPORTATION ALGORITHM, PHASE II (STEPPING STONE METHOD)

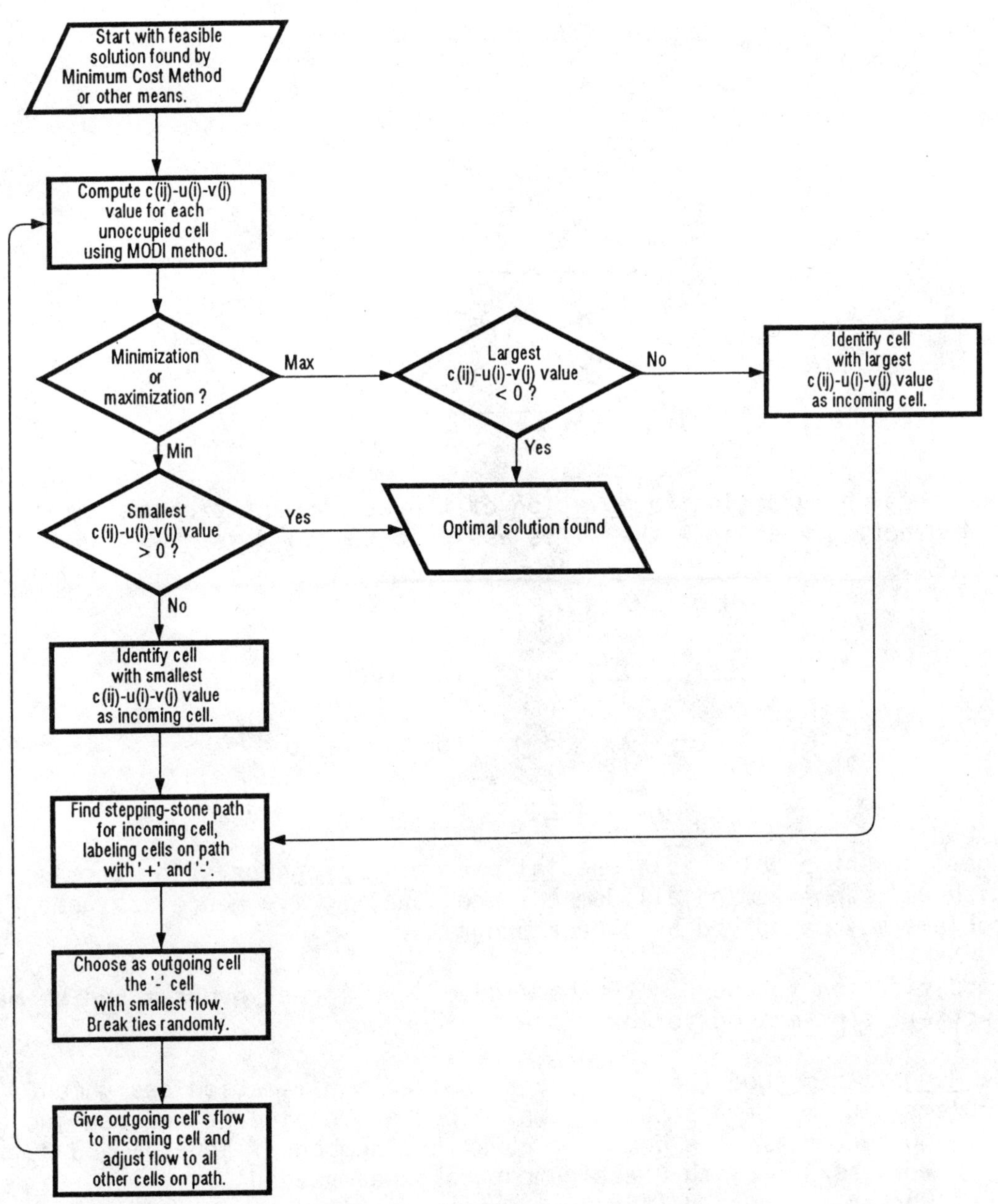
Start with feasible solution found by Minimum Cost Method or other means.
Compute c(ij)-u(i)-v(j) value for each unoccupied cell using MODI method.
Minimization or maximization ?
Max
Min
Largest c(ij)-u(i)-v(j) value < 0 ?
No
Yes
Identify cell with largest c(ij)-u(i)-v(j) value as incoming cell.
Smallest c(ij)-u(i)-v(j) value > 0 ?
Yes
No
Optimal solution found
Identify cell with smallest c(ij)-u(i)-v(j) value as incoming cell.
Find stepping-stone path for incoming cell, labeling cells on path with '+' and '-'.
Choose as outgoing cell the '-' cell with smallest flow. Break ties randomly.
Give outgoing cell's flow to incoming cell and adjust flow to all other cells on path.

ASSIGNMENT PROBLEM

1. An <u>assignment problem</u> seeks to minimize the total cost assignment of m workers to m jobs, given that the cost of worker i performing job j is c_{ij}. It assumes all workers are assigned and each job is performed.

2. The <u>network representation</u> of an assignment problem with three workers and three jobs is:

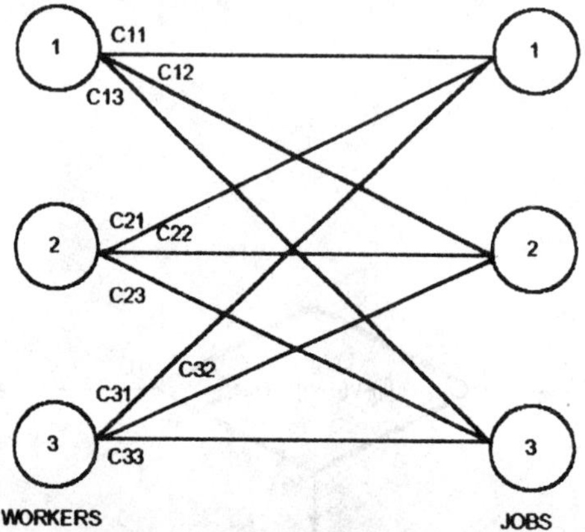

3. The <u>linear programming formulation</u> of the assignment problem using $x_{ij} = 0$ or 1 denoting whether worker i is assigned to job j is:

$$\text{MIN} \quad \sum_{i}\sum_{j} c_{ij}x_{ij}$$

$$\text{S.T.} \quad \sum_{j} x_{ij} = 1 \quad \text{for each worker } i$$

$$\sum_{i} x_{ij} = 1 \quad \text{for each job } j$$

$$x_{ij} \geq 0 \quad \text{for all } i \text{ and } j.$$

4. An assignment problem is a <u>special case of a transportation problem</u> in which all supplies and all demands are equal to 1; hence assignment problems may be solved as linear programs.

5. A modification to the <u>right-hand side</u> of the linear program can be made if a worker is permitted to work more than 1 job.

6. The <u>Hungarian method</u> (see next page) solves minimization assignment problems with m workers and m jobs. Special considerations can include:
   (a) number of workers does not equal the number of jobs -- add dummy workers/jobs with 0 assignment costs as needed
   (b) worker i cannot do job j -- assign c_{ij} = +M.
   (c) maximization objective -- create an <u>opportunity loss matrix</u> subtracting all profits for each job from the maximum profit for that job before beginning the Hungarian method.

HUNGARIAN METHOD

It is assumed that the problem is a minimization problem and that dummy workers/jobs have been added so that the total number of workers equals the total number of jobs.

1. For each row, subtract the minimum number in that row from all numbers in that row.

2. Then, for each column, subtract the minimum number in that column from all numbers in that column.

3. Draw the minimum number of lines to cover all zeroes (see below.) If this number = m, STOP -- an assignment can be made. Otherwise, go to Step 4.

4. Determine the minimum uncovered number (call it d).
   (a) Subtract d from uncovered numbers.
   (b) Add d to numbers covered by two lines.
   (c) Numbers covered by one line remain the same.
   Then, go to Step 3.

Finding the Minimum Number of Lines and Determining the Optimal Solution

1. Find a row or column with only one unlined zero and circle it. (If all rows/columns have two or more unlined zeroes choose an arbitrary zero and circle it.)

2. If the circle is in a row with one zero, draw a line through its column. If the circle is in a column with one zero, draw a line through its row. A heuristic approach when all rows and columns have two or more zeroes is to draw a line through one with the most zeroes, breaking ties arbitrarily.

3. Repeat step 2 until all circles are lined. This determines the minimum number of lines. If this minimum number equals m, the circles provide the optimal assignment.

FLOW CHART OF HUNGARIAN METHOD

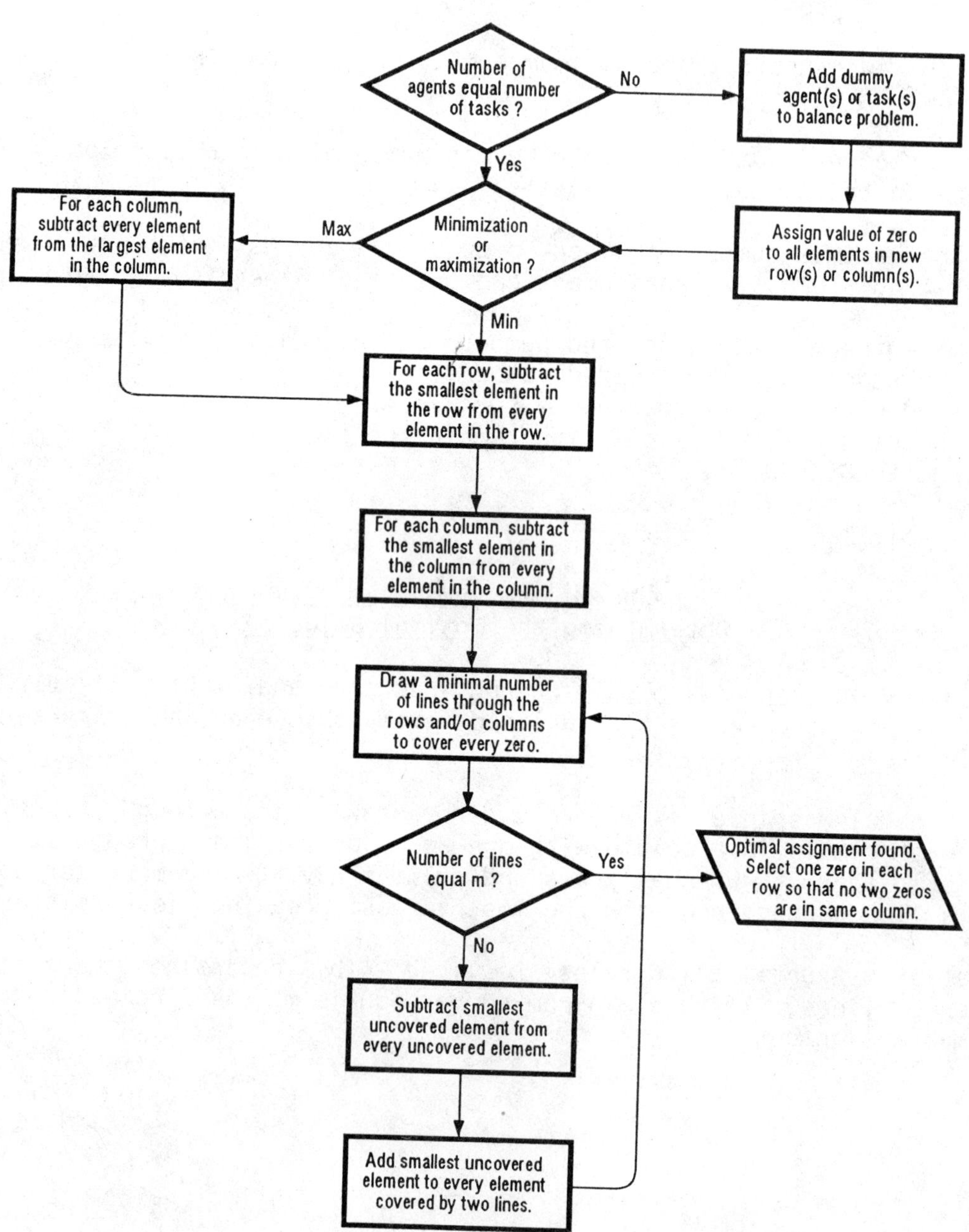
Number of agents equal number of tasks ?
No
Add dummy agent(s) or task(s) to balance problem.
Yes
Assign value of zero to all elements in new row(s) or column(s).
Minimization or maximization ?
Max
For each column, subtract every element from the largest element in the column.
Min
For each row, subtract the smallest element in the row from every element in the row.
For each column, subtract the smallest element in the column from every element in the column.
Draw a minimal number of lines through the rows and/or columns to cover every zero.
Number of lines equal m ?
Yes
Optimal assignment found. Select one zero in each row so that no two zeros are in same column.
No
Subtract smallest uncovered element from every uncovered element.
Add smallest uncovered element to every element covered by two lines.

TRANSSHIPMENT PROBLEM

1. Transshipment problems are transportation problems in which a shipment may move through intermediate nodes (transshipment nodes) before reaching a particular destination node.

2. The network representation for a transshipment problem with two sources, three intermediate nodes, and two destinations is given below:

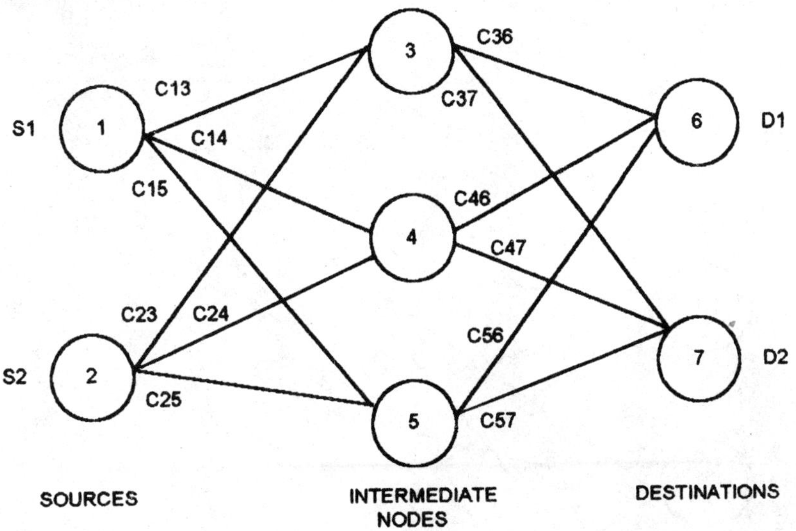

3. The linear programming formulation for the transshipment problem with x_{ij} representing the shipment from node i to node j is:

$$\text{MIN} \quad \sum_{ij}\sum c_{ij}x_{ij}$$

$$\text{S.T.} \qquad \sum_j x_{ij} \le s_i \qquad \text{for each origin } i$$

$$\sum_i x_{ik} - \sum_j x_{kj} = 0 \qquad \text{for each intermediate node } k$$

$$\sum_i x_{ij} = d_j \qquad \text{for each destination } j$$

$$x_{ij} \ge 0 \qquad \text{for all } i \text{ and } j.$$

4. Conversion of transshipment problems to large transportation problems for solution, but for computer programs without such codes, they may be solved by general purpose linear programming codes.

ILLUSTRATED PROBLEMS

> **NOTE:** The coefficient values used in dummy rows and dummy columns in transportation tables and assignment matrices are always zero, regardless of whether you are maximizing or minimizing.
> In the case of infeasible (unallowed) shipments or assignments, use as your coefficients a very large negative number when maximizing and a very large positive number when minimizing.

PROBLEM 1

Given the following minimum cost transportation network:

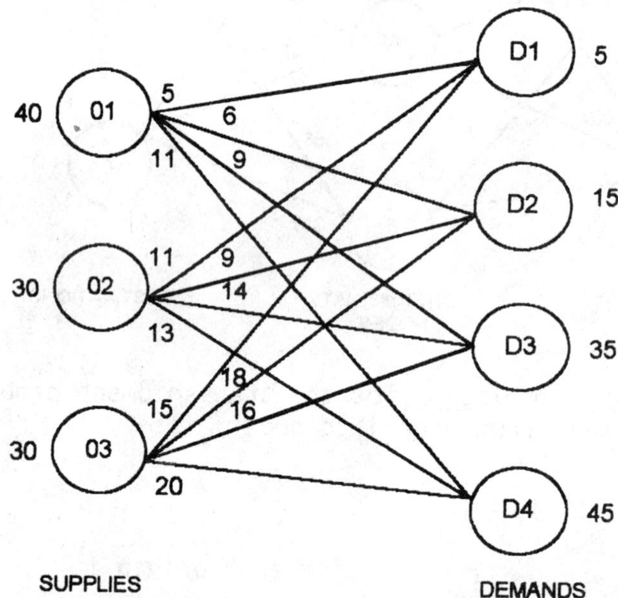

a) Use the Least Cost Method to get an initial solution.

b) Use the MODI Method to determine the reduced costs of the unoccupied cells.

c) What is the value of the current solution?

d) By how much will the next transportation tableau improve the value of the objective function over this solution?

e) Solve the problem by the stepping stone method.

SOLUTION 1

Let us first develop the transportation tableau:

	D1	D2	D3	D4	SUPPLY
O1	5	6	9	11	40
O2	11	9	14	13	30
O3	15	18	16	20	30
DEMAND	5	15	35	45	

a) Least Cost Method:

Iteration 1

	D1	D2	D3	D4	S_i
O1	5	6	9	11	40
O2	11	9	14	13	30
O3	15	18	16	20	30
D_j	5	15	35	45	

Least cost is 5 for O1-D1.
Remaining supply for O1 = 40.
Remaining demand for D1 = 5.
Assign 5 units to O1-D1.
Reduce S_1 by 5 to 35.
Eliminate the D1 column.

Iteration 2

	D1	D2	D3	D4	S_i
O1		6	9	11	35
O2		9	14	13	30
O3		18	16	20	30
D_j		15	35	45	

Least cost is 6 for O1-D2.
Remaining S_1 = 35.
Remaining D_2 = 15.
Assign 15 units to O1-D2.
Reduce S_1 by 15 to 20.
Eliminate the D2 column.

Iteration 3

	D1	D2	D3	D4	S_i
O1			9	11	20
O2			14	13	30
O3			16	20	30
D_j			35	45	

Least cost is 9 for O1-D3.
Remaining S_1 = 20.
Remaining D_3 = 35.
Assign 20 units to O1-D3.
Eliminate the O1 row.
Reduce D_3 by 20 to 15.

Iteration 4

	D1	D2	D3	D4	S_i
O1					
O2			14	13	30
O3			16	20	30
D_j			15	45	

Least Cost is 13 for O2-D4.
Remaining S_2 = 30.
Remaining D_4 = 45.
Assign 30 units to O2-D4.
Eliminate the O2 row.
Reduce D_4 by 30 to 15.

Iteration 5

This leaves the one row O3 with S_3 = 30. Assign 15 to O3-D3 and 15 to O3-D4 to complete the least cost assignment.

	D1		D2		D3		D4	
	amount	cost	amount	cost	amount	cost	amount	cost
O1	5	5	15	6	20	9		11
O2		11		9		14	30	13
O3		15		18	15	16	15	20

b) To calculate the reduced costs for the unoccupied cells, first calculate the u_i's and the v_j's.

1. Set $u_1 = 0$.

2. Since $u_1 + v_j = c_{1j}$ for occupied cells in row 1, $v_1 = 5$, $v_2 = 6$, and $v_3 = 9$.

3. Now since $u_3 + v_3 = c_{33}$ for occupied cell (3,3), $u_3 + 9 = 16$ or $u_3 = 7$.

4. Now since $u_3 + v_4 = c_{34}$ for occupied cell (3,4), $7 + v_4 = 20$ or $v_4 = 13$.

5. Finally since $u_2 + v_4 = c_{24}$ for occupied cell (2,4), $u_2 + 13 = 13$ or $u_2 = 0$.

Now the reduced costs can be calculated for the unoccupied cells by:

Unoccupied Cell	Reduced Cost = $c_{ij} - u_i - v_j$
(1,4)	11 - 0 - 13 = -2
(2,1)	11 - 0 - 5 = 6
(2,2)	9 - 0 - 6 = 3
(2,3)	14 - 0 - 9 = 5
(3,1)	15 - 7 - 5 = 3
(3,2)	18 - 7 - 6 = 5

Thus the tableau at this iteration is:

	D1	D2	D3	D4	u_i
O1	5 | 5	15 | 6	20 | 9	(-2) | 11	0
O2	(6) | 11	(3) | 9	(5) | 14	30 | 13	0
O3	(3) | 15	(5) | 18	15 | 16	15 | 20	7
v_j	5	6	9	13	

c) The value of the current solution is the sum of the allocations times the unit costs:

$$Z = 5(5) + 15(6) + 20(9) + 30(13) + 15(16) + 15(20) = \$1225.$$

d) The unoccupied cell with the most negative reduced cost is cell (1,4), with a reduced cost of -2. The stepping stone path would be to add to cell (1,4) subtract from occupied cell (3,4), add to occupied cell (3,3) and subtract from occupied cell (1,3). Along this path subtractions are made from cells (3,4) and (1,3). The allocations $X_{34} = 15$ and $X_{13} = 20$. The minimum is 15, and so the total cost will change by (-\$2)x15 = -\$30, i.e. a \$30 reduction.

e) (c) and (d) are the first two steps of the transportation stepping stone algorithm. Thus, all shipments at the corners of the stepping stone path will be changed by subtracting 15 from the subtraction cells and adding 15 to the addition cells. Thus the changes are:

$$X_{14} = 0 + 15 = 15$$
$$X_{34} = 15 - 15 = 0 \quad \text{(blank for next tableau)}$$
$$X_{33} = 15 + 15 = 30$$
$$X_{13} = 20 - 15 = 5$$

The resulting tableau is:

	D1	D2	D3	D4	u_i
O1	5 [5]	15 [6]	5 [9]	15 [11]	0
O2	(4) [11]	(1) [9]	(3) [14]	30 [13]	2
O3	(3) [15]	(5) [18]	30 [16]	(2) [20]	7
v_j	5	6	9	11	

In this tableau, the circled numbers are the reduced costs calculated as follows:

1. Set $u_1 = 0$.
2. Since all cells in row 1 are occupied and $u_1 + v_j = c_{ij}$ for occupied cells, $v_1 = 5$; $v_2 = 6$; $v_3 = 9$; $v_4 = 11$.
3. Since $v_4 = 11$ and cell (2,4) is occupied, $u_2 + 11 = 13$ or $u_2 = 2$.
4. Since $v_3 = 9$ and cell (3,3) is occupied, $u_3 + 9 = 16$ or $u_3 = 7$.

Now the reduced costs can be calculated for the unoccupied cells by:

Unoccupied Cell	Reduced Cost = $c_{ij} - u_i - v_j$	Unoccupied Cell	Reduced Cost = $c_{ij} - u_i - v_j$
(2,1)	11 - 2 - 5 = 4	(3,1)	15 - 7 - 5 = 3
(2,2)	9 - 2 - 6 = 1	(3,2)	18 - 7 - 6 = 5
(2,3)	14 - 2 - 9 = 3	(3,4)	20 - 7 - 11 = 2

Since all the reduced costs are non-negative, this tableau is optimal. To summarize, the optimal solution is:

From	To	Shipment	Cost
O1	D1	5	25
O1	D2	15	90
O1	D3	5	45
O1	D4	15	165
O2	D4	30	390
O3	D3	30	480

	Total Cost	=	$1,195

PROBLEM 2

Building Brick Company (BBC) has orders for 80 tons of bricks at three suburban locations as follows: Northwood -- 25 tons, Westwood -- 45 tons, and Eastwood -- 10 tons. BBC has two plants, each of which can produce 50 tons per week. How should end of week shipments be made to fill the above orders given the following delivery cost per ton:

	Northwood	Westwood	Eastwood
Plant 1	24	30	40
Plant 2	30	40	42

SOLUTION 2

Since total supply = 100 and total demand = 80, a dummy destination is created with demand of 20 and 0 unit costs.

	Northwood	Westwood	Eastwood	Dummy	Supply
Plant 1	24	30	40	0	50
Plant 2	30	40	42	0	50
Demand	25	45	10	20	

Least Cost Starting Procedure: (See problem 1 for more details.)

1. Tie for least cost (0), arbitrarily select X_{14}. Allocate 20. Reduce S_1 by 20 to 30 and delete the Dummy column.

2. Of the remaining cells the least cost is 24 for X_{11}. Allocate 25. Reduce S_1 by 25 to 5 and eliminate the Northwood column.

3. Of the remaining cells the least cost is 30 for X_{12}. Allocate 5. Reduce the Westwood column to 40 and eliminate the Plant 1 row.

4. Since there is only one row with two cells left, make the final allocations of 40 and 10 to X_{22} and X_{23} respectively.

Thus, the initial tableau is on the next page. To determine the u_i's and v_j's using the MODI method:

Iteration 1

1. Set $u_1 = 0$

2. Since $u_1 + v_j = c_{1j}$ for occupied cells in row 1, then $v_1 = 24$, $v_2 = 30$, $v_4 = 0$.

3. Since $u_i + v_2 = c_{i2}$ for occupied cells in column 2, then $u_2 + 30 = 40$, hence $u_2 = 10$.

4. Since $u_2 + v_j = c_{2j}$ for occupied cells in row 2, then $10 + v_3 = 42$, hence $v_3 = 32$.

Calculate the reduced costs (circled numbers) by $c_{ij} - u_i + v_j$.

Unoccupied Cell	Reduced Cost
(1,3)	40 - 0 - 32 = 8
(2,1)	30 - 24 - 10 = -4
(2,4)	0 - 10 - 0 = -10

	Northwood	Westwood	Eastwood	Dummy	u_i
Plant 1	25 [24]	5 [30]	(8) [40]	20 [0]	0
Plant 2	(-4) [30]	40 [40]	10 [42]	(-10) [0]	10
v_j	24	30	32	0	

The stepping stone path for cell (2,4) is (2,4), (1,4), (1,2), (2,2). The allocations in the subtraction cells are 20 and 40, respectively. The minimum is 20, and hence reallocate 20 along this path. Thus for the next tableau:

X_{24} = 0 + 20 = 20 (0 is its current allocation)
X_{14} = 20 - 20 = 0 (blank for the next tableau)
X_{12} = 5 + 20 = 25
X_{22} = 40 - 20 = 20

The other occupied cells remain the same.

Iteration 2

The reduced costs are found by calculating the u_i's and v_j's for this tableau.

1. Set $u_1 = 0$.

2. Since $u_1 + v_j = c_{1j}$ for occupied cells in row 1, then $v_1 = 24$, $v_2 = 30$.

3. Since $u_i + v_2 = c_{i2}$ for occupied cells in column 2, then $u_2 + 30 = 40$, or $u_2 = 10$.

4. Since $u_2 + v_j = c_{2j}$ for occupied cells in row 2, then $10 + v_3 = 42$ or $v_3 = 32$; and, $10 + v_4 = 0$ or $v_4 = -10$.

Calculate the reduced costs (circled numbers) by $c_{ij} - u_i + v_j$.

Unoccupied Cell	Reduced Cost
(1,3)	40 - 0 - 32 = 8
(1,4)	0 - 0 - (-10) = 10
(2,1)	30 - 10 - 24 = -4

	Northwood	Westwood	Eastwood	Dummy	u_i
Plant 1	25 [24]	25 [30]	(8) [40]	(10) [0]	0
Plant 2	(-4) [30]	20 [40]	10 [42]	20 [0]	10
v_j	24	30	36	-6	

The most negative reduced cost is = -4 determined by X_{21}. The stepping stone path for this cell is (2,1),(1,1),(1,2),(2,2). The allocations in the subtraction cells are 25 and 20 respectively. Thus the new solution is obtained by reallocating 20 on the stepping stone path. Thus for the next tableau:

$X_{21} = 0 + 20 = 20$ (0 is its current allocation)
$X_{11} = 25 - 20 = 5$
$X_{12} = 25 + 20 = 45$
$X_{22} = 20 - 20 = 0$ (blank for the next tableau)

The other occupied cells remain the same.

Iteration 3

The reduced costs are found by calculating the u_i's and v_j's for this tableau.

1. Set $u_1 = 0$

2. Since $u_1 + v_j = c_{1j}$ for occupied cells in row 1, then $v_1 = 24$ and $v_2 = 30$.

3. Since $u_i + v_1 = c_{i1}$ for occupied cells in column 2, then $u_2 + 24 = 30$ or $u_2 = 6$.

4. Since $u_2 + v_j = c_{2j}$ for occupied cells in row 2, then $6 + v_3 = 42$ or $v_3 = 36$, and $6 + v_4 = 0$ or $v_4 = -6$.

Calculate the reduced costs (circled numbers) by $c_{ij} - u_i + v_j$.

Unoccupied Cell	Reduced Cost
(1,3)	40 - 0 - 36 = 4
(1,4)	0 - 0 - (-6) = 6
(2,2)	40 - 6 - 30 = 4

This gives the tableau on the next page. Since all the reduced costs are non-negative, this is the optimal tableau.

	Northwood	Westwood	Eastwood	Dummy	u_i
Plant 1	24 5	30 45	40 (4)	0 (6)	0
Plant 2	30 20	40 (4)	42 10	0 20	6
v_j	24	30	36	-6	

Thus the optimal solution is:

From	To	Amount	Cost
Plant 1	Northwood	5	120
Plant 1	Westwood	45	1,350
Plant 2	Northwood	20	600
Plant 2	Eastwood	10	420

		Total Cost =	$2,490

PROBLEM 3

Telly's Toy Company produces three kinds of dolls called Bertha, Holly, and Shari. Maximum production quantities for the dolls are 1,000, 2,000, and 2,000 per week, respectively. These dolls are purchased by three large department stores: Shears, Nichols and Words. Each department store wishes 1,500 total dolls per week form Telly's. However, Words does not want any Bertha dolls.

Because of past commitments and the sizes of other orders from Telly's, unit profits per doll vary from store to store for each style of doll. These are summarized as follows:

	Shears	Nichols	Words
Bertha	$ 5	$10	X
Holly	$16	$ 8	$ 9
Shari	$12	$ 9	$11

a) Set the problem up as a maximization transportation problem.

b) Give the "highest profit" starting solution.

c) Solve the problem using MODI to determine the reduced costs.

SOLUTION 3

a) The origins are the dolls, the destinations are the stores. Since potential supply exceeds demand by 500, a dummy destination is added with a demand of 500 and with unit profits of 0. The profit for shipment from Bertha to Words is -M (a large negative number.) The shipments will be in terms of hundreds of dolls shipped.

b) Starting solution: (See problems 1 and 2 for more details)

Iteration	Maximum Profit	Cell	Assignment	Eliminate
1	16	(H,S)	15	S column
2	11	(S,W)	15	W column
3	10	(B,N)	10	B row
4	9	(S,N)	5	S row & N col.
(Degeneracy! Also assign a 0 anywhere left in Shari row or Nichols column before they are deleted, say, in (S,D).)				
5	0	(H,D)	5	Finished

Thus the first assignment tableau becomes:

	Shears	Nichols	Words	Dummy
Bertha	[5]	10 [10]	[-M]	[0]
Holly	15 [16]	[8]	[9]	5 [0]
Shari	[12]	5 [9]	15 [11]	0 [0]

Calculate the u_i's and v_j's (See problems 1 & 2 for details):

1. $u_1 = 0$.
2. Since $u_1 = 0$, then $v_2 = 10$.
3. Since $v_2 = 10$, then $u_3 = -1$.
4. Since $u_3 = -1$, then $v_3 = 12$ and $v_4 = 1$.
5. Since $v_4 = 1$, then $u_2 = -1$.
6. Since $u_2 = -1$, then $v_1 = 17$.

Calculate the reduced costs ($c_{ij}-u_i-v_j$) for unoccupied cells. The resulting transportation tableau is:

	Shears	Nichols	Words	Dummy	u_i
Bertha	(-12) [5]	10 [10]	(-M) [-M]	(-1) [0]	0
Holly	15 [16]	(-1) [8]	(-2) [9]	5 [0]	-1
Shari	(-4) [12]	5 [9]	15 [11]	0 [0]	-1
v_j	17	10	12	1	

In a maximization problem we choose the unoccupied cell with the highest reduced cost. There are no occupied cells with positive reduced costs, so this gives the optimal solution:

Dolls	Store	Shipment	Profit
Bertha	Nichols	1000	$10,000
Holly	Shears	1500	$24,000
Shari	Nichols	500	$ 4,500
Shari	Words	1500	$16,500

Total Profit = $55,000

PROBLEM 4

A contractor pays his subcontractors a fixed fee plus mileage for work performed. On a given day the contractor is faced with three electrical jobs associated with various projects. He has four electrical subcontractors which are located at various places throughout the area. Given below are the distances between the subcontractors and the projects.

		Project		
		A	B	C
Subcontractors	Westside	50	36	16
	Federated	28	30	18
	Goliath	35	32	20
	Universal	25	25	14

How should the contractors be assigned to minimize total costs?

SOLUTION 4

This is an assignment problem that needs a dummy job (column). Now let us draw the network representation of this problem:

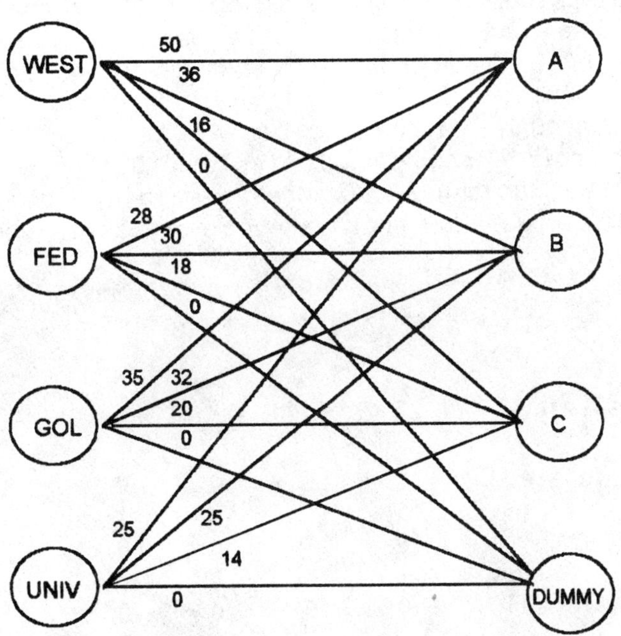

Since the Hungarian algorithm requires that there be the same number of rows as columns, add a Dummy column so that the first tableau is:

	A	B	C	Dummy
Westside	50	36	16	0
Federated	28	30	18	0
Goliath	35	32	20	0
Universal	25	25	14	0

Step 1: Subtract minimum number in each row from all numbers in that row. Since each row has a zero, we would simply generate the same matrix above.

Step 2: Subtract the minimum number in each column from all numbers in the column. For A it is 25, for B it is 25, for C it is 14, for Dummy it is 0. This yields:

	A	B	C	Dummy
Westside	25	11	2	0
Federated	3	5	4	0
Goliath	10	7	6	0
Universal	0	0	0	0

Step 3: Draw the minimum number of lines to cover all zeroes.

Although one can "eyeball" this minimum, use the following algorithm. If a "remaining" row has only one zero, draw a line through the column. If a remaining column has only one zero in it, draw a line through the row.

Note that row W has one 0, (column D); draw a line through column D. Then column A has one "remaining" 0, (row U); draw a line through row U. Now there are no more zeros uncovered.

	A	B	C	Dummy
Westside	25	11	(2)	0
Federated	3	5	4	0
Goliath	10	7	6	0
Universal	-- 0 ---	0 ---	0 ---	0 --

Step 4: The minimum uncovered number is 2 (circled above).

Step 5: Subtract 2 from uncovered numbers; add 2 to all numbers covered by two lines. This gives:

	A	B	C	Dummy
Westside	23	9	0	0
Federated	1	3	2	0
Goliath	8	5	4	0
Universal	0	0	0	2

Step 3: Draw the minimum number of lines to cover all zeroes. Column A has one 0 (row U) -- draw a line through row U. Row F has one 0 remaining (column D) -- draw a line through column D. Column C has one 0 remaining (row W) -- draw a line through row W.

	A	B	C	Dummy
Westside	23	9	0	0
Federated	(1)	3	2	0
Goliath	8	5	4	0
Universal	0	0	0	2

Step 4: The minimum uncovered number is 1 (circled).

Step 5: Subtract 1 from uncovered numbers; add 1 to numbers covered by two lines. This gives:

	A	B	C	Dummy
Westside	23	9	0	1
Federated	0	2	1	0
Goliath	7	4	3	0
Universal	0	0	0	3

Step 4: The minimum number of lines to cover all 0's is four. Thus, there is a minimum-cost assignment of 0's with this tableau. The optimal assignment is:

Subcontractor	Project	Distance	
Westside	C	16	
Federated	A	28	
Universal	B	25	Total distance
(Goliath)	(unassigned)	--	is 69 miles

PROBLEM 5

A foreman is trying to assign crews to produce the maximum number of parts per hour of a certain product. He has three crews and four possible work centers. The estimated number of parts per hour for each crew at each work center is summarized below:

	Work Center			
	WC1	WC2	WC3	WC4
Crew 1	15	20	18	30
Crew 2	20	22	26	30
Crew 3	25	26	27	30

Solve for the optimal assignment of crews to work centers.

SOLUTION 5

This is a maximization assignment problem with fewer rows than columns. First add a row of zeroes (dummy crew). Then construct an opportunity loss matrix as follows. Find the maximum number in each column, 25 for column 1, 26 for column 2, 27 for column 3 and 30 for column 4. Then for each number in a column, replace it with the difference between that number and the corresponding maximum number in that column. This yields:

	WC1	WC2	WC3	WC4
Crew 1	10	6	9	0
Crew 2	5	4	1	0
Crew 3	0	0	0	0
Dummy	25	26	27	30

Now apply the Hungarian algorithm.

Step 1: Subtract the minimum number in each row from all numbers in that row. Note that only the bottom row is changed.

	WC1	WC2	WC3	WC4
Crew 1	10	6	9	0
Crew 2	5	4	1	0
Crew 3	0	0	0	0
Dummy	0	1	2	5

Step 2: Subtract the minimum number in each column from all numbers in the corresponding column. Since there is a zero in each column the above matrix is left unchanged.

Step 3: Draw the minimum number of lines to cover all 0's.

	WC1	WC2	WC3	WC4
Crew 1	10	6	9	0
Crew 2	5	4	(1)	0
Crew 3	0	0	0	0
Dummy	0	(1)	2	5

Step 4: The minimum uncovered number is 1 (circled).

Step 5: Subtract 1 from uncovered numbers. Add 1 to numbers covered by two lines. This yields:

	WC1	WC2	WC3	WC4
Crew 1	10	5	8	0
Crew 2	5	3	0	0
Crew 3	1	0	0	1
Dummy	0	0	1	5

It will now take four lines to cover all 0's and an optimal solution is:

Crew	Work Center	Parts/Hour
Crew 1	WC4	30
Crew 2	WC3	26
Crew 3	WC2	26
--	WC1	--
Total Parts Per Hour	=	82

PROBLEM 6

Thomas Industries and Washburn Corporation supply three firms (Zrox, Hewes, Rockwright) with customized shelving for its offices. They both order shelving from the same two manufacturers, Arnold Manufacturers and Supershelf, Inc. Because of long standing contracts based on past orders, unit costs from the manufacturers to the suppliers are given below:

	Thomas	Washburn
Arnold	5	8
Supershelf	7	4

The chart below gives the cost to install the shelving at the various locations:

	Zrox	Hewes	Rockwright
Thomas	1	5	8
Washburn	3	4	4

Currently weekly demands by the users are 50 for Zrox, 60 for Hewes, and 40 for Rockwright. Both Arnold and Supershelf can supply at most 75 units to its customers.

a) Draw the network representation for this problem.

b) Formulate this problem as a transshipment linear program.

SOLUTION 6

a) Arnold Manufacturers and Supershelf are manufacturers (origins) and Zrox, Hewes, and Rockwright are customers (destinations). Thomas and Washburn represent transshipment points (middlemen) supplying Arnold and Supershelf products to their customers. The network representation is on the next page.

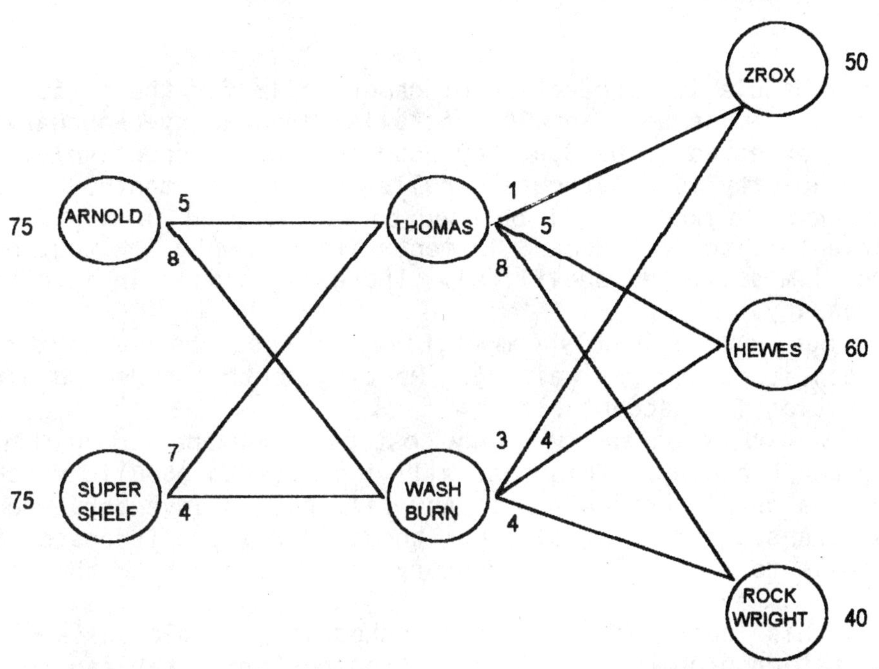

b) Linear Programming Formulation

Define the decision variables:

X_{ij} = amount shipped from manufacturer i to supplier j
X_{jk} = amount shipped from supplier j to customer k
i = 1(Arnold), 2(Supershelf)
j = 3(Thomas), 4(Washburn)
k = 5(Zrox), 6(Hewes), 7(Rockwright)

Define Objective: Minimize Overall Shipping Costs:

$$\text{MIN} \quad 5X_{13} + 8X_{14} + 7X_{23} + 4X_{24} + 1X_{35} + 5X_{36} + 8X_{37} + 3X_{45} + 4X_{46} + 4X_{47}$$

Define the constraints:

Amount Out of Arnold: $X_{13} + X_{14} \leq 75$
Amount Out of Supershelf: $X_{23} + X_{24} \leq 75$

Amount Through Thomas: $X_{13} + X_{23} - X_{35} - X_{36} - X_{37} = 0$
Amount Through Washburn: $X_{14} + X_{24} - X_{45} - X_{46} - X_{47} = 0$

Amount Into Zrox: $X_{35} + X_{45} = 50$
Amount Into Hewes: $X_{36} + X_{46} = 60$
Amount Into Rockwright: $X_{37} + X_{47} = 40$

Non-negativity of Variables: $X_{ij} \geq 0$, for all i and j.

PROBLEM 7

Fodak must schedule its production of camera film for the first four months of the year. Film demand (in 000s of rolls) in January, February, March and April is expected to be 300, 500, 650 and 400, respectively. Fodak's production capacity is 500 thousand rolls of film per month.

Film produced in month i can be used to meet demand in month i or can be held in inventory to meet demand in month i+1 or month i+2 (but not later due to the film's limited shelflife). There is no film in inventory at the start of January.

The film business is highly competitive, so Fodak cannot afford to lose sales or keep its customers waiting. Meeting month i's demand with month i+1's production is unacceptable.

The film's production and delivery cost per thousand rolls will be $500 in January and February. This cost will increase to $600 in March and April due to a new labor contract. Any film put in inventory requires additional transport costing $100 per thousand rolls. It costs $50 per thousand rolls to hold film in inventory from one month to the next.

a) Modeling this least-cost production scheduling problem as a transportation problem, develop the transportation tableau (overlooking the need for a dummy row or column).

b) Modeling this same problem as a transshipment problem, draw the network representation.

c) How might the network in (b) be changed if there was no limit on the length of time film could be held in inventory?

SOLUTION 7 a)

	Jan. Demand	Feb. Demand	Mar. Demand	Apr. Demand	Production Capacity
January Production	500	650	700	+M	500
February Production	+M	500	650	700	500
March Production	+M	+M	600	750	500
April Production	+M	+M	+M	600	500
Demand	300	500	650	400	

Note in the above tableau that there are numerous unacceptable "routes", resulting from two restrictions: 1) demand cannot be kept waiting, and 2) film cannot be held in inventory more than two months. We use +M as the cost for an unacceptable route since our objective is cost minimization.

b) The source nodes in this transshipment problem are the four months of production. The destination nodes are the four months of demand. The intermediate nodes are the first three months' ending inventory (there is no reason to be holding any inventory at the end of April).

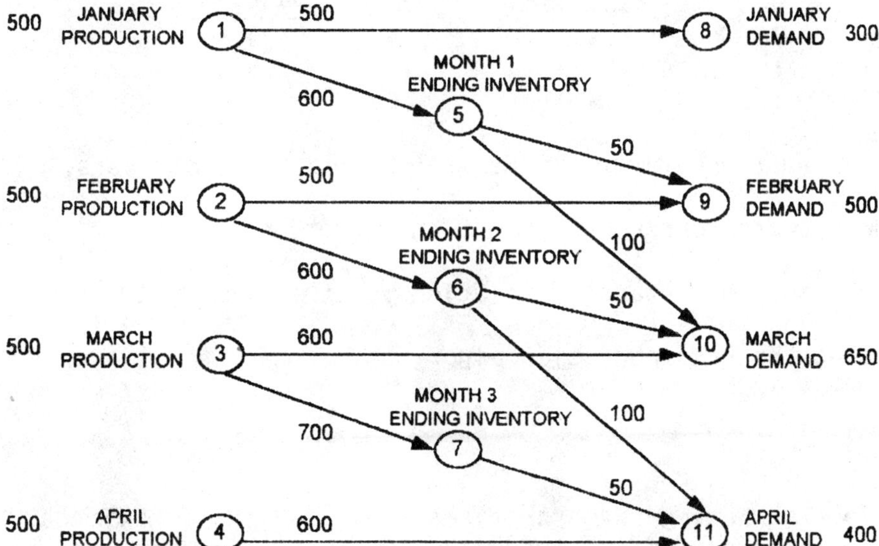

c)

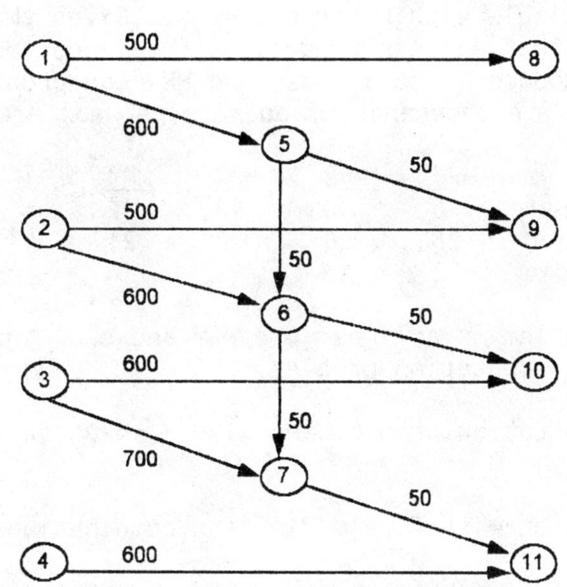

ANSWERED PROBLEMS

PROBLEM 8

The Navy has 9,000 pounds of material in Albany, Georgia which it wishes to ship to three installations: San Diego, Norfolk, and Pensacola. They require 4,000, 2,500, and 2,500 pounds, respectively. The following gives the shipping costs per pound for truck, railroad, and airplane transit.

	San Diego	Norfolk	Pensacola
Truck	\$12	\$ 6	\$ 5
Railroad	\$20	\$11	\$ 9
Airplane	\$30	\$26	\$28

Laws require equal allotment of shipping among the 3 carriers.

a) Draw the network representation of this problem.

b) Give the least cost starting solution for this problem.

c) Solve using the transportation algorithm.

PROBLEM 9

There are four marketing research firms (MR1, MR2, MR3, MR4) that Hairways has faith in to advertise its products. Hairways has just come out with a new hairspray and they wish to have 30 newspaper ads, 15 television ads, and 25 radio ads available within three months. Given the size of the firms it is expected that MR1 can produce 15 total ads, MR2 can produce 25 total ads, MR3 can produce 10 total ads, and MR4 can produce 20 total ads. The bids submitted (in thousands of dollars per ad) are:

	MR1	MR2	MR3	MR4
Newspaper	16	10	12	12
Television	26	20	30	21
Radio	22	15	23	14

a) Formulate this problem as a linear program and show that it fits the structure of a transportation problem.

b) Solve as a transportation problem and give a solution with six media-firm combinations.

c) Give another solution with five media-firm combinations.

d) Give another solution with seven media-firm combinations.

PROBLEM 10

The city of Francene has 25 contracts up for bids in each of four different departments: Sanitation, Police Services, Parks Department, and Administration.

Three different consulting firms are bidding on the contracts: Ace Consulting, Band Corporation, and QM Associates. Ace has personnel for 40 contracts, Band for 40, and QM for 30. Because contracts are similar within each department, each firm is able to set a fixed bid per contract for each department. The bid price (in $1000s per contract) is summarized below:

	Sanitation	Police	Parks	Administration
Ace	10	15	14	16
Band	15	18	8	10
QM	12	12	12	12

How should the contracts be awarded and how much will the city spend?

PROBLEM 11

Independent Auditors (IA) has committed 100 of its auditors in three locations (35 from its Los Angeles branch, 30 from its Chicago branch, and 35 from its New York branch) to audit firms in three cities: 25 for Denver, 35 for Atlanta, and 40 for New York. Because of possible charges of conflicts of interest, no New York based IA auditor will audit a New York firm.

Taking into account all costs and revenues, and the following profit table giving the average profit per auditor (in $1000's), solve for IA's optimal distribution of auditors.

	Denver	Atlanta	New York
Los Angeles	25	18	10
Chicago	30	35	20
New York	14	24	X

PROBLEM 12

Emily Rodd, manager of Camp Pinnacle, must assign her five head counselors to cabins for the summer. The counselors have cabin assignment preferences (based on cabin size, location, condition and other factors). The counselors' cabin preference ratings on a 1-to-9 scale (9 being most favorable) are listed below:

	Cabin				
	1	2	3	4	5
Abbey	3	9	7	5	5
Babbs	6	8	3	5	7
Carla	2	8	5	2	7
Diane	7	4	2	2	9
Ellsa	6	8	5	2	5

Help Emily make the counselor-cabin assignments that will maximize the sum of the preference ratings achieved.

PROBLEM 13

In addition to Pine City's established microcomputer firm, Local Computer, there are three new microcomputer firms that have opened up in the area. In an effort to establish good relations, Manny's Manufacturing plans on buying one computer system from each of the new firms and two from Local Computer. Manny's has five plants, each with different needs, and hence Manny needs to install five different systems. The bids (in $1,000's) from the firms are:

	Plant				
	P1	P2	P3	P4	P5
Computer Town	10	12	14	18	20
Computer World	11	13	15	14	18
Universal Comp	6	14	24	20	19
Local Computer	14	15	16	22	25

a) Give a network representation for this problem.

b) Solve the problem using the Hungarian Method.

c) Suppose Computer World did not have the system needed by P5. How would this have affected the first assignment matrix? How would this have affected the optimal solution?

d) Suppose Computer World did not have the systems needed by P4 or P5. How would this have affected the first assignment matrix? How would this have affected the optimal solution?

PROBLEM 14

A plant manager for a sporting goods manufacturer is in charge of assigning the manufacture of four new aluminum products to four different departments. Because of varying expertise and workloads, the different departments can produce the new products at various rates. If only one product is to be produced by each department and the daily output rates are given in the table below, which department should manufacture which product to maximize total daily product output? (Note: Department 1 does not have the facilities to produce golf clubs.)

Department	Bats	Tennis Rackets	Golf Clubs	Racquetball Rackets
1	100	60	X	80
2	100	80	140	100
3	110	75	150	120
4	85	50	100	75

PROBLEM 15

RVW (Restored Volkswagens) buys 15 used VW's at each of two car auctions each week held at different locations. It then transports the cars to repair shops it contracts with. When they are restored to RVW's specifications, RVW sells 10 each to three different used car lots.

There are various costs associated with the average purchase and transportation prices from each auction to each repair shop. Also there are transportation costs from the repair shops to the used car lots. RVW is concerned with minimizing its total cost given the costs in the table below.

a) Given the costs below, draw a network representation for this problem.

	Repair Shops	
	S1	S2
Auction 1	550	500
Auction 2	600	450

	Used Car Lots		
	L1	L2	L3
S1	250	300	500
S2	350	650	450

b) Formulate this problem as a transshipment linear programming model.

TRUE/FALSE

16. In order to use the special solution procedures for the transportation problem (Stepping Stone and MODI), it is assumed that the cost per unit of shipment between an origin and a destination is independent of the number of items shipped.

17. If a transportation problem has four origins and five destinations, the LP formulation of the problem will have nine constraints.

18. In a transportation problem, if the total supply is greater than the total demand, a dummy origin is added prior to using its special purpose algorithm.

19. The transportation, assignment, and transshipment problems are all special cases of linear programming models known as network models and can be solved by the simplex method.

20. In the stepping stone method, when two cells are simultaneously reduced to zero, degeneracy occurs and one of the two cells must stay occupied with a zero quantity.

21. In a transportation problem with total supply equal to total demand, if there are four origins and seven destinations, and there is a unique optimal solution, the optimal solution will utilize 11 shipping routes.

22. If the optimal transportation tableau has an occupied cell with a zero allocation, then there are alternate optimal solutions.

23. Before using the Hungarian method for a maximization problem with three workers and four jobs to be assigned, first an opportunity cost matrix would be calculated and then a row of zeroes would be added.

24. A transshipment problem is a generalization of the transportation problem in which certain nodes are neither supply nodes nor destination nodes.

25. The assignment problem is a special case of the transportation problem in which all supply and demand values equal one.

26. The stepping stone procedure does not always improve the solution found in the first phase of the transportation simplex method.

27. An opportunity loss matrix in an assignment problem is obtained by subtracting each element in the matrix from the largest element in the matrix.

28. All of the transportation costs associated with a dummy origin or a dummy destination are zero, regardless of whether you are maximizing or minimizing.

29. The optimal solution to a transportation problem will never include a shipment from a dummy origin.

30. Transshipment problem allows shipments both in and out of some nodes while transportation problems do not.

Chapter 12
Integer Linear Programming

KEY CONCEPTS

CONCEPT	ILLUSTRATED PROBLEMS	ANSWERED PROBLEMS
All-Integer Linear Program	1,2	5,6,11
Mixed-Integer Linear Program	2	11
ILP: Maximization	1,3	5,6,7,10
ILP: Minimization	2	11
Rounding LP Solution	1	5,10
Graphical Solution	1,2	6
0-1 Integer Linear Program	3,4	8,9
Special 0-1 Constraints	3	8,9

REVIEW

1. A linear program in which all the variables are restricted to be integers is called an integer linear program (ILP). If only a subset of the variables are restricted to be integers, the problem is called a mixed integer linear program (MILP).

2. Binary variables are variables whose values are restricted to be 0 or 1. If all variables are restricted to be 0 or 1, the problem is called a 0-1 or binary integer program.

3. Many practical applications involve only binary integer variables and hence many computer codes are written only for this case (such as LINDO/PC). Binary expansion is a mathematical technique which may be used to convert any integer variable into the sum of binary variables.

4. Computer codes based on a branch-and-bound solution procedure are available for solving integer linear programs. These codes are much slower than codes for linear programs.

5. Rounding the values of the variables obtained by solving the linear programming problem may yield an infeasible solution or a solution that might be feasible but not optimal for the ILP or MILP.

6. For problems in which X_i and and X_j represent binary variables designating whether projects i and j have been completed, the following special constraints may be formulated:

   (a) At most k out of n projects will be completed: $\sum_j X_j \leq k$

   (b) Project j is conditional on project i: $X_j - X_i \leq 0$

   (c) Project i is a corequisite for project j: $X_j - X_i = 0$

   (d) Projects i and j are mutually exclusive: $X_i + X_j \leq 1$.

7. Sensitivity analysis information for integer linear programming does not have the same connotation as that for linear programming and should be either discarded or used with great caution. In fact, small changes in the coefficients of an integer program can cause large changes in its optimal solution or even cause the problem to be infeasible.

ILLUSTRATED PROBLEMS

PROBLEM 1

Given the following all-integer linear program:

$$\begin{aligned} \text{MAX} \quad Z &= 3X_1 + 2X_2 \\ \text{S.T.} \quad 3X_1 + X_2 &\leq 9 \\ X_1 + 3X_2 &\leq 7 \\ -X_1 + X_2 &\leq 1 \\ X_1, X_2 &\geq 0 \text{ and integer} \end{aligned}$$

a) Solve the problem as a linear program ignoring the integer constraints. Show that the optimal solution to the linear program gives fractional values for both X_1 and X_2.

b) What is the solution obtained by rounding fractions greater than of equal to 1/2 to the next larger number? Show that this solution is not a feasible solution.

c) What is the solution obtained by rounding down all fractions? Is it feasible?

d) Enumerate all points in the linear programming feasible region in which both X_1 and X_2 are integers, and show that the feasible solution obtained in (c) is not optimal and that in fact the optimal integer is not obtained by any form of rounding.

SOLUTION 1

a) From the graph on the next page, the optimal solution to the linear program is $X_1 = 2.5$, $X_2 = 1.5$, $Z = 10.5$.

b) By rounding the optimal solution of $X_1 = 2.5$, $X_2 = 1.5$ to $X_1 = 3$, $X_2 = 2$, this point lies outside the feasible region.

c) By rounding the optimal solution down to $X_1 = 2$, $X_2 = 1$, we see that this solution indeed is an integer solution within the feasible region, and substituting in the the objective function, it gives $Z = 8$.

d) There are eight feasible integer solutions in the linear programming feasible region with Z values as follows:

	X_1	X_2	Z	
1.	0	0	0	
2.	1	0	3	
3.	2	0	6	
4.	3	0	9	<==== optimal
5.	0	1	2	
6.	1	1	5	
7.	2	1	8	<==== part (c) solution
8.	1	2	7	

$X_1 = 3$, $X_2 = 0$ is the optimal solution. Rounding the LP solution ($X_1 = 2.5$, $X_2 = 1.5$) would not have been optimal.

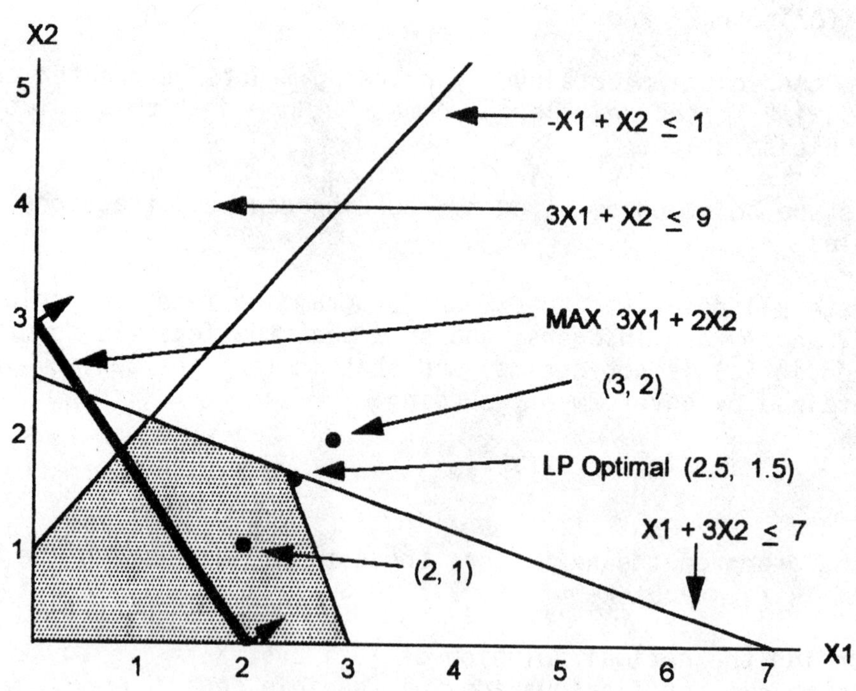

PROBLEM 2

Given the following problem:

$$\text{MIN } Z = 2X_1 + X_2$$

$$\text{S.T.} \quad X_1 + 3X_2 \geq 5$$

$$8X_1 + 3X_2 \geq 17$$

$$X_1, X_2 \geq 0$$

a) Solve for the optimal solution to the linear program.

b) Suppose only X_2 were restricted to be an integer. What is the optimal solution to this mixed integer linear program?

c) Suppose both X_1 and X_2 were restricted to be integers. Determine the optimal solution to the all-integer linear program.

d) Make a comment about the relative optimal values of the objective functions for the lnear program, mixed integer program, and the all-integer program.

SOLUTION 2

a)

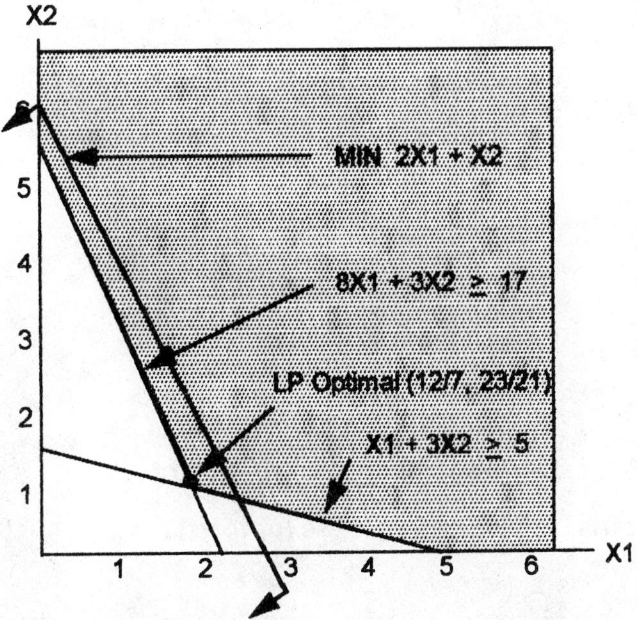

The optimal solution is X_1 = 1 5/7, X_2 = 1 2/21, Z = 4 11/21.

b) Since only X_2 must be integer, the solution must lie on a line of constant integer value for X_2, i.e. $X_2 = 0$, or $X_2 = 1$, etc. The graph below indicates that for each integer value for X_2 the minimum value of Z is attained at the minimum value for X_1.

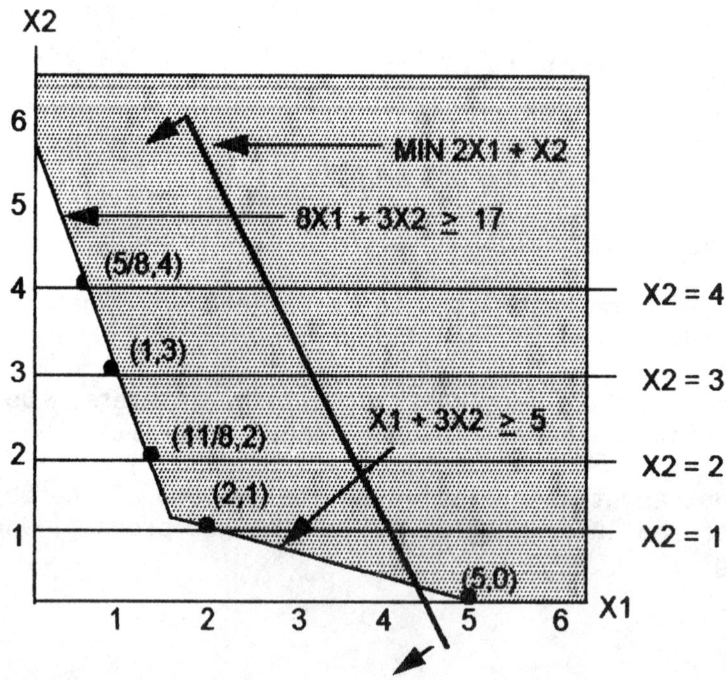

The following table summarizes the corresponding values for X_1 and Z for increasing values of X_2.

X_2	Smallest Feasible X_1	Z
0	5	10
1	2	5
2	1 3/8	4 3/4
3	1	5
4	5/8	5 1/4

(For higher values of X_2, Z continues to increase.)

Hence, the optimal mixed integer solution is $X_1 = 1\ 3/8$, $X_2 = 2$, $Z = 4\ 3/4$.

c) The graph below indicates feasible integer points that are closest to the constraint boundaries. It can be observed that the optimal solution to the all-integer problem is attained both at X1 = 2, X2 = 1 and at X1 = 1, X2 = 3. Both give Z = 5.

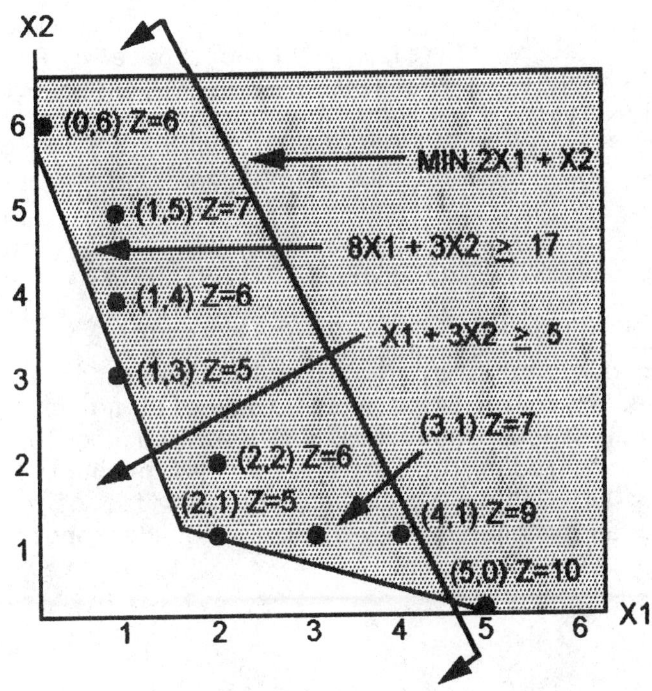

d) The optimal value for the linear program is "better" than for the mixed integer program, which in turn is better than that for the all-integer program.

PROBLEM 3

Metropolitan Microwaves, Inc. is planning to expand its operations into other electronic appliances. The company has identified seven new product lines it can carry. The required initial investment and floor space and the expected rate of return on each line.

Product Line	Initial Investment	Floor Space (Sq.Ft.)	Expected Rate Of Return
1. Black & White TVs	$ 6,000	125	8.1%
2. Color TVs	12,000	150	9.0
3. Large Screen TVs	20,000	200	11.0
4. VHS VCRs	14,000	40	10.2
5. Beta VCRs	15,000	40	10.5
6. Video Games	2,000	20	14.1
7. Home Computers	32,000	100	13.2

Metropolitan has decided that they should not stock large screen TVs unless they stock either B&W or color TVs. Also, they will not stock both types of VCRs, and they will stock video games if they stock color TVs. Finally, the company wishes to introduce at least three new product lines.

If the company has $45,000 to invest and 420 sq. ft. of floor space available, formulate an integer linear program for Metropolitan to maximize its overall expected rate of return.

SOLUTION 3

Define variables: X_j = 1 if product line j is introduced; = 0 otherwise.

Define objective function: Maximize total overall expected return:

$$\text{MAX } .081(6000)X_1 + .09(12000)X_2 + .11(20000)X_3 + .102(14000)X_4 + .105(15000)X_5 + .141(2000)X_6 + .132(32000)X_7$$

Define constraints:

1) Money: $6X_1 + 12X_2 + 20X_3 + 14X_4 + 15X_5 + 2X_6 + 32X_7 \leq 45$

2) Space: $125X_1 + 150X_2 + 200X_3 + 40X_4 + 40X_5 + 20X_6 + 100X_7 \leq 420$

3) Stock large screen TVs only if stock B&W or color TVs:
$X_1 + X_2 \geq X_3$ or $X_1 + X_2 - X_3 \geq 0$

4) Not stock both types of VCRs: $X_4 + X_5 \leq 1$

5) Stock video games if they stock color TV's: $X_2 - X_6 \geq 0$.

6) At least 3 new lines: $X_1 + X_2 + X_3 + X_4 + X_5 + X_6 + X_7 \geq 3$

7) Variables are 0 or 1: X_j = 0 or 1 for j = 1,,,7.

PROBLEM 4

Tom's Tailoring has five idle tailors and four custom garments to make. The estimated time (in hours) it would take each tailor to make each garment is listed below. (An 'X' in the table indicates an unacceptable tailor-garment assignment.)

	Tailor				
Garment	1	2	3	4	5
Wedding gown	19	23	20	21	18
Clown costume	11	14	X	12	10
Admiral's uniform	12	8	11	X	9
Bullfighter's outfit	X	20	20	18	21

Formulate an integer program for determining the tailor-garment assignments that minimize the total estimated time spent making the four garments. No tailor is to be assigned more than one garment and each garment is to be worked on by only one tailor.

SOLUTION 4

This problem can be formulated as a 0-1 integer program. The LP solution to this problem will automatically be integer (0-1).

Define the decision variables:

X_{ij} = 1 if garment i is assigned to tailor j; = 0 otherwise.

Number of decision variables = [(number of garments)(number of tailors)] - (number of unacceptable assignments) = [4(5)] - 3 = 17.

Define the objective function:

Minimize total time spent making garments:

$$\text{MIN } 19X_{11} + 23X_{12} + 20X_{13} + 21X_{14} + 18X_{15} + 11X_{21} + 14X_{22} + 12X_{24} + 10X_{25} + 12X_{31} + 8X_{32} + 11X_{33} + 9X_{35} + 20X_{42} + 20X_{43} + 18X_{44} + 21X_{45}$$

Define the constraints:

Exactly one tailor per garment:

1) $X_{11} + X_{12} + X_{13} + X_{14} + X_{15} = 1$
2) $X_{21} + X_{22} + X_{24} + X_{25} = 1$
3) $X_{31} + X_{32} + X_{33} + X_{35} = 1$
4) $X_{42} + X_{43} + X_{44} + X_{45} = 1$

No more than one garment per tailor:

5) $X_{11} + X_{21} + X_{31} \leq 1$
6) $X_{21} + X_{22} + X_{23} + X_{24} \leq 1$
7) $X_{31} + X_{33} + X_{34} \leq 1$
8) $X_{41} + X_{42} + X_{44} \leq 1$
9) $X_{51} + X_{52} + X_{53} + X_{54} \leq 1$

Nonnegativity: $X_{ij} \geq 0$ for i = 1,..,4 and j = 1,..,5

NOTE: This problem is a classic assignment problem. A specialized solution procedure for this type of problem is covered in Chapter 11.

ANSWERED PROBLEMS

PROBLEM 5

Given the following all-integer linear program:

$$\text{MAX } Z = 15X_1 + 2X_2$$

$$\text{S.T.} \quad 7X_1 + X_2 \leq 23$$

$$3X_1 - X_2 \leq 5$$

$$X_1, X_2 \geq 0 \text{ and integer}$$

a) Solve the problem as an LP, ignoring the integer constraints.

b) What solution is obtained by rounding up fractions greater than or equal to 1/2? Is this the optimal integer solution?

c) What solution is obtained by rounding down all fractions? Is this the optimal integer solution? Explain.

d) Show that the optimal solution to the all-integer problem gives a lower Z value than the optimal Z value for the LP.

e) Why is the optimal Z value for the ILP problem always less than or equal to the corresponding LP's optimal Z value? When would they be equal? Comment on the MILP's optimal Z compared to the corresponding LP & ILP.

PROBLEM 6

Given the following all-integer linear programming problem:

$$\text{MAX } Z = 3X_1 + 10X_2$$

$$\text{S.T.} \quad 2X_1 + X_2 \leq 5$$

$$X_1 + 6X_2 \leq 9$$

$$X_1 - X_2 \geq 2$$

$$X_1, X_2 \geq 0 \text{ and integer}$$

a) Solve the problem graphically as a linear program.

b) Show that there is only one integer point and it is optimal.

c) Suppose the third constraint was changed to $X_1 - X_2 \geq 2.1$. What is the new optimal solution to the LP? ILP?

PROBLEM 7

Given the following all-integer linear programming problem:

$$\text{MAX } Z = 5X_1 + 4X_2$$

$$\begin{aligned} \text{S.T.} \quad 4X_1 + X_2 &\leq 10 \\ 5X_1 + 3X_2 &\leq 15 \\ X_1 + X_2 &\leq 4 \\ X_1, X_2 &\geq 0 \text{ and integer} \end{aligned}$$

a) Solve the LP relaxation of this problem. Does this provide an upper bound or a lower bound for the value of the objective function for the integer programming problem?

b) Solve by inspection for the optimal solution to the integer program.

c) Suppose the objective function were changed to MAX $Z = 5X_1 + 3X_2$. What is the new optimal solution to this problem?

PROBLEM 8

Tower Engineering Corporation is considering undertaking several proposed projects for the next fiscal year. The projects, the number of engineers and the number of support personnel required for each project, and the expected profits for each project are summarized in the following table:

	Project 1	2	3	4	5	6
Engineers Required	20	55	47	38	90	63
Support Personnel Required	15	45	50	40	70	70
Profit ($1,000,000s)	1.0	1.8	2.0	1.5	3.6	2.2

Formulate an integer program that maximizes Tower's profit subject to the following management constraints:

(1) Use no more than 175 engineers
(2) Use no more than 150 support personnel
(3) If either project 6 or project 4 is done, both must be done
(4) Project 2 can be done only if project 1 is done
(5) If project 5 is done, project 3 must not be done and vice versa
(6) No more than three projects are to be done.

PROBLEM 9

Kloos Industries has projected the availability of capital over each of the next three years to be $850,000, $1,000,000, and $1,200,000, respectively. It is considering four options for the disposition of the capital:

(1) Research and development of a promising new product
(2) Plant expansion
(3) Modernization of its current facilities
(4) Investment in a valuable piece of nearby real estate

Monies not invested in these projects in a given year will NOT be available for following year's investment in the projects.

The expected benefits three years hence from each of the four projects and the yearly capital outlays of the four options are summarized in the table below in $1,000,000's.

In addition, Kloos has decided to undertake exactly two of the projects, and if plant expansion is selected, it will also modernize its current facilities.

Options	Capital Outlays Year 1	Year 2	Year 3	Projected Benefits
New Product R&D	.35	.55	.75	5.2
Plant Expansion	.50	.50	0	3.6
Modernization	.35	.40	.45	3.2
Real Estate	.50	0	0	2.8

Formulate this problem as a binary programming problem.

PROBLEM 10

A business manager for a grain distributor is asked to decide how many containers of each of two grains to purchase to fill its 1,600 pound capacity warehouse. The table below summarizes the container size, availability, and expected profit per container upon distribution.

Grain	Container Size	Containers Available	Container Profit
A	500 lbs.	3	$1,200
B	600 lbs.	2	$1,500

a) Formulate as a linear program with the decision variables representing the number of containers purchased of each grain. Solve for the optimal solution.

b) What would be the optimal solution if you were not allowed to purchase fractional containers?

c) There are three possible results from rounding an LP solution to obtain an integer solution:
(1) the rounded optimal LP solution will be the optimal IP solution;
(2) the rounded optimal LP solution gives a feasible, but not optimal IP solution;
(3) the rounded optimal LP solution is an infeasible IP solution.

For this problem (i) round <u>down</u> all fractions; (ii) round <u>up</u> all fractions; (iii) round <u>off</u> (to the nearest integer) all fractions (NOTE: Two of these are equivalent.) Which result above (1, 2, or 3) occurred under each rounding method?

PROBLEM 11

Given the following problem:

$$\text{MIN } Z = 4X_1 + 7X_2$$

$$\text{S.T.} \quad X_1 + 6X_2 \geq 14$$

$$2X_1 + 5X_2 \geq 22$$

$$3X_1 + X_2 \geq 10$$

$$X_1, X_2 \geq 0$$

a) Solve the mixed integer problem where X_1 is required to be integer.

b) Using (a), solve the all-integer linear program.

TRUE/FALSE

12. The optimal solution to a linear program gave $X_1 = 2.58$ and $X_2 = 1.32$. If X_1 and X_2 were restricted to be integers, then $X_1 = 3$, $X_2 = 1$ will give a feasible solution, but not necessarily an optimal integer solution.

13. The objective function coefficients are all integers for an ILP. The optimal solution to the linear program is $X_1 = 2.58$, $X_2 = 1.32$, and $z = 14.28$. The solution was rounded to $X_1 = 3$, $X_2 = 1$ and $z = 14$, and this is a feasible solution. Then this must be the optimal solution to the ILP.

14. Project 5 must be completed before project 6 is started. The constraint would be: $X_5 - X_6 \leq 0$.

15. If the LP relaxation of an integer program has a feasible solution, then the integer program has a feasible solution.

16. A mixed-integer linear program involves both discrete and continuous variables.

17. The optimal solution to an integer linear program still must occur at an extreme point of the feasible region formed by the functional constraints.

18. If at most three of five projects are to be completed, the constraint would be: $X_1 + X_2 + X_3 + X_4 + X_5 \leq 3$.

19. Multiple-choice constraints involve binary variables.

20. The classic assignment problem can be modeled as a 0-1 integer linear program.

21. An optimal integer solution of $X_1 = 3$, $X_2 = 5$, $z = 150$ has been found for an ILP. For the linear programming formulation, the range of optimality for C_1 was between 15 and 30 with a current $C_1 = 20$. Then if C_1 is increased to 21 in the ILP, the new optimal value of the objective function must be 153.

22. For a minimization ILP, a lower bound is found when any integer solution is determined.

23. For some types of ILP problems their LP relaxation solutions are optimal.

24. The value of the optimal solution to any mixed-integer linear program involving minimization will be less than or equal to the solution to its LP relaxation.

25. Generally, the optimal solution to an integer linear program is less sensitive to the constraint coefficients than is a linear program.

26. The use of integer variables involves a tradeoff between modeling flexibility and solution difficulty.

Chapter 13
Project Management: PERT/CPM

KEY CONCEPTS

CONCEPT	ILLUSTRATED PROBLEMS	ANSWERED PROBLEMS
Construction of PERT Networks	1,2	6,8,12,13
PERT Analysis with Certain Times	1	6,7,9
PERT Analysis with Uncertain Times	2,4	8,10,11
Activity Earliest/Latest Times	1,2,5	7,9
Time/Cost Analysis	3,4	9-13
LP Formulation for Crashing	3	12,13
PERT/Cost	5	14

REVIEW

1. PERT (Program Evaluation Review Technique) is used to plan the scheduling of individual activities that make up a project.

2. A PERT network can be constructed to model the precedence of the activities. The arcs of the network represent the activities. The nodes of the network represent points in time when an activity or a group of activities have been completed. The nodes are numbered so that each activity begins at a lower numbered node and ends at a higher numbered node. Dummy activities having 0 completion times can be created to help indicate that the proper set of activities has been completed prior to the start of another activity.

3. PERT can be used to determine the earliest/latest start and finish times for each activity, the entire project completion time and the slack time for each activity. (See algorithm at the end of the Review.)

4. A critical path for the network is a path consisting of activities with zero slack.

5. In the three-time estimate approach, the time to complete an activity is assumed to follow a Beta distribution. Its mean is $t = (a + 4m + b)/6$, and its variance is $\sigma^2 = ((b-a)/6)^2$. Here a = the optimistic completion time estimate, b = the pessimistic completion time estimate, and m = the most likely completion time estimate.

6. In the three-time estimate approach, the critical path is determined as if the mean times for the activities were fixed times. The overall project completion time is assumed to have a normal distribution with mean equal to the sum of the means along the critical path and variance equal to the sum of the variances along the critical path.

7. In the CPM (Critical Path Method) approach to project scheduling, it is assumed that the normal time to complete an activity, t_j, which can be met at a normal cost, c_j, can be crashed to a reduced time, t_j', under maximum crashing for an increased cost, c_j'.

8. Using CPM, activity j's maximum time reduction, M_j, may be calculated by: $M_j = t_j - t_j'$. It is assumed that its cost per unit reduction, K_j, is linear and can be calculated by: $K_j = (c_j' - c_j)/M_j$.

9. Linear programming may be used to solve a CPM problem to minimize the crashing costs needed to complete a project within a specified time limit. (See formulation at the end of the Review.)

10. PERT/COST is a technique for monitoring costs during a project. Work packages (groups of related activities) with estimated budgets and completion times are evaluated.

11. A cost status report may be calculated by determining the cost overrun or underrun for each work package. These are calculated by subtracting the budgeted cost from the actual cost of the work package. For work in progress, these may be determined by subtracting the prorated budget cost from the actual cost to date. The overall project cost overrun or underrun at a particular time during a project is determined by summing the individual cost overruns and underruns to date of the work packages.

LINEAR PROGRAM FOR PROJECT CRASHING

Notation

(Note: activity ij starts at node i, ends at node j)

T = required completion time of the project

x_i = time represented by node i

y_{ij} = the amount activity ij is crashed

M_{ij} = maximum amount activity ij can be crashed

K_{ij} = cost per time unit to crash activity ij

τ_{ij} = normal time to complete activity ij

Formulation

$$\text{MIN} \quad \sum_i \sum_j K_{ij} y_{ij}$$

S.T.

$$x_N \le T \quad \text{where N is the completion node}$$

$$y_{ij} \le M_{ij} \quad \text{for each activity ij}$$

$$-x_i + x_j + y_{ij} \ge \tau_{ij} \quad \text{for each activity ij}$$

$$x_i,\ y_{ij} \ge 0$$

PERT ANALYSIS ALGORITHM

PERT networks assume all activities are directed from lower numbered nodes to higher numbered nodes.

1. Make a forward pass through the network as follows: Move sequentially from node 1 to node 2 to node 3, etc. At a given node i, consider all activities beginning at node i. For each of these activities, (i,j), beginning at node i:

   (a) Earliest Start Time = the maximum of all earliest finish times ending at node i. (For node 1 this is 0.)

   (b) Earliest Finish Time = (Earliest Start Time) + (Time to complete activity (i,j)).

   The project completion time is the maximum of the Earliest Finish Times at the completion node.

2. Make a backwards pass through the network as follows: Move sequentially backwards from the last node, N, to node N-1, to node N-2, etc. At a given node, j, consider all activities ending at node j. For each of these activities, (i,j):

   (a) Latest Finish Time = the minimum of the latest start times beginning at node j. (For node N, this is the project completion time.)

   (b) Latest Start Time = (Latest Finish Time) - (Time to complete activity (i,j)).

3. Calculate the slack time for each activity by:

   Slack = (Latest Start) - (Earliest Start) or
   = (Latest Finish) - (Earliest Finish).

   A critical path is a path of activities, from node 1 to N, with 0 slack times.

FLOW CHART FOR PROJECT CRASHING

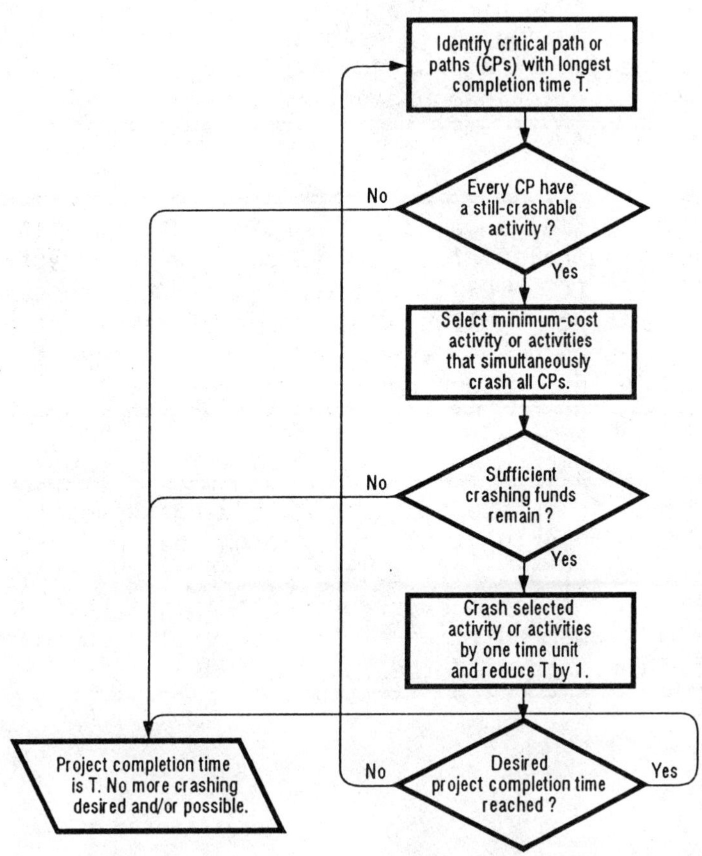
Identify critical path or paths (CPs) with longest completion time T.
Every CP have a still-crashable activity ?
No
Yes
Select minimum-cost activity or activities that simultaneously crash all CPs.
Sufficient crashing funds remain ?
No
Yes
Crash selected activity or activities by one time unit and reduce T by 1.
Desired project completion time reached ?
No
Yes
Project completion time is T. No more crashing desired and/or possible.

ILLUSTRATED PROBLEMS

NOTE: Two reasons for using dummy activities in project networks are: (1) Two (or more) arcs should not have both a common starting node and a common finish node because many PERT/CPM computer programs will erroneously treat these multiple arcs as one. (2) An arc must not enter node i unless it is a prerequisite to every arc exiting node i; otherwise, precedence is inaccurately depicted.

NOTE: One way to partially check the accuracy of your activity earliest/latest time calculations is to compute every activity's slack two ways: Slack = (LS - ES) = (LF - EF) If the preceding is not true, you have an error! Also, the number of different values in your slack column should not exceed (but does not have to equal) the number of paths in the project network.

NOTE: If you are only interested in identifying the critical path and expected project completion time, there might be an easier approach than determining every activity's earliest start and finish times. List (if there are not too many) every path in the network and, for each one, sum the expected times of the activities on that path. You are looking for the path with the largest sum.

PROBLEM 1

Kraft's Kustom Kars is in the business of producing custom automobile assemblies. In particular, Kraft operates a shop that builds and assembles the body and frame of the cars.

Kraft's operations begin with the processing of initial paperwork. This must be done before any other operations are commenced. Once the paperwork has been completed, the body of the car can be built in Room A and the frame of the car can be built in Room B. When the body is built, it is transferred to Room C for finishing work. Similarly, when the frame is built, it is transferred to Room D for finishing work.

When both are built, although not necessarily finished, the final paperwork can be completed. When both the body and frame are finished, they are transported to the assembly Room E, where the body is mounted to the frame.

In the frame building room, Room B, certain chemicals are used which must be completely eliminated by a thorough washdown to prevent gaseous fumes from becoming a health hazard. The project is considered complete when the final paperwork has been completed, the body has been mounted to the frame, and Room B has been completely washed down.

The table below gives the expected completion times in hours for each activity of the project.

Activity	Description	Completion Time
A	Initial Paperwork	3
B	Build Body	3
C	Build Frame	2
D	Finish Body	3
E	Finish Frame	7
F	Final Paperwork	3
G	Mount Body to Frame	6
H	Room B Washdown	2

a) Draw the PERT network that corresponds to this problem.

b) Find the earliest and latest start and finish times for each activity of the project. How long should the project take?

c) Which activities must not be delayed if the project is to be completed in the time calculated in part (b)?

d) Suppose the body finish operation (D) were delayed four hours. By how much would the entire project be delayed?

SOLUTION 1

Before constructing the PERT network, summarize in the following table the immediate predecessor activities for each activity.

Activity	Immediate Predecessors	Completion Times (Hrs.)
A	--	3
B	A	3
C	A	2
D	B	3
E	C	7
F	B,C	3
G	D,E	6
H	C	2

To construct a PERT network, there must be a node for the completion of each distinct entry in the immediate predecessor column as well as a beginning node and and ending node. (There could be others.) Number the nodes such that arrows point from a lower number node to a higher number node.

The result is:

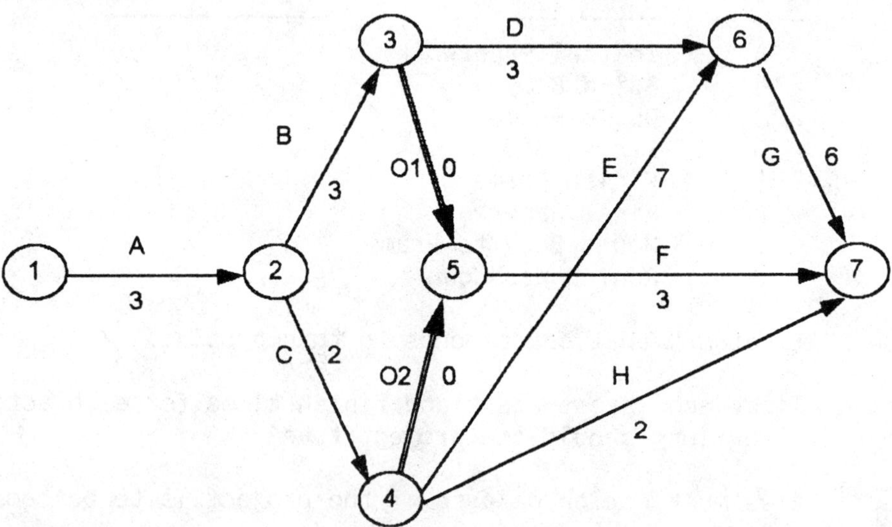

(NOTE: Node 5 represents the time point when both B and C are completed, since node 3 is the time point when only B is completed and node 4 is the time point when only C is completed. Thus, dummy activities, O1 and O2, were created to connect nodes 3 and 5, and nodes 4 and 5 respectively to give the proper precedence relation meaning to node 5. They both have a 0 completion time.)

b) The earliest start time (ES) for activities from node 1 is 0. Then the earliest finish time (EF) for an activity is given by: EF = ES + (completion time). Then ES for an activity = max (EF for all activities into its start node). These appear on the top of the arrow as [ES,EF].

The forward pass to calculate ES and EF:

Start Node	Activity	Earliest Start (ES)	Earliest Finish(EF)
1	A	0	0 + 3 = 3
2	B	3	3 + 3 = 6
	C	3	3 + 2 = 5
3	D	6	6 + 3 = 9
	01	6	6 + 0 = 6
4	02	5	5 + 0 = 5
	E	5	5 + 7 = 12
	H	5	5 + 2 = 7
5	F	MAX(5,6)=6	6 + 3 = 9
6	G	MAX(9,12)=12	12 + 6 = 18

The max(EF at node 7) = 18, so the completion time of the project is 18.

The backwards pass to calculate LF and LS:

End Node	Activity	Latest Finish (LF)	Latest Start (LS)
7	H	18	18 - 2 = 16
	G	18	18 - 6 = 12
	F	18	18 - 3 = 15
6	E	12	12 - 7 = 5
	D	12	12 - 3 = 9
5	01	15	15 - 0 = 15
	02	15	15 - 0 = 15
4	C	MIN(15,5,16)=5	5 - 2 = 3
3	B	MIN(9,15)=9	9 - 3 = 6
2	A	MIN(6,3)=3	3 - 3 = 0

This gives the completed network at the top of the next page.

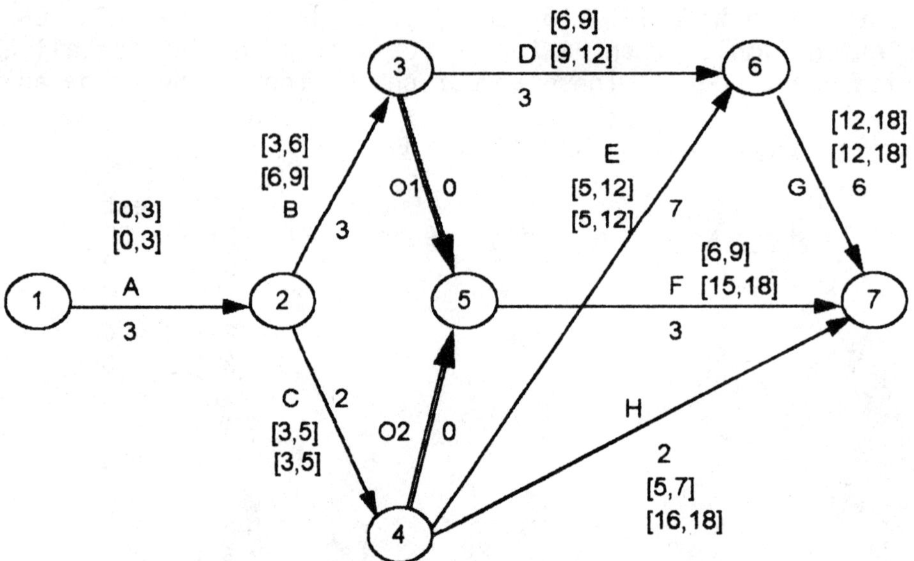

The slack time for each activity (LS - ES) is summarized below:

Activity	ES	EF	LS	LF	Slack
A	0	3	0	3	0
B	3	6	6	9	3
C	3	5	3	5	0
D	6	9	9	12	3
E	5	12	5	12	0
F	6	9	15	18	9
G	12	18	12	18	0
H	5	7	16	18	11

c) Activities A, C, E, G have 0 slack times -- they form the critical path.

d) Activity D has a slack of 3. Hence a 4 hour delay in D would delay the entire project 4 - 3 = 1 hour.

PROBLEM 2

The following project has been analyzed:

Activity	Immediate Predecessors	Optimistic Time (Hrs.)	Most Likely Time (Hrs.)	Pessimistic Time (Hrs.)
A	--	4	6	8
B	--	1	4.5	5
C	A	3	3	3
D	A	4	5	6
E	A	0.5	1	1.5
F	B,C	3	4	5
G	B,C	1	1.5	5
H	E,F	5	6	7
I	E,F	2	5	8
J	D,H	2.5	2.75	4.5
K	G,I	3	5	7

a) Construct the PERT network for this problem.

b) Solve for the expected earliest and latest start and finish times for each activity.

c) Identify the critical path and give the estimated project completion time.

d) What is the probability the project will be completed within one day (24 hours)?

SOLUTION 2

a) Nodes are needed for the start node, the finish node, the completion of A, completion of B, completion of C, completion of E and F, completion of D and H, and the completion of G and I:

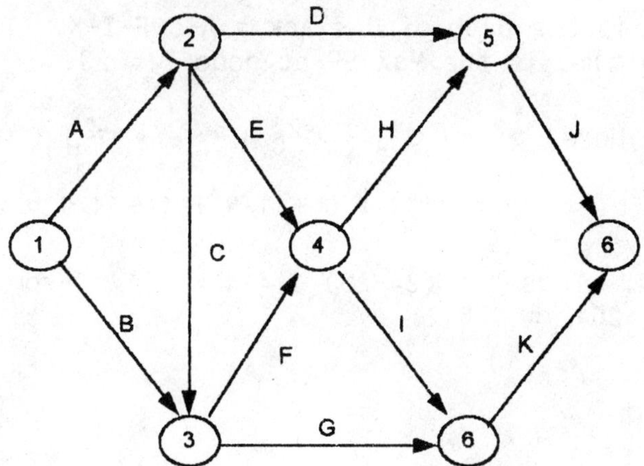

b) Calculate the expected times, t, and variances, σ^2, for each activity.

$$t = (a + 4m + b)/6 \qquad \sigma^2 = ((b-a)/6)^2$$

Activity	Expected Time	Variance
A	6	4/9
B	4	4/9
C	3	0
D	5	1/9
E	1	1/36
F	4	1/9
G	2	4/9
H	6	1/9
I	5	1
J	3	1/9
K	5	4/9

Thus, using the algorithm illustrated in problem 1, we have:

Activity	ES	EF	LS	LF	Slack
A	0	6	0	6	0
B	0	4	5	9	5
C	6	9	6	9	0
D	6	11	15	20	9
E	6	7	12	13	6
F	9	13	9	13	0
G	9	11	16	18	7
H	13	19	14	20	1
I	13	18	13	18	0
J	19	22	20	23	1
K	18	23	18	23	0

c) The critical path is the path of 0 slack = A-C-F-I-K. The estimated project completion time is the Max EF at node 7 = 23.

d) $z = (24 - 23)/\sigma$. Here, $\sigma^2 = \sigma^2_A + \sigma^2_C + \sigma^2_F + \sigma^2_H + \sigma^2_K$

$$= 4/9 + 0 + 1/9 + 1 + 4/9 = 2.$$

Hence, $\sigma = 1.414$. Thus $z = (24-23)/1.414 = .71$. From appendix B, $P(z < .71) = .5 + .2612 = .7612$.

PROBLEM 3

National Business Machines (NBM) has just developed a new microcomputer it plans to put into full scale production in a few months. The table and the PERT network below show the precedence relations and give the activity times and costs under normal operations and maximum crashing for a daily operation production of 1000 microcomputers at its local plant.

NBM plans three eight-hour shifts per day and desires to know the minimum cost of producing the 1000 microcomputers within the 24-hour period. Set up a linear program, which when solved, would yield this information.

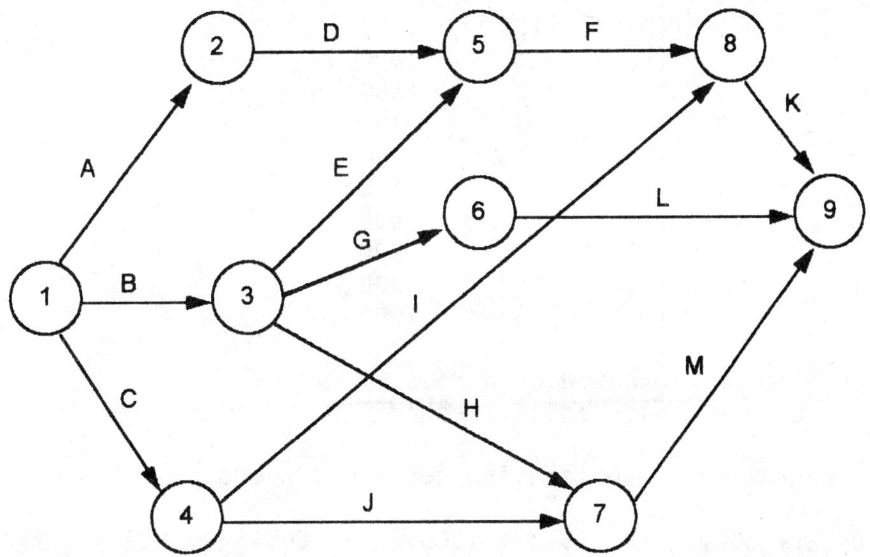

Activity*	Normal Time	Normal Cost	Crash Time	Crash Cost
1-2 (A)	2	$2,000	1.5	$3,000
1-3 (B)	4	3,000	3	3,500
1-4 (C)	1	1,500	1	1,500
2-5 (D)	4	5,300	2.5	8,000
3-5 (E)	6	5,400	5	7,000
5-8 (F)	10	6,000	8	9,000
3-6 (G)	8	4,800	5	9,900
3-7 (H)	2	2,800	1	2,900
4-8 (I)	5	4,500	4	5,000
4-7 (J)	12	6,000	6	9,600
8-9 (K)	7	7,000	4	9,700
6-9 (L)	11	8,800	9	9,200
7-9 (M)	4	1,000	1	7,000

* Activity 12 starts at node 1 and ends at node 2, etc.

SOLUTION 3

First prepare a chart giving maximum crashing,
M = (Normal Time) - (Time Under Maximum Crashing)
and the marginal cost per hour for crashing,
K = ([Cost Under Maximum Crashing] - [Normal Cost])/M

Activity	M	K
1-2 (A)	0.5	2000
1-3 (B)	1	500
1-4 (C)	0	0
2-5 (D)	1.5	1800
3-5 (E)	1	1600
5-8 (F)	2	1500
3-6 (G)	3	1700
3-7 (H)	1	100
4-8 (I)	1	500
4-7 (J)	6	600
8-9 (K)	3	900
6-9 (L)	2	200
7-9 (M)	3	2000

Define: x_i = time represented by node i
y_{ij} = time activity ij is crashed

The linear program must minimize the total extra cost:

$$\text{MIN } 2000y_{12} + 500y_{13} + 0y_{14} + 1800y_{25} + 1600y_{35} + 1500y_{58} + 1700y_{36} + 100y_{37} + 500y_{48} + 600y_{47} + 900y_{89} + 200y_{69} + 2000y_{79}$$

Subject to:
(1) The project must be completed within 24 hours: $x_9 \leq 24$
(2) The amount an activity is crashed cannot exceed its maximum crashing:

$$\begin{aligned}
y_{12} &\leq 0.5 \\
y_{13} &\leq 1 \\
y_{14} &\leq 0 \\
y_{25} &\leq 1.5 \\
y_{35} &\leq 1 \\
y_{58} &\leq 2 \\
y_{36} &\leq 3 \\
y_{37} &\leq 1 \\
y_{48} &\leq 1 \\
y_{47} &\leq 6 \\
y_{89} &\leq 3 \\
y_{69} &\leq 2 \\
y_{79} &\leq 3
\end{aligned}$$

(3) For each activity:
(Time at end node) $\geq$ (Time at Start Node) + [(Normal Activity Time) - (Amount of Time the Activity is crashed)]

$$x_9 \geq x_7 + 4 - y_{79}$$
$$x_9 \geq x_6 + 11 - y_{69}$$
$$x_9 \geq x_8 + 7 - y_{89}$$

$$x_8 \geq x_4 + 5 - y_{48}$$
$$x_8 \geq x_5 + 10 - y_{58}$$

$$x_7 \geq x_4 + 12 - y_{47}$$
$$x_7 \geq x_3 + 2 - y_{37}$$

$$x_6 \geq x_3 + 8 - y_{36}$$

$$x_5 \geq x_3 + 6 - y_{35}$$
$$x_5 \geq x_2 + 4 - y_{25}$$

$$x_4 \geq x_1 + 1 - y_{14}$$

$$x_3 \geq x_1 + 4 - y_{13}$$

$$x_2 \geq x_1 + 2 - y_{12}$$

(4) Non-negativity of the variables:

$$x_i \geq 0 \quad \text{for all } i$$
$$y_{ij} \geq 0 \quad \text{for all } j$$

PROBLEM 4

Given the following PERT network for Gus's Painters:

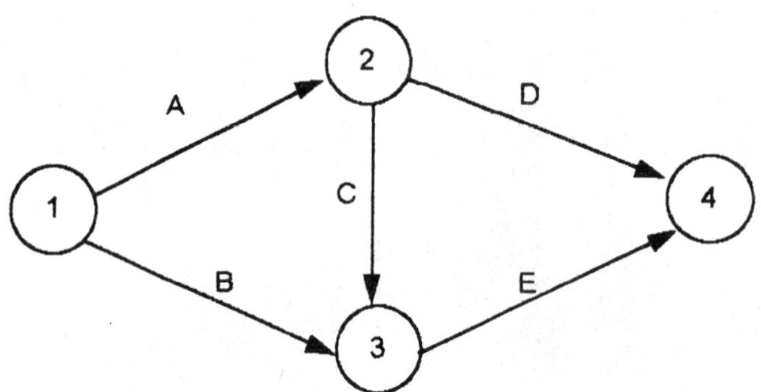

The following means and standard deviations were calculated for the activities:

Activity	t	σ
A	6	2
B	3	1
C	6	1
D	15	2
E	12	2

There is a $100,000 bonus for completing the project in 26 weeks. Currently activity E is assigned to Wilson Brothers. Gus has the option of hiring Jones Inc. for activity E. Their expected completion time for activity E is 8 weeks (with a standard deviation of 2), but they will cost Gus $15,000 more to do E than Wilson Brothers. Should Gus hire Jones?

SOLUTION 4

Analysis using Wilson Brothers to do E:

Activity	ES	EF	LS	LF
A	0	6	0	6
B	0	3	9	12
C	6	12	6	12
D	6	21	9	21
E	12	24	12	24

Hence the critical path is A - C - E and the overall expected project completion time is 24.

The variance of the critical path is:

$$\sigma^2 = \sigma^2_A + \sigma^2_C + \sigma^2_E = (2)^2 + (1)^2 + (2)^2 = 9. \quad \text{Thus } \sigma = 3.$$

To find the probability of completing the project in 26 weeks, calculate,

$$z = (26 - 24)/3 = .67.$$

Thus the probability of finishing in 26 weeks is $P(Z < .67)$. From appendix A, the table gives the $P(0 < Z < .67) = .2486$. Therefore the probability of completing the project within 26 weeks is .5 + .2486 = .7486.

Thus the expected bonus using Wilson Brothers to do E is:

$$(.486)(100{,}000) + (.2514)(0) = \$74{,}860.$$

Analysis using Jones, Inc. do E:

Activity	ES	EF	LS	LF
A	0	6	0	6
B	0	3	10	13
C	6	12	7	13
D	6	21	6	21
E	12	20	13	21

Hence the critical path is A - D and the overall expected project completion time is 21. The variance of the critical path is:

$$\sigma^2 = \sigma^2_A + \sigma^2_D = (2)^2 + (2)^2 = 8. \quad \text{Thus } \sigma = 2.828.$$

To find the probability of completing the project in 26 weeks, calculate,

$$z = (26 - 21)/2.828 = 1.77.$$

Thus the probability of finishing in 26 weeks is $P(Z < 1.77)$. From Appendix A, the table gives the $P(0 < Z < 1.77) = .4616$. Therefore the probability of completing the project within 26 weeks is .5 + .4616 = .9616.

Thus the expected bonus using Jones, Inc. to do E is:

$$(.9616)(100{,}000) + (.0384)(0) = \$96{,}160.$$

Decision:

The difference in expected returns between the two firms is: \$96,160 - \$74,860 = \$21,300. Since this is greater than the \$15,000 cost to hire Jones, Inc., Gus should hire Jones, Inc.

PROBLEM 5

For the PERT network below, the project cost of each activity was $6000. After the eleventh week the following data has been forwarded to management concerning the project status:

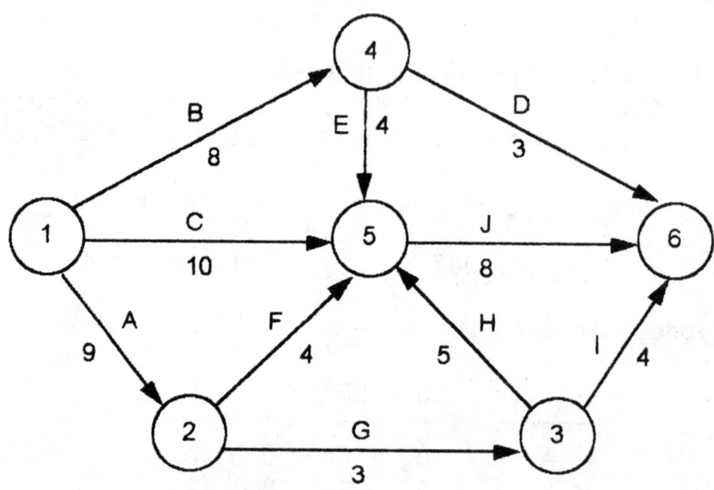

Activity	Actual Cost	% Complete
A	$6,200	100
B	$5,700	100
C	$5,600	90
D	0	0
E	$1,000	25
F	$5,000	75
G	$2,000	50
H	0	0
I	0	0
J	0	0

a) Solve for the earliest and latest start and finish times for each activity as well as the expected overall completion time.

b) Do the total expenditures to date represent an overall cost overrun or overall cost underrun?

c) Is the project being completed on time?

d) What corrective action, if any, do you recommend?

SOLUTION 5

a) Solving the PERT network for the ES, EF, LS, LF, and slack times by the method illustrated in problem 1, we can summarize:

Activity	ES	EF	LS	LF	Slack
A	0	9	0	9	0
B	0	8	5	13	5
C	0	10	7	17	7
D	8	11	22	25	14
E	8	12	13	17	5
F	9	13	13	17	4
G	9	12	9	12	0
H	12	17	12	17	0
I	12	16	21	25	9
J	17	25	17	25	0

The overall project completion time is 25 weeks.

b) Use the following formula for each activity:

Value = (proportion complete) X (amount budgeted).

This gives the following table of costs:

Activity	Actual Cost	Value	Difference
A	$6,200	(1.00)x6000 = 6000	$ 200
B	5,700	(1.00)x6000 = 6000	- 300
C	5,600	(.90)x6000 = 5400	200
D	0	0	0
E	1,000	(.25)x6000 = 1500	- 500
F	5,000	(.75)x6000 = 4500	500
G	2,000	(.50)x6000 = 3000	-1000
H	0	0	0
I	0	0	0
J	0	0	0
TOTALS	$25,500	$26,400	-$ 900

Based on these values, the project is currently experiencing a $900 cost underrun.

c) Consider the PERT diagram at week 11. The times reflect that 11 weeks have already passed and the activity completion times are the times remaining for each activity. For instance, activity C is 90% complete, and thus has 10% of 10 (= 1) week remaining. The PERT diagram then is:

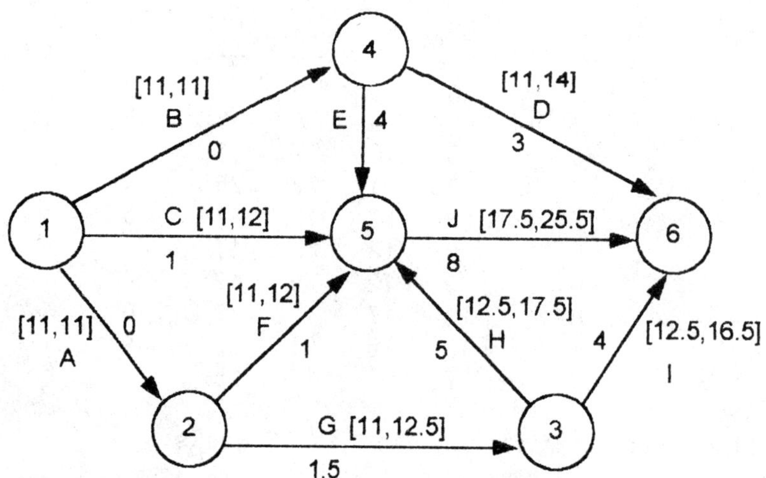

Note that the overall completion time is now 25.5 weeks or a .5 week delay.

d) Management should consider using some of the $900 cost savings and apply it to activity G to assist in a more rapid completion of this activity (and hence the entire project).

ANSWERED PROBLEMS

PROBLEM 6

Consider a project which has been modeled as follows:

Activity	Immediate Predecessors	Completion Time (hrs.)
A	---	7
B	---	10
C	A	4
D	A	30
E	A	7
F	B,C	12
G	B,C	15
H	E,F	11
I	E,F	25
J	E,F	6
K	D,H	21
L	G,J	25

a) Draw the PERT network for this project and determine project's expected completion time and its critical path.

b) Can activities E and G be performed simultaneously without delaying the minimum project completion time?

c) Can one person perform A, G, and I without delaying the project?

d) By how much can activities G and L be delayed without delaying the entire project?

e) How much would the project be delayed if activity G were delayed by 7 hours and activity L by 4 hours? Explain.

PROBLEM 7

Given the following PERT network of tasks with completion times in hours for scheduling interns in a hospital:

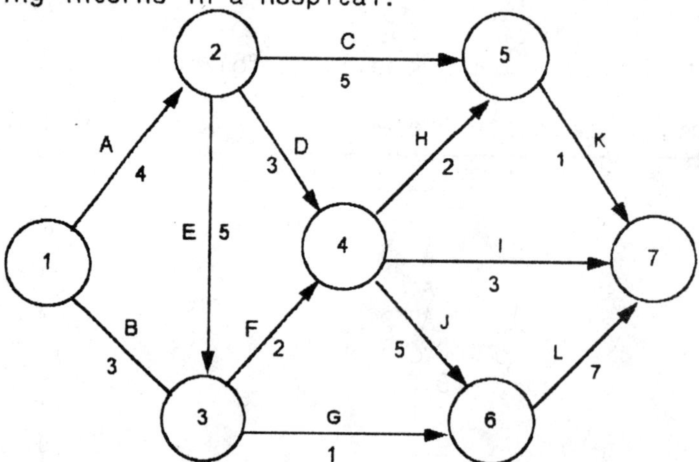

a) Given that interns start at midnight (00:00), construct a chart giving the ES, EF, LS, LF, and slack for each activity.

b) What is the critical path and project completion time?

c) If an intern can do any job and works a 24-hour shift, show that all the jobs can be completed by two interns. (Hint: One intern is assigned the critical path jobs, but be sure to schedule the remaining activities within the limits in (a).)

PROBLEM 8

A project consists of five activities. Naturally the paint mixing precedes the painting activities. Also, both ceiling painting and floor sanding must be done prior to floor buffing.

Activity	Optimistic Time (hrs.)	Most Likely Time (hrs.)	Pessimistic Time (hrs.)
Floor sanding	3	4	5
Floor buffing	1	2	3
Paint mixing	0.5	1	1.5
Wall painting	1	2	9
Ceiling painting	1	5.5	7

a) Construct a PERT network for this problem.

b) What is the expected completion time of this project?

c) What is the probability that the project can be completed within 9 hrs.?

PROBLEM 9

Given the following PERT network modeling new home construction by Bonanza Development:

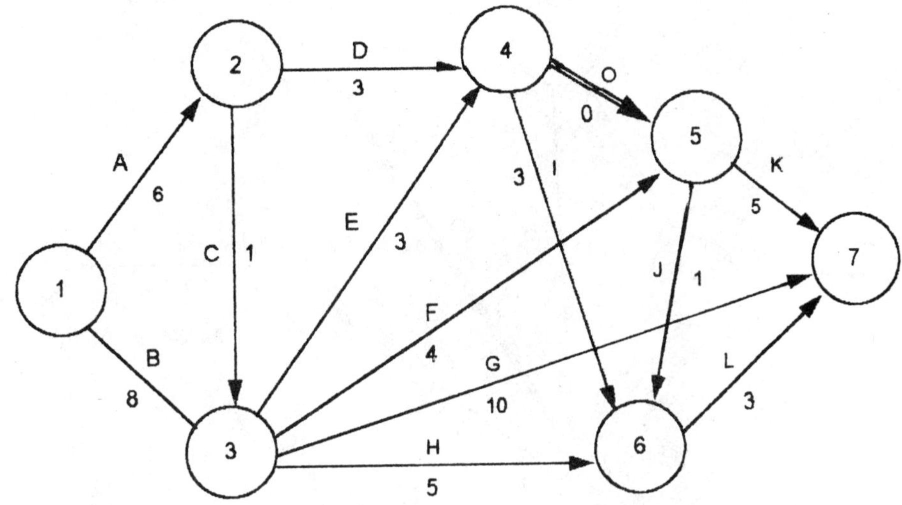

a) Prepare a table of the earliest and latest start and finish times and slack times for each activity in Bonanza's project.

b) What is the critical path and the expected project completion time?

c) Reliable Plumbers, the subcontractor performing activity J, is going to be delayed 5 weeks. If the project is delayed, it will cost Bonanza \$2000 per week of delay of the entire project. Reliable is charging \$3000 for the plumbing.

Bonanza has three options:
(1) Keep Reliable Plumbers.
(2) Cancel the contract with Reliable Plumbers and hire Local Plumbers, Inc. Local Plumbers, however, will take two weeks to do activity J, and will charge \$7000.
(3) Bonanza can train its own employees who are currently performing activity E to do the work. This involves a two-week training period as soon as activity E is done. Then it is expected it will take them three weeks to perform activity J. The cost of the training is \$800 per week and the cost of them doing activity J is \$1,000 per week.

Which alternative do you recommend to Bonanza? Explain.

PROBLEM 10

Consider the following PERT network with estimated times in weeks. The project is scheduled to begin on May 1.

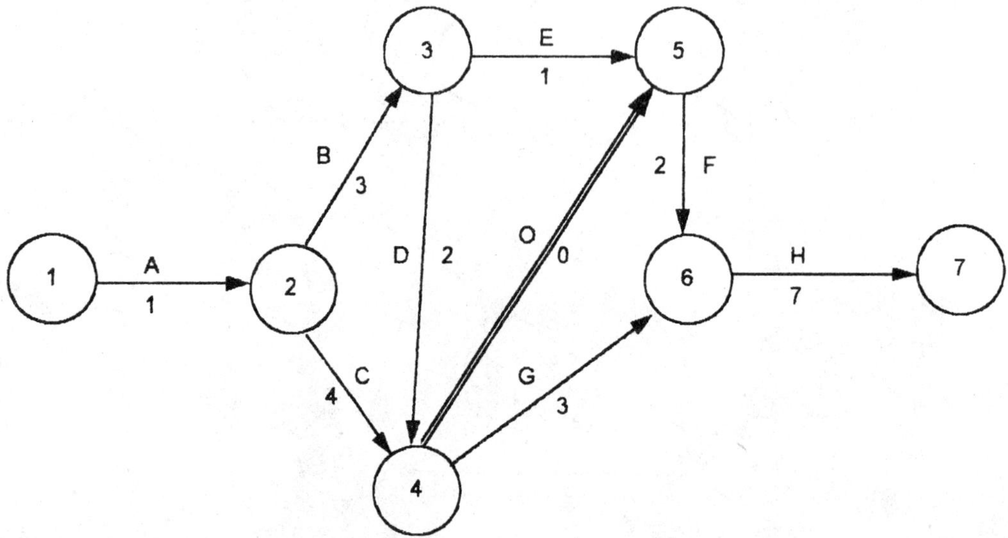

The three-time estimate approach was used to calculate the expected times (on the arcs) and the following table gives the variance for each activity:

Activity	Variance
A	1.1
B	.5
C	1.2
D	.8
E	.3
F	.6
G	.6
H	1.0

a) Give the expected project project completion date and the critical path.

b) By what date are you 99% sure the project will be completed?

c) The project has a target completion date of August 28 (17 weeks). If the project is completed by August 28, the profit on the project will be $10,000. If work is not completed by August 28, a $5,000 penalty will be incurred, reducing the project's profit to $5,000. For $2,000 more than is currently being spent for a firm to do activity H, a more experienced firm can complete the activity in just 5 weeks. Should this offer be accepted? (Assume the variance for H will not change.)

PROBLEM 11

Consider the following PERT network.

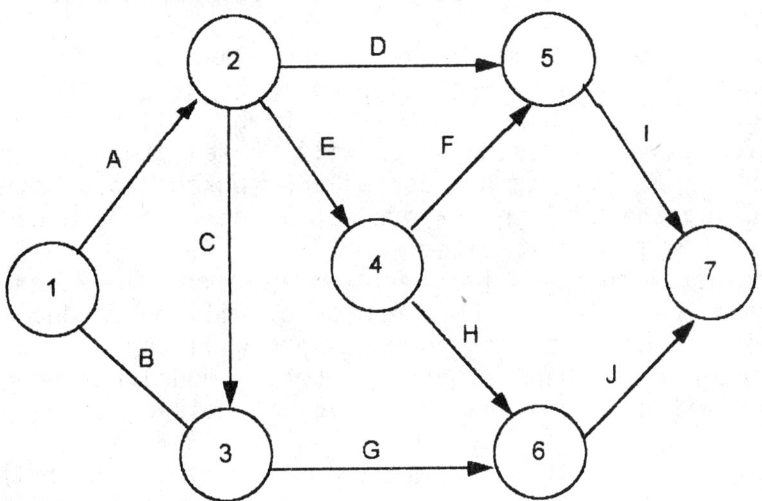

The following chart has been prepared giving the optimistic time (a), the most likely time (m), and the pessimistic time (b), in weeks for each activity.

Activity	a	m	b
A	2	8	14
B	3	12	21
C	2	5	8
D	4	5	12
E	1	3	17
F	2	3	10
G	3	9	15
H	7	8	9
I	3	11	13
J	7	10	13

a) Determine the critical path, expected project completion time, and standard deviation of the project completion time.

b) Management insists that the project be completed in 36 weeks and will be charged a $100,000 fine for any time overrun. If, at a cost of $3,000, the expected completion time of activity A could be reduced by 2 weeks, should the extra money be spent? (Assume A's variance does not change.)

c) Why is considering only critical path activities for project completion time not always a good assumption in probabilistic cases? (HINT: Consider activity E.)

PROBLEM 12

Plane, Inc. is a manufacturer of heavy equipment and is considering introducing a new line of small steamrollers. Development is to proceed as follows.

A feasibility study will first be performed. Upon receiving a successful feasibility report, a manufacturing building is to be secured and a project leader hired. Once the building is secured, Plane will be committed to the project. Therefore an advertising group will be selected and the raw materials for the manufacturing process will be purchased. When, in addition to securing the building, a project leader has been named, a manufacturing staff will be recruited.

After the manufacturing staff has been selected and the raw materials purchased, a prototype model of the steamroller will be produced. Following the completion of the prototype, work will begin on a production run of 100 steamrollers. When both the prototype model has been built and the advertising staff selected, an intensive advertising campaign will be launched.

The development phase of this project will be complete with the production of the first 100 steamrollers and the initiation of the advertising campaign.

Two separate costs analyses have been prepared. One is effective under current (normal) conditions, while the other is effective if the development phase of the activities is "crashed". These are summarized below. (Times are in weeks.)

	Normal		Crash	
Activity	Time	Cost	Time	Cost
Feasibility Study (A)	6	$ 80,000	5	$100,000
Building Purchased (B)	4	100,000	4	100,000
Project Leader Hired (C)	3	50,000	2	100,000
Advertising Staff Selected (D)	6	150,000	3	300,000
Materials Purchased (E)	3	180,000	2	250,000
Manufacturing Staff Hired (F)	10	300,000	7	480,000
Prototype Manufactured (G)	2	100,000	2	100,000
Production Run of 100 (H)	6	450,000	5	800,000
Advertising Campaign (I)	8	350,000	4	650,000

a) Draw the PERT network for this problem.

b) Write a linear program for determining the minimum cost of completing this project in half a year (=26 weeks).

c) What assumptions are made in calculating the "marginal" costs for the activities?

d) Interpret the meaning of the shadow price that would be associated with the constraint that set the maximum completion time to 26 weeks.

PROBLEM 13

Joseph King has ambitions to be mayor of Williston, North Dakota. Joe has determined the breakdown of the steps to the nomination and has estimated normal and crash costs and times for the campaign as follows (times are in weeks):

Activity	Normal Time	Normal Cost	Crash Time	Crash Cost	Immediate Predecessors
A. Solicit Volunteers	6	$5,000	2	$10,000	---
B. Initial "Free" Exposure	3	$4,000	3	$ 4,000	---
C. Raise Money	10	$4,000	6	$12,000	A
D. Organize and co-ordinate Schedule	4	$1,000	2	$ 2,000	A
E. Hire Advertising Firm	2	$1,500	1	$ 2,000	B
F. Arrange Major TV Interview	3	$4,000	1	$ 8,000	B
G. Advertising Campaign	5	$7,000	4	$12,000	C,E
H. Personal Campaigning	7	$8,000	5	$20,000	D,F

a) Joe King is not a wealthy man and would like to organize a four month (16 week) campaign at minimum cost. Write a linear program that, when solved, would accomplish this task.

b) Dan Wetzel is an independent who is also trying to make a bid to become mayor of Williston. He has promised a clean campaign, one that he will initially finance on his own. He has $50,000 to invest in his campaign. Being a student of recent successful political campaigns, he knows that his best chance to win is be a "fresh new face" at nomination time. Hence he wishes to keep the entire campaign from beginning to end at a minimum. Write a linear program that, when solved, will minimize the total time of the campaign while keeping expenditures to a maximum of $50,000.

PROBLEM 14

Consider the following PERT network:

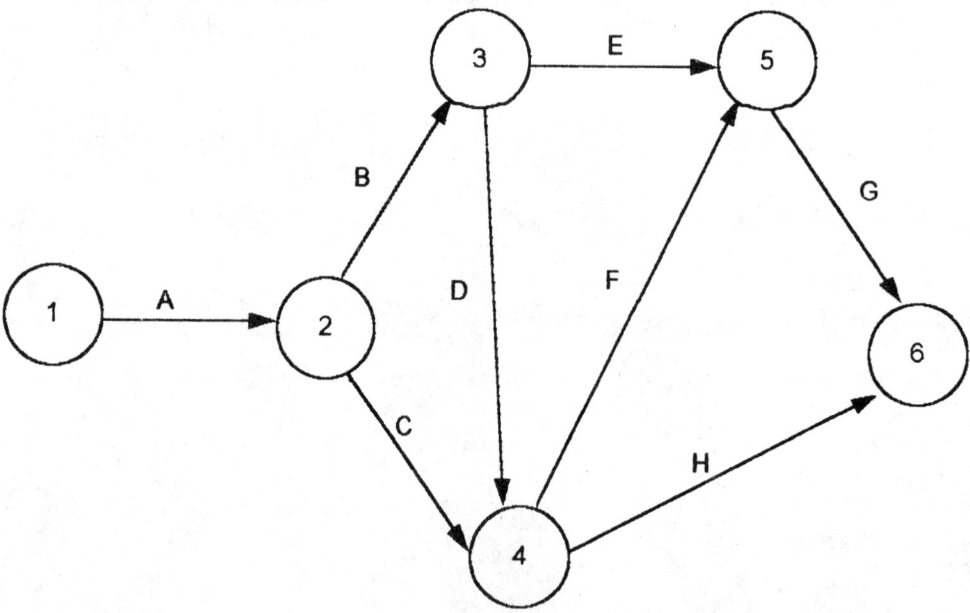

The estimated times (in weeks) and costs to do each activity are summarized below along with the actual status after 12 weeks.

Activity	Time	Expected Cost	Cost Through 12 Weeks	Percent Complete In 12 Weeks
A	4	$200	$200	100
B	3	$600	$525	100
C	4	$500	$480	100
D	2	$500	$515	100
E	5	$725	$600	60
F	2	$250	$130	50
G	5	$800	$ 0	0
H	6	$780	$400	50

a) Given the current status of the project, does it appear as if the project will be completed in its minimum expected time?

b) Is the project currently in a cost overrun or cost underrun posture?

c) What corrective action, if any, do you recommend? Should the project leader report to management that an overall cost overrun is inevitable?

TRUE/FALSE

15. The only purpose of dummy activities in PERT is to keep the precedence relations correct.

16. In PERT, it is assumed that the amount of time to complete any one activity is independent of the amount of time to complete any other activity in the project.

17. In PERT, an activity's most likely time is the same as its expected time.

18. In PERT, it is assumed that the underlying distribution for each activity in the three-time estimate approach is a normal distribution.

19. In a given PERT problem, activities F and G are on the critical path. If each is delayed two weeks, then in all cases, the project will be delayed four weeks.

20. The difference between an activity's earliest finish and latest finish equals the difference between its earliest start and latest start.

21. In a given PERT problem, activities F and G are not on the critical path and each has two weeks slack time. If both are delayed by two weeks each, then in all cases, the project will not be delayed.

22. An activity originating at a node can be started as soon as any one of the activities terminating at that node is finished.

23. In a given PERT problem, activity F is on the critical path. If its time is reduced by five weeks, then in all cases, the overall project completion time will be reduced by five weeks.

24. In PERT, the critical path is the path of longest distance through the network.

25. In CPM, the marginal cost per week's saving of an activity's completion time is valid only between its normal time and the time after maximum crashing.

26. It is possible to have more than one critical path at a time.

27. In CPM, if activity B's normal completion time is 8 weeks and normal cost is $10,000, and its completion time after maximum crashing is 5 weeks at a cost of $15,000, then the assumption is that if $13,000 is spent on activity B, its completion time is 6.8 weeks.

28. Work package G is 80% completed and it has been budgeted for $50,000. To date $45,000 has been expended on this work package. Work package G is in a cost underrun situation.

29. A critical activity can be part of a noncritical path.

Chapter 14
Inventory Management: Independent Demand

KEY CONCEPTS

CONCEPT	ILLUSTRATED PROBLEMS	ANSWERED PROBLEMS
Economic Order Quantity Model	1	9,10,13,18
Economic Production Lot Size Model	2	10,11,18,19
Planned Shortage Model	3	12,13,20
Quantity Discount Model	4	14,24,25
EOQ Model With Stochastic Demand	5	15,26
Reorder Point Based on Service Level	5	15,21,26
Single Period Inventory Model:		
Normal Demand Distribution	6	16,22
Uniform Demand Distribution	8	23
Periodic Review Systems	7	17,27

REVIEW

1. The study of inventory models is concerned with two basic questions: (1) how much should be ordered each time, and (2) when should the reordering occur. The objective is to minimize total variable cost over a specified time period (assumed to be annual in the following review).

2. Potential variable costs include:
   (1) Ordering cost -- salaries and expenses of processing an order, regardless of the order quantity
   (2) Holding cost -- usually a percentage of the value of the item assessed for keeping an item in inventory (including finance costs, insurance, security costs, taxes, warehouse overhead, and other related variable expenses)
   (3) Backorder cost -- costs associated with being out of stock when an item is demanded (including lost goodwill)
   (4) Purchase cost -- the actual price of the items
   (5) Other Costs

3. The simplest inventory models assume demand and the other parameters of the problem to be deterministic and constant. The deterministic models covered in this chapter are: a) economic order quantity (EOQ), b) economic production lot size, c) EOQ with planned shortages, and d) EOQ with quantity discounts.

4. The most basic of the deterministic inventory models is the economic order quantity (EOQ). The variable costs in this model are annual holding cost and annual ordering cost. For the EOQ, these two costs are equal.

5. The economic production lot size model is a variation of the basic EOQ model. A replenishment order is not received in one lump sum as it is in the basic EOQ model. Instead, inventory is replenished gradually as the order is produced (which requires the production rate to be greater than the demand rate). This model's variable costs are annual holding cost and annual set-up cost (equivalent to ordering cost). For the optimal lot size, these two costs are equal.

6. A stockout (or shortage) is a demand that cannot be immediately satisfied. A backorder is a stockout in which the customer waits until the next replenishment order arrives and then the demand is satisfied.

7. With the EOQ with planned shortages model, a replenishment order does not arrive at or before the inventory position drops to zero. Instead, shortages occur until a predetermined backorder quantity is reached, at which time the replenishment order arrives. The variable costs in this model are annual holding, backorder, and ordering. For the optimal order and backorder quantity combination, the sum of the annual holding and backordering costs equals the annual ordering cost

8. The EOQ with quantity discounts model is applicable where a supplier offers a lower purchase cost when an item is ordered in larger quantities. This model's variable costs are annual holding, ordering and purchase costs.

9. EOQ-based inventory models give results that are rather insensitive to changes in the parameters. Small and sometimes even moderate changes in costs, demands, etc. will have only minor effects on overall total costs.

10. The decision maker must determine if a set of assumptions is appropriate for his particular problem. If the assumptions are approximately correct, employing them will simplify the solution procedure, but the results should only be used as guidelines for an inventory policy.

11. There may be reasons, not built into the model, for modifying the results of a model (such as rounding a reorder time from 12.8 days to 2 weeks to simplify reordering and make bookkeeping control easier).

12. In many cases demand (or some other factor) is not known with a high degree of certainty and a probabilistic inventory model should actually be used. These models tend to be more complex than deterministic models. The probabilistic models covered in this chapter are: a) single-period order quantity, b) reorder-point quantity, and c) periodic-review order quantity.

13. A single-period order quantity model (sometimes called the newsboy problem) deals with a situation in which only one order is placed for the item and the demand is probabilistic. If the period's demand exceeds the order quantity, the demand is not backordered and revenue (profit) will be lost. If demand is less than the order quantity, the surplus stock is sold at the end of the period (usually for less than the original purchase price).

14. A firm's inventory position consists of the on-hand inventory plus on-order inventory (all amounts previously ordered but not yet received). An inventory item is reordered when the item's inventory position reaches a predetermined value, referred to as the reorder point.

15. The <u>reorder point</u> represents the quantity available to meet demand during lead time. <u>Lead time</u> is the time span starting when the replenishment order is placed and ending when the order arrives.

16. Under deterministic conditions, when both demand and lead time are constant, the reorder point associated with EOQ-based models is relatively simple to determine. The reorder point is set equal to <u>lead time demand</u>.

17. Under probabilistic conditions, when demand and/or lead time varies, the reorder point often includes safety stock. <u>Safety stock</u> is the amount by which the reorder point exceeds the expected (average) lead time demand.

18. The amount of safety stock in a reorder point determines the odds (chance) of a stockout during lead time. The complement of this chance is called the service level. <u>Service level</u>, in this context, is defined as the probability of not incurring a stockout during any one lead time. Also, it is the long-run proportion of lead times in which no stockouts occur.

19. A <u>periodic review system</u> is one in which the inventory level is checked and reordering is done only at specified points in time (at fixed intervals usually). Assuming the demand rate varies, the order quantity will vary from one review period to another. This is in contrast to the <u>continuous review system</u> in which inventory is monitored continuously and an order (of a fixed amount) can be placed whenever the reorder point is reached.

20. At the time a <u>periodic-review order quantity</u> is being decided, the concern is that the on-hand inventory and the quantity being ordered is enough to satisfy demand from the time this order is placed until the next order is received (not placed).

DETERMINISTIC INVENTORY MODELS -- ASSUMPTIONS/RESULTS

I. ECONOMIC ORDER QUANTITY (EOQ)

Assumptions

1. Demand is constant throughout the year at D items per year.
2. Ordering cost: $\$C_o$ per order.
3. Holding cost: $\$C_h$ per item in inventory per year.
4. Purchase cost per unit is constant (no quantity discount).
5. Delivery time (lead time) is constant.
6. Planned shortages are not permitted.

Results

1. Optimal order quantity: $Q^* = \sqrt{2DC_o/C_h}$

2. Number of orders per year: D/Q^*

3. Time between orders (cycle time): Q^*/D years

4. Total annual cost: $[(1/2)Q^*C_h] + [DC_o/Q^*]$
   (holding + ordering)

II. ECONOMIC PRODUCTION LOT SIZE

Assumptions

1. Demand occurs at a constant rate of D items per year.
2. Production rate is P items per year (and $P>D$).
3. Set-up cost: $\$C_o$ per run.
4. Holding cost: $\$C_h$ per item in inventory per year.
5. Purchase cost per unit is constant (no quantity discount).
6. Set-up time (lead time) is constant.
7. Planned shortages are not permitted.

Results

1. Optimal production lot-size: $Q^* = \sqrt{2DC_o/[(1-D/P)C_h]}$

2. Number of production runs per year: D/Q^*

3. Time between set-ups (cycle time): Q^*/D years

4. Total annual cost: $[(1/2)(1-D/P)Q^*C_h] + [DC_o/Q^*]$
   (holding + ordering)

III. PLANNED-SHORTAGE ORDER QUANTITY

Assumptions

1. Demand occurs at a constant rate of D items per year.
2. Ordering cost: $\$C_o$ per order.
3. Holding cost: $\$C_h$ per item in inventory per year.
4. Backorder cost: $\$C_b$ per item backordered per year.
5. Purchase cost per unit is constant (no quantity discount).
6. Set-up time (lead time) is constant.
7. Planned shortages are permitted (backordered demand units are withdrawn from a replenishment order when it is delivered).

Results

1. Optimal order quantity: $Q^* = \sqrt{2DC_o/C_h}\ \sqrt{(C_h+C_b)/C_b}$
2. Maximum number of backorders: $S^* = Q^*(C_h/(C_h+C_b))$
3. Number of orders per year: D/Q^*
4. Time between orders (cycle time): Q^*/D years
5. Total annual cost: $[C_h(Q^*-S^*)^2/2Q^*] + [DC_o/Q^*] + [S^{*2}C_b/2Q^*]$
   (holding + ordering + backordering)

IV. QUANTITY-DISCOUNT ORDER QUANTITY

Assumptions

1. Demand occurs at a constant rate of D items per year.
2. Ordering Cost: $\$C_o$ per order.
3. Holding Cost: $\$C_h = \$C_iI$ per item in inventory per year (note holding cost is based on the cost of the item, C_i).
4. Purchase Cost: $\$C_1$ per item if the quantity ordered is between 0 and X_1, $\$C_2$ if the order quantity is between X_1 and X_2, etc.
5. Delivery time (lead time) is constant.
6. Planned shortages are not permitted.

Results

1. Optimal order quantity: use procedure on the next page to determine Q^*
2. Number of orders per year: D/Q^*
3. Time between orders (cycle time): Q^*/D years
4. Total annual cost: $[(1/2)Q^*C_h] + [DC_o/Q^*] + DC$
   (holding + ordering + purchase)

FLOW CHART OF QUANTITY DISCOUNT PROCEDURE

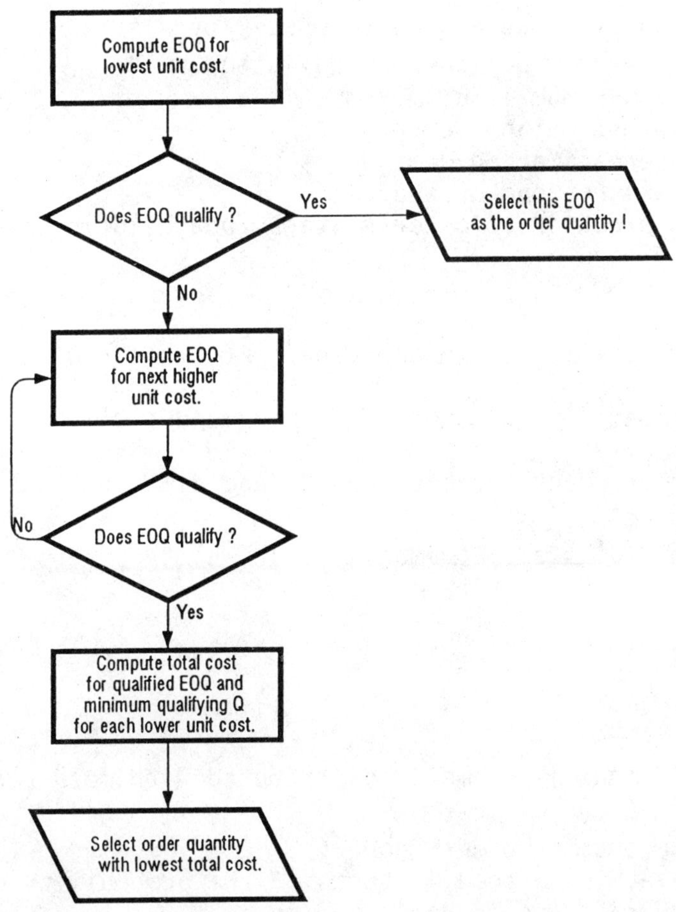
Compute EOQ for lowest unit cost.
Does EOQ qualify ?
Yes
Select this EOQ as the order quantity !
No
Compute EOQ for next higher unit cost.
No
Does EOQ qualify ?
Yes
Compute total cost for qualified EOQ and minimum qualifying Q for each lower unit cost.
Select order quantity with lowest total cost.

PROBABILISTIC INVENTORY MODELS -- ASSUMPTIONS/RESULTS

I. SINGLE-PERIOD ORDER QUANTITY

Assumptions

1. Period demand follows a known probability distribution.
   a. normal: mean is μ, standard deviation is σ
   b. uniform: minimum is a, maximum is b
2. Cost of overestimating demand: $\$c_o$
3. Cost of underestimating demand: $\$c_u$
4. Shortages are not backordered.
5. Period-end stock is sold for salvage (not held in inventory).

Results

1. Optimal probability of no shortage: $P(\text{demand} \leq Q^*) = c_u/(c_u+c_o)$
2. Optimal probability of shortage: $P(\text{demand} > Q^*) = 1 - c_u/(c_u+c_o)$
3. Optimal order quantity, based on demand distribution --
   a) normal: $Q^* = \mu + z\sigma$
   b) uniform: $Q^* = a + P(\text{demand} \leq Q^*)(b-a)$

II. REORDER POINT

Assumptions

1. Lead-time demand is normally distributed with mean μ and standard deviation σ.
2. Approximate optimal order quantity: EOQ
3. Service level is defined in terms of the probability of no stockouts during lead time and is reflected in z.
4. Shortages are not backordered.
5. Inventory position is reviewed continuously.

Results

1. Reorder point: $r = \mu + z\sigma$
2. Safety stock: $z\sigma$
3. Average inventory: $1/2(Q) + z\sigma$
4. Total annual cost: $[(1/2)Q^*C_h] + [z\sigma C_h] + [DC_o/Q^*]$
   (holding(normal) + holding(safety) + ordering)

III. PERIODIC-REVIEW ORDER QUANTITY

Assumptions

1. Inventory position is reviewed at constant intervals (periods).
2. Demand during review period plus lead time period is normally distributed with mean μ and standard deviation σ.
3. Service level is defined in terms of the probability of no stockouts during a review period and is reflected in z.
4. On-hand inventory at ordering time: I
5. Shortages are not backordered.
6. Lead time is less than the length of the review period.

Results

1. Replenishment level: $M = \mu + z\sigma$
2. Order quantity: $Q = M - I$

ILLUSTRATED PROBLEMS

PROBLEM 1

Bart's Barometer Business (BBB) is a retail outlet which deals exclusively with weather equipment. Currently BBB is trying to decide on an inventory and reorder policy for home barometers.

These cost BBB $50 each and demand is about 500 per year distributed fairly evenly throughout the year. Reordering costs are $80 per order and holding costs are figured at 20% of the cost of the item. BBB is open 300 days a year (6 days a week and closed two weeks in August). Lead time is 60 working days.

a) Develop a total variable cost model for this system.

b) What is the optimal reorder quantity and reorder point?

c) How many times per year would BBB reorder?

d) What total annual variable cost does the model give?

e) Given your answer to (b) and (c), choose a more convenient order quantity. Compare the resulting total cost with (d) and comment.

SOLUTION 1

a) Total Costs = (Holding Cost) + (Ordering Cost) $= [C_h(Q/2)] + [C_o(D/Q)]$
$TC = [.2(50)(Q/2)] + [80(500/Q)] = 5Q + (40{,}000/Q)$

b) $Q^* = \sqrt{2DC_o/C_h} = \sqrt{2(500)(80)/10} = 89.44 \approx 90$

Lead time is m = 60 days, and daily demand is d = 500/300 or 1.667. Thus the reorder point r = (1.667)(60) = 100. Bart should reorder 90 barometers when his inventory position reaches 100, i.e. 10 on hand and one outstanding order.

c) Number of reorder times per year = (500/90) = 5.56 or once every (300/5.56) = 54 working days -- about every 9 weeks.

d) TC = 5(90) + (40,000/90) = 450 + 444 = $894.

e) It might be more convenient to order 100 at a time and order 5 times per year (every 10 weeks). This total cost is TC = 5(100) + (40,000/100) = 500 + 400 = $900. This $6 difference represents only a 0.6% change in total cost.

PROBLEM 2

Non-Slip Tile Company (NST) has been using production runs of 100,000 tiles, 10 times per year to meet the demand of 1,000,000 tiles annually. The set-up cost is $5,000 per run and holding cost is estimated at 10% of the manufacturing cost of $1 per tile. The production capacity of the machine is 500,000 tiles per month. The factory is open 365 days per year.

a) Develop a model for the total annual variable cost for this problem.

b) What production schedule do you recommend?

c) How much is NST losing annually with their present production schedule?

d) How long is the machine idle between production runs?

e) What is the maximum number of tiles in inventory under the current policy? under the optimal policy?

f) What fraction of time is the machine producing tiles?

SOLUTION 2

This is an economic production lot size problem with $D = 1{,}000{,}000$, $P = 6{,}000{,}000$, $C_h = .10$, $C_o = 5{,}000$.

a) $TC = (\text{Holding Costs}) + (\text{Set-Up Costs})$
$= [C_h(Q/2)(1 - D/P)] + [DC_o/Q] = .04167Q + 5{,}000{,}000{,}000/Q$

b) $Q^* = \sqrt{2DC_o/[C_h(1-D/P)]} = \sqrt{2(1{,}000{,}000)(5{,}000)/[.1(1-1/6)]} = 346{,}410$

The number of runs per year = D/Q^* = 2.89 times per year

c) Optimal TC = .04167(346,410) + 5,000,000,000/346,410 = $28,868
Current TC = .04167(100,000) + 5,000,000,000/100,000 = $54,167
Difference = 54,167 - 28,868 = $25,299

d) There are 2.89 cycles per year, so each cycle lasts (365/2.89) = 126.3 days. The time to produce 346,410 per run = 346,410/6,000,000)365 = 21.1 days. The machine is idle 126.3 - 21.1 = 105.2 days between runs.

e) Current maximum inventory = $(1-D/P)Q^*$ = (1-1/6)100,000 = 83,333.
Optimal maximum inventory = (1-1/6)346,410 = 288,675.

f) The machine is producing tiles D/P = 1/6 of the time.

PROBLEM 3

Hervis Rent-a-Car has a fleet of 2,500 Rockets serving the Los Angeles area. All Rockets are maintained at a central garage. On the average, eight Rockets per month require a new engine. Engines cost \$850 each. There is also a \$120 order cost (independent of the number of engines ordered).

Hervis has an annual holding cost rate of 30% on engines. It takes two weeks to obtain the engines after they are ordered. For each week a car is out of service, Hervis loses \$40 profit.

a) Determine Hervis' optimal order policy for engines.

b) How many days after receiving an order does Hervis run out of engines? How long is Hervis without any engines per cycle?

SOLUTION 3

This can be modeled as a planned shortage model with the following annual data: $D = 8 \times 12 = 96$; $C_o = \$120$; $C_h = .30(850) = \$255$; $C_b = 40 \times 52 = 2080$.

a) $Q^* = \sqrt{2DC_o/C_h}\ \sqrt{(C_h+C_b)/C_b} = \sqrt{2(96)(120)/255}\ \sqrt{(255+2080)/2080} = 10.07 \approx 10$

$S^* = Q^*(C_h/(C_h+C_b)) = 10(255/(255+2080)) = 1.09 \approx 1$

Demand is 8 per month or 2 per week. Since lead time is 2 weeks, lead time demand is 4. Thus, since the optimal policy is to order 10 to arrive when there is one backorder, the order should be placed when there are 3 engines remaining in inventory.

b) Inventory exists for $C_b/(C_b+C_h) = 2080/(255+2080) = .8908$ of the order cycle. (Note, $(Q^*-S^*)/Q^* = .8908$ also, before Q^* and S^* are rounded.) An order cycle is $Q^*/D = .1049$ years = 38.3 days. Thus, Hervis runs out of engines .8908(38.3) = 34 days after receiving an order. Hervis is out of stock for approximately 38 - 34 = 4 days.

PROBLEM 4

Nick's Camera Shop carries Zodiac instant print film. The film normally costs Nick \$3.20 per roll, and he sells it for \$5.25. Zodiac film has a shelf life of 18 months. Nick's average sales are 21 rolls per week. His annual inventory holding cost rate is 25% and it costs Nick \$20 to place an order with Zodiac.

If Zodiac offers a 7% discount on orders of 400 rolls or more, a 10% discount for 900 rolls or more, and a 15% discount for 2000 rolls or more, determine Nick's optimal order quantity.

SOLUTION 4

This can be modeled as a quantity discount problem with the following annual data: $D = 21(52) = 1092$; $C_h = .25(C_i)$; $C_o = 20$.

For each unit-price, starting with the lowest and working up, determine the most economical, feasible order quantity.

For $C_4 = .85(3.20) = \$2.72$:

To receive a 15% discount Nick must order at least 2,000 rolls. Unfortunately, the film's shelf life is 18 months. The demand in 18 months (78 weeks) is 78 X 21 = 1638 rolls of film, if he ordered 2,000 rolls he would have to scrap 372 of them. This would cost more than the 15% discount would save.

For $C_3 = .90(3.20) = \$2.88$:

$$Q_3^* = \sqrt{2DC_o/C_h} = \sqrt{2(1092)(20)/[.25(2.88)]} = 246.31 \text{ (not feasible)}$$

The most economical, feasible quantity for C_3 is $Q_3^* = 900$.

For $C_2 = .93(3.20) = \$2.976$:

$$Q_2^* = \sqrt{2DC_o/C_h} = \sqrt{2(1092)(20)/[.25(2.976)]} = 242.30 \text{ (not feasible)}$$

The most economical, feasible quantity for C_2 is $Q_2^* = 400$.

For $C_1 = 1.00(3.20) = \$3.20$ (no discount):

$$Q_1^* = \sqrt{2DC_o/C_h} = \sqrt{2(1092)(20)} = 233.67 \approx 234$$ (feasible, so we stop computing Qs. In this problem we have no more Qs anyway.)

Compute the total cost for the most economical, feasible order quantity in each price category for which a Q^* was computed.

$$TC_i = (1/2)(Q_i^* C_h) + (DC_o/Q_i^*) + DC_i$$

$$TC_3 = (1/2)(900)(.720) + ((1092)(20)/900) + (1092)(2.880) = \$3493$$
$$TC_2 = (1/2)(400)(.744) + ((1092)(20)/400) + (1092)(2.976) = \$3453$$
$$TC_1 = (1/2)(234)(.800) + ((1092)(20)/234) + (1092)(3.200) = \$3681$$

Comparing the total costs for 234, 400 and 900, the lowest total annual cost is \$3453. Nick should order 400 rolls at a time.

PROBLEM 5

Robert's Drugs is a drug wholesaler supplying 55 independent drug stores. Roberts wishes to determine an optimal inventory policy for Comfort brand headache remedy. Sales of Comfort are relatively constant as the past 10 weeks of data indicate:

Week	Sales (cases)	Week	Sales (cases)
1	110	6	120
2	115	7	130
3	125	8	115
4	120	9	110
5	125	10	130

a) Each case of Comfort costs Roberts $10 and Roberts uses a 14% annual holding cost rate for its inventory. If the cost to prepare a purchase order for Comfort is $12, determine the optimal inventory ordering quantity for Comfort.

b) The lead time for a delivery of Comfort has averaged four working days. Lead time has therefore been estimated as having a normal distribution with a mean of 80 cases and a standard deviation of 10 cases. Roberts wants at most a 2% probability of selling out of Comfort during this lead time. What should be Roberts' reorder point?

c) On the basis of parts (a) and (b) determine the total annual inventory cost for Comfort.

SOLUTION 5

a) The average sales over the 10 week period is 120 cases. Hence $D = 120 \times 52 = 6{,}240$ cases per year; $C_h = (.14)(10) = 1.40$; $C_o = 12$.

$$Q^* = \sqrt{2DCo/Ch} = \sqrt{2(6240)(12)/1.40} = 327$$

b) Lead time demand is normally distributed with $\mu = 80$, $\sigma = 10$. Since Roberts wants at most a 2% probability of selling out of Comfort, the corresponding z value (see Appendix C) is 2.06. That is, $P(z > 2.06) = .0197$ (about .02). Roberts should reorder Comfort when supply reaches $\mu + z\sigma = 80 + 2.06(10) = 101$ cases. The safety stock is 21 cases.

c) The total annual cost of this solution is:

Ordering: $(DC_o/Q^*) = ((6240)(12)/327)$	=	$229
Holding--Normal: $(1/2)Q^*C_o = (1/2)(327)(1.40)$	=	$229
Holding--Safety Stock: $C_h(21) = (1.40)(21)$	=	$ 29
Total	=	$487

PROBLEM 6

The publishers of the Fast Food Restaurant Menu Book wish to determine how many copies to print. There is a fixed cost of $5,000 to produce the book and the incremental profit per copy is $.45. Sales for this edition are estimated to be normally distributed. The most likely sales volume is 12,000 copies and they believe there is a 5% chance that sales will exceed 20,000.

a) If any unsold copies of the book can be sold at salvage at a $.55 loss, how many copies should be printed?

b) If any unsold copies of the book can be sold at salvage at a $.65 loss, how many copies should be printed? Comment.

SOLUTION 6

a) μ = 12,000. To find σ note that z = 1.65 corresponds to a 5% tail probability. Therefore, (20,000 - 12,000) = 1.65σ or σ = 4848.

Using incremental analysis with C_o = .55 and C_u = .45, $(C_u/(C_u+C_o))$ = .45/(.45+.55) = .45.

Find Q^* such that $P(D \leq Q^*)$ = .45. From Appendix C, z = -.12 gives this probability. Thus, Q^* = 12,000 - .12(4848) = 11,418 books.

b) Using incremental analysis as above but with C_o = .65, $(C_u/(C_u+C_o))$ = .45/(.45 + .65) = .4091.

Find Q^* such that $P(D \leq Q^*)$ = .4091. From Appendix C, z = -.23 gives this probability. Thus, Q^* = 12,000 - .23(4848) = 10,885 books.

However, since this is less than the breakeven volume of 11,111 books (= 5000/.45), no copies should be printed because if the company produced only 10,885 copies it will not recoup its $5,000 fixed cost of producing the book.

NOTE: A common mistake is thinking that the probability of having a stockout in some period is equivalent to the portion of the period's demand that will be backordered or lost, when demand is stochastic. A .10 stockout probability does NOT mean that ninety percent of demand will be satisfied. This point applies to all of the stochastic models in this chapter.

PROBLEM 7

Joe Walsh is a salesman for the Ace Brush Company. Every three weeks he contacts Dollar Department Store so that they may place an order to replenish their stock.

Weekly demand for Ace brushes at Dollar approximately follows a normal distribution with a mean of 60 brushes and a standard deviation of 9 brushes. Once Joe submits an order, the lead time until Dollar receives the brushes is one week.

Dollar would like at most a 2% chance of running out of stock during any replenishment period. If Dollar has 75 brushes in stock when Joe contacts them, how many should they order?

SOLUTION 7

This can be modeled as a periodic review problem with probabilistic demand. The review period plus the following lead time totals 4 weeks. This is the amount of time that will elapse before the next brush shipment arrives.

Weekly demand is normally distributed with:

Mean weekly demand, μ	$= 60$
Weekly standard deviation, σ	$= 9$
Weekly variance, σ^2	$= 81$

Thus the distribution of demand for 4 weeks is normal with:

Mean demand over 4 weeks, μ	$= 4\text{x}60 = 240$
Variance of demand over 4 weeks, σ^2	$= 4\text{x}81 = 324$
Standard deviation over 4 weeks, σ	$= (324)^{\frac{1}{2}} = 18$

The replenishment level, M, is given by the formula $M = \mu + z\sigma$, where z is determined by the desired stockout probability. For a 2% stockout probability (2% tail area in Appendix C), $z = 2.05$. Thus, $M = 240 + 05(18) = 277$.

As the store currently has 75 brushes in stock, Dollar should order:
$277 - 75 =$ 202 brushes from Joe. The safety stock is $z\sigma = (2.05)(18) = 37$ brushes.

NOTE: The standard deviation (SD) of the "whole" does NOT equal the sum of the SDs of the "parts". For example, if the SD of daily demand equals 10, the SD of two-day demand does NOT equal 20.

However, the variance (VAR) of the "whole" does equal the sum of the VARs of the "parts". So, for this example, the VAR of two-day demand is 200 and the SD of two-day demand equals $\sqrt{200} = 14.14$ or $\sqrt{2}$ days(10) $= 14.14$.

PROBLEM 8

Mark Hall manages a small greeting card shop that sells artificial Christmas trees during the six weeks prior to Christmas. Based on past experience and current circumstances, Mark estimates that he will sell somewhere between 20 and 80 trees and that the actual number is equally likely to fall anywhere in that range.

A tree costs Mark \$28.00 and he sells it for \$46.00. Due to very limited storage space, Mark is forced to sell any trees that remain after Christmas at half price (\$23.00).

a) What is the optimal probability of stocking out (having more demand than supply)?

b) How many trees should Mark order?

c) Based on your order quantity in (b), what is the probability that Mark will have ten or more trees to sell at a discount after Christmas?

SOLUTION 8

This can be modeled as a single-period problem with uniform demand. The demand limits are a = 20 and b = 80. $C_u = 46 - 28 = \$18$; $C_o = 28 - 23 = \$5$.

a) Using incremental analysis, the optimal probability of NOT running out of stock is:

$$P(D \leq Q^*) = C_u/(C_u+C_o) = 18/(18+5) = .7826$$

Thus, the optimal probability of stocking out is:

$$P(D > Q^*) = 1 - P(D \leq Q^*) = 1 - .7826 = .2174$$

b) The optimal order quantity is:

$$Q^* = a + P(D \leq Q^*)(b-a) = 20 + .7826(80-20) = 20 + 46.956 = 67 \text{ trees.}$$

c) If Mark orders 67 trees and later is left with ten or more of them, demand would have to be less than or equal to 57 trees. The probability of this is:

$$P(D \leq 57) = (57-a)/(b-a) = (57-20)/(80-20) = 37/60 = .6167 \approx .62$$

ANSWERED PROBLEMS

PROBLEM 9

Terri's Tie Shop (TTS) is the exclusive retail outlet for Trophy Ties. Although Trophy Tie demand was slightly higher in December (Christmas) and June (Father's Day), it was relatively constant throughout last year:

Month	Demand	Month	Demand	Month	Demand
Jan	75	May	69	Sep	74
Feb	70	Jun	85	Oct	70
Mar	72	Jul	68	Nov	76
Apr	76	Aug	75	Dec	90

The average cost of a Trophy Tie is $4 to TTS. TTS figures inventory costs at 15% yearly and reorder costs are $25 per order. There is no reason to assume demand will change much this year.

a) What is the average monthly demand?

b) Assume demand is constant throughout the year and the lead time is two months. Determine an optimal inventory policy for the model.

c) What is the total annual variable costs of the model?

d) Make some suggestions to modify the inventory policy of the model to fit the "real" problem. Comment.

PROBLEM 10

One decision faced by many manufacturing firms is whether to make or buy a particular component of the manufacturing process. Harrison Sound Corporation manufactures stereo systems. The company has a choice of either manufacturing the digital display unit for the Model 243 receiver themselves or purchasing the unit from Allied Electronics.

Allied will charge Harrison $7.50 per unit and Harrison estimates the cost of placing an order with Allied at $48.

On the other hand, if Harrison manufactures the units themselves, there will be a set-up cost for production of $1,600, an annual production rate of 50,000 units a year is possible, and the per unit production cost will be $7.00 (in addition to the set-up cost).

a) If Harrison expects the annual demand for these display units to be about 10,000, and the holding cost rate is 20%, determine the total annual variable costs of both policies.

b) Which policy would you recommend to management? Why?

PROBLEM 11

National Business Machines (NBM) is trying to develop the effective use of one of its production lines which produces transistors for circuits of computers. In general, allowing for defectives, NBM needs 1,000,000 transistors per year for their NBM 470 series.

A production rate of 3,000,000 per year is possible if the production line were in continuous operation 24 hours a day, 365 days a year. The cost of storing a transistor is $1 per year. Production set-up costs $4,000 and takes two weeks.

a) What is the optimal number of transistors NBM should make per production run?

b) What will be the number of production runs per year?

c) What is the duration of a production run?

d) If workers have (and must take) vacation between the end of one production run and the start-up of another, how much vacation time do they get per year? (Note they participate in the set-up).

PROBLEM 12

Andy's Auto Parts has been stocking an unusually fine grade of racing oil on which it makes a $.10 per quart profit. Demand has been 2,000 quarts per week. Storage costs are $.01 per quart per week. Reorder costs are $10 per order. If Andy allows backorders, he figures his demand will drop to 1,900 quarts per week. Andy will, however, give a $.03 per week discount per can backordered.

a) Derive an optimal inventory policy for Andy.

b) Based on your answer in (a), what is the maximum time a backordered customer would have to wait?

PROBLEM 13

Wiley's TV Town sells Apex large screen TV's. Weekly demand has averaged 20 Apex TV's per week. Wiley makes a gross profit of $50 per TV sold (not including inventory costs). Holding costs are $260 per TV per year and reorder costs are $32 per order. Lead time is 1 week.

a) Determine: (1) the optimal number of TV's Wiley should order; (2) his reorder point; and, (3) his yearly net profit.

b) Wiley is considering allowing backorders. Wiley intends to offer customers a discount of $20 per week for each week the customer must wait for his TV. Wiley estimates that this policy will result in a drop in demand to 19 TV's per week. Order and holding costs will remain the same. Should Wiley adopt this policy? Why or why not?

PROBLEM 14

Rosato's Pizza Parlor uses tomato sauce at a fairly constant rate of 3600 cans per year. It costs Rosato $40 to place an order for tomato sauce. The holding cost rate is 30 percent per can per year.

Shipping cost, based on weight, must be paid by Rosato and a can of tomato paste weighs 15 pounds. Both the shipping cost and the purchase cost depend on the order quantity. Using the information below, determine the most economical number of cans to order at one time. (Hint: Start by converting the shipping cost discount schedule from pounds to cans.)

Shipping Cost		Purchase Cost	
Pounds	Cost/Pound	Quantity	Cost/Can
1 - 1799	$0.26	1 - 149	$17.80
1800 - 4499	0.23	150 - 349	17.50
4500 or more	0.20	350 or more	17.40

NOTE: A common mistake is to think that the EOQ equation (square-root equation) ALWAYS determines the optimal order quantity. This is not true for quantity discount problems. Recall that an optimal solution must be a feasible solution. With quantity discounts, an EOQ-derived order quantity must be checked to see if it is feasible (falls in the required range).

PROBLEM 15

Kelly's Service Station does a large business in tune-ups. Demand has been averaging 210 spark plugs per week. Holding costs are $.01 per plug per week and reorder costs are estimated at $10 per order.

Kelly does not want to be out of stock on more than 1% of his orders. There is a one day delivery time. The standard deviation of demand is five plugs per day. Assume a normal distribution of demand during lead time and a 7-day work week.

a) What inventory policy do you suggest for Kelly's station?

b) What is the average amount of safety stock for the reorder point in (a)?

c) What are the total variable weekly costs including safety stock costs?

PROBLEM 16

Winkies Donuts is a small chain of donut shops in Lemon County. Winkies' success is built largely around its jelly donut. Recently, Winkies management has received a number of complaints concerning store #17 running out of jelly donuts late in the afternoon. Thus, Winkies has undertaken a study of the store's operations. The study has indicated the following:

(1) Afternoon demand for jelly donuts is approximately normally distributed with mean 150 and standard deviation 30 donuts.
(2) The cost to manufacture a jelly donut is $.09.
(3) The selling price is $.20.
(4) Donuts unsold at the end of the day are given to a charity which gives Winkies a tax savings of $.03 per donut.

Winkies management feels there is a goodwill loss of $.75 for each sale lost when it is out of stock of jelly donuts. Based on this information, how many jelly donuts should the baker prepare for the afternoon?

PROBLEM 17

A lawn and garden shop that is open for business seven days a week orders bags of grass seed every OTHER Monday. Lead time for seed orders is 5 days. On Monday, at ordering time, a clerk found 112 bags of seed in stock, and so he ordered 198 bags. Daily demand for grass seed is normally distributed with a mean of 15 bags and a standard deviation of four bags.

The manager would like to know what the probability is that a grass seed stockout will occur before the NEXT order arrives.

PROBLEM 18

Zak's Zippers is contemplating manufacturing their own zippers rather than distributing the zippers it receives from ZZZ, Inc. Zak's figures it must sell the zipper at the same price or else the yearly demand of 4,000 dozen zippers will be greatly affected.

Presently the purchase cost per dozen zippers is $10, whereas the proposed manufacturing cost for labor and raw materials is estimated at $8 per dozen. In any event, the holding costs are estimated at 20% of the purchase or manufacturing cost of the item. Reorder costs are currently $40 per order. Set-up costs for a production run are estimated at $400.

If Zak's can lease a machine capable of making 8,000 dozen zippers per year at an annual cost of $5,000, should Zak's make their own zippers?

PROBLEM 19

Rancher Jim's Luncheon Meat Company produces fresh luncheon meats. Demand is for 300,000 pounds of meat annually. Rancher Jim has his choice of two machines to process the meats. The annual lease costs and annual processing capacities are given below:

	Annual Lease Cost	Annual Processing Capacity
Machine I	$10,000	250,000 lbs.
Machine II	$12,000	1,000,000 lbs.

Set-up costs are $1,000 per run and holding costs are $.10 per pound per year. Rancher Jim's gross profit is $.20 per pound (not including annual lease, set-up or holding costs).

a) Show that Machine II gives the maximum profit for processing.

b) Why would you likely recommend machine I for Rancher Jim?

PROBLEM 20

Honest Archie's Appliance Co. has a policy of giving loaner TV's to customers who purchase a set from Archie when he is out of stock of they model they want. As soon as Archie gets the set in stock, he delivers the new set and picks up the loaner from the customer.

Demand at Archie's for the Apex 19-inch remote control TV is 5 units per week. The sets have an annual holding cost of $55. The cost to place an order for the sets is $80, and it typically takes three weeks for the sets to arrive after the order is placed.

a) If the loaner TV's cost Archie $3 per week to rent, determine his optimal order policy.

b) What is the total annual variable cost of this policy?

PROBLEM 21

Clearview Optical gives a customer a complimentary carrying case with each pair of eye glasses bought. Lead time demand for these cases is normally distributed with a mean of 230 cases and a standard deviation of 42 cases.

a) If Clearview reorders cases when inventory reaches 285 cases, what is the probability that there will be a stockout during lead time?

b) If Clearview desires a .05 probability of a stockout during lead time, what should the reorder point be for glass cases?

PROBLEM 22

Amazing Bakers sells bread to 40 supermarkets. It costs Amazing $1,250 per day to operate its plant. The profit per loaf of bread sold in the supermarket is $.025. Any unsold bread is returned to be sold at the Amazing Thrift store at a loss of $.015.

a) If sales follow a normal distribution with μ = 70,000 and σ = 5,000 per day, how many loaves should Amazing bake daily?

b) Amazing is considering a different sales plan for which the profit per loaf of bread sold in the supermarket is $.03 and the loss per loaf bread returned is $.018. If μ = 60,000 and σ = 4,000 per day, how many loaves should Amazing bake daily?

PROBLEM 23

Every year in early October Steven King buys pumpkins of one size from a farmer in Maine and then hires an artist to carve bewitching faces in them. He then tries to sell them at his produce stand in a public market in Boston.

The farmer charges Steven $2.50 per pumpkin and the artist is paid $2.00 per carved pumpkin. Steven sells a carved pumpkin for $8.00. Any pumpkins not sold by 5:00 p.m. on Halloween are donated to Steven's favorite children's hospital. Steven pays the artist $0.75 per pumpkin to rush the pumpkins to the hospital for the youngsters to enjoy.

Steven estimates the demand for his pumpkins this season to be uniformly distributed within a range of 30 to 70.

a) How many pumpkins should Steven have available for sale?

b) Based on your answer to (a), what is the probability that Steven will be short five or more pumpkins?

PROBLEM 24

Bank Drugs sells Jami Michelle lipstick. The Jami Michelle Company offers a 6% discount on orders of at least 500 tubes, a 10% discount on orders of at least 1,000 tubes, a 12% discount on orders of at least 1,800 tubes and a 15% discount on orders at least 2,500 tubes.

Bank sells an average of 40 tubes of Jami Michelle lipstick weekly. The normal price paid by Bank drugs is $1 per tube. If it costs Bank $30 to place an order, and Bank's annual holding cost rate is 27%, determine the optimal order policy for Bank Drugs.

PROBLEM 25

A company has the following choices for purchasing a product for which demand is 100 per week.

Option	Purchase Cost/Item	Quantity
I	$10.00	0 - 599
II	$ 9.80	600 or more
III	$ 9.90	exactly 100

Under option III, the ordering company will have no paperwork as the 100 items will be delivered every week automatically. Thus under option III, the only work associated with an order is in filing an invoice which is assumed to have zero cost. Otherwise reorder costs are $75 per order.

If holding costs are .5% per week, what is the optimal order quantity?

PROBLEM 26

Demand for the Kansas Systems Model 402 printer at the Computer Town chain of computer stores has averaged 35 units per week with a standard deviation of 10 units per week.

The units cost Computer Town $910 each and there is a $500 order cost. Computer Town's an annual holding cost rate is 20%.

The lead time for these printers is approximately a month with lead time demand being normally distributed with a mean of 140 units and a standard deviation of 20 units.

a) If Computer Town wants to experience an average of at most one stockout per year on these printers, determine an optimal inventory policy for the store.

b) Determine the annual cost of the policy for Computer Town.

c) If Computer Town was just starting to stock printers, use the data above to determine how many printers they should order.

PROBLEM 27

Chez Paul Restaurant orders special styrofoam "doggy bags" for its customers once a month and lead time is one week. Weekly demand for doggy bags is approximately normally distributed with an average of 120 bags and a standard deviation of 25.

Chez Paul wants at most a 3% chance of running out of doggy bags during the replenishment period. If he has 150 bags in stock when he places an order, how many additional bags should he order? What is the safety stock in this case?

TRUE/FALSE

28. At the optimal order quantity, Q^*, in the EOQ model, annual order costs equal annual holding costs.

29. If an item's per-unit backorder cost is greater than its per-unit holding cost, no intentional shortage should be planned.

30. At the optimal order quantity for the quantity discount model, the sum of the annual holding and ordering costs is minimized.

31. As lead time for an item increases, the cycle time increases.

32. If an item's per-unit backorder cost equals one-half of its per-unit holding cost, it is optimal to plan to incur the first shortage one-third of the way through the order cycle.

33. If the annual production rate for an item increases, then the optimal production lot size, Q^*, will also increase.

34. When demand increases by 100 percent, the economic order quantity increases by less than 50 percent.

35. If the cost of underestimating demand, C_u, is greater than the cost of overestimating demand, C_o, the optimal single-period order quantity is greater than expected demand.

36. An assumption in the economic production lot size model is that there is storage capacity to hold the entire production lot.

37. In the EOQ model, an item's optimal order quantity, Q^*, cannot be greater than its annual demand, D.

38. The single-period inventory model is most applicable to items that are perishable or have seasonal demand.

39. In the single-period inventory model, an increase in the item's salvage value will cause a decrease in the optimal order quantity.

40. To avoid a stockout of a periodic-review item, the item's order quantity plus inventory on hand at ordering time must last until the time the item can be ordered again.

41. If the optimal production lot size decreases, average inventory increases.

42. In the EOQ model, the doubling of both the ordering and holding costs would result in no change in the optimal order quantity.

Chapter 15
Inventory Management: Dependent Demand

KEY CONCEPTS

CONCEPT	ILLUSTRATED PROBLEMS	ANSWERED PROBLEMS
Dependent vs. Independent Demands	1-4	5-14
Inputs to MRP Systems	1	6,11
Determining Net Requirements Using MRP Planning Worksheets	2,3	7,8,12,13
Lot Sizing and Safety Stock Fixed Order Size Rule Lot for Lot Rule Safety Stock	2-4	5,7-10,12-14
MRP and Time Phased Production Schedules	4	5,9,10,14

REVIEW

1. Material Requirements Planning (MRP) is used to control a manufacturing inventory system. The major function of an MRP system is to translate the demand for finished goods into detailed inventory requirements for all their components. MRP serves as part of a data processing system whose function is to monitor and control the status of production and perform inventory control. Its objective is to have the right components available at the right time in order to minimize inventory holding costs and ensure a smooth flow of materials.

2. One goal of MRP is to minimize the investment in manufacturing inventories. Another goal is to ensure all new materials, parts and subassemblies are available when needed, thus preventing production delays from occurring.

3. MRP exploits the dependence of demand between the finished good and the components making up the good to achieve inventory holding cost savings.

4. The time periods appropriate for the firm are called time buckets. A planning horizon consists of an appropriate number of time buckets.

5. One input to an MRP system is the master production schedule (MPS) which summarizes requirements and deadlines for finished goods over the planning horizon. Another input is the bill of materials (BOM) which is a structured parts list detailing the sequencing of the assembly of the product. A third input is an MRP inventory record for each raw material, part or subassembly showing everything affecting the inventory level over the planning horizon.

6. One graphical representation of a bill of materials is known as a product structure tree. In this representation, the finished product is shown at the top of the hierarchy (level 0). At the level below this (level 1) are the parts or subassemblies making up the finished product. In the next level (level 2) are the parts or subassemblies making up the subassemblies of level 1, etc.

7. The parts or subassemblies shown at each level of the hierarchy are said to be the parent of the parts or subassemblies directly below them in the hierarchy. Each item in the bill of materials, except for the end product, has a parent.

8. Information contained in the inventory record can be classified as either: (1) inventory transaction information; or, (2) planning information. Inventory transaction information includes events such as the receipt of goods from a supplier, the disbursement of items from inventory to satisfy production, the occurrence of scrap, etc. Planning information includes lead time, safety stock, lot sizing method, etc.

9. In manufacturing there is often a dependent demand between different components. In this case, (Net Component Requirements) = (Gross Component Requirements) - (Number of Components in Inventory). The gross component requirement is the quantity of the component necessary to support production at the next higher level of assembly. Both net and gross requirements are assumed to refer to requirements at the beginning of each time bucket.

10. An MRP planning worksheet is useful for calculating how much to order and when to order each part or subassembly over the planning horizon.

11. The net requirements calculation enables one to determine the required additions to inventory. An order placed during a previous planning period but scheduled to arrive during the current planning period is called a scheduled receipt. An order placed during the current planning period is referred to as a planned order release. Its arrival is known as a planned order receipt. Items are normally assumed to arrive at the beginning of each time bucket.

12. Two commonly use methods for determining the amount of inventory to order during the planning period are the fixed order size and the lot for lot rules.

13. The fixed order size rule is appropriate for purchased components when such a lot size is necessary to take advantage of quantity discounts, when an economic order quantity (EOQ) rule is being used, or when batches must be of a certain size due to equipment capacities.

14. The lot for lot rule has the lot size equal to the net requirement for the period in which the lot will become available. In this case, the planned order receipts are identical to the net requirements for each time bucket.

15. Safety stock can be used to buffer the production system against unexpected events. These include uncertainty about gross requirements, lead times, defective parts, pilferage, etc. Safety stock is indicated in the MRP planning worksheet as a projected balance in each time bucket. In calculating net requirements, it should be included in the total for the gross requirements.

16. MRP also determines the date the net requirements are needed by a procedure called time phasing. In time phasing, a production plan for components is developed by working backwards from the desired completion date of the finished product through the various manufacturing stages.

17. Time phasing is used to determine the appropriate planning horizon for each subassembly or parent corresponding to the planning horizon for the end product. An MRP worksheet can then be prepared for the part or subassembly over this planning horizon.

18. The process of generating net requirements for components from the MPS for an end product is called BOM explosion.

19. A successful implementation of an MRP system is dependent upon accurate record keeping. Due to the fact that large amounts of data and records must be processed and stored in an MRP, such systems employ a fairly sophisticated computer information system.

20. Two approaches used to update MRP records are the regeneration and the net change approaches. With regeneration, the records for all items are updated periodically. With net change, the MRP system recalculates net requirements whenever changes make it necessary; however, only the records affected by the new or revised information are updated.

21. Capacity requirements planning is the process of determining the time-phased labor and machine resources necessary to meet the MPS. The integration of capacity requirements with the MRP leads to what is often referred to as a closed loop MRP system.

22. Just-in-time (JIT) inventory management reflects a philosophy of eliminating all sources of waste including unnecessary inventory.

23. In order for JIT to function effectively, changes in the design of the production layout and material flow process may be required as well as reduction in setup times.

24. A key component of the coordination of JIT production is an information system called Kanban (the Japanese word for "card"). The type and number of units required by the production process are written on Kanbans which are used to indicate withdrawal and production of units through the production process. In this manner the entire manufacturing operation is synchronized to the final assembly stage.

25. The total quality concept is critical to the implementation of the JIT philosophy. Lot sizes are small and inventory levels are minimal; there is no safety stock to replace nonconforming or defective units. Hence, a JIT system requires a trusting partnership between suppliers and the manufacturer in order to obtain materials on time and with zero defects.

ILLUSTRATED PROBLEMS

PROBLEM 1

Columbia Mopeds is a manufacturer of off-road mopeds. It imports moped frames from Asia and adds an engine, gas tank and wheels to produce a finished moped. The following product structure tree represents the bill of materials for its dual carburetor model 621 moped.

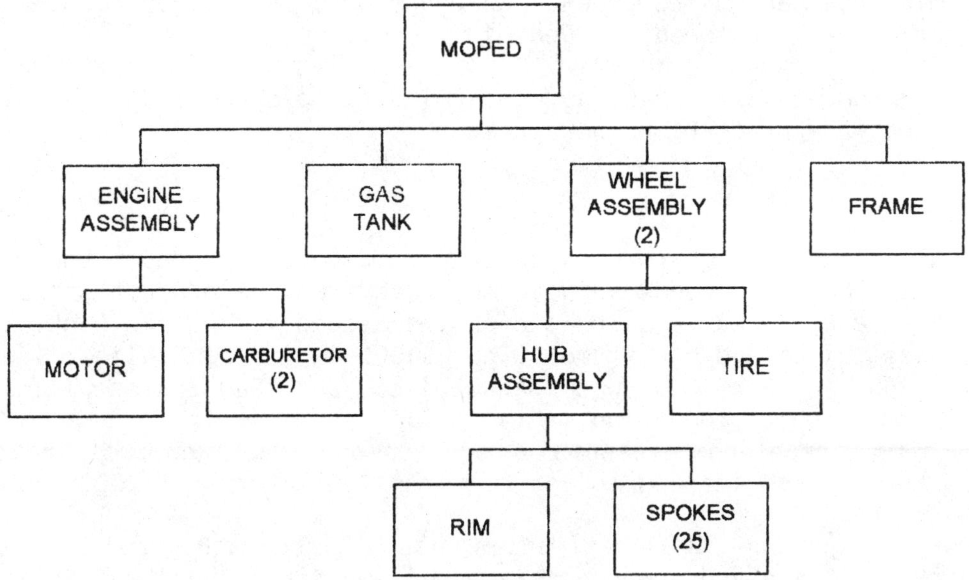

The final assembly of the engine, gas tank, wheels, and frame to produce a moped takes one week.

Lead times for the other components are as follows:

Component	Lead Time (Weeks)
Engine Assembly	1
Motor	1
Carburetor	2
Gas Tank	2
Wheel Assembly	1
Tire	3
Hub	1
Rim	1
Spokes	2
Frame	3

The company is currently planning production for weeks 10 through 16. Based on existing orders and demand forecasts, the master production schedule is as follows:

WEEK	10	11	12	13	14	15	16
PRODUCTION QUANTITY	1000	0	1300	800	0	1400	900

a) Determine how many units of each component will be needed to support the production of 1000 mopeds in week 10.

b) Based on the answer to part a), determine the planned order release date to support the production in week 10.

SOLUTION 1

a) To find the gross requirements of each component to support the production of 1000 mopeds in week 10, note from the product structure tree that each moped requires one engine assembly, one gas tank, two wheel assemblies and one frame. Thus, 1000 engine assemblies, 1000 gas tanks, 2000 (= 2 x 1000) wheel assemblies, and 1000 frames will be needed to support production.

Note that each engine assembly requires one motor and two carburetors. Hence the 1000 engine assemblies require 1000 motors and 2000 carburetors.

Now consider the 2000 wheel assemblies. Since each wheel assembly requires one tire and one hub assembly, 2000 tires and 2000 hub assemblies will be required to produce 2000 wheel assemblies.

Finally, note that each of the 2000 hub assemblies requires one rim and 25 spokes. Thus, 2000 rims and 50,000 (= 25 x 2000) spokes will be needed to produce 2000 hub assemblies.

The resulting unit requirements are summarized below:

Item	Units
Moped	1000
Engine Assembly	1000
Motor	1000
Carburetor	2000
Gas Tank	1000
Wheel Assembly	2000
Tire	2000
Hub	2000
Rim	2000
Spokes	50000
Frame	1000

b) To determine the planned order release (POR) date for each of the components required to support the production of 1000 mopeds in week 10, note that each of the four level 1 components (engine assembly, gas tank, wheel assembly, and frame) must be available in week 10. Given that the lead time for the engine assembly is one week, its POR date should be week 9 (= 10 - 1).

Similarly, as the lead time for gas tanks is two weeks, its POR date should be week 8 (= 10 - 2). Following the same reasoning, the POR date for the wheel assembly should be week 9 (= 10 - 1) and for the frame, week 7 (= 10 - 3).

Considering the level 2 components, observe that in order to have engine assemblies ready for assembly in week 9 (their POR date), the motor and carburetor must be available by week 9. Given that the motors have a one-week lead time, this means they should have a POR date of week 8 (= 9 - 1). Similarly, the POR date for the carburetors should be week 7 (= 9 - 2).

Similarly, for the level 2 components of the wheel assemblies, the POR date for the tires should be week 6 (= 9 - 3), and the POR date for the hubs should be week 8 (= 9 - 1).

Finally, consider the level 3 components whose parent is the hub. Since the POR date for the hub is week 8 and the lead time for the rim is one week, the POR date for rims should be week 7 (= 8 - 1). Similarly, since the lead time for spokes is 2 weeks, their POR date should be week 6 (= 8 - 2).

These results are summarized in the table below:

Item	Planned Order Release Date (Week)
Moped	10
Engine Assembly	9
Motor	8
Carburetor	7
Gas Tank	8
Wheel Assembly	9
Tire	6
Hub	8
Rim	7
Spokes	6
Frame	7

PROBLEM 2

Consider the data from problem 1). Assume there is a projected balance of 400 gas tanks at the beginning of week 10 and a scheduled receipt of 900 gas tanks in week 10. Columbia Mopeds uses a lot for lot rule for ordering gas tanks, and it desires a safety stock of 200 gas tanks. Determine the MRP worksheet for gas tanks during the period from week 10 through week 16.

SOLUTION 2

From problem 1) the following chart gives the gross requirements for gas tanks:

WEEK	10	11	12	13	14	15	16
GROSS REQUIREMENTS	1000	0	1300	800	0	1400	900

A lot for lot rule is used for gas tanks and the following information regarding the gas tanks is given:

Projected balance at the beginning of week 10:	400
Scheduled receipt of gas tanks in week 10:	900
Desired safety stock of gas tanks:	200
Lead time for gas tanks:	2 weeks

Therefore, the data can initially be put into the following MRP worksheet:

ITEM:: GAS TANK LEAD TIME: 2		WEEK						
LOT SIZE: L-F-L SAFETY STOCK: 200		10	11	12	13	14	15	16
GROSS REQUIREMENTS		1000	0	1300	800	0	1400	900
SCHEDULED RECEIPTS		900						
PROJECTED BALANCE	400							
NET REQUIREMENTS								
PLANNED ORDER RECEIPTS								
PLANNED ORDER RELEASES								

To complete the worksheet, begin at week 10. Since there is a projected balance of 400 gas tanks at the beginning of week 10 and scheduled receipts of 900 gas tanks in week 10 (assumed to arrive at the beginning of the week), a total of 1300 (= 400 + 900) gas tanks are available at the beginning of week 10.

As the gross requirements in week 10 are for 1000 gas tanks, this leaves a projected balance of 300 (= 400 + 900 - 1000) at the end of week 10 (i.e. at the beginning of week 11). Since 300 gas tanks is greater than the desired safety stock of 200 gas tanks, there are no net requirements in week 10 and therefore no planned order receipts. The worksheet now looks as follows:

ITEM:: GAS TANK LEAD TIME: 2		WEEK						
LOT SIZE: L-F-L SAFETY STOCK: 200		10	11	12	13	14	15	16
GROSS REQUIREMENTS		1000	0	1300	800	0	1400	900
SCHEDULED RECEIPTS		900						
PROJECTED BALANCE	400	300						
NET REQUIREMENTS		0						
PLANNED ORDER RECEIPTS								
PLANNED ORDER RELEASES								

There are no gross requirements for week 11. Thus, the projected balance at the end of week 11 (the beginning of week 12) remains at 300 and there are no net requirements for week 11.

In week 12, however, there are gross requirements for 1300 gas tanks. In addition, 200 gas tanks must remain in inventory as safety stock. Hence, the total requirement for week 12 is 1500 (= 1300 + 200) gas tanks. Since there is a projected balance of 300 at the beginning of week 12, the net requirement for week 12 is 1200 (= 1300 + 200 - 300) gas tanks.

As a lot for lot rule is being used, this means that there should be a planned order receipt of 1200 gas tanks in week 12. (This is assumed to occur at the beginning of the week). Since the lead time for gas tanks is two weeks, this means that there should be a planned order release for the 1200 gas tanks in week 10 (= 12 - 2).

The MRP worksheet would now look as follows:

ITEM:: GAS TANK LEAD TIME: 2		WEEK						
LOT SIZE: L-F-L SAFETY STOCK: 200		10	11	12	13	14	15	16
GROSS REQUIREMENTS		1000	0	1300	800	0	1400	900
SCHEDULED RECEIPTS		900						
PROJECTED BALANCE	400	300	300	200				
NET REQUIREMENTS		0	0	1200				
PLANNED ORDER RECEIPTS				1200				
PLANNED ORDER RELEASES		1200						

The same approach is used to calculate the net requirements for week 13. The formula for determining the net requirments using the lot for lot rule is:

(Net Requirements) = (Gross Requirements) + (Projected Balance)
 - (Desired Safety Stock)

The projected balance at the end of the week will equal the desired safety stock. Hence net requirements for week 13 will be 800 (= 800 + 200 - 200), and the projected balance at the end of the week will be 200. Because a lot for lot rule is being used, this implies there should be a planned order receipt of 800 gas tanks in week 13. Given the two week lead time, the planned order release of these 800 gas tanks would be week 11.

Now the MRP worksheet would be:

ITEM:: GAS TANK LEAD TIME: 2		WEEK						
LOT SIZE: L-F-L SAFETY STOCK: 200		10	11	12	13	14	15	16
GROSS REQUIREMENTS		1000	0	1300	800	0	1400	900
SCHEDULED RECEIPTS		900						
PROJECTED BALANCE	400	300	300	200	200			
NET REQUIREMENTS		0	0	1200	800			
PLANNED ORDER RECEIPTS				1200	800			
PLANNED ORDER RELEASES		1200	800					

In week 14, since the gross requirements are 0, the net requirements will also be 0 and there will be no planned order receipt. The projected balance at the end of week 14 will remain at the safety stock level of 200 units.

For week 15, 1400 gas tanks are required. Hence, the net requirements for this week will be 1400 (= 1400 +200 - 200). Thus, there should be a planned order receipt of 1400 units in week 15. These should have a planned order release date of week 13 (= 15 - 2). The projected balance at the end of week 15 will be 200 units. Now, the MRP worksheet is:

ITEM:: GAS TANK LEAD TIME: 2		WEEK						
LOT SIZE: L-F-L SAFETY STOCK: 200		10	11	12	13	14	15	16
GROSS REQUIREMENTS		1000	0	1300	800	0	1400	900
SCHEDULED RECEIPTS		900						
PROJECTED BALANCE	400	300	300	200	200	200	200	
NET REQUIREMENTS		0	0	1200	800	0	1400	
PLANNED ORDER RECEIPTS				1200	800		1400	
PLANNED ORDER RELEASES		1200	800		1400			

For week 16, the gross requirements of 900 translates into net requirements of 900 (= 900 + 200 - 200), and a planned order receipt of 900. The planned order release date for this order will be week 14 (= 16 - 2). The projected balance at the end of week 16 will then be equal to the desired safety stock of 200 units. Thus the completed MRP worksheet for weeks 10 through 16 is:

ITEM:: GAS TANK LEAD TIME: 2		WEEK						
LOT SIZE: L-F-L SAFETY STOCK: 200		10	11	12	13	14	15	16
GROSS REQUIREMENTS		1000	0	1300	800	0	1400	900
SCHEDULED RECEIPTS		900						
PROJECTED BALANCE	400	300	300	200	200	200	200	200
NET REQUIREMENTS		0	0	1200	800	0	1400	900
PLANNED ORDER RECEIPTS				1200	800		1400	900
PLANNED ORDER RELEASES		1200	800		1400	900		

PROBLEM 3

Consider the Columbia Moped data in problem 1). Assume there is a projected balance of 600 frames at the beginning of week 10 and a scheduled receipt of 2000 frames in week 10. The firm uses a fixed order size of 2000 frames and desires no safety stock of frames.

a) Determine the MRP worksheet for frames over the time period from week 10 through week 16.

b) How would the answer to a) change if Columbia Mopeds desired a minimum safety stock of 300 frames?

SOLUTION 3

a) From problem 1), the following chart gives the weekly gross requirements for frames:

WEEK	10	11	12	13	14	15	16
GROSS REQUIREMENTS	1000	0	1300	800	0	1400	900

Recall the fixed order size rule (order size = 2000) is used for frames and the following information regarding the frames is given:

Projected balance at the beginning of week 10:	600
Scheduled receipt of gas tanks in week 10:	2000
Desired safety stock of gas tanks:	0
Lead time for gas tanks:	3 weeks

This data gives the following partially completed MRP worksheet

ITEM:: FRAME	LEAD TIME: 3		WEEK						
LOT SIZE: 2000	SAFETY STOCK: 0		10	11	12	13	14	15	16
GROSS REQUIREMENTS			1000	0	1300	800	0	1400	900
SCHEDULED RECEIPTS			2000						
PROJECTED BALANCE		600							
NET REQUIREMENTS									
PLANNED ORDER RECEIPTS									
PLANNED ORDER RELEASES									

Note that there are 2600 frames (the 600 projected balance plus the 2000 scheduled receipt) available for week 10, but only 1000 frames are required. Hence the projected balance at the end of week 10 (the beginning of week 11) is 1600 (= 600 + 2000 - 1000). Thus, there are no net requirements and no planned order receipts are necessary.

Since the gross requirements in week 11 are 0, the projected balance at the end of week 11 remains at 1600 units. Hence, there are no net requirements and no planned order receipts for week 11.

The MRP worksheet now looks as follows:

ITEM:: FRAME — LEAD TIME: 3		WEEK						
LOT SIZE: 2000 — SAFETY STOCK: 0		10	11	12	13	14	15	16
GROSS REQUIREMENTS		1000	0	1300	800	0	1400	900
SCHEDULED RECEIPTS		2000						
PROJECTED BALANCE	600	1600	1600					
NET REQUIREMENTS		0	0					
PLANNED ORDER RECEIPTS								
PLANNED ORDER RELEASES								

In week 12, the gross requirements of 1300 are less than the projected balance of 1600 units. Therefore, the net requirements and the planned order receipts for week 12 are 0. The projected balance is now 300 (= 1600 - 1300).

The MRP worksheet is now:

ITEM:: FRAME — LEAD TIME: 3		WEEK						
LOT SIZE: 2000 — SAFETY STOCK: 0		10	11	12	13	14	15	16
GROSS REQUIREMENTS		1000	0	1300	800	0	1400	900
SCHEDULED RECEIPTS		2000						
PROJECTED BALANCE	600	1600	1600	300				
NET REQUIREMENTS		0	0	0				
PLANNED ORDER RECEIPTS								
PLANNED ORDER RELEASES								

In week 13, the gross requirements of 800 frames exceed the projected balance of 300 at the beginning of the week. The net requirements for week 13 would then be 500 (= 800 - 300). Hence there must be a planned order receipt. As the lot size is 2000, this is the planned order receipt. Since the lead time is 3 weeks, the planned order release date for this order must be week 10 (= 13 - 3). This order will leave a projected balance of 1500 (= 2000 - 500) at the end of week 13.

Now the MRP worksheet is:

ITEM:: FRAME LEAD TIME: 3		WEEK						
LOT SIZE: 2000 SAFETY STOCK: 0		10	11	12	13	14	15	16
GROSS REQUIREMENTS		1000	0	1300	800	0	1400	900
SCHEDULED RECEIPTS		2000						
PROJECTED BALANCE	600	1600	1600	300	1500			
NET REQUIREMENTS		0	0	0	500			
PLANNED ORDER RECEIPTS					2000			
PLANNED ORDER RELEASES		2000						

Since the gross requirements for week 14 are 0, there are no net requirements and no planned order receipt and the projected balance at the end of week 14 remains at 1500.

In week 15, the gross requirements of 1400 units is less than the projected balance of 1500 units at the beginning of the week. Thus the net requirements and the planned order receipts are both 0. However, the projected balance at the end of week 15 is now 100 (= 1500 - 1400).

The MRP worksheet is now:

ITEM:: FRAME LEAD TIME: 3		WEEK						
LOT SIZE: 2000 SAFETY STOCK: 0		10	11	12	13	14	15	16
GROSS REQUIREMENTS		1000	0	1300	800	0	1400	900
SCHEDULED RECEIPTS		2000						
PROJECTED BALANCE	600	1600	1600	300	1500	1500	100	
NET REQUIREMENTS		0	0	0	500	0	0	
PLANNED ORDER RECEIPTS					2000			
PLANNED ORDER RELEASES		2000						

In week 16, the gross requirements of 900 units exceed that of the projected balance of 100 units. Hence the net requirements in week 16 are 800 units (= 900 - 100). Thus, there must be a planned order receipt in week 16 of the fixed order size of 2000. Given the 3 week lead time, the planned order release of these 2000 units must be week 13 (= 16 - 3). The projected balance at the end of week 16 will be 1200 units (= 2000 - 800).

The complete MRP worksheet is:

ITEM:: FRAME LEAD TIME: 3		WEEK						
LOT SIZE: 2000 SAFETY STOCK: 0		10	11	12	13	14	15	16
GROSS REQUIREMENTS		1000	0	1300	800	0	1400	900
SCHEDULED RECEIPTS		2000						
PROJECTED BALANCE	600	1600	1600	300	1500	1500	100	1200
NET REQUIREMENTS		0	0	0	500	0	0	800
PLANNED ORDER RECEIPTS					2000			2000
PLANNED ORDER RELEASES		2000			2000			

b) Now consider a desired safety stock of 300. Note in the final answer to part a) that the projected balance exceeds the desired safety stock level of 300 in weeks 10 through 14. In week 13, however, the true net requirements are 800 (= gross requirements (800) + safety stock (300) - projected balance at the end of week 12 (300)).

In week 15, the completed worksheet in part a) shows a projected balance of only 100. This is less than the desired safety stock of 300. Hence the new net requirements for week 15 is 200 units (= gross requirements (1400) + safety stock (300) - projected balance at the end of week 14 (1500)).

Therefore there should be a planned order receipt of the fixed size of 2000 in week 15. Since there is a 3 week lead time, this means a planned order release date of week 12 (= 15 - 3).

The projected balance at the end of week 15 will then be 2100 units (= projected balance at the end of week 14 (1500) + planned order receipt for week 15 (2000) - gross requirements in week 15 (1400)).

The MRP worksheet with this data is as follows:

ITEM:: FRAME	LEAD TIME: 3		WEEK						
LOT SIZE: 2000	SAFETY STOCK:	300	10	11	12	13	14	15	16
GROSS REQUIREMENTS			1000	0	1300	800	0	1400	900
SCHEDULED RECEIPTS			2000						
PROJECTED BALANCE		600	1600	1600	300	1500	1500	2100	
NET REQUIREMENTS			0	0	0	800	0	200	
PLANNED ORDER RECEIPTS						2000		2000	
PLANNED ORDER RELEASES			2000		2000				

In week 16, the gross requirements of 500 plus the desired safety stock of 300 does not exceed the projected balance of 2100 at the beginning of week 16 (end of week 15). Hence, the net requirements are 0 and there is no planned order receipt.

Then the projected balance at the end of week 16 will be 1200 units (= 2100 - 900).

Thus the completed MRP worksheet when a safety stock of 300 is desired is as follows:

ITEM:: FRAME	LEAD TIME: 3		WEEK						
LOT SIZE: 2000	SAFETY STOCK:	300	10	11	12	13	14	15	16
GROSS REQUIREMENTS			1000	0	1300	800	0	1400	900
SCHEDULED RECEIPTS			2000						
PROJECTED BALANCE		600	1600	1600	300	1500	1500	2100	1200
NET REQUIREMENTS			0	0	0	800	0	200	0
PLANNED ORDER RECEIPTS						2000		2000	
PLANNED ORDER RELEASES			2000		2000				

PROBLEM 4

Consider the Columbia Moped data of Problem 1. Assume the following:

(1) the projected balance for wheel assemblies at the start of week 12 is 400;
(2) the projected balance for tires at the start of week 11 is 700;
(3) the projected balance for hubs at the start of week 11 is 300;
(4) the projected balance for spokes at the start of week 10 is 25,000;
(5) there are no scheduled receipts for wheel assemblies, tires, hubs, or spokes;
(6) Columbia uses a lot for lot rule for wheel assemblies, hubs, and spokes, but uses a fixed order size of 3000 for tires;
(7) Columbia desires no safety stock for wheel assemblies or hubs, but desires a minimum safety stock of 600 tires and a minimum safety stock of 20,000 spokes at all times.

Determine the MRP worksheets for weeks 6 through 12 for wheel assemblies, tires, hubs, and spokes to support the production of 1300 mopeds in week 12.

SOLUTION 4

Wheel Assemblies

From the data in problem 1), note that two wheel assemblies are required for each moped and they must be available in the week production is planned. Since 1300 mopeds are to be produced in week 12, the gross requirements for wheel assemblies to support production in week 12 will be 2600 (= 1300 x 2).

As the projected balance of wheel assemblies at the beginning of week 12 is 400 and there is no safety stock requirement, the net requirement for wheel assemblies in week 12 will be 2200 units (= 2600 - 400).

Since a lot for lot rule is used for wheel assemblies there will be a planned order receipt of 2200 units in week 12. As lead time for wheel assemblies is one week, these units will have a planned order release date of week 11 (= 12 - 1).

Thus the required MRP worksheet for wheel assemblies is:

ITEM:: WHEEL ASSEMBLY LEAD TIME: 1		WEEK						
LOT SIZE: L-F-L SAFETY STOCK: 0		6	7	8	9	10	11	12
GROSS REQUIREMENTS								2600
SCHEDULED RECEIPTS								
PROJECTED BALANCE							400	0
NET REQUIREMENTS								2200
PLANNED ORDER RECEIPTS								2200
PLANNED ORDER RELEASES							2200	

Tires

From the data in problem 1), note that there is one tire for each wheel assembly. From the above MRP worksheet for wheel assemblies, observe that there is a planned order release of 2200 wheel assemblies in week 11. Thus the gross requirements are for 2200 tires in week 11.

There is a projected balance of 700 tires at the beginning of week 11 and Columbia desires a minimum safety stock of 600 tires. Hence the net requirements for tires in week 11 will be 2100 (= gross requirements (2200) + safety stock (600) - projected balance (700)).

Given a positive net requirement, using the fixed lot size rule with lot size of 3000, there should be a planned order receipt in week 11 equal to the lot size of 3000. As there is a 3 week lead time for tires, this order should have a planned release date of week 8 (= 11 - 3).

Thus the MRP for tires is:

ITEM:: TIRE LEAD TIME: 3		WEEK						
LOT SIZE: 3000 SAFETY STOCK: 600		6	7	8	9	10	11	12
GROSS REQUIREMENTS							2200	
SCHEDULED RECEIPTS								
PROJECTED BALANCE						700	1500	
NET REQUIREMENTS							2100	
PLANNED ORDER RECEIPTS							3000	
PLANNED ORDER RELEASES				3000				

Hub Assemblies

As with tires, one hub assembly is required for each wheel assembly. Hence the gross requirements for hub assemblies will be 2200 in week 11.

Since the projected balance of hub assemblies at the beginning of week 11 is 300 and there are no safety stock requirements, the net requirements for hub assemblies in week 11 will be 1900 (= 2200 - 300). Because a lot for lot rule is used for hubs, the planned order receipt in week 11 will be 1900. Since there is a one week lead time for hubs, the planned order release date will be week 10 (= 11 - 1).

The MRP worksheet for hub assemblies is:

ITEM:: HUB ASSEMBLY LEAD TIME: 1		WEEK						
LOT SIZE: L-F-L SAFETY STOCK: 0		6	7	8	9	10	11	12
GROSS REQUIREMENTS							2200	
SCHEDULED RECEIPTS								
PROJECTED BALANCE						300	0	
NET REQUIREMENTS							1900	
PLANNED ORDER RECEIPTS							1900	
PLANNED ORDER RELEASES						1900		

Spokes

From the data in problem 1), note that each hub assembly requires 25 spokes. From the hub assembly MRP worksheet, there is a planned order release date for 1900 hub assemblies in week 10. This means there are gross requirements at the beginning of week 10 for 47,500 (= 1900 x 25) spokes.

Since there is a projected balance of 25,000 spokes at the beginning of week 10 and a desired safety stock of 20,000 spokes, this means the net requirements for spokes is week 10 will be 42,500 (= gross requirements (47,500) + safety stock (20,000) - projected balance (25,000)).

Given that the lot for lot rule is used for spokes, a planned order receipt for 42,500 spokes is required for week 10. Since the lead time for spokes is two weeks, this order has a planned order release date of week 8 (= 10 - 2).

Thus the MRP worksheet for spokes is:

ITEM:: SPOKE LEAD TIME: 2		WEEK						
LOT SIZE: L-F-L SAFETY STOCK: 20000		6	7	8	9	10	11	12
GROSS REQUIREMENTS						47500		
SCHEDULED RECEIPTS								
PROJECTED BALANCE					25000	20000		
NET REQUIREMENTS						42500		
PLANNED ORDER RECEIPTS						42500		
PLANNED ORDER RELEASES				42500				

ANSWERED PROBLEMS

PROBLEM 5

Consider the data for Columbia Moped in problem 1). The projected balance of engine assemblies at the beginning of week 12 is 200, the projected balance of motors at the beginning of week 11 is 500, and the projected balance of carburetors at the beginning of week 11 is 0.

Columbia desires no safety stock for engine assemblies and carburetors, but a safety stock of 500 for motors. It uses a lot for lot rule for engine assemblies, carburetors, and motors.

Compute the MRP worksheet for each of the three components over the period from week 6 through week 12 in order to support the production of 1300 mopeds in week 12.

PROBLEM 6

Innovative Products, Inc. manufactures "charcoal" barbecue grills for indoor use. The following product structure tree represents the bill of materials:

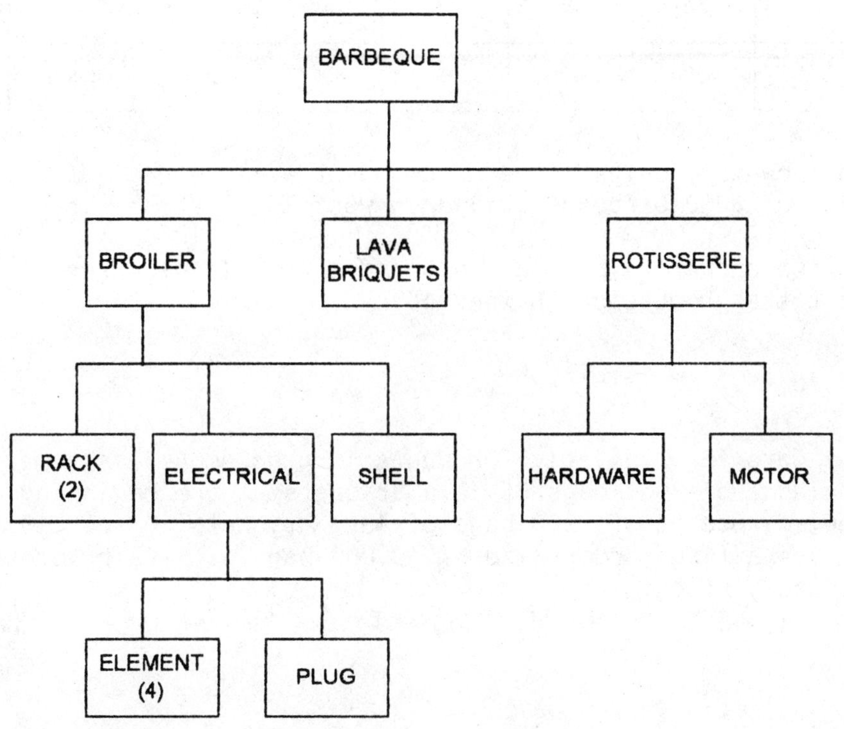

The final assembly of the broiler, lava briquets, and rotisserie into the barbecue takes one week. Lead times for the other components are as follows:

Component	Lead Time (Weeks)
Broiler	1
Rack	2
Electrical	1
Element	2
Plug	1
Shell	2
Lava Briquets	1
Rotisserie	1
Hardware	2
Motor	1

Innovative Products is currently planning production for weeks 15 through 20. Based on existing orders and demand forecasts, the production schedule is as follows:

WEEK	15	16	17	18	19	20
PRODUCTION QUANTITY	6000	9000	0	8000	6000	5000

a) Determine how many units of each component will be needed to support the production of 6000 barbecue grills in week 15.

b) Based on the answer to part a), determine the planned order release date to support the production in week 15.

PROBLEM 7

Consider the data for Innovative Products in problem 6). Assume there is a projected balance of 3000 bags of lava briquets at the beginning of week 15 and a scheduled receipt of 7000 bags of lava briquets in week 15. Innovative uses a fixed order size of 10,000 bags of lava briquets and desires no safety stock.

Determine the MRP worksheet for bags of lava briquets for weeks 15 through 20.

PROBLEM 8

Consider the data for Innovative Products in problem 6). Assume a lot for lot rule is used for rotisseries. There is a scheduled receipt of 7000 rotisseries in week 15 and a projected balance of 2000 rotisseries at the beginning of week 15. Innovative Products desires a safety stock of 2000 rotisseries.

a) Determine the MRP worksheet for rotisseries for weeks 15 through 20.

b) How would the MRP worksheet change if there were no safety stock requirement?

PROBLEM 9

Consider the data for Innovative Products in problem 6). Innovative Products uses a lot for lot rule for broilers, electrical units, elements, and plugs. No safety stock for these items is desired.

There are no schedule receipts for broilers and electrical units during week 11 through week 15. There is, however, a scheduled receipt of 16000 elements in week 13 and 4000 plugs in week 12.

Determine the MRP worksheets for week 11 through week 15 to support the production of 6000 barbecue grills in week 15 for broilers, electrical units, elements, and plugs.

PROBLEM 10

Consider the data for Innovative Products in problem 6). Innovative Products uses a lot for lot rule for hardware and motors. There are no scheduled receipt of hardware or motors during weeks 15 through 20.

While Innovative Products has not desired any safety stock for hardware and motors in the past, beginning with this planning period (week 15 through week 20), it desires a safety stock of 2000 units of hardware and 1500 motors.

Determine the MRP worksheets over the time frame from week 15 through 20 to support the production of 5000 barbecues in week 20 for:

a) hardware

b) motors

c) How would the answer to part a) change if there was a scheduled receipt of 4000 units of hardware in week 19?

PROBLEM 11

Weber Appliance manufactures the La Guillotine model 406 food processor. The following product structure tree represents the bill of materials:

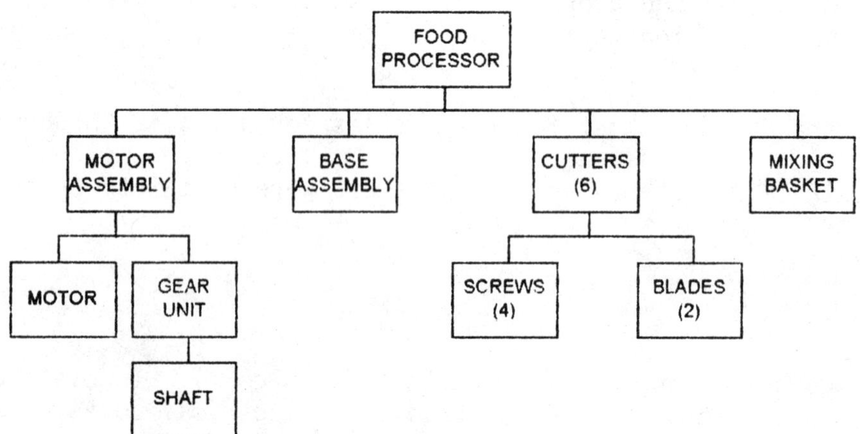

The final assembly of the motor base, mixing basket, and blades takes one week. Lead times for the other components are as follows:

Component	Lead Time (Weeks)
Motor Assembly	1
Motor	3
Gear Unit	1
Shaft	1
Base Assembly	2
Mixing Basket	1
Cutters	1
Screws	2
Blades	4

Weber is currently planning production for week 12 through 17. Based on existing orders and demand forecasts, the master production schedule is as follows:

WEEK	12	13	14	15	16	17
PRODUCTION QUANTITY	1600	1200	1500	1400	1800	2000

a) Determine how many units of each component will be needed to support production of the 1500 units in week 14.

b) Based on the answer to part a), determine the planned order release dates to support the production in week 14.

PROBLEM 12

Consider the data for Weber Appliance in problem 11). Weber uses a fixed lot size of 2500 for ordering mixing baskets and desires no safety stock for these items. There is no projected balance of mixing baskets at the beginning of week 12, but there is a scheduled receipt of 2500 mixing baskets in week 12.

Below is a partially completed MRP worksheet for mixing baskets over the period from week 12 through week 17.

a) Complete the MRP worksheet for mixing baskets.

b) How would the MRP worksheet change if there were a projected balance of 600 mixing baskets at the beginning of week 12?

ITEM:: MIXING BASKET	LEAD TIME: 1		WEEK					
LOT SIZE: 2500	SAFETY STOCK: 0		12	13	14	15	16	17
GROSS REQUIREMENTS			1600	1200	1500	1400	1800	2000
SCHEDULED RECEIPTS			2500					
PROJECTED BALANCE		0						
NET REQUIREMENTS								
PLANNED ORDER RECEIPTS								
PLANNED ORDER RELEASES								

PROBLEM 13

Consider the data for Weber Appliance in problem 11). Weber projects a balance of 800 base assemblies at the beginning of week 12 and a scheduled receipt of 2000 base assemblies in week 12. Weber uses a fixed order size of 2000 base assemblies and desires no safety stock of these assemblies.

a) Determine the MRP worksheet for base assemblies over the time frame from week 11 through week 17.

b) How would the answer to part a) change if the firm desired a safety stock of 500 base assemblies?

PROBLEM 14

Consider the data for Weber Appliance in problem 11). Weber uses a lot for lot rule for cutters, screws, and blades. There are no scheduled deliveries for these items during the period from week 7 through week 12. Weber desires no safety stock for these items.

The projected balance at the beginning of week 11 is zero for both cutters and screws, but is 4000 for blades.

Determine the MRP worksheets over the time frame from week 7 through week 12 for cutters, screws, and blades to support the production of 1600 food processors during week 12.

TRUE/FALSE

15. Using a lot for lot rule will never result in a larger inventory position than using a fixed order rule.

16. The three key inputs to an MRP are the master production schedule, the bill of materials, and inventory records.

17. In an MRP system, only the end product does not have a parent.

18. The master production schedule shows how the finished good is assembled from its subcomponents.

19. In managing manufacturing inventories, an MRP system enables savings in inventory holding costs by taking into account the dependent nature of demand.

20. The bill of materials contains inventory transaction information and planning information for each component.

21. Planned order releases always follow planned order receipts.

22. In a given time period, gross requirements (including necessary safety stock) will never be less than net requirements.

23. Two approaches to updating MRP records are the regeneration and the net change approach.

24. The process of generating net requirements for components from the MPS for an end item is called an MPS explosion.

25. A planned order receipt is the result of a scheduled receipt.

26. The time difference between a planned order release and its corresponding planned order receipt is called lead time.

27. Capacity requirements are not a consideration in a closed-loop MRP system.

28. A production system based on the just-in-time philosophy relies heavily on safety stock.

29. A push system of production is more likely to cause a buildup of system inventory than is a pull system of production.

Chapter 16

Waiting Line Models

KEY CONCEPTS

CONCEPT	ILLUSTRATED PROBLEMS	ANSWERED PROBLEMS
Poisson Arrival Process	1	10
Exponential Service Time Distribution	1	10
Queuing Systems		
M/M/1	1,4,5	10-15,17
M/M/k	2,3	11,15,16,18
M/M/1 w/Finite Calling Population	6	23
M/G/1	7	19
M/G/k w/Blocked Customers Cleared	8	20,21
M/D/1	9	22
Economic Analysis of Queuing Systems	3,4,5	11,14,16,17

* Note: <u>Unless otherwise stated</u>, all problems in this chapter assume a Poisson arrival process, exponential service time distribution, first-come-first-served queue discipline and unlimited potential queue length.

REVIEW

1. Queuing theory is the study of waiting lines. Four characteristics of a queuing system are: (1) the manner in which customers arrive; (2) the time required for service; (3) the priority determining the order of service; and (4) the number and configuration of servers in the system.

2. In general, the arrival of customers into the system is a random event. Frequently the arrival pattern is modeled as a Poisson process. The Poisson distribution defines the probability of x arrivals during a specified time period as:

$$P(x) = \lambda^x e^{-\lambda}/(x!)$$

   Here λ is the mean number of arrivals during the specified period and $e = 2.71828...$ Appendix D provides a table of the quantity $e^{-\lambda}$ for specified values of λ. Sample data should be collected to determine the appropriateness of using the Poisson distribution as well as estimating the value for λ.

3. Service time is also usually a random variable. A distribution commonly used to describe this time is the exponential distribution. The exponential distribution has a probability density function:

$$f(t) = \mu e^{-\mu t}$$

   Here μ is the mean number of customers that can be served in a specified time period.

4. For the exponential distribution, the cumulative probability:

$$P(t \leq T) = 1 - e^{-\mu T}$$

   Thus the probability of a service taking longer than T is $e^{-\mu T}$.

5. The most common queue discipline is first come, first served (FCFS). An elevator is an example of last come, first served (LCFS) queue discipline.

6. A three part code of the form A/D/k is used to describe various queuing systems. Here, A identifies the arrival distribution, D the service (departure) distribution and k the number of servers for the system.

   Frequently used symbols for the arrival and service processes are: M - Markov distributions (Poisson/exponential), D - Deterministic (constant) and G - General distribution (with a known mean and variance).

   Thus the notation, M/M/k refers to a queuing situation in which arrivals occur according to a Poisson distribution, service times follow an exponential distribution and there are k servers each working at an identical service rate.

7. In order for an M/M/k system not to have an *infinitely large queue*, λ must be less than $k\mu$, where λ is the mean arrival rate and μ is the mean service rate for each server.

8. For a single server system, one defines the ratio λ/μ as the *utilization factor* for the queue. This can be thought of as the long run proportion of time the server is busy, the probability there is someone in the system, or the probability that an arriving customer must wait for service.

9. In determining the most economical queuing system configuration or evaluating service parameters for the system, one is frequently interested in long run or *steady state* results. For steady state results to exist, $\lambda < \mu$ for an M/M/1 or an M/G/1 queue, and $\lambda < k\mu$ for an M/M/k queue.

10. Notation used for various queue measures are as follows:

    P_0 = *probability* the service facility is idle
    P_n = *probability* of n units in the system
    P_w = *probability* an arriving unit must wait for service
    L_q = average *number of units* in the queue awaiting service
    L = average *number of units* in the system
    W_q = average *time* a unit spends in the queue awaiting service
    W = average *time* a unit spends in the system
    λ = the average arrival *rate*
    μ = the average service *rate* for each server
    $1/\lambda$ = the average *time* between arrivals
    $1/\mu$ = the average service *time*
    σ = the standard deviation of the service *time*

11. For nearly all queuing systems, there is a relationship between the average time a unit spends in the system or queue and the average number of units in the system or queue. These relationships, known as *Little's flow equations* are:

$$L = \lambda W \quad \text{and} \quad L_q = W_q$$

12. When the queue discipline is FCFS, *analytical formulas* have been derived for several different queuing models including the following: M/M/1, M/M/k, M/G/1, M/G/k with blocked customers cleared, and M/M/1 with a finite calling population. These formulas are presented on the next few pages.

13. Analytical formulas are not available for all possible queuing systems. In this event, insights may be gained through a *simulation* of the system.

STEADY STATE RESULTS

Quantity	M/M/1 Queues	M/M/k Queues	M/G/1 Queues*
P_0	$1-\frac{\lambda}{\mu}$	$\frac{1}{\sum_{n=0}^{k-1}\frac{(\lambda/\mu)^n}{n!}+\frac{(\lambda/\mu)^k}{k!}(\frac{k\mu}{k\mu-\lambda})}$	$1-\frac{\lambda}{\mu}$
P_n	$(\frac{\lambda}{\mu})^n P_0$	$\frac{(\lambda/\mu)^n}{n!}P_0$ for n ≤ k $\frac{(\lambda/\mu)^n}{k!k^{(n-k)}}P_0$ for n > k	No formula
L_q	$\frac{\lambda^2}{\mu(\mu-\lambda)}$	$\frac{\lambda\mu(\lambda/\mu)^k}{(k-1)!(k\mu-\lambda)^2}P_0$	$\frac{\lambda^2\sigma^2+(\lambda/\mu)^2}{2(1-\lambda/\mu)}$
L	$L_q+\frac{\lambda}{\mu}$	$L_q+\frac{\lambda}{\mu}$	$L_q+\frac{\lambda}{\mu}$
W_q	$\frac{L_q}{\lambda}$	$\frac{L_q}{\lambda}$	$\frac{L_q}{\lambda}$
W	$W_q+\frac{1}{\mu}$	$W_q+\frac{1}{\mu}$	$W_q+\frac{1}{\mu}$
P_w	$\frac{\lambda}{\mu}$	$\frac{1}{k!}(\frac{\lambda}{\mu})^k(\frac{k\mu}{k\mu-\lambda})P_0$	$\frac{\lambda}{\mu}$

Note:

* In the M/G/1 queue, if G is the exponential distribution, then $\sigma = 1/\mu$ and the above formulas reduce to those given for the M/M/1 queue.

STEADY STATE RESULTS

Quantity	M/D/1 Queues	M/G/k Queues With Blocked Customers Cleared	M/M/1 Queues* with Finite Calling Population (Size N)
P_0	$1-\frac{\lambda}{\mu}$	$\frac{1}{\sum_{i=0}^{k}(\lambda/\mu)^i/i!}$	$\frac{1}{\sum_{n=0}^{N}\frac{N!}{(N-n)!}(\frac{\lambda}{\mu})^n}$
P_n	No formula	$\frac{(\lambda/\mu)^n/n!}{\sum_{i=0}^{k}(\lambda/\mu)^i/i!}$	$\frac{N!}{(N-n)!}(\frac{\lambda}{\mu})^n P_0$
L_q	$\frac{(\lambda/\mu)^2}{2(1-\lambda/\mu)}$	No queue	$N-\frac{\lambda+\mu}{\lambda}(1-P_0)$
L	$L_q+\frac{\lambda}{\mu}$	$\frac{\lambda}{\mu}(1-P_k)$	$L_q+(1-P_0)$
W_q	$\frac{L_q}{\lambda}$	No queue	$\frac{L_q}{(N-L)\lambda}$
W	$W_q+\frac{1}{\mu}$	$\frac{1-P_k}{\mu}$	$W_q+\frac{1}{\mu}$
P_w	$\frac{\lambda}{\mu}$	No waiting	$1-P_0$

Note:

* In the finite calling population model, λ represents the mean arrival rate for each unit.

ILLUSTRATED PROBLEMS

> **NOTE:** Students frequently confuse <u>rates</u> and <u>times</u> in this chapter. They are not the same; they have an inverse relationship. The equations throughout the chapter assume λ and μ are <u>rates</u>. If you are given average interarrival time or service time, use the inverse.
>
> Also, λ and μ should be stated in the same unit of time (per hour, for example). Finally, be careful converting the standard deviation of service times σ from one unit of time to another. (It might be easier to convert the arrival rate's time basis to that of the service rate.)

> **NOTE:** Economic analysis of queuing systems usually involves a tradeoff between the cost of service and the <u>cost of waiting</u>. To get the latter, you might be inclined to multiple the waiting cost per unit per time period, c_W, by the average wait time in the system, W. If you take this approach you are not finished until you also multiply by the average number of units entering the system per hour, λ. You get the same results by simply multiplying c_W by L, the average number of units in the system.

<u>PROBLEM 1</u>

Joe Ferris is a stock trader on the floor of the New York Stock Exchange for the firm of Smith, Jones, Johnson, and Thomas, Inc. Stock transactions arrive at a mean rate of 20 per hour. Each order received by Joe requires an average of two minutes to process.

a) What is the probability that no orders are received within a 15-minute period?

b) What is the probability that exactly 3 orders are received within a 15-minute period?

c) What is the probability that more than 6 orders arrive within a 15-minute period?

d) What is the mean service rate per hour?

e) What percentage of the orders will take less than one minute to process?

f) What percentage of the orders will be completed in exactly 3 minutes?

g) What percentage of the orders will take more than 3 minutes to process?

h) What is the average time an order must wait from the time Joe receives the order until its processing is finished (i.e. its turnaround time)?

i) What is the average number of orders Joe has waiting to be processed?

j) What percentage of the time is Joe processing orders?

SOLUTION 1

Orders arrive at a mean rate of 20 per hour or one order every 3 minutes. Therefore, in a 15 minute interval the average number of orders arriving will be $\lambda = 15/3 = 5$. From Appendix D note that $e^{-5} = .0067$.

a) $P(x = 0) = (5^0e^{-5})/0! = e^{-5} = .0067$.

b) $P(x = 3) = (5^3e^{-5})/3! = 125(.0067)/6 = .1396$.

c) $P(x > 6) = 1 - P(x = 0) - P(x = 1) - P(x = 2) - P(x = 3) - P(x = 4) - P(x = 5) - P(x = 6) = 1 - .762 = .238$.

d) Since Joe Ferris' average processing time is 2 minutes (= 2/60 hr.), the mean service rate, μ, is μ = 1/(mean service time), or 60/2 = 30/hr.

e) Since the units are expressed in hours, $P(T \leq 1 \text{ minute}) = P(T \leq 1/60 \text{ hour})$. Using the exponential distribution, $P(T \leq t) = 1 - e^{-\mu t}$. Hence,

$$P(T \leq 1/60) = 1 - e^{-30(1/60)} = 1 - e^{-.5} = 1 - .6065 = .3935.$$

f) Since the exponential distribution is a continuous distribution, the probability a service time exactly equals any specific quantity is 0.

g) The percentage of orders requiring more than 3 minutes to process is:

$$P(T > 3/60) = e^{-30(3/60)} = e^{-1.5} = .2231.$$

h) This is an M/M/1 queue with λ = 20 per hour and μ = 30 per hour. The average time an order waits in the system is:

$$W = 1/(\mu - \lambda) = 1/(30 - 20) = 1/10 \text{ hour or 6 minutes.}$$

i) The average number of orders waiting in the queue is:

$$L_q = \lambda^2/[\mu(\mu - \lambda)] = (20)^2/[(30)(30-20)] = 400/300 = 4/3.$$

j) The percentage of time Joe is processing orders is equivalent to the utilization factor, λ/μ. Thus, the percentage of time he is processing orders is: $\lambda/\mu = 20/30 = 2/3$ or 66 2/3%.

PROBLEM 2

Smith, Jones, Johnson, and Thomas, Inc. (see problem 1) has begun a major advertising campaign which it believes will increase its business 50%. To handle the increased volume, the company has hired an additional floor trader, Fred Hanson, who works at the same speed as Joe Ferris.

a) Why will Joe Ferris alone not be able to handle the increase in orders?

b) What is the probability that neither Joe nor Fred will be working on an order at any point in time?

c) What is the average turnaround time for an order with both Joe and Fred working?

d) What is the average number of orders waiting to be filled with both Joe and Fred working?

SOLUTION 2

We first note that the new arrival rate of orders, λ, is 50% higher than that of problem 1. Thus, $\lambda = 1.5(20) = 30$ per hour.

a) Since Joe Ferris processes orders at a mean rate of $\mu = 30$ per hour, then $\lambda = \mu = 30$ and the utilization factor is 1. This implies the queue of orders will grow infinitely large. Hence, Joe alone cannot handle this increase in demand.

b) This is now an M/M/2 queuing system with $\lambda = 30$, $\mu = 30$, $k = 2$ and $\lambda/\mu = 1$. The probability that neither Joe nor Fred will be working is:

$$P_0 = \frac{1}{\sum_{n=0}^{k-1}\frac{(\lambda/\mu)^n}{n!} + \frac{(\lambda/\mu)^k}{k!}\left(\frac{k\mu}{k\mu-\lambda}\right)}$$

$$= \frac{1}{[(1 + (1/1!)(30/30)^1] + [(1/2!)(1)^2][2(30)/(2(30)-30)]}$$

$$= 1/(1 + 1 + 1)$$

$$= 1/3$$

c) The average turnaround time is the average waiting time in the system, W. $W = L/\lambda$ and $L = L_q + (\lambda/\mu)$. Now,

$$L_q = \frac{\lambda\mu(\lambda/\mu)^k}{(k-1)!(k\mu-\lambda)^2} P_0$$

$$= \frac{(30)(30)(30/30)^2}{(1!)((2)(30)-30))^2}(1/3)$$

$$= 1/3$$

Hence, $L = 1/3 + (30/30) = 4/3$. $W = (4/3)/30 = 4/90$ hr. = 2.67 min.

d) The average number of orders waiting to be filled is L_q. This was calculated above in part (c) as 1/3.

PROBLEM 3

The advertising campaign of Smith, Jones, Johnson and Thomas, Inc. (see problems 1 and 2) was so successful that business actually doubled. The mean rate of stock orders arriving at the exchange is now 40 per hour and the company must decide how many floor traders to employ. Each floor trader hired can process an order in an average time of 2 minutes.

Based on a number of factors the brokerage firm has determined the average waiting cost per minute for an order to be $.50. Floor traders hired will earn $20 per hour in wages and benefits. Using this information compare the total hourly cost of hiring 2 traders with that of hiring 3 traders.

SOLUTION 3

The hourly cost can be modeled as
(Total Hourly Salary Cost) + (Total Hourly Cost for Orders in the System)
= ($20/trader/hour) x (Number of Traders) + ($30 waiting cost/hour)
x (average number of orders in the system) = 20k + 30L.

Thus, L must be determined for k = 2 traders and for k = 3 traders with λ = 40/hour and μ = 30/hour (since the average service time is 2 minutes).

k = 2

$$P_0 = \frac{1}{\sum_{n=0}^{k-1} \frac{(\lambda/\mu)^n}{n!} + \frac{(\lambda/\mu)^k}{k!}\left(\frac{k\mu}{k\mu-\lambda}\right)}$$

$$= \frac{1}{[1+[(1/1!)(40/30)]+[(1/2!)(40/30)^2(60/(60-40))]} = \frac{1}{1+(4/3)+(8/3)} = 1/5$$

Thus,

$$L_q = \frac{\lambda\mu(\lambda/\mu)^k}{(k-1)!(k\mu-\lambda)^2} P_0$$

$$= \frac{40(30)(40/30)^2}{1!(2(30)-40)^2} = 16/15$$

Hence, $L = L_q + (\lambda/\mu) = 16/15 + 4/3 = 12/5$.
Thus, the total Cost = (20)(2) + 30(12/5) = \$112.00 per hour

k = 3

Using the same formulas for k = 3:

$$P_0 = \frac{1}{[1+(1/1!)(40/30)+(1/2!)(40/30)^2] + [(1/3!)(40/30)^3(90/(90-40))]}$$

$$= \frac{1}{[1 + 4/3 + 8/9] + [32/45]} = 15/59$$

Hence, $L_q = \frac{(30)(40)(40/30)^3}{(2!)(3(30)-40)^2}(15/59) = 128/885$ (=.1446)

Thus, L = 128/885 + 40/30 = 1308/885 (= 1.4780).
Total Cost = (20)(3) + 30(1308/885) = \$104.35 per hour

Thus, the cost of having 3 traders is less than that of 2 traders.

PROBLEM 4

Frederick's Auto Company currently receives an average of 22 letters a day and has a typist who can type a letter in an average time of 20 minutes. It is considering taking some relief action to ease the typist's workload. It can either hire an additional typist (who also works at an average rate of one letter per 20 minutes) at a cost of $40 per day or it can lease one of three models of word processing systems listed below:

Model	Cost Per Day	Increase in Typist's Efficiency
I	$37	50%
II	$39	75%
III	$43	150%

Frederick's has determined that the cost of a letter waiting to be mailed is $.80/hour. If typists work 8 hours/day, what action should be taken?

SOLUTION 4

For each of the 5 alternatives, determine the average number of letters in the system and the total daily cost. The total daily cost = (Extra typist cost or Lease Cost) + 6.40L, where $6.40 is $.80/hour times 8 hours/day.

Another Typist

This is an M/M/2 system with $\lambda = 22$, $\mu = 24$ and $k = 2$. Using the formulas from the review section we compute $P_0 = .3714$ and $L = 1.16$. Hence Total Cost = 40 + (6.40)(1.16) = $47.42.

Lease Machine 1

This is an M/M/1 system with $\lambda = 22$ and $\mu = (1.5)(24) = 36$. Using the formulas from the review section for an M/M/1 system, $L = 22/(36-22) = 1.57$. Total Cost = 37 + (6.40)(1.57) = $47.05.

Lease Machine 2

This is an M/M/1 system with $\lambda = 22$ and $\mu = (1.75)(24) = 42$. $L = 22/(42-22) = 1.1$. Total cost = 39 + (6.40)(1.1) = 46.04.

Lease Machine 3

This is an M/M/1 system with $\lambda = 22$ and $\mu = (2.5)(24) = 60$. $L = 22/(60-22) = .58$. Total cost = 43 + (6.40)(.58) = 46.71.

No Action

This is an M/M/1 system with $\lambda = 22$ and $\mu = 24$. $L = 22/(24-22) = 11$. Total cost = 0 + (6.40)(11) = $70.40.

Thus the best course of action is to lease Machine II.

PROBLEM 5

Jerry's Jewelry Store is seeking a salesman for its evening shift. Three applicants with former experience have applied for the position, each demanding different salaries. Jerry has contacted the former supervisor of each who has supplied him with information on average service times for each applicant. The applicant's salary demands and average service times are as follows:

Applicant	Hourly Wage	Average Service Time
Martha Miller	\$ 6	6 min.
Ken Weeks	\$10	5 min.
Eddie Smith	\$14	4 min.

Customers arrive to the store at the average rate of 8 per hour and you have estimated the cost of having a customer in the store to be \$4 per customer per hour (for security, customer relations, etc.) Which applicant should Jerry hire?

SOLUTION 5

For each applicant calculate the total hourly cost = (Hourly Wage) + 4L, where L is the average number of customers in the system. Each case is an M/M/1 queuing system with $\lambda = 8$.

Martha Miller

Since the average service time is 6 min., the average service rate, $\mu = 1/6$ per minute or 10 per hour.

$L = 8/(10-8) = 4$. Thus total hourly cost = $6 + (4)(4) = \$22$.

Ken Weeks

Since the average service time is 5 min., the average service rate, $\mu = 1/5$ per minute or 12 per hour.

$L = 8/(12-8) = 2$. Thus total hourly cost = $10 + (4)(2) = \$18$.

Eddie Smith

Since the average service time is 4 min., the average service rate, $\mu = 1/4$ per minute or 15 per hour.

$L = 8/(15-8) = 8/7$. Total hourly cost = $14 + (4)(8/7) = \$18.56$.

Based on this study, hire Ken Weeks.

PROBLEM 6

Biff Smith is in charge of maintenance for four of the rides at the Algorithmland Amusement Park: the Pivot, the Traveling Salesman's Adventure, Minimax Regret, and the CPM Crash. On the average, each ride operates four hours before needing repair. When repair is needed, the average repair time is 10 minutes.

Assuming that the time between machine repairs and the service times follow exponential distributions, determine the following:

a) the proportion of time Biff is idle

b) the average time a ride is "down" for repairs

> **NOTE:** For an M/M/1 system with a finite calling population, the arrival rate is the average number of times one unit from the finite population arrives per time period, not the average number of total arrivals per time period.

SOLUTION 6

This problem can be modeled as an M/M/1 queue with a finite calling population of size N = 4 (rides). Here

$$\lambda = 1/(4 \text{ hours}) = .25 \text{ per hour}$$
$$\mu = 60/(10 \text{ minutes}) = 6 \text{ per hour.}$$
$$\lambda/\mu = .25/6 = 1/24$$

a) The proportion of time Biff is idle is P_0:

$$P_0 = \frac{1}{\sum_{n=0}^{N} \frac{N!}{(N-n)!}\left(\frac{\lambda}{\mu}\right)^n}$$

$$P_0 = \frac{1}{\frac{4!}{4!}(1/24)^0+\frac{4!}{3!}(1/24)^1+\frac{4!}{2!}(1/24)^2+\frac{4!}{1!}(1/24)^3+\frac{4!}{0!}(1/24)^4}$$

$$= \frac{1}{1 + 4(1/24)^1 + 12(1/24)^2 + 24(1/24)^3 + 24(1/24)^4} = .840825$$

Hence, Biff is idle approximately 84% of the time.

b) To find the average time a ride is "down" for repairs we need to calculate W. This is given by the formula:

$$W = W_q + \frac{1}{\mu} \text{ where } W_q = \frac{L_q}{(N-L)\lambda},\ L_q = N - \frac{\lambda+\mu}{\lambda}(1-P_0) \text{ and } L = L_q + (1-P_0)$$

Substituting the appropriate values gives:

L_q = 4 - ((.25+6)/.25)(1-.840825) = .020625

L = .020625 + (1-.840825) = .1798

Wq = .020625/((4-.1798).25) = .02159573

W = .02159573 + 1/6 = .18826 hours or 11.3 minutes

PROBLEM 7

The Bowmar University Student Union has one self service copying machine. On the average, 12 customers per hour arrive to make copies. (The arrival process follows a Poisson distribution.) The time to copy documents follows approximately a <u>normal</u> distribution with a mean of two and one-half minutes and a standard deviation of 30 seconds.

The Union president has received several complaints from students regarding the long lines at the copying machine. On the basis of this information determine:

a) the average number of customers waiting or using the copy machine.

b) the probability an arriving customer must wait in line.

c) the proportion of time the copy machine is idle.

d) the average time a customer must wait in line before using the copy machine.

SOLUTION 7

This situation can be modeled as an M/G/1 system with

λ = 12 per hour = 12/60 =.2/minute
$1/\mu$ = 2.5 minutes
μ = 1/(2.5) = .4 per minute
σ = 30 seconds = .5 minutes

a) The average number of customers waiting or using the copy machine is:

$$L = L_q + \frac{\lambda}{\mu} \quad \text{where } L_q = \frac{\lambda^2\sigma^2 + (\lambda/\mu)^2}{2(1-\lambda/\mu)}$$

Substituting the appropriate values gives:

$$L_q = \frac{(.2)^2(.5)^2 + (.2/.4)^2}{2(1-(.2/.4)} = .26 \qquad \text{Thus } L = .26 + (.2/.4) = .76$$

b) The probability an arriving customer must wait in line is:

$P_W = \lambda/\mu = .2/.4 = .5$

c) The proportion of time the copy machine is idle is:

$P_0 = 1 - \lambda/\mu = 1 - .2/.4 = .5$

d) The average time a customer must wait in line before using the copy machine is:

$W_q = L_q/\lambda = .26/.2 = 1.3$ minutes

PROBLEM 8

Several firms are over the counter (OTC) market makers of Probabillistics stock. A broker wishing to trade this stock for a client will call on these firms to execute the order. If the market maker's phone line is busy, a broker will immediately try calling another market maker to transact the order.

Richardson and Company is one such OTC market maker. It estimates that on the average, a broker will try to call to execute a stock transaction every two minutes. The time required to complete the transaction averages 75 seconds. The firm has four traders staffing its phones.

Assume calls arrive according to a Poisson distribution.

a) What percentage of its potential business will be lost by Richardson?

b) What percentage of its potential business would be lost if only three traders staffed its phones?

SOLUTION 8

This problem can be modeled as an M/G/k system with block customers cleared with:

$$1/\lambda = 2 \text{ minutes} = 2/60 \text{ hour}$$
$$\lambda = 60/2 = 30 \text{ per hour}$$
$$1/\mu = 75 \text{ seconds} = 75/60 \text{ minutes} = 75/3600 \text{ hours}$$
$$\mu = 3600/75 = 48 \text{ per hour}$$

a) As there are four traders staffing the phones, k = 4, and the system will be blocked when there are four customers in the system. Hence, the answer is P_4. To find P_4, first find P_0 by:

$$P_0 = \frac{1}{\sum_{i=0}^{k} (\lambda/\mu)^i / i!} \quad \text{where } k = 4$$

$$= \frac{1}{1 + (30/48) + (30/48)^2/2! + (30/48)^3/3! + (30/48)^4/4!}$$

$$= \frac{1}{1 + (.625) + (.625)^2/2 + (.625)^3/6 + (.625)^4/24}$$

$$= .536$$

$$\text{Now, } P_4 = \frac{(\lambda/\mu)^4}{4!} P_0 = \frac{(30/48)^4}{24}(.536) = .003$$

Thus with four traders 0.3% of the potential customers are lost.

b) In this case k = 3, and the answer is P_3. Recalculate P_0:

$$P_0 = \frac{1}{1 + (30/48) + (30/48)^2/2! + (30/48)^3/3!} = .537$$

$$\text{Now, } P_3 = \frac{(\lambda/\mu)^3}{3!} P_0 = \frac{(30/48)^3}{6}(.537) = .022$$

Thus with three traders 2.2% of the potential customers are lost.

PROBLEM 9

The long distance viewing scope at the scenic rest stop on Interstate 20 provides two minutes of viewing for $.25. People wanting to use the scope arrive according to a Poisson distribution with a mean rate of 15 per hour.

a) What fraction of time is the scope idle?

b) What is the average number of sightseers waiting to use the scope?

c) What is the average time a sightseer waits to use the scope?

SOLUTION 9

This situation can modeled as an M/D/1 system with

$$\begin{aligned} \lambda &= 15 \text{ per hour} \\ 1/\mu &= 2 \text{ minutes} = 2/60 \text{ hour} \\ \mu &= 60/2 = 30 \text{ per hour} \\ \sigma &= 0 \end{aligned}$$

a) The fraction of time the scope is idle is the complement of the utilization factor:

$$1 - \lambda/\mu = 1 - 15/30 = .5$$

b) The average number of customers waiting in line is:

$$L_q = \frac{(\lambda/\mu)^2}{2(1 - \lambda/\mu)} = \frac{(15/30)^2}{2(1- 15/30)} = .25 \text{ people}$$

c) The average time a customer must wait to use the scope is:

$$W_q = L_q/\lambda = .25/15 = .01667 \text{ hours or } 1.0 \text{ minutes.}$$

ANSWERED PROBLEMS

PROBLEM 10

Customers arrive at the Roney Tax Preparation office at an average rate of one per hour. The average time it takes Ms. Roney to prepare a customer's income tax form is 45 minutes.

a) What is the probability of no customers arriving in 2 hours?

b) What is the probability that an income tax form is finished within 45 minutes from the time it is started?

c) What is the average time a customer spends waiting to see Ms. Roney?

d) What is the probability Ms. Roney has 3 customers in the office (i.e. 2 waiting customers plus the one being served)?

PROBLEM 11

Ms. Roney is contemplating a computer system to help her with her income tax preparation (see problem 9). She estimates that such a system will reduce the average time to prepare a return from 45 minutes to 30 minutes. The computer leases for $40 per day.

Ms. Roney estimates the average cost to her of having a waiting customer (due to good will, lost sales, etc.) is $3 per hour. She is open 10 hours per day.

a) Should she lease the computer?

b) If Ms. Roney has the option of hiring another tax preparer for $60 per day who works at the same speed she does, should she do this rather than lease the computer?

PROBLEM 12

The postmaster at the Oak Hill Post Office expects the mean arrival rate of people to her customer counter will soon increase by fifty percent due to a large apartment complex being built.

Currently, the mean arrival rate is 15 people per hour. The postmaster can serve an average of 25 people per hour.

By what percentage must the postmaster's mean service rate increase when the apartment complex is completed in order that the average time spent at the post office remains at its current value?

PROBLEM 13

Cars travel down Main Street at the rate of 20,000 per hour. The probability of any of these cars stopping at the drive-in window of the Burger Prince Restaurant is .002. Cars at Burger Prince are serviced at the mean rate of 60 per hour.

a) What is the average arrival rate to the drive-in window?

b) What is the average number of cars waiting to be served?

c) What is the average number of cars both being served and waiting to be served?

d) What is the probability an arriving car to the Burger Prince Restaurant must wait for service?

e) Management believes that if the number of cars waiting to be served was reduced to less than 1, the probability a car would stop at the drive-in window would increase to .003 and is contemplating implementing changes to speed up service. Given the increased arrival rate, what is the minimum value of the service rate that will meet management's objective?

PROBLEM 14

Cabinet Crafters manufactures specially designed kitchen cabinets and bathroom vanities. One piece of machinery used on most projects is a stationary router. The average number of times carpenters use the router daily is 20 and the average time required for each use is 15 minutes.
The company is planning to purchase a digital router which should reduce the average time required for each use to 12 minutes. The digital router will cost an additional $60 per day. If carpenters earn an average of $20 per hour and work 9 hours per day, determine whether or not Cabinet Crafters should purchase the digital router.

PROBLEM 15

Shear's Department Store has 2 catalog order desks, one at each entrance to the store. On the average, a customer arrives at each order desk every 12 minutes. The service rate at each order desk is an average of 8 customers per hour.
Shear's is considering consolidating its two desks into one location staffed by two order clerks. They would continue to serve customers at the mean rate of 8 customers per hour. Shear's figures it would not lose customers under this arrangement and hence arrivals to this single desk would occur every 6 minutes on the average.
For each configuration of the catalog order desks determine:

a) the average number of customers waiting to be served

b) the probability no customers are present in the entire system

c) the average time a customer spends at the order desk(waiting time plus service time)

d) the probability both clerks are busy

e) should Shear's consolidate its catalog order desks? Explain.

PROBLEM 16

The insurance department at Shear's has two agents, each working at a mean speed of 8 customers per hour. Customers arrive at the insurance desk at a mean rate of one every six minutes and form a single queue.

Management feels that some customers are going to find the wait at the desk too long and take their business to Word's, Shear's competitor. In order to reduce the time required by an agent to serve a customer Shear's is contemplating installing one of two minicomputer systems: System A which leases for $18 per day and will increase an agent's efficiency by 25%; or, System B which leases for $23 per day and will increase an agent's efficiency by 50%. Agents work 8-hour days.

If Shear's estimates its cost of having a customer in the system at $3 per hour, determine if Shear's should install a new minicomputer system, and if so, which one.

PROBLEM 17

A company has tool cribs where workmen draw parts. Two men have applied for the position of distributing parts to the workmen. George Fuller is fresh out of trade school and expects a $6 per hour salary. His average service time is 4 minutes. John Cox is a veteran who expects $12 per hour. His average service time is 2 minutes. A workman's time is figured at $10 per hour. Workmen arrive to draw parts at an average rate of 12 per hour.

a) What is the average waiting time a workman would spend in the system under each applicant?

b) Which applicant should be hired?

PROBLEM 18

Dollar Supermarkets currently has 5 checkout positions. On the average, one customer per minute enters the store and spends an average of 55 minutes choosing his items. Each checker can check out a customer in an average of 4 minutes.

a) What is the average time a customer will spend in the store?

b) Management is considering reducing the number of checkout positions to 3 and hiring baggers. This would reduce the average time required to check out a customer to 2.5 minutes. Would this reduce the average waiting time?

PROBLEM 19

Ted "Tank" Fuller operates a small Texxon gas station that has one gas pump. The arrival rate of vehicles to the pump follows a Poisson probability distribution having a mean of 10 per hour. The time it takes Tank to service a vehicle follows a normal distribution with a mean of 4 minutes and a standard deviation of 1.5 minutes.

a) What is the utilization factor for the gas pump?

b) What is the average length of time a gas customer spends waiting for service to begin?

c) What is the average number of full-service vehicles at the gas station?

d) What is the probability that the servicing of a vehicle will take no more than 7 minutes (excluding the queue wait)?

PROBLEM 20

Tom's Towing Service operates three tow trucks and relies solely on towing requests from the city police department. If Tom has a truck available when the police need one, Tom is always their first choice. However, if he does not have a truck available, the police will select an alternative company rather than wait.

On the average, the police request a tow truck once every 50 minutes. Tom estimates his average tow job takes 90 minutes.

a) Is Tom achieving at least 50 percent utilization of his fleet of tow trucks? (HINT: start by determining the average number of his trucks being used.)

b) What percentage of the police department's towing business is Tom losing because he has only three trucks?

PROBLEM 21

Quick Clean Rooter cleans out clogged drains. Due to the competitive nature of the drain cleaning business, if a customer calls Quick Clean and finds the line busy, they immediately try another company and Quick Clean loses the business.

Quick Clean management estimates that on the average, a customer tries to call Quick Clean every three minutes and the average time to take a service order is 200 seconds. The company wishes to hire enough operators so that at most 4% of its potential customers get the busy signal.

a) How many operators should be hired to meet this objective?

b) Given your answer to a), what is the probability that all the operators are idle?

PROBLEM 22

The Quick Snap photo machine at the Lemon County bus station takes four snapshots in exactly 75 seconds. Customers arrive at the machine according to a Poisson distribution at the mean rate of 20 per hour.

On the basis of this information, determine the following:

a) the average number of customers waiting to use the photo machine

b) the average time a customer spends in the system

c) the probability an arriving customer must wait for service.

PROBLEM 23

Andy Archer, Ph.D., is a training consultant for six mid-sized manufacturing firms. On the average, each of his six clients calls him for consulting assistance once every 25 days. Andy typically spends an average of five days at the client's firm during each consultation.

Assuming that the time between client calls follows an exponential distribution, determine the following:

a) the average number of clients Andy has on backlog

b) the average time a client must wait before Andy arrives to it

c) the proportion of the time Andy is busy.

TRUE/FALSE

24. For a single server queue, the average time a customer spends in the system is equal to the average time a customer spends in the waiting line plus the average service time.

25. In order to obtain analytical results for a queuing problem one must assume an exponential service time.

26. For a single server queuing system, the average number of customers in the waiting line is one less than the average number in the system.

27. In queuing notation L_q is the average time a customer spends in the waiting line.

28. Little's flow equations apply to any queuing system regardless of the arrival distribution, service time distribution, and number of channels.

29. For an M/M/1 queue, the sum of the utilization factor plus P_0 equals 1.

30. Queue discipline refers to the assumption that a customer has the patience to remain in a slow moving queue.

31. For an M/M/2 system, the probability that the system is empty plus the probability an arriving customer must wait for service equals 1.

32. If some maximum number of customers are allowed in a queuing system at one time, the system has a finite calling population.

33. Assuming the same arrival rates, the average number of customers in the system for an M/M/1 system is the same as that for an M/M/2 system if the average service time in the M/M/2 system is twice as long as for the M/M/1 system.

34. For an M/M/k system, the average number of customers in the system equals the customer arrival rate times the average time a customer spends waiting in the system.

35. Simulation may be used to obtain results for queuing systems.

36. For an M/M/1 queuing system, if the service rate, μ, is doubled, the average wait in the system, W, is cut in half.

37. A multiple-channel system has more than one waiting line.

38. Even when the mean service rate of the queuing system cannot be increased, a reduction in the service time variation will reduce the average length of the waiting line.

Chapter 17
Computer Simulation

KEY CONCEPTS

CONCEPT	ILLUSTRATED PROBLEMS	ANSWERED PROBLEMS
Simulation of:		
One Event	1,2	9
Two Events	3	7,8,10,11,14
Multiple Events	4	13,15
Comparison of Expected and Simulated Outcomes	1,6	9,10
Simulation of Decision Alternatives	2	7,10,11,14
Simulation Applications:		
Inventory Systems	2	10,11,13
Waiting Lines	3,4	8,12,15
Markov Processes	5	16
Project Times	6	9

REVIEW

1. Computer simulation is one of the most frequently employed management science techniques. It is typically used to model random processes that are too complex to be solved by analytical methods.

2. One begins a computer simulation by developing a mathematical statement of the problem. The model should be realistic yet solvable within the speed and storage constraints of the computer system being used. Input values for the model as well as probability estimates for the random variables must then be determined.

3. Random variable values are utilized in the model through a technique known as Monte Carlo simulation. Here each random variable is mapped to a set of numbers so that each time one number in that set is generated, the corresponding value of the random variable is given as an input to the model. The mapping is done in such a way that the likelihood that a particular number is chosen is the same as the probability that the corresponding value of the random variable occurs.

4. Because a computer program generates random numbers for the mapping according to some formula, the numbers are not truly generated in a random fashion. However, using standard statistical tests, the numbers can be shown to appear to be drawn from a random process. These numbers are called pseudo-random numbers. Appendix E is a table of pseudo-random digits.

5. In a fixed time simulation model, time periods are incremented by a fixed amount. For each time period a different set of data from the input sequence is used to calculate the effects on the model.

6. In a next event simulation model, time periods are not fixed but are determined by the data values from the input sequence.

7. The computer program that performs the simulation is called a simulator. Flowcharts can be useful in writing such a program. While this program can be written in any general purpose language (e.g. BASIC, FORTRAN, PL/1, etc.) special languages which reduce the amount of code which must be written to perform the simulation have been developed. Some of these are SIMSCRIPT, GASP, DYNAMO, and SLAM.

8. Validation of both the model and the method used by the computer to carry out the calculations is extremely important. Models which do not accurately reflect real world behavior cannot be expected to generate meaningful results. Likewise, errors in programming can result in nonsensical results.

9. Validation is generally done by having an expert review the model and the computer code for errors. If possible, the simulation should be run using actual past data. Predictions from the simulation model should be compared with historical results.

10. Experimental design is an important consideration in the simulation process. Issues such as the length of time of the simulation and the treatment of initial data outputs from the model must be addressed prior to collecting and analyzing output data. Through careful development of the simulation model, one can reduce the time required for the computer run without sacrificing the accuracy of the results.

11. Normally one is interested in results for the steady state (long run) operation of the system being modelled. Hence, the initial data inputs to the simulation generally represent a start-up period for the process and it may be important that the data outputs for this start-up period be neglected for predicting this long run behavior.

12. For each policy under consideration by the decision maker, the simulation is run by considering a long sequence of input data values (given by a pseudo-random number generator). Whenever possible, different policies should be compared by using the same sequence of input data.

13. Among the advantages of computer simulation is the ability to gain insights into the model solution which may be impossible to attain through other techniques. Also, once the simulation has been developed, it provides a convenient experimental laboratory to perform "what if" and sensitivity analysis.

14. Two major disadvantages of simulation are: (1) a large amount of time may be required to develop the simulation; and, (2) there is no guarantee that the solution obtained will actually be optimal. Simulation is, in effect, a trial and error method of comparing different policy inputs. It does not determine if some input which was not considered could have provided a better solution for the model.

FLOW CHART OF
COMPUTER SIMULATION PROCESS

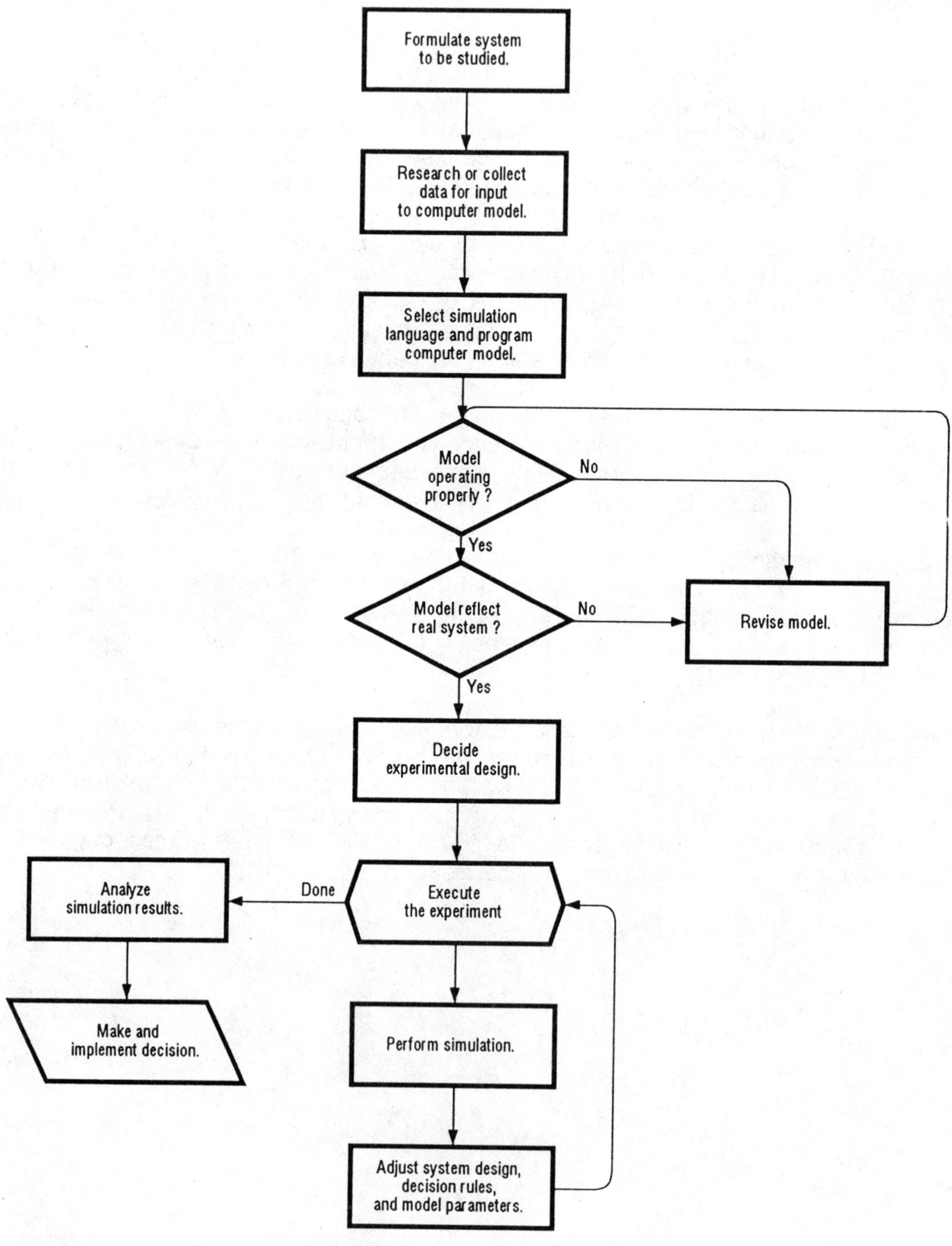

ILLUSTRATED PROBLEMS

> **NOTE:** Several of the problems in this chapter relate to topics of other chapters such as inventory, waiting lines, markov processes, and projects. Where applicable, you are encouraged to compare your simulation results with those of analytic procedures covered in other chapters. However, you might find significant differences that are due most likely to the small number of simulation trials performed.

PROBLEM 1

The price change of shares of Probablistics, Inc. has been observed over the past 50 trades. The frequency distribution is as follows:

Price Change	Frequency (Number of Trades)
-3/8	4
-1/4	2
-1/8	8
0	20
+1/8	10
+1/4	3
+3/8	2
+1/2	1
TOTAL	50

a) Develop a relative frequency distribution for this data.

b) If the current price per share of Probablistics is 23, use random numbers to simulate the price per share over the next 20 trades. (For random numbers, use the first two numbers at the bottom of column 1 of Appendix E and move up.)

c) Compare this price with the expected price one would obtain based on the probability distribution.

SOLUTION 1

a) To develop a relative frequency distribution for this data, divide the frequency of each price by the total number of trades. The results are shown in the table below.

b) To develop a simulation for the future prices, assign a random number to each price change so that the probability of seeing a certain price corresponds to its probability (relative frequency).

One such assignment of numbers is:

Price Change	Relative Frequency	Random Numbers
-3/8	.08	00 - 07
-1/4	.04	08 - 11
-1/8	.16	12 - 27
0	.40	28 - 67
+1/8	.20	68 - 87
+1/4	.06	88 - 93
+3/8	.04	94 - 97
+1/2	.02	98 - 99
	TOTAL 1.00	

According to the instructions, the first random number will be 21, the second 84, etc. The simulated results are:

Trade Number	Random Number	Price Change	Stock Price
1	21	-1/8	22 7/8
2	84	+1/8	23
3	07	-3/8	22 5/8
4	30	0	22 5/8
5	94	+3/8	23
6	57	0	23
7	57	0	23
8	19	-1/8	22 7/8
9	84	+1/8	23
10	84	+1/8	23 1/8
11	62	0	23 1/8
12	32	0	23 1/8
13	71	+1/8	23 1/4
14	94	+3/8	23 5/8
15	04	-3/8	23 1/4
16	97	+3/8	23 5/8
17	58	0	23 5/8
18	67	0	23 5/8
19	78	+1/8	23 3/4
20	14	-1/8	23 5/8

c) Based on the probability distribution, the expected price change per trade can be calculated by: $(.08)(-3/8) + (.04)(-1/4) + (.16)(-1/8) + (.40)(0) + (.20)(1/8) + (.06)(1/4) + (.04)(3/8) + (.02)(1/2) = .005$

The expected price change for 20 trades is $(20)(.005) = .10$. Hence, the expected stock price after 20 trades is $23 + .10 = 23.10$. This is lower than the simulated price of 23.625.

PROBLEM 2

Shelly's Supermarket has just installed a postage stamp vending machine. Based on one month of operation, Shelly's estimates the number of postage stamps sold per day can be approximated by the following distribution:

Number Sold Per Day	Probability
20	.10
30	.15
40	.20
50	.25
60	.20
70	.10

Shelly's makes a $.02 profit per postage stamp. The vending machine holds 230 stamps and it costs Shelly's $2.00 in labor to fill the machine.

a) Determine the mean number of stamps sold per day.

b) Determine the mean time until the machine is empty.

c) Assume that Shelly's adopts the following policy. Shelly's will fill the machine at the beginning of every n-th day, where n is the answer found in part (b). Conduct a 20-day simulation and determine the expected profit per day. Assume the machine must be filled on the first day. (Use the first two numbers of column 3 of Appendix E, beginning at the top for the random numbers.)

d) Suppose Shelly's fills the machine every (n-1)-th day. Repeat the 20-day simulation and compare the answer with that of part (c). Which policy would you recommend?

SOLUTION 2

The flow chart on the next page can assist in setting up the simulations.

a) The mean number of stamps sold daily =
(.10)(20)+(.15)(30)+(.20)(40)+(.25)(50)+(.20)(60)+(.10)(70) = 46.

b) The mean time until the machine is empty is:
(Machine capacity)/(Mean number of stamps sold per day) = 230/46 = 5 days.

Flow Chart of Vending Machine Simulation

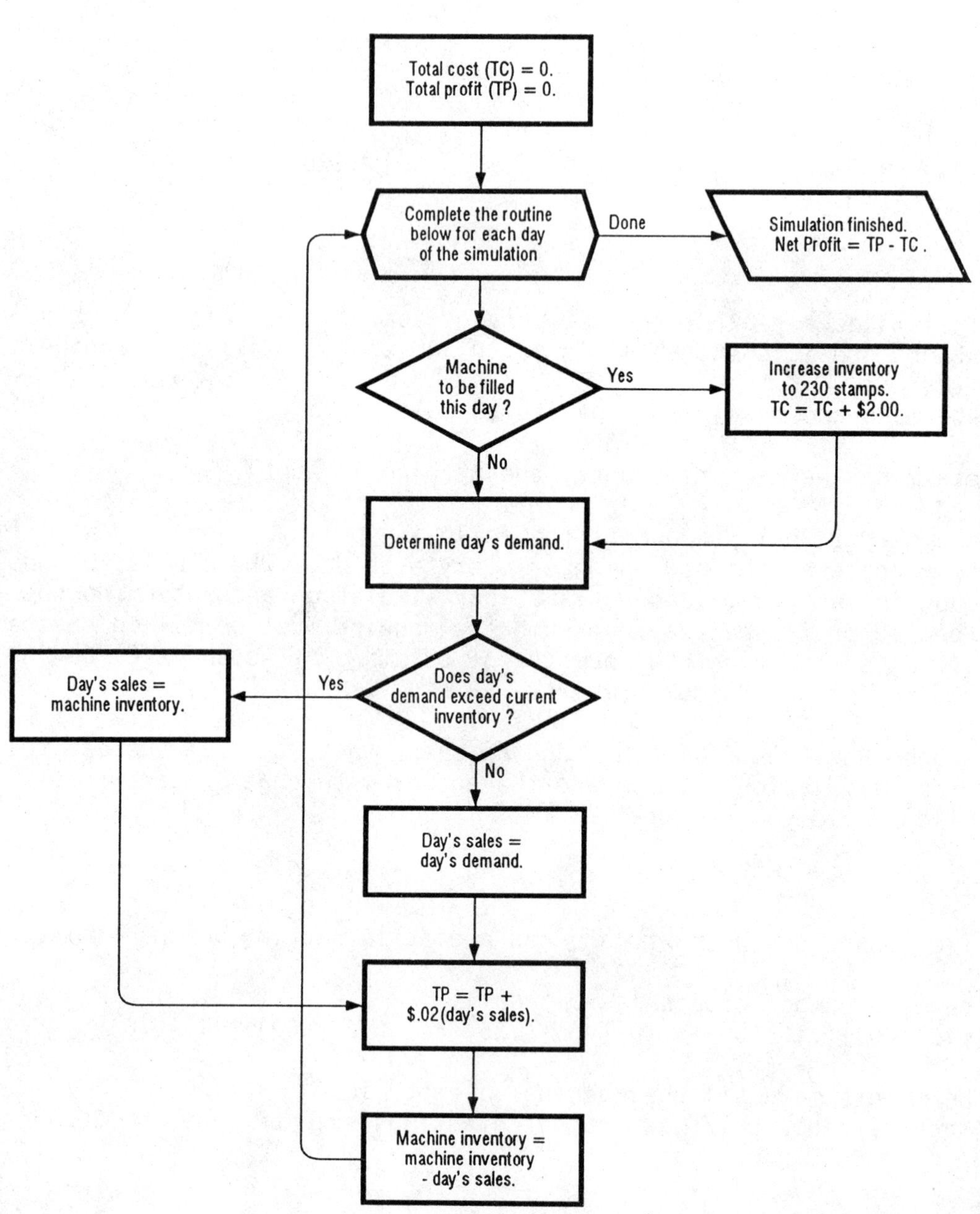
Total cost (TC) = 0.
Total profit (TP) = 0.
Complete the routine below for each day of the simulation
Done
Simulation finished.
Net Profit = TP - TC .
Machine to be filled this day ?
Yes
Increase inventory to 230 stamps.
TC = TC + $2.00.
No
Determine day's demand.
Does day's demand exceed current inventory ?
Yes
Day's sales = machine inventory.
No
Day's sales = day's demand.
TP = TP + $.02(day's sales).
Machine inventory = machine inventory - day's sales.

Assuming Shelly's fills the machine every fifth day, determine a set of random numbers corresponding to each sales level.

Number Sold Per Day	Range Of Numbers
20	00 - 09
30	10 - 24
40	25 - 44
50	45 - 69
60	70 - 89
70	90 - 99

Following the instructions of using the first two numbers in column 3 of Appendix E generates the following simulation:

Day	Random Number	Demand	Number Of Stamps Left In Machine	Profit From Sale Of Stamps	Cost Of Refilling Machine	Daily Profit
1	71	60	170	1.20	2.00	- .80
2	95	70	100	1.40	--	1.40
3	83	60	40	1.20	--	1.20
4	44	40	0	.80	--	.80
5	34	40	0	0*	--	0
6	49	50	180	1.00	2.00	-1.00
7	88	60	120	1.20	--	1.20
8	56	50	70	1.00	--	1.00
9	05	20	50	.40	--	.40
10	39	40	10	.80	--	.80
11	75	60	170	1.20	2.00	- .80
12	12	30	140	.60	--	.60
13	03	20	120	.40	--	.40
14	59	50	70	1.00	--	1.00
15	29	40	30	.80	--	.80
16	77	60	170	1.20	2.00	- .80
17	76	60	110	1.20	--	1.20
18	57	50	60	1.00	--	1.00
19	15	30	30	.60	--	.60
20	53	50	0	.60**	--	.60

Total Profit = $9.60

* 0 since the machine was empty
** .60 since there were only 30 stamps left in the machine

Expected Profit per Day = (9.60)/20 = $.48.

d) In order to compare the two policies, the same set of input data should be generated. Thus the simulation below has the same input for daily demand as that of part (c). In this part, the machine is to be filled every fourth day.

Day	Random Number	Demand	Number Of Stamps Left In Machine	Profit From Sale Of Stamps	Cost Of Refilling Machine	Daily Profit
1	71	60	170	1.20	2.00	- .80
2	95	70	100	1.40	--	1.40
3	83	60	40	1.20	--	1.20
4	44	40	0	.80	--	.80
5	34	40	190	0	2.00	-1.20
6	49	50	140	1.00	--	1.00
7	88	60	80	1.20	--	1.20
8	56	50	30	1.00	--	1.00
9	05	20	210	.40	2.00	-1.60
10	39	40	170	.80	--	.80
11	75	60	110	1.20	--	1.20
12	12	30	80	.60	--	.60
13	03	20	210	.40	2.00	-1.60
14	59	50	160	1.00	--	1.00
15	29	40	120	.80	--	.80
16	77	60	60	1.20	--	1.20
17	76	60	170	1.20	2.00	- .80
18	57	50	120	1.00	--	1.00
19	15	30	90	.60	--	.60
20	53	50	40	.60	--	1.00

Total Profit = $8.80

Expected Daily Profit = $ .44

Based on the results of this simulation, Shelly's should fill the machine every fifth day rather than every fourth day.

PROBLEM 3

Wayne International Airport primarily serves domestic air traffic. Occasionally, however, a chartered plane from abroad will arrive with passengers bound for Wayne's two great amusement parks, Algorithmland and Giffith's Cherry Preserve.

Whenever an international plane arrives at the airport the two customs inspectors on duty set up operations to process the passengers.

Incoming passengers must first have their passports and visas checked. This is handled by one inspector. The time required to check a passenger's passports and visas can be described by the following probability distribution:

Time Required to Check a Passenger's Passport and Visa	Probability
20 seconds	.20
40 seconds	.40
60 seconds	.30
80 seconds	.10

After having their passports and visas checked, the passengers next proceed to the second customs official who does baggage inspections. Passengers form a single waiting line with the official inspecting baggage on a first come, first served basis.

The time required for baggage inspection has the following probability distribution:

Time Required For Baggage Inspection	Probability
No Time	.25
1 minute	.60
2 minutes	.10
3 minutes	.05

a) If a chartered plane from abroad lands at Wayne Airport with 80 passengers, use simulation to determine how long it will take for the first 20 passengers to clear customs. (From Appendix E, use the first two digits in column 8 for passport control and the first two digits in column 9 for baggage inspection.)

b) What is the average length of time a customer waits before having his bags inspected after he clears passport control? How is this estimate biased?

SOLUTION 3

The problem is easiest to set up as a next-event simulation model. The random number mappings are:

Time Required to Check a Passenger's Passport and Visa	Probability	Random Numbers
20 seconds	.20	00 - 19
40 seconds	.40	20 - 59
60 seconds	.30	60 - 89
80 seconds	.10	90 - 99

Time Required For Baggage Inspection	Probability	Random Numbers
No Time	.25	00 - 24
1 minute	.60	25 - 84
2 minutes	.10	85 - 94
3 minutes	.05	95 - 99

For each passenger the following information must be recorded:
(1) When his service begins at the passport control inspection
(2) The length of time of this service
(3) When his service begins at the baggage inspection
(4) The length of time of this service

Note the following relationships:

(1) Time a passenger begins service by the passport inspector = (Time the previous passenger started passport service) + (Time of previous passenger's passport service)

(2) Time a passenger begins being served by the baggage inspector depends on whether or not the passenger must wait in line for this service. Thus,
   If passenger does not wait in line for baggage inspection:
      Time a passenger begins being served by the baggage inspector = (Time passenger completes service with the passport control inspector)
   If the passenger does wait in line for baggage inspection:
      Time a passenger begins being served by the baggage inspector = (Time previous passenger completes service with the baggage inspector)

(3) Time a customer completes service at the baggage inspector = (Time customer begins service with baggage inspector) + (Time required for baggage inspection).

The following table describes the simulation: (service times in minutes)

	Passport Control				Baggage Inspections			
Passenger Number	Time Begin	Random Number	Service Time	Time End	Time Begin	Random Number	Service Time	Time End
1	0:00	93	1:20	1:20	1:20	13	0:00	1:20
2	1:20	63	1:00	2:20	2:20	08	0:00	2:20
3	2:20	26	:40	3:00	3:00	60	1:00	4:00
4	3:00	16	:20	3:20	4:00	13	0:00	4:00
5	3:20	21	:40	4:00	4:00	68	1:00	5:00
6	4:00	26	:40	4:40	5:00	40	1:00	6:00
7	4:40	70	1:00	5:40	6:00	40	1:00	7:00
8	5:40	55	:40	6:20	7:00	27	1:00	8:00
9	6:20	72	1:00	7:20	8:00	23	0:00	8:00
10	7:20	89	1:00	8:20	8:20	64	1:00	9:20
11	8:20	49	:40	9:00	9:20	36	1:00	10:20
12	9:00	64	1:00	10:00	10:20	56	1:00	11:20
13	10:00	91	1:20	11:20	11:20	25	1:00	12:20
14	11:20	02	:20	11:40	12:20	88	2:00	14:20
15	11:40	52	:40	12:20	14:20	18	0:00	14:20
16	12:20	69	1:00	13:20	14:20	74	1:00	15:20
17	13:20	29	:40	14:00	15:20	75	1:00	16:20
18	14:00	96	1:20	15:20	16:20	29	1:00	17:20
19	15:20	95	1:20	16:40	17:20	80	1:00	18:20
20	16:40	84	1:00	17:40	18:20	25	1:00	19:20

For example, passenger 1 begins being served by the passport control inspector immediately. His service time is 1:20 (80 seconds) at which time he goes to the baggage inspector who waves him through without inspection.

Passenger 2 begins service with passport inspector 1:20 minutes (80 seconds) after arriving there (as this is when passenger 1 is finished) and requires 1:00 minute (60 seconds) for passport inspection. He is waved through baggage inspection as well. The process continues in this manner.

a) Passenger 20 clears customs after 19 minutes 20 seconds.

b) For each passenger calculate his waiting time (in seconds): (Baggage Inspection Begins) - (Passport Control Ends) = 0+0+0+40+0+20+20+40+40+0+20+20+0+40+120+60+80+60+40+40 = 640 seconds. This gives an average of 640/20 = 32 seconds per passenger. This is a biased estimate because we assume that the simulation began with the system empty, resulting in underestimated average waiting time.

PROBLEM 4

Attendees at the National Management Science Society (NMSS) Conference register by first standing in line to pay their fees. They then proceed to a designated line based on the first letter of their last name to collect their conference materials.

At the conference, it is planned to have three different parallel lines for the collection of materials: one each for people whose last names begin with A-H, I-Q, and R-Z respectively.

During each minute of the morning registration period it is anticipated that attendees will arrive to pay their fees according to the following distribution:

Number of Arrivals	Probability
0	.30
1	.30
2	.30
3	.10

The time to pay one's fees is either one minute or two minutes depending upon whether one uses a check or credit card. The probability of a one-minute time is .60.

After paying his fees, an attendee then goes to the correct line for the conference materials. At this year's conference 35% of the attendees have last names beginning with A-H, 36% with last names beginning with I-Q, and 29% with last names beginning with R-Z. The time required to pick up conference materials is fixed at 2 minutes.

a) Simulate the waiting line for the first 30 attendees during the morning registration. From Appendix E, use column 3 to generate the number of arrivals in any given minute, column 4 to generate registration fee service time, and column 5 to generate the first letter of the last name. Assume registration begins at 8:00 AM.

b) What is the average size of the waiting line to pay fees (not including the person being served), and the average customer waiting time to pay fees based on this simulation?

c) What is the percentage of time each of the three individuals who distribute conference materials is working?

SOLUTION 4

a) For each minute, record the number of arrivals at the fee desk. Then for each arrival determine how long he must wait in line to pay fees, his service time to pay fees, which conference material line is joined, and his waiting and service time in that material line.

Random numbers are needed for the number of arrivals in a given minute to the fee line, the length of service time in the fee line, and first letter of the last name to determine to which conference material line the attendee will proceed. The random number mappings are:

Number of Arrivals	Probability	Random Numbers
0	.30	00 - 29
1	.30	30 - 59
2	.30	60 - 89
3	.10	90 - 99

Service Time To Pay Fees	Probability	Random Numbers
1 minute	.60	00 - 59
2 minutes	.40	60 - 99

First Letter Of Last Name	Probability	Random Numbers
A-H	.35	00 - 34
I-Q	.36	35 - 70
R-Z	.29	71 - 99

The simulation then flows chronologically through the events listed as headings on the simulation chart on the next page:

1. Time period begins with Q customers waiting to pay fees. (Q can be determined from the number of previous customers with end times in the fee pay line greater than this time period.)
2. Determine the number of arrivals in the period, #.
3. For each distinct arrival, I, determine begin, wait, and end times in the fee pay line.
4. For each distinct arrival, determine the last name and the begin, wait and end times in the conference material line.
5. Repeat until 30 customers have arrived.

b) The average length of the waiting line to pay fees is the average of the entries in the column Q over the 26 time intervals observed, including the 10 at the beginning of 8:26. This is 181/26 = 6.96. The average time a customer waits to pay his fees is the average of the entries in the Fee Pay Wait column over the 30 arrivals = 248/30 = 8.267 minutes.

c) To determine the percentage of time each of the three people who are distributing conference materials are working, take the total amount of time each works and divide by the total length of the simulation (= 42 minutes since 8:41 is the earliest the next arrival could want material service.)

A-H worker = 20/42 = .476 or 47.6%
I-Q worker = 29/42 = .690 or 69.0%
R-Z worker = 8/42 = .190 or 19.0%

Arrivals				Fee Pay						Conference Materials				
Time	RN	#	Q	I	Wait	Begin	RN	Time	End	RN	Name	Wait	Begin	End
8:00	71	2	0	1	0	8:00	51	1	8:01	15	A-H	0	8:01	8:03
				2	1	8:01	79	2	8:03	08	A-H	0	8:03	8:05
8:01	95	3	1	3	2	8:03	09	1	8:04	19	A-H	1	8:05	8:07
				4	3	8:04	67	2	8:06	45	I-Q	0	8:06	8:08
				5	5	8:06	15	1	8:07	76	R-Z	0	8:07	8:09
8:02	83	2	3	6	5	8:07	58	1	8:08	42	I-Q	0	8:08	8:10
				7	6	8:08	04	1	8:09	38	I-Q	1	8:10	8:12
8:03	44	1	5	8	6	8:09	78	2	8:11	47	I-Q	1	8:12	8:14
8:04	34	1	5	9	7	8:11	30	1	8:12	82	R-Z	0	8:12	8:14
8:05	49	1	5	10	7	8:12	56	1	8:13	37	I-Q	1	8:14	8:16
8:06	88	2	6	11	7	8:13	75	2	8:15	49	I-Q	1	8:16	8:18
				12	9	8:15	75	2	8:17	43	I-Q	1	8:18	8:20
8:07	56	1	7	13	10	8:17	05	1	8:18	37	I-Q	2	8:20	8:22
8:08	05	0	7											
8:09	39	1	6	14	9	8:18	49	1	8:19	11	A-H	0	8:19	8:21
8:10	75	2	6	15	9	8:19	70	2	8:21	45	I-Q	1	8:22	8:24
				16	11	8:21	25	1	8:22	55	I-Q	2	8:24	8:26
8:11	12	0	8											
8:12	03	0	7											
8:13	59	1	6	17	9	8:22	26	1	8:23	89	R-Z	0	8:23	8:25
8:14	29	0	6											
8:15	77	2	6	18	8	8:23	10	1	8:24	09	A-H	0	8:24	8:26
				19	9	8:24	46	1	8:25	67	I-Q	1	8:26	8:28
8:16	76	2	7	20	9	8:25	16	1	8:26	84	R-Z	0	8:26	8:28
				21	10	8:26	64	2	8:28	51	I-Q	0	8:28	8:30
8:17	57	1	9	22	11	8:28	72	2	8:30	67	I-Q	0	8:30	8:32
8:18	15	0	9											
8:19	53	1	8	23	11	8:30	50	1	8:31	14	A-H	0	8:31	8:33
8:20	37	1	8	24	11	8:31	15	1	8:32	10	A-H	1	8:33	8:35
8:21	46	1	9	25	11	8:32	79	2	8:34	52	I-Q	0	8:34	8:36
8:22	85	2	9	26	12	8:34	22	1	8:35	03	A-H	0	8:35	8:37
				27	13	8:35	51	1	8:36	02	A-H	1	8:37	8:39
8:23	24	0	10											
8:24	53	1	9	28	12	8:36	01	1	8:37	09	A-H	2	8:39	8:41
8:25	72	2	9	29	12	8:37	47	1	8:38	13	A-H	3	8:41	8:43
				30	13	8:38	88	2	8:40	42	I-Q	0	8:40	8:42
8:26			10	Simulation Over										
TOTALS		--	---		--			--						
26		30	181		248			40						

In 42 minutes (8:00-8:41) the number of minutes busy were A-H: 20, I-Q: 29, R-Z: 8

PROBLEM 5

Mark is a specialist at repairing large metal-cutting machines that use laser technology. His repair territory consists of the cities of Austin, San Antonio, and Houston. His day-to-day repair assignment locations can be modeled as a Markov process. The transition matrix is as follows:

This Day's Location		Next Day's Location: Austin	San Antonio	Houston
	Austin	.60	.15	.25
	San Antonio	.20	.75	.05
	Houston	.15	.05	.80

a) Show the random number assignments that can be used to simulate Mark's next day location when his current location is Austin, San Antonio, and Houston.

b) Assume Mark is currently in Houston. Simulate where Mark will be over the next 25 days. What percentage of time will Mark be in each of the three cities? (Use column 8 of Appendix E.)

c) Repeat the simulation in part b with Mark currently in Austin. (Use column 9 of Appendix E.) Compare the percentages with those found in part b.

SOLUTION 5

a)

Currently in Austin: Next-Day Location	Random Numbers	Currently in San Antonio: Next-Day Location	Random Numbers	Currently in Houston: Next-Day Location	Random Numbers
Austin	00 - 59	Austin	00 - 19	Austin	00 - 14
San Ant.	60 - 74	San Ant.	20 - 94	San Ant.	15 - 19
Houston	75 - 99	Houston	95 - 99	Houston	20 - 99

b) Starting in Houston

Day	Random Number	Day's Location
1	93	Houston
2	63	Houston
3	26	Houston
4	16	San Ant.
5	21	San Ant.
6	26	San Ant.
7	70	San Ant.
8	55	San Ant.
9	72	San Ant.
10	89	San Ant.
11	49	San Ant.
12	64	San Ant.
13	91	San Ant.
14	02	Austin
15	52	Austin
16	69	San Ant.
17	29	San Ant.
18	96	Houston
19	95	Houston
20	84	Houston
21	61	Houston
22	09	Austin
23	06	Austin
24	00	Austin
25	63	San Ant.

Austin = 5/25 = 20%
San Antonio = 13/25 = 52%
Houston = 7/25 = 28%

c) Starting in Austin

Day	Random Number	Day's Location
1	13	Austin
2	08	Austin
3	60	San Ant.
4	13	Austin
5	68	San Ant.
6	40	San Ant.
7	40	San Ant.
8	27	San Ant.
9	23	San Ant.
10	64	San Ant.
11	36	San Ant.
12	56	San Ant.
13	25	San Ant.
14	88	San. Ant.
15	18	Austin
16	74	San Ant.
17	75	San Ant.
18	29	San Ant.
19	80	San Ant.
20	25	San Ant.
21	05	Austin
22	64	San Ant.
23	71	San Ant.
24	83	San Ant.
25	74	San Ant.

Austin = 5/25 = 20%
San Antonio = 20/25 = 80%
Houston = 0/25 = 0%

PROBLEM 6

Consider the following house renovation project.

Job and Description	Expected Completion Time (in days)
A - Remove old roof shingles	2
B - Plaster walls and ceilings	4
C - Lay new roof shingles	3
D - Paint exterior	4
E - Paint walls and ceilings	5
F - Hang new gutters	2
G - Install exterior lights	2
H - Lay wall-to-wall carpet	2

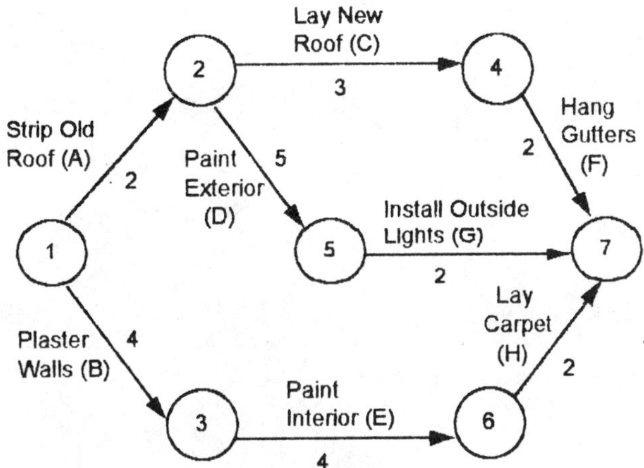

For each job the probabilities of being completed 1 day earlier than expected, on time, 1 day later than expected, and 2 days later than expected are .2, .5, .2, and .1, respectively.

a) Determine the critical path(s) and the project's expected completion time.

b) Do a five trial simulation using the last digit of column 4 of Appendix E for the random numbers to determine the average completion time of the project. Compare this result with your answer to part (a).

SOLUTION 6

a) A path in this context is a set of successive jobs that lead from the project network's starting node (node 1) to the finish node (node 7). There are three different paths in the network. They are A-C-F, A-D-G, and B-E-H. The critical (longest) path consists of jobs B-E-H.

The project's expected completion time is the sum of the expected completion times of the jobs on the critical path. Thus, the expected project completion time is 4+4+2=10 days.

b) The random number mappings are as follows. Note only single digit random numbers need be generated.

Job Completion Time	Probability	Random Numbers
Expected time minus 1 day	.2	0,1
Expected time	.5	2,3,4,5,6
Expected time plus 1 day	.2	7,8
Expected time plus 2 days	.1	9

The table on the following page describes the simulation. Note that due to the randomness of job times, a path other than B-E-H was critical in four out of the five trials.

Job	RN	Job's Exp. Time	Time Adjustment	Job's Act. Time	Critical Path and Proj. Compl. Time
A	2	2	0	2	
B	5	4	0	4	
C	1	3	-1	2	
D	2	5	0	5	
E	0	4	-1	3	
F	7	2	+1	3	
G	8	2	+1	3	
H	1	2	-1	1	A-D-G = 10
A	7	2	+1	3	
B	5	4	0	4	
C	8	3	+1	4	
D	5	5	0	5	
E	5	4	0	4	
F	1	2	-1	1	
G	5	2	0	2	
H	0	2	-1	1	A-D-G = 10
A	8	2	+1	3	
B	8	4	+1	5	
C	2	3	0	3	
D	5	5	0	5	
E	6	4	0	4	
F	7	2	+1	3	
G	4	2	0	2	
H	4	2	0	2	B-E-H = 11
A	7	2	+1	3	
B	2	4	0	4	
C	3	3	0	3	
D	6	5	0	5	
E	7	4	+1	5	
F	6	2	0	2	
G	3	2	0	2	
H	4	2	0	2	A-D-G = 12
A	8	2	+1	3	
B	5	4	0	4	
C	1	3	-1	2	
D	2	5	0	5	
E	2	4	0	4	
F	5	2	0	2	
G	9	2	+2	4	
H	6	2	0	2	A-D-G = 12

Average project completion time is (10+10+11+12+12)/5 = 11 days.

ANSWERED PROBLEMS

PROBLEM 7

Susan Winslow has two alternative routes to travel from her home in Olport to her office in Lewisburg. She can travel on Freeway 5 to Freeway 57 or on Freeway 55 to Freeway 91. The time distributions are as follows:

Freeway 5		Freeway 57		Freeway 55		Freeway 91	
Time	Relative Frequency	Time	Relative Frequency	Time	Relative Frequency	Time	Relative Frequency
5	.30	4	.10	6	.20	3	.30
6	.20	5	.20	7	.20	4	.35
7	.40	6	. 35	8	.40	5	.20
8	.10	7	.20	9	.20	6	.15
		8	.15				

Do a five day simulation of each of the two combinations of routes using columns 1, 2, 3, and 4 of Appendix E for the random numbers. Based on this simulation, which routes should Susan take if her objective is to minimize her total travel time?

PROBLEM 8

The Rumson Post Office serves a small rural town. In any one minute interval during a Saturday morning either 0, 1, 2, or 3 customers arrive with the following probabilities: P(0) = .40; P(1) = .30; P(2) = .20; P(3) = .10.

The only clerk working on Saturday at the post office is Mrs. Smith. Her service time per customer is also a random variable with the following distribution of 1, 2, or 3 minutes per service: P(1) = .80; P(2) = .15; P(3) = .05.

If the system starts empty, simulate the waiting line over a 10 minute interval. Use Appendix E, column 1 to generate the number of arrivals and column 2 to generate service times. What is the average number of customers waiting in line for service?

PROBLEM 9

Consider the following PERT problem.

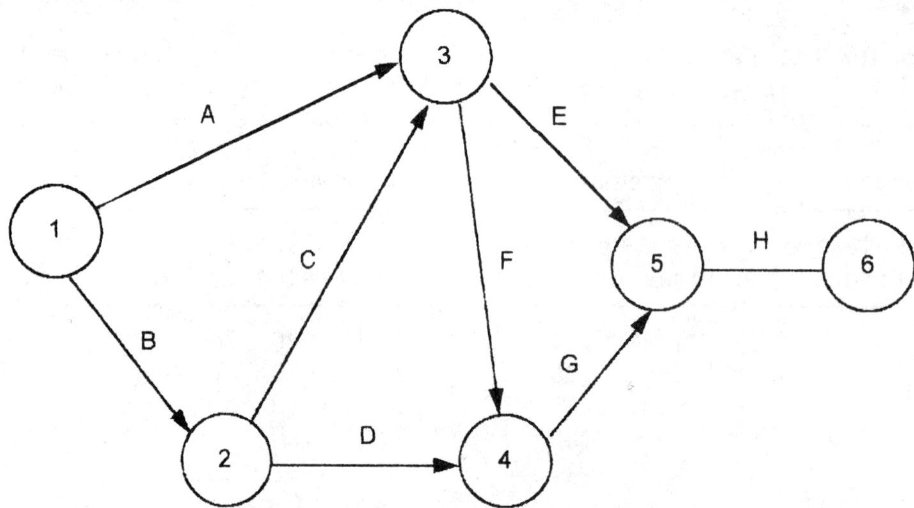

The expected completion time for each job is given below:

Job	Expected Completion Time in Weeks
A	7
B	4
C	3
D	6
E	5
F	3
G	3
H	4

a) Determine the critical path(s) and expected completion time of this project.

b) Suppose that each job has a 25% chance of being completed in a week less than its expected completion time and a 25% chance of being completed in a week more than its expected completion time. Do a five trial simulation using the last two digits of column 6 of Appendix E for the random numbers to determine the average completion time of this project. Compare this answer to part (a).

PROBLEM 10

Demand for mopeds at the Easy Rider Bike Shop is either 0, 1, 2, or 3 per day with the following probability distribution:

Demand	Probability
0	.15
1	.25
2	.35
3	.25

Each working day a moped remains in inventory costs Easy Rider $2 per moped. It costs Easy Rider $30 to process an order.

The delivery time required to obtain new mopeds from the wholesaler is also random with the following distribution:

Delivery Time (in Working Days)	Probability
1	.20
2	.60
3	.20

Easy Rider has adopted the policy of offering customers an $8 per day discount for each working day they must wait for a moped if Easy Rider is out of stock.

a) Assume Easy Rider is open 200 days per year and delivery time is exactly two working days. Further, assume that although demand varies, it is actually constant at the level of average demand. What would be the optimal order policy?

b) Do a 20 day simulation using the answer you obtained in part (a) assuming a current inventory of 6 mopeds and that delivery time and demand follow the distributions given above. Use the first two digits in column 2 of Appendix E to generate demands and the first two digits of column 3 to generate lead times. What is the average inventory cost per day, where inventory holding costs are assessed on ending inventory?

PROBLEM 11

Miller's Carpets runs a store that carries a certain style of carpet. Over the weeks Miller's has collected data concerning the demand for the number of rolls of this brand of carpet:

Weekly Demand	Probability
0	.10
1	.20
2	.20
3	.20
4	.20
5	.10

Miller's policy has been to reorder 8 rolls whenever its inventory reached 4 rolls or less at the end of the week. Current inventory is 5 rolls. Reordering costs are $40 per order and holding costs are $2 per roll per week. Stockout costs are $10 per occurrence and these sales are lost.
Lead time for an order has been observed to be:

Weeks	Probability
1	.40
2	.50
3	.10

a) Conduct an 8 week simulation of Miller's situation and determine the total cost for this period. Use column 4 of Appendix E for demand and column 6 for lead times.

b) Miller's has been offered a new policy. The wholesaler will automatically deliver 3 rolls to Miller's at the end of each week for a weekly service charge of $12. This eliminates reorder costs and lead times. Should Miller's accept this new policy or keep its current policy?

PROBLEM 12

Customers at Winkies Donuts can either eat their doughnut purchase on the premises or carry it out. Winkies estimates that 35% of its morning business customers enjoy their doughnuts on the premises.

Customers eating their doughnuts on the premises either buy one or two doughnuts and nearly always order a beverage. Winkies estimates the following profits and probabilities hold for service times of the on-the-premises customers:

Service Times	Probability	Expected Profit
25 seconds	.15	$ .08
50 seconds	.60	$ .23
75 seconds	.25	$ .34

Carry-out customers typically purchase a couple of doughnuts or a dozen. Winkies estimates the following profits and probabilities hold for the service times of carry-out customers:

Service Times	Probability	Expected Profit
50 seconds	.30	$ .15
100 seconds	.70	$ .90

During any 25 second interval, either 0, 1, or 2 customers will arrive at Winkies with the following probability distribution:

Customers	Probability
0	.75
1	.16
2	.09

Winkies has only one morning sales clerk on duty.

a) Conduct a 10 minute simulation of sales at Winkies. Using Appendix E, use column 1 for number of arrivals in 25 seconds, column 2 for the eat-in/carry-out decision, column 3 for on-the-premises and carry-out service times.

b) What is the expected profit during this period?

c) What percentage of the time is the server busy?

d) What is the average number of customers at Winkies?

PROBLEM 13

Honest Archie's Appliance Company has decided to cease selling microwave ovens. Archie has slashed prices on the three models he has in stock -- Amana, Litton, and Tappan. He currently has 3 Amanas, 2 Littons, and 4 Tappans left in stock.

Because of his low prices, Archie expects to have from one to four customers come into his store each day inquiring about the ovens. Archie believes the following daily probabilities hold:

Customers	Probability
1	.50
2	.30
3	.10
4	.10

For each inquiry, Archie believes the following probabilities hold: P(not interested in any purchase) = .30; P(desires Amana) = .30; P(desires Litton) = .25; P(desires Tappan) = .15.

If a customer desires a particular brand of oven that Archie is sold out of, Archie will try to sell the customer the brand of oven in which his current stock is the largest. (If there is a tie, he chooses the one that had the largest initial stock.) Archie believes there is a 25% chance he will be successful in convincing the person to switch to that brand and a 75% chance of losing the sale.

Do a simulation to determine the number of days it will take Archie to sell out his stock of microwave ovens. Use column 7 of Appendix E for arriving customers, column 8 for oven preference, and column 9 for brand switching.

PROBLEM 14

As the owner of a rent-a-car agency you have determined the following statistics:

Number of Potential Rentals Daily	Probability	Length of Car Rental Per Rent	Probability
0	.10	1 day	.50
1	.15	2 days	.30
2	.20	3 days	.15
3	.30	4 days	.05
4	.25		

The gross profit is $40 per car per day rented. When there is demand for a car when none is available there is a goodwill loss of $80 and the rental is lost. Each day a car is unused costs you $5 per car. Your firm initially has 4 cars.

a) Conduct a 10 day simulation of this business using column 1 of Appendix E for demand and column 2 for rental length.

b) If your firm can obtain another car for $200 for 10 days should you take the extra car?

PROBLEM 15

Scooper Dooper is a small ice cream parlor located next to the Lemonville exit of the Metropolitan Subway Line. Arriving customers to Scooper Dooper purchase either ice cream cones, malts, or sundaes. The following table gives the approximate service time required, expected profit, and the probability of each type of purchase:

Purchase	Probability	Service Time Required	Expected Profit
Ice Cream Cone	.75	30 seconds	$.12
Malt	.15	60 seconds	$.22
Sundae	.10	90 seconds	$.30

The store is small, holding a maximum of four customers. Customers who find the store full go elsewhere for their ice cream.

Management estimates that during the lunch hour in each 30 second interval there will be either 0, 1, 2, or 3 arrivals with the following probability distribution:

Number of Arrivals	Probability
0	.30
1	.40
2	.20
3	.10

Simulate the operation of the Scooper Dooper ice cream parlor for a 15 minute period during the lunch hour. From Appendix E, use column 1 to generate the number of arrivals and column 2 to determine the type of purchase.

a) What is the expected profit earned during this period?

b) What percentage of the customers are lost due to a full store?

c) What is the average size of the waiting line?

PROBLEM 16

Three airlines compete on the route between New York and Los Angeles. Stanton Marketing has performed an analysis of first class business travelers to determine their airline choice.

Stanton has modeled this choice as a Markov process and has determined the following transition probabilities.

		Next Airline		
		A	B	C
Last Airline	A	.50	.30	.20
	B	.30	.45	.25
	C	.10	.35	.55

a) Show the random number assignments that can be used to simulate the first class business traveler's next airline when her last airline is A, B, and C.

b) Assume the traveler used airline C last. Simulate which airline the traveler will be using over her next 25 flights. What percentage of her flights are on each of the three airlines? (Use column 3 of Appendix E.)

TRUE/FALSE

17. Given the accuracy of computers, it is not necessary to validate a simulation program.

18. Using the next event simulation approach, the time between system updates is variable.

19. A random number mapping always maps a set of occurrences to numbers between 00 and 99.

20. Computer simulation requires a special purpose simulation language.

21. In comparing different policies using simulation, one should use the same set of random numbers whenever possible.

22. Flowcharts are useful in designing a simulation program.

23. In Monte Carlo simulation, outcomes are determined by choosing a random number and selecting the outcome corresponding to that number.

24. A computer simulator is a device which acts like a computer but is not a computer.

25. One is guaranteed an optimal solution to a problem using simulation.

26. A typical way to avoid start-up problems in simulation is to run the program for a specified time without recording any data corresponding to the simulation.

27. Probabilistic inputs to a Monte Carlo simulation must follow a discrete probability distribution.

28. If there are no probabilistic components in a problem, there is no reason to use computer simulation to solve it.

29. Simulation is a trial-and-error approach to problem solving.

30. If a computer simulator is correctly programmed, there will be no difference between the simulated and real distributions for a probabilistic component.

31. If a computer simulator is properly programmed, different random number sequences will not cause different output results.

Chapter 18
Multicriteria Decision Problems

KEY CONCEPTS

CONCEPT	ILLUSTRATED PROBLEMS	ANSWERED PROBLEMS
Goal Programming		
Formulations	1-3	8-10
Graphical Solution	1	8
Computer Solution	2	9
Analytic Hierarchy Process		
Pairwise Comparison Matrices	4-7	11-15
Priority Vectors	4-7	11-15
Overall Priorities	6,7	12-15
Consistency	4	12,13
Hierarchy Construction	7	13,14

REVIEW

1. Goal programming may be used to solve linear programs with multiple objectives. Each objective may be viewed as a "goal".

2. An approach to goal programming is to satisfy goals in a priority sequence. Second-priority goals are pursued without reducing the first-priority goals; third-priority goals are pursued without reducing first- or second-priority goals, etc.

3. In goal programming, d_i^+ and d_i^- are the amounts a targeted goal i is overachieved or underachieved, respectively. Usually only one of d_i^+ or d_i^- is considered detrimental.

4. For each priority level, the objective function is to minimize the (weighted) sum of the goal deviations. Previous "optimal" achievements of goals are added to the constraint set so that they are not degraded while trying to achieve lesser priority goals. The goals themselves are added to the constraint set with d_i^+ and d_i^- acting as the surplus and slack variables.

5. Infeasible linear programming problems can be reformulated as goal programs so that some reasonable solution may be attained.

6. The Analytic Hierarchy Process (AHP), is a procedure designed to quantify managerial judgments of the relative importance of each of several conflicting criteria used in the decision making process.

7. Computer packages can be used for evaluating AHPs. The AHP developed in this chapter is based on one such package, EXPERT CHOICE.

GOAL PROGRAMMING APPROACH

Assuming all of the objectives (goals) and functional constraints in the problem have been identified:

1. Decide the priority level of each goal.

2. If a priority level has more than one goal, for each goal i decide the weight, w_i, to be placed on the deviation(s), d_i^+ and/or d_i^-, from the goal.

3. Set up the initial linear program as follows:

   (Assume d_1^+ and d_2^- are the detrimental deviations from first priority goals 1 and 2, respectively.)

   $$\text{MIN} \quad w_1 d_1^+ + w_2 d_2^-$$

   S.T. Functional Constraints, and
   Goal Constraints

4. Solve this linear program. (Assume that the optimal value of the objective function is k.) If there is a lower priority level, go to step 5; otherwise, a final optimal solution has been reached.

5. Consider the next-lower priority level goals and formulate a new objective function based on these goals. Add a constraint requiring the achievement of the next-higher priority level goals to be maintained. The new linear program is:

   (Assume d_3^+ and d_4^- are the detrimental deviations associated with the current priority level goals.)

   $$\text{MIN} \quad w_3 d_3^+ + w_4 d_4^-$$

   S.T. Functional Constraints,
   Goal Constraints, and
   $w_1 d_1^+ + w_2 d_2^- = k$

   Go to step 4. (Repeat steps 4 and 5 until all priority levels have been examined. Each time, solve a linear program with a lesser priority goal for the objective function and with the optimal achieved amounts of higher priority goals as added constraints.)

ANALYTIC HIERARCHY PROCESS

1. The first step is:
   (a) list an overall goal for the process;
   (b) list criteria that make up the relevant factors that contribute to achieving the goal;
   (c) list the (n) possible decision alternatives for each of the individual criterion.

*** For each criterion, perform steps 2 through 5 ***

2. Develop a pairwise comparison matrix for a criterion by rating the relative importance between each pair of decision alternatives. The matrix lists the alternatives horizontally and vertically and has the numerical ratings comparing the horizontal (first) alternative with the vertical (second) alternative. Ratings are given as follows:

Compared to the second alternative, the first alternative is:	Numerical rating
extremely preferred	9
very strongly preferred	7
strongly preferred	5
moderately preferred	3
equally preferred	1

   Intermediate numeric ratings of 8, 6, 4, 2 can be assigned. A reciprocal rating (i.e. 1/9, 1/8, 1/7, etc.) is assigned when the second alternative is preferred to the first. The value of 1 is always assigned when comparing an alternative with itself.

3. Develop the normalized matrix by dividing each number in a column of the pairwise comparison matrix by its column sum.

4. Develop the priority vector for the criterion by averaging each row of the normalized matrix. These row averages form the priority vector of alternative preferences with respect to the particular criterion. The values in this vector sum to 1.

5. The consistency of the subjective input in the pairwise comparison matrix can be measured by calculating a consistency ratio. (See details below.) A consistency ratio of less than .1 is good. For consistency ratios which are greater than .1, the subjective input should be re-evaluated.

6. After steps 2 through 5 has been performed for all criteria, the results of step 4 are summarized in a priority matrix by listing the decision alternatives horizontally and the criteria vertically. The column entries are the priority vectors for each criterion.

7. Develop a criteria pairwise development matrix in the same manner as that used to construct alternative pairwise comparison matrices by using subjective ratings (step 2). Similarly, normalize the matrix (step 3) and develop a criteria priority vector (step 4).

8. Develop an overall priority vector by multiplying the criteria priority vector (from step 7) by the priority matrix (from step 6).

Determining the Consistency Ratio

1. For each row of the pairwise comparison matrix, determine a weighted sum by summing the multiples of the entries by the priority of its corresponding (column) alternative.

2. For each row, divide its weighted sum by the priority of its corresponding (row) alternative.

3. Determine the average, λ_{max}, of the results of step 2.

4. Compute the consistency index, CI, of the n alternatives by:

$$CI = (\lambda_{max} - n)/(n - 1).$$

5. Determine the random index, RI, from the the following chart:

Number of Decision Alternatives, n	Random Index, RI
3	0.58
4	0.90
5	1.12
6	1.24
7	1.32
8	1.41

6. Determine the consistency ratio, CR, as follows:

$$CR = CR/RI.$$

FLOW CHART OF ANALYTIC HIERARCHY PROCESS

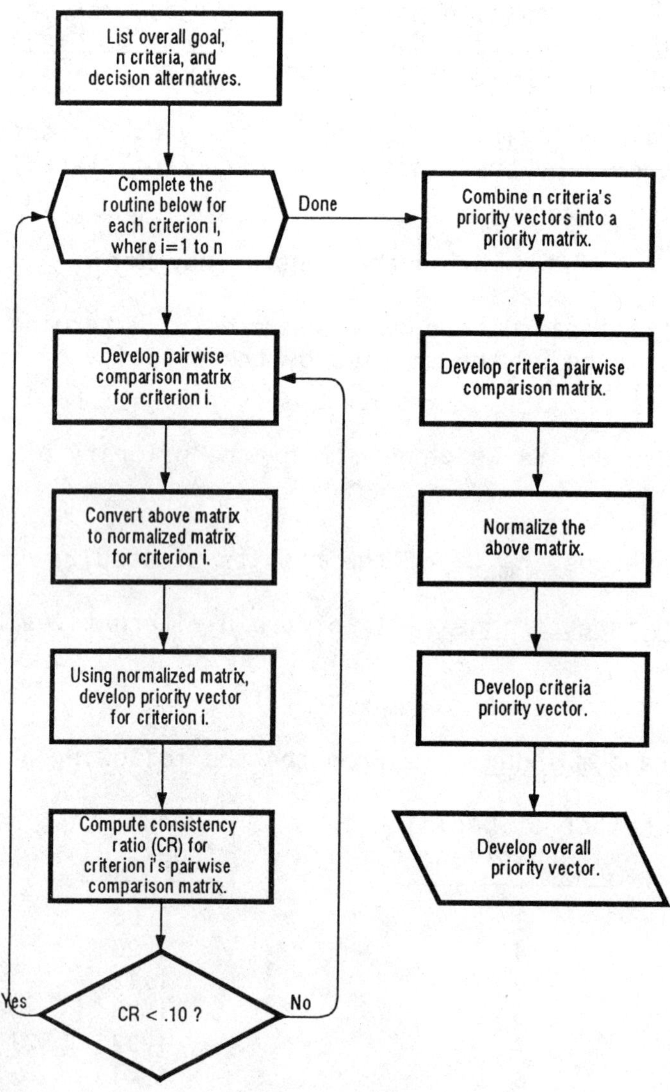
List overall goal, n criteria, and decision alternatives.
Complete the routine below for each criterion i, where i=1 to n
Done
Combine n criteria's priority vectors into a priority matrix.
Develop pairwise comparison matrix for criterion i.
Develop criteria pairwise comparison matrix.
Convert above matrix to normalized matrix for criterion i.
Normalize the above matrix.
Using normalized matrix, develop priority vector for criterion i.
Develop criteria priority vector.
Compute consistency ratio (CR) for criterion i's pairwise comparison matrix.
Develop overall priority vector.
Yes
CR < .10 ?
No

ILLUSTRATED PROBLEMS

> **NOTE:** Priorities and weights are not synonymous in goal programming. Think of priorities as absolute, firm, preemptive. No tradeoffs occur in the achievement of goals with different priorities. However, tradeoffs can occur in the achievement of goals with the same priority and different weights.

PROBLEM 1

Conceptual Products is a computer company that produces the CP286 and the CP386 computers. The computers use different mother boards produced in abundant supply by the company, but use the same cases and disk drives. The CP286 models use two floppy disk drives and no hard disks whereas the CP386 models use one floppy disk drive and one hard disk drive.

The disk drives and cases are bought from vendors. There are 1000 floppy disk drives, 500 hard disk drives, and 600 cases available to Conceptual Products on a weekly basis. It takes one hour to manufacture a CP286 and its profit is $200 and it takes one and one-half hours to manufacture a CP386 and its profit is $500.

The company has four goals which are given below.

Priority 1: Meet a state contract of 200 CP286 machines weekly. (Goal 1)
Priority 2: Make at least 500 total computers weekly. (Goal 2)
Priority 3: Make at least $250,000 weekly. (Goal 3)
Priority 4: Use no more than 400 man-hours per week. (Goal 4)

a) Formulate this problem as a goal program.

b) Solve graphically for the solution that best meets the goals of Conceptual Products as stated above.

c) Suppose Conceptual Products combined goals 3 and 4 into one priority level, Priority 3. What would be the recommendation under the following conditions:

(1) Each goal was equally desirable.
(2) Each $1000 underachieved from its profit goal was three times as important as an extra man-hour.
(3) Each $1000 underachieved from its profit goal was five times as important as an extra man-hour.

SOLUTION 1

a) Variables

X_1 = the number of CP286 computers produced weekly
X_2 = the number of CP386 computers produced weekly

Functional Constraints

Availability of floppy disk drives: $2X_1 + X_2 \leq 1000$

Availability of hard disk drives: $X_2 \leq 500$

Availability of cases: $X_1 + X_2 \leq 600$

Goals

Define: d_i^- = the amount the right hand side of goal i is deficient
d_i^+ = the amount the right hand side of goal i is exceeded

(1) 200 CP286 computers weekly: $X_1 + d_1^- - d_1^+ = 200$

(2) 500 total computers weekly: $X_1 + X_2 + d_2^- - d_2^+ = 500$

(3) \$250(in thousands) profit: $.2X_1 + .5X_2 + d_3^- - d_3^+ = 250$

(4) 400 total man-hours weekly: $X_1 + 1.5X_2 + d_4^- - d_4^+ = 400$

Non-negativity: $X_1, X_2, d_i^-, d_i^+ \geq 0$ for all i

Objective Functions

Priority 1: Minimize the amount the state contract is not met:
MIN d_1^-

Priority 2: Minimize the number under 500 computers produced weekly:
MIN d_2^-

Priority 3: Minimize the amount under \$250,000 earned weekly:
MIN d_3^-

Priority 4: Minimize the man-hours over 400 used weekly:
MIN d_4^+

Summary

Using the notation P_j to denote the priority level of the objective functions, the problem becomes:

$$\text{MIN} \quad P_1(d_1^-) + P_2(d_2^-) + P_3(d_3^-) + P_4(d_4^+)$$

$$\begin{aligned}
\text{S.T.} \quad & 2X_1 + X_2 && \leq 1000 \\
& +X_2 && \leq 500 \\
& X_1 + X_2 && \leq 600 \\
& X_1 + d_1^- - d_1^+ && = 200 \\
& X_1 + X_2 + d_2^- - d_2^+ && = 500 \\
& .2X_1 + .5X_2 + d_3^- - d_3^+ && = 250 \\
& X_1 + 1.5X_2 + d_4^- - d_4^+ && = 400 \\
& X_1, X_2, d_1^-, d_1^+, d_2^-, d_2^+, d_3^-, d_3^+, d_4^-, d_4^+ && \geq 0
\end{aligned}$$

b) To solve graphically, first graph the functional constraints as below. Then graph the first goal: $X_1 = 200$ and note that there is a set of points that exceeds $X_1 = 200$, i.e. where $d_1^- = 0$.

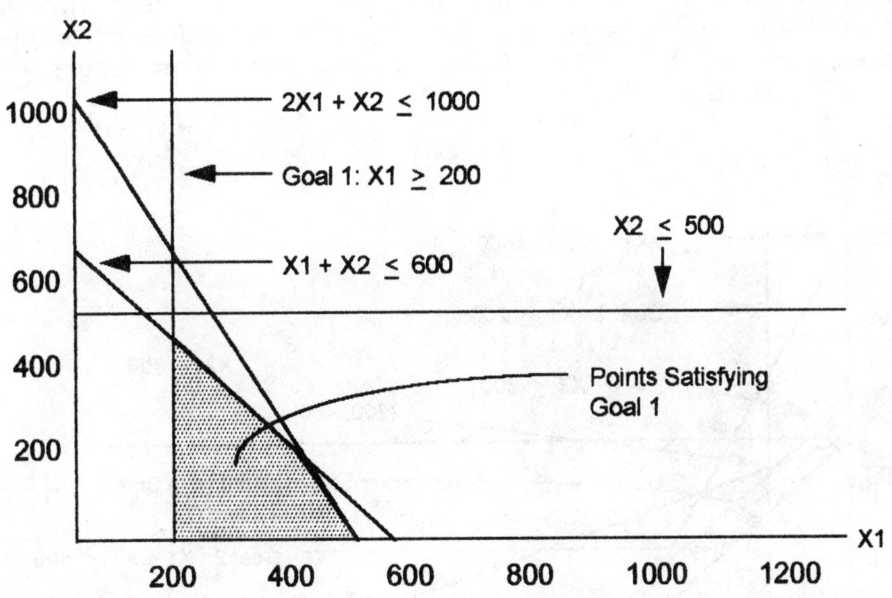

Now add goal 1 as $X_1 \geq 200$ and graph goal 2: $X_1 + X_2 = 500$ as below. Note there is still a set of points satisfying the first goal that also satisfies this second goal, i.e. where $d_2^- = 0$.

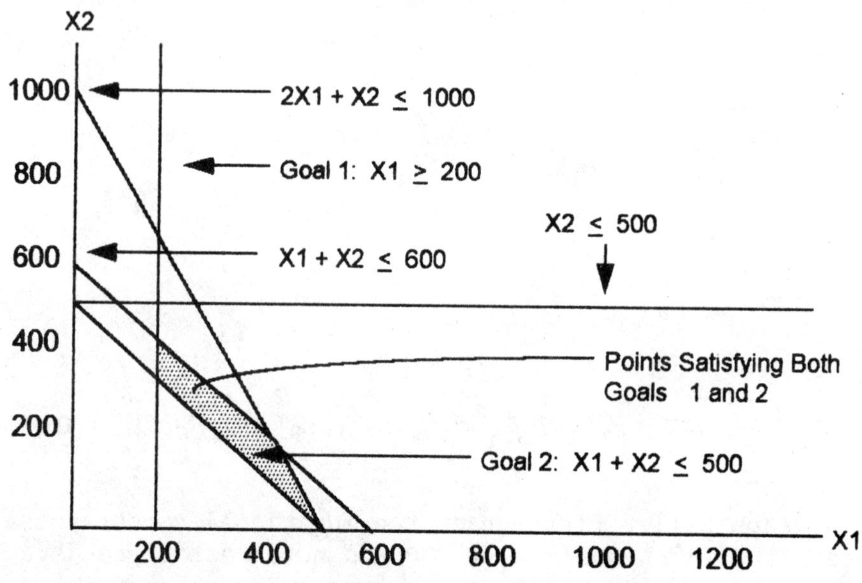

Now add goal 2 as: $X_1 + X_2 \geq 500$, and graph goal 3: $.2X_1 + .5X_2 = 250$. Note that no points satisfy the previous functional constraints and goals as well as this constraint. Thus to MIN d_3^-, this minimum value is achieved when we MAX .2X1 + .5X2. We note that this occurs at $X_1 = 200$, $X_2 = 400$, so that $.2X_1 + .5X_2 = 240$ or $d_3^- = 10$.

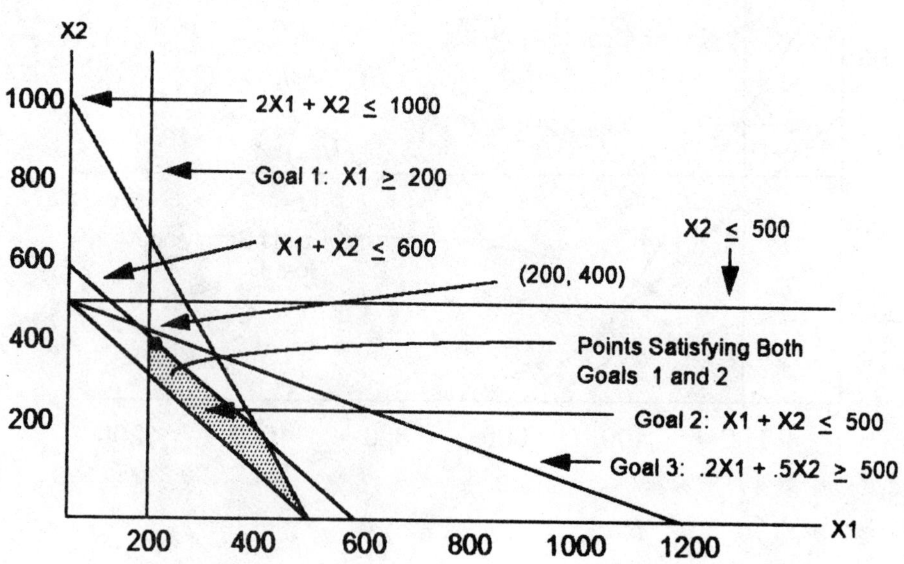

Since this is the only point the meets goal three with only a \$10(thousand) deficiency, priority 4's objective becomes irrelevant. This is because if we add the constraint: $.2X_1 + .5X_2 = 240$, there is only one feasible point. This is our recommendation of $X_1 = 200$, $X_2 = 400$. Thus the recommendations is to make 200 CP286 computers and 400 CP386 computers weekly.

c) The first two priorities were met by a set of points and it was shown that there was no point that met the first two goals and goal 3. Similarly, by looking at the top graph on the previous page, it is seen that there are no points that meet the first two priorities and goal 4. Since both will not be achieved,

$$d_3^- = 250 - .2X_1 - .5X_2$$

$$d_4^+ = X_1 + 1.5X_2 - 400.$$

Case (1): MIN $d_3^- + d_4^+ = \text{MIN } .8X_1 + X_2 - 150$

Case (2): MIN $3d_3^- + d_4^+ = \text{MIN } .4X_1 + 350$

Case (3): MIN $5d_3^- + d_4^+ = \text{MIN } -X_2 + 850$

Ignoring the constant in each of the above, it can be seen in the next three graphs that Case (1) is minimized at $X_1 = 500$, $X_2 = 0$; Case (2) is minimized by all points on the line $X_1 = 200$ between $X_2 = 300$ and $X_2 = 400$; and,Case (3) is minimized where X_2 takes on its maximum value, i.e. at $X_1 = 200$, $X_2 = 400$.

CASE (1)

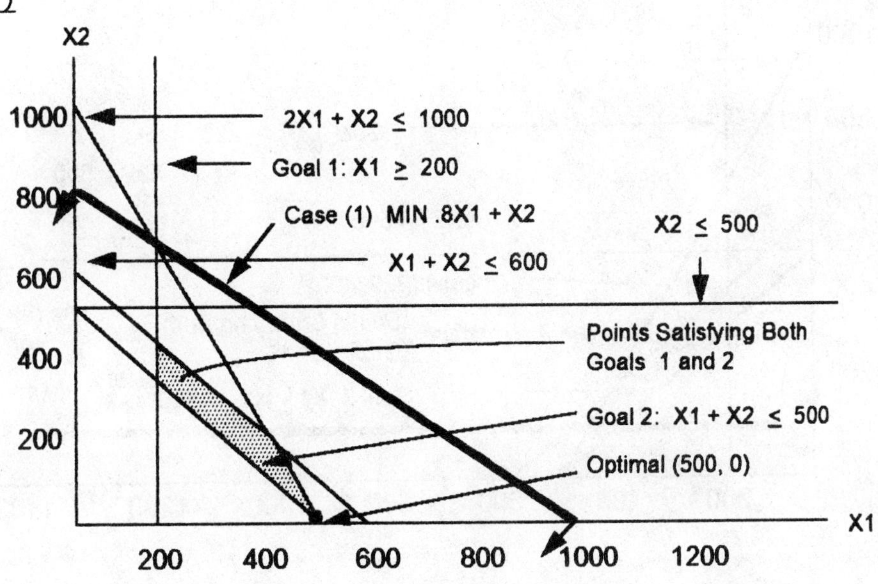

CASE (2)

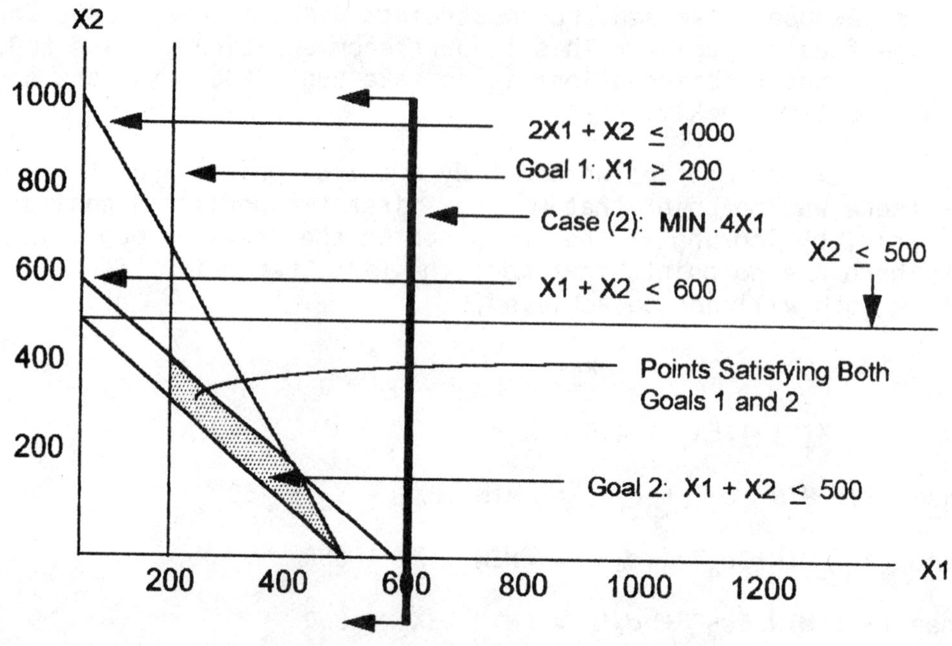

Line between (200, 300) and (200, 400) is optimal

CASE (3)

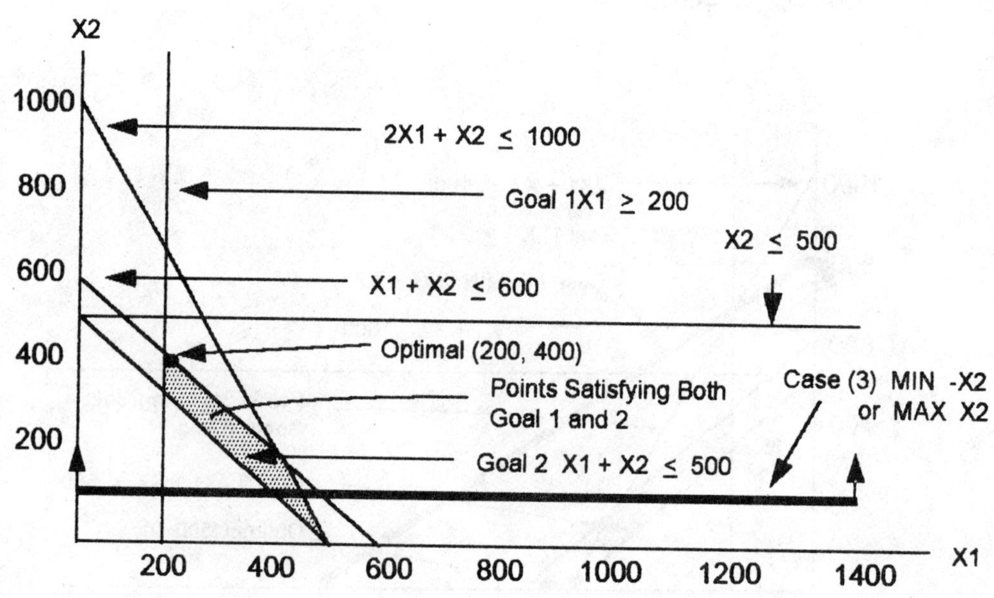

PROBLEM 2

Suppose in problem 1, Conceptual Products made a third computer, the CP486 which requires two floppy disks and a hard disk. It takes two hours to manufacture and the profit is $900. Use a computer program such as the Management Scientist to solve the goal program of Case (3) in part (c) of problem 1.

SOLUTION 2

The goal programming formulation is now:

$$\text{MIN } P_1(d_1^-) + P_2(d_2^-) + P_3(5d_3^-) + P_3(d_4^+)$$

$$\begin{array}{llll}
\text{S.T.} & 2X_1 + X_2 + X_3 & \leq 1000 & \text{(floppy disks)} \\
 & X_2 + X_3 & \leq 500 & \text{(hard disks)} \\
 & X_1 + X_2 + X_3 & \leq 600 & \text{(cases)} \\
\text{(Priority 1)} & X_1 + d_1^- - d_1^+ & = 200 & \text{(Goal 1: contract)} \\
\text{(Priority 2)} & X_1 + X_2 + X_3 + d_2^- - d_2^+ & = 500 & \text{(Goal 2: total)} \\
\text{(Priority 3)} & .2X_1 + .5X_2 + .9X_3 + d_3^- - d_3^+ & = 250 & \text{(Goal 3: profit)} \\
\text{(Priority 3)} & X_1 + 1.5X_2 + 2X_3 + d_4^- - d_4^+ & = 400 & \text{(Goal 4: man-hours)}
\end{array}$$

$$X_1, X_2, d_i^-, d_i^+ \geq 0 \quad \text{for all } i$$

Priority 1 Program

The following was input into the MANAGEMENT SCIENTIST:

```
MIN  D1MINUS
S.T.  2X1 +    X2 +    X3                          < 1000

               X2 +    X3                          <  500

       X1 +    X2 +    X3                          <  600

       X1                 + D1MINUS - D1PLUS =    200

       X1 +    X2 +    X3 + D2MINUS - D2PLUS =    500

     .2X1 +   .5X2 +  .9X3 + D3MINUS - D3PLUS =    250

       X1 + 1.5X2 +   2X3 + D4MINUS - D4PLUS =    400
```

The following output was attained:

OBJECTIVE FUNCTION VALUE = 0.000

VARIABLE	VALUE	REDUCED COSTS
X1	200.000	0.000
X2	0.000	0.000
X3	233.333	0.000
D1MINUS	0.000	1.000
D1PLUS	0.000	0.000
D2MINUS	66.667	0.000
D2PLUS	0.000	0.000
D3MINUS	0.000	0.000
D3PLUS	0.000	0.000
D4MINUS	0.000	0.000
D4PLUS	266.667	0.000

Thus the priority 1 objective is met since the value of the objective function, D1MINUS = 0.

Priority 2 Program

Add to the constraints on the previous page a constraint requiring the priority 1 objective to be maintained at 0: D1MINUS = 0, and change the objective to the priority 2 objective: MIN D2MINUS.

The following output is generated:

OBJECTIVE FUNCTION VALUE = 0.000

VARIABLE	VALUE	REDUCED COSTS
X1	285.714	0.000
X2	0.000	0.000
X3	214.286	0.000
D1MINUS	0.000	0.000
D1PLUS	85.714	0.000
D2MINUS	0.000	1.000
D2PLUS	0.000	0.000
D3MINUS	0.000	0.000
D3PLUS	0.000	0.000
D4MINUS	0.000	0.000
D4PLUS	314.286	0.000

Thus the priority 2 objective is met since the value of the objective function, D2MINUS, = 0.

Priority 3 Program

Add to the previous constraints, a constraint requiring that the priority 2 objective to be maintained at 0: D2MINUS = 0, and change the objective to the priority 3 objective: MIN 5 D3MINUS + D4PLUS.

The following output is generated:

OBJECTIVE FUNCTION VALUE = 314.286

VARIABLE	VALUE	REDUCED COSTS
X1	285.714	0.000
X2	0.000	0.071
X3	214.286	0.000
D1MINUS	0.000	0.000
D1PLUS	85.714	0.000
D2MINUS	0.000	0.000
D2PLUS	0.000	0.714
D3MINUS	0.000	3.571
D3PLUS	0.000	1.429
D4MINUS	0.000	1.000
D4PLUS	314.286	0.000

Thus the optimal recommendation is to produce 285.714286 CP286 computers weekly and 214.285714 CP486 computers weekly. All goals will be met except goal 4. 314.285714 extra man-hours or a total of 714.285714 man-hours will be used.

PROBLEM 3

The campaign headquarters of Jerry Black, a candidate for the Board of Supervisors, has 100 volunteers. With one week to go in the election, there are three major strategies remaining: media advertising, door-to-door canvassing, and telephone campaigning. It is estimated that each phone call will take approximately four minutes and each door-to-door personal contact will average seven minutes. These times include time between contacts for breaks, transportation, dialing, etc. Volunteers who work on advertising will not be able to handle any other duties. Each ad will utilize the talents of three workers for the entire week.

Volunteers are expected to work 12 hours per day during the final seven days of the campaign. At a minimum, Jerry Black feels he needs 30,000 phone contacts, 20,000 personal contacts, and three advertisements during the last week. However, he would like to see 50,000 phone contacts and 50,000 personal contacts made and five advertisements developed. It is felt that advertising is 50 times as important as personal contacts which in turn is twice as important as phone contacts.

Formulate this problem as a goal program with a single weighted priority to determine how the work should be distributed during the final week of the campaign.

SOLUTION 3

Define variables

X_1 = number of volunteers doing phone work during the week
X_2 = number of volunteers making personal contacts during week
X_3 = number of volunteers preparing advertising during the week

Define goals

1) 50,000 phone contacts:
   d_1^+ and d_1^- = the amount this quantity is overachieved and underachieved, respectively
2) 50,000 personal contacts:
   d_2^+ and d_2^- = the amount this quantity is overachieved and underachieved, respectively
3) 5 advertisements:
   d_3^+ and d_3^- = the amount this quantity is overachieved and underachieved respectively

Define objective

It would not hurt Jerry Black if his goals were exceeded, however since the importance of his goals are in the ratio 1:2:100, the goal programming objective function would be:

$$\text{MIN} \quad d_1^- + 2d_2^- + 100d_3^-$$

Define constraints

There are (7 days) x (12 hours per day) x (60 minutes per hour) = 5040 minutes per worker. Thus a phone worker could make 5040/4 = 1260 phone calls in the week. And a door-to-door canvasser could make 5040/7 = 720 personal contacts during the week.

Linear Programming Constraints

1) At least 30,000 phone contacts: $1260X_1 \geq 30{,}000$

2) At least 20,000 personal contacts: $720X_2 \geq 20{,}000$

3) At least 3 advertisements: $(1/3)X_3 \geq 3$

4) 100 volunteers: $X_1 + X_2 + X_3 = 100$

Goal Constraints

5) Make 50,000 phone contacts: $1260X_1 - d_1^+ + d_1^- = 50{,}000$

6) Make 50,000 personal contacts: $720X_2 - d_2^+ + d_2^- = 50{,}000$

7) Design 5 advertisements: $(1/3)X_3 - d_3^+ + d_3^- = 5$

Non-negativity of Variables

$X_1, X_2, X_3, d_1^+, d_1^-, d_2^+, d_2^-, d_3^+, d_3^- \geq 0$

PROBLEM 4

Designer Gill Glass must decide which of three manufacturers will develop his "signature" toothbrushes. Three factors seem important to Gill: (1) his costs; (2) reliability of the product; and, (3) delivery time of the orders.

The three manufacturers are Cornell Industries, Brush Pik, and Picobuy. Cornell Industries will sell toothbrushes to Gill Glass for $100 per gross, Brush Pik for $80 per gross, and Picobuy for $144 per gross. Gill has decided that in terms of price, Brush Pik is moderately preferred to Cornell and very strongly preferred to Picobuy. In turn Cornell is strongly to very strongly preferred to Picobuy.

a) Form the pairwise comparison matrix for cost.

b) Calculate the normalized matrix for cost.

c) Determine the priority vector for cost.

d) Are Gill Glass's responses to cost consistent? Explain.

SOLUTION 4

a) Since Brush Pik is moderately preferred to Cornell, Cornell's entry in the Brush Pik row is 3 and Brush Pik's entry in the Cornell row is 1/3.

Since Brush Pik is very strongly preferred to Picobuy, Picobuy's entry in the Brush Pik row is 7 and Brush Pik's entry in the Picobuy row is 1/7.

Since Cornell is strongly to very strongly preferred to Picobuy, Picobuy's entry in the Cornell row is 6 and Cornell's entry in the Picobuy row is 1/6.

All diagonal entries are 1. Hence:

Pairwise comparison matrix for cost

	Cornell	Brush Pik	Picobuy
Cornell	1	1/3	6
Brush Pik	3	1	7
Picobuy	1/6	1/7	1

b) To determine normalized matrix, divide each entry in the matrix by its corresponding column sum. For Cornell the column sum = 1 + 3 + 1/6 = 25/6. For Brush Pik the column sum is 1/3 + 1 + 1/7 = 31/21. For Picobuy the column sum is 6 + 7 + 1 = 14. This gives:

<u>Normalized matrix for cost</u>

	Cornell	Brush Pik	Picobuy
Cornell	6/25	7/31	6/14
Brush Pik	18/25	21/31	7/14
Picobuy	1/25	3/31	1/14

c) The priority vector is determined by averaging the row entries in the normalized matrix. Converting to decimals we get:

<u>Priority vector for cost</u>

$$\begin{array}{ll} \text{Cornell:} & (6/25 + 7/31 + 6/14)/3 = \\ \text{Brush Pik:} & (18/25 + 21/31 + 7/14)/3 = \\ \text{Picobuy:} & (1/25 + 3/31 + 1/14)/3 = \end{array} \begin{bmatrix} .298 \\ .632 \\ .069 \end{bmatrix}$$

d) To check consistency,

(1) Multiply each column of the pairwise comparison matrix by its priority:

$$.298 \begin{bmatrix} 1 \\ 3 \\ 1/6 \end{bmatrix} + .632 \begin{bmatrix} 1/3 \\ 1 \\ 1/7 \end{bmatrix} + .069 \begin{bmatrix} 6 \\ 7 \\ 1 \end{bmatrix} = \begin{bmatrix} .923 \\ 2.009 \\ .209 \end{bmatrix}$$

(2) Divide these number by their priorities to get:

$$\begin{aligned} .923/.298 &= 3.097 \\ 2.009/.632 &= 3.179 \\ .209/.069 &= 3.029 \end{aligned}$$

(3) Average the above results to get λ_{max}.

$$\lambda_{max} = (3.097 + 3.179 + 3.029)/3 = 3.102$$

(4) Compute the consistence index, CI, for two terms by:

$$CI = (\lambda_{max} - n)/(n - 1) = (3.102 - 3)/2 = .051.$$

(5) Compute the consistency ratio, CR, by CI/RI, where RI = .58 for 3 factors:

$$CR = CI/RI = .051/.58 = .088$$

Since the consistency ratio, CR, is less than .10, this is well within the acceptable range for consistency.

PROBLEM 5

Referring to problem (4), Gill Glass has determined that for reliability, Cornell is very strongly preferable to Brush Pik and equally to moderately preferable to Picobuy. Also, Picobuy is strongly preferable to Brush Pik.

Regarding delivery time, Cornell is equally preferred with Picobuy. Both Cornell and Picobuy are very strongly to extremely preferable to Brush Pik.

a) Construct pairwise comparison matrices for reliability and for delivery time.

b) Construct priority vectors for reliability and delivery time.

SOLUTION 5

a) Pairwise comparison matrix for reliability

	Cornell	Brush Pik	Picobuy
Cornell	1	7	2
Brush Pik	1/7	1	5
Picobuy	1/2	1/5	1

Pairwise comparison matrix for delivery time

	Cornell	Brush Pik	Picobuy
Cornell	1	8	1
Brush Pik	1/8	1	1/8
Picobuy	1	8	1

b) For reliability the column sums are 23/14, 41/5, and 8. Dividing each entry by its corresponding column sum, we get:

Normalized matrix for reliability

	Cornell	Brush Pik	Picobuy
Cornell	14/23	35/41	2/8
Brush Pik	2/23	5/41	5/8
Picobuy	7/23	1/41	1/8

Priority vector for reliability

$$\begin{array}{rl} \text{Cornell:} & (14/23 + 35/41 + 2/8)/3 = \\ \text{Brush Pik:} & (\ 2/23 + \ 5/41 + 5/8)/3 = \\ \text{Picobuy:} & (\ 7/23 + \ 1/41 + 1/8)/3 = \end{array} \begin{bmatrix} .571 \\ .278 \\ .151 \end{bmatrix}$$

For delivery time the column sums are 17/8, 17, and 17/8 respectively.

Dividing each entry by its corresponding column sum gives:

Normalized matrix for delivery time

	Cornell	Brush Pik	Picobuy
Cornell	8/17	8/17	8/17
Brush Pik	1/17	1/17	1/17
Picobuy	8/17	8/17	8/17

Priority vector for delivery time

$$\begin{array}{rl} \text{Cornell:} & (8/17 + 8/17 + 8/17)/3 \\ \text{Brush Pik:} & (1/17 + 1/17 + 1/17)/3 \\ \text{Picobuy:} & (8/17 + 8/17 + 8/17)/3 \end{array} = \begin{bmatrix} .471 \\ .059 \\ .471 \end{bmatrix}$$

PROBLEM 6

The accounting department at Gill Glass (problems (4) and (5)) has determined that in terms of criteria, cost is extremely preferred to delivery time and very strongly preferred to reliability, and that reliability is very strongly preferred to delivery time.

a) Construct a pairwise comparison matrix for the criteria.

b) Construct a normalized pairwise matrix for the criteria.

c) Determine a priority vector for the criteria.

d) Determine an overall priority vector for the decision alternatives based on the criteria of the accounting dept.

SOLUTION 6

a) Pairwise comparison matrix for criteria

	Cost	Reliability	Delivery
Cost	1	7	9
Reliability	1/7	1	7
Delivery	1/9	1/7	1

b) The column sums are 79/63, 57/7, and 17 respectively. Dividing each entry by its corresponding column sum gives:

Normalized matrix for criteria

	Cost	Reliability	Delivery
Cost	63/79	49/57	9/17
Reliability	9/79	7/57	7/17
Delivery	7/79	1/57	1/17

c) Average the rows of the normalized matrix to get:

Priority vector for criteria

$$\begin{array}{lll} \text{Cost:} & (63/79 + 49/57 + 9/17)/3 & = \\ \text{Reliability:} & (\ 9/79 + \ 7/57 + 7/17)/3 & = \\ \text{Delivery:} & (\ 7/79 + \ 1/57 + 1/17)/3 & = \end{array} \begin{bmatrix} .729 \\ .216 \\ .055 \end{bmatrix}$$

d) The overall priorities are determined by multiplying the priority vector of the criteria by the priorities for each decision alternative for each objective:

Priority Vector for criteria -> [.729 .216 .055]

	Cost	Reliability	Delivery
Cost	63/79	49/57	9/17
Reliability	9/79	7/57	7/17
Delivery	7/79	1/57	1/17

(Priority Matrix)

<u>Overall</u> <u>priority</u> <u>vector</u>

Cornell: (.729)(.298) + (.216)(.571) + (.055)(.471) = .366

Brush Pik: (.729)(.632) + (.216)(.278) + (.055)(.059) = .524

Picobuy: (.729)(.069) + (.216)(.151) + (.055)(.471) = .109

Thus, Brush Pik appears to be the overall recommendation.

PROBLEM 7

A student has one quantitative elective left to select to complete his graduation requirements. The two quantitative electives that are available are an advanced management science class (MS) and an advanced statistics class (STAT). Two factors which are important to the student in his selection process are relevance (R) and difficulty (D). The student formulated the following pairwise consistency matrices:

Criteria

	R	D
R	1	1/3
D	3	1

Relevance

	MS	STAT
MS	1	1/3
STAT	3	1

Difficulty

	MS	STAT
MS	1	5
STAT	1/5	1

a) Draw the hierarchy for this decision problem.

b) Compute the priorities for each of the pairwise comparison matrices.

c) Determine an overall priority for the course selection process.

SOLUTION 7

a) First, list the overall goal: Select the best course. Then, list the evaluation criteria: Relevance, Difficulty. Last, list the alternatives: Management Science, Statistics.

b) Priority Vectors:

Relevance

The column sums are 4 and 4/3 respectively. Dividing the entries by the column sums yields the following normalized matrix:

	MS	STAT
MS	1/4	1/4
STAT	3/4	3/4

Averaging the rows gives the following priority vector for relevance:

$$\begin{array}{r} \text{MS} \\ \text{STAT} \end{array} \begin{bmatrix} 1/4 \\ 3/4 \end{bmatrix}$$

Difficulty

The column sums are 6/5 and 6 respectively. Dividing the entries by the column sums yields the following normalized matrix:

	MS	STAT
MS	5/6	5/6
STAT	1/6	1/6

Averaging the rows gives the following priority vector for difficulty:

$$\begin{matrix} \text{MS} \\ \text{STAT} \end{matrix} \begin{bmatrix} 5/6 \\ 1/6 \end{bmatrix}$$

Criteria

The column sums are 4 and 4/3 respectively. Dividing the entries by the column sums yields the following normalized matrix:

	Rel.	Dif.
Rel.	1	1/3
Dif.	3	1

Averaging the rows gives the following priority vector for criteria:

$$\begin{matrix} \text{Relevance} \\ \text{Difficulty} \end{matrix} \begin{bmatrix} 1/4 \\ 3/4 \end{bmatrix}$$

c) Determine the overall priorities for MS and STAT by multiplying their relevance and difficulty vectors by their priority:

Priority vector for criteria --> [1/4 3/4]

	Rel.	Dif.
Rel.	1/4	5/6
Dif.	3/4	1/6

(Priority Matrix)

Overall priority vector

$$\begin{matrix} \text{MS:} & (.25)(.25) + (.75)(.833) = \\ \text{STAT:} & (.25)(.75) + (.75)(.167) = \end{matrix} \begin{bmatrix} .6875 \\ .3125 \end{bmatrix}$$

Thus, MS appears to be the overall recommendation.

ANSWERED PROBLEMS

PROBLEM 8

Alfax Industries is trying to promote a new product which it recently developed. It wishes to restrict advertising to television and radio ads. Television ads cost $50,000 each to produce and radio ads $15,000 each. Each television ad will require the use of three Alfax marketing employees and each radio ad will require one. There are 24 persons in the marketing department. Management requires a minimum of six total ads monthly.

Alfax has set the following goals for the production of ads:

(1) Do not exceed a monthly advertising budget of $250,000.
(2) Do not use more than 50% of its marketing personnel on this project.
(3) Produce at least 4 television ads monthly.
(4) Produce at least 4 radio ads monthly.

a) Using the goals as simple constraints, formulate the constraint set for this problem and show it is infeasible.

b) Solve the above goal program graphically with four levels of priority.

c) Suppose goals (3) and (4) were within the same priority level but with the goal of producing at least 4 television ads monthly deemed twice as important as making 4 radio ads. Resolve this problem with three levels of priority.

PROBLEM 9

Barry College has received a $200,000 donation for its scholarship fund to be used for $3000 athletic scholarships, $2500 minority scholarships and $2000 women's scholarships. The donor, an avid sports fan, has stipulated at least 20 athletic scholarships must be awarded.

The Board of Trustees of Barry College has three levels of priority for awarding the scholarships:

(1) It would like at least 80 total scholarships.
(2) It would like no more than 25% of the scholarships to be athletic scholarships.
(3) It would like at least 25 athletic scholarships, 40 minority scholarships, and 30 women's scholarships. (Meeting the target for minorities is viewed as three times as important as meeting the target for athletes or women.)

Formulate a goal program for Barry College and solve by a computer package such as the Management Scientist.

PROBLEM 10

Universal Electric (UE) has facilities all over the United States. Currently UE has 150,000 employees, 5,000 of which are in management positions. The government contends that UE is delinquent in its Affirmative Action policies and will take action if UE does not rectify the situation.

Although UE currently has 12,000 minority employees (8% of its total), only 50 are in management positions (or 1% of the management positions). UE has submitted a plan to the federal government which expresses that UE has a target of 20% minority employees by the end of the year. In negotiating with various minority groups, UE has promised that by the end of the year, at least 10% of its management positions will be held by minorities.

Attrition rates of all employees (both management and otherwise) are 8% for non-minorities, 4% for minorities. Because of a good year, UE will create 6,000 new positions, 200 of which will be in management. However, the mandate from the top is that it would be unwise from a community relations point of view, if more than 2/3 of the new employee positions and more than 2/3 of the promotions to management positions be minorities.

Assume all management positions will be filled in-house and hence all hiring will be for non-management positions. Further assume violations of the company mandate have the same weight as not meeting the goal of 10% minority management positions. However, not meeting federal standards is considered three times more serious.

Formulate this problem as a goal programming problem with a single weighted priority.

PROBLEM 11

Consider a beauty pageant in which there are three finalists. They are to be judged on (1) evening gown; (2) swim suit; and, (3) answering a corny question posed by an equally corny MC. The three finalists are Miss Northern State, Miss Central State, and Miss Southern State.

It is known that Judge Jones believes that swim suit is strongly more important than evening gown appearance and extremely more important than answering the question. Further, he feels that the evening gown appearance is very strongly more important than answering the question.

In the evening gown competition, Miss Central State performed very strongly compared to Miss Southern State and strongly compared to Miss Northern State. Miss Northern State compared equally to moderately more strongly than Miss Southern State.

In the swim suit competition, Miss Southern State was extremely preferred to both Miss Northern State or Miss Central State and Miss Northern State was moderately preferred to Miss Central State.

In the question competition, Miss Northern State was extremely preferred to Miss Southern State and strongly preferred to Miss Central State. Miss Central State was moderately preferred to Miss Southern State.

Judge Jones has 100 points to distribute among the three finalists. Using his observations and preferences, how should he divide his 100 points between the three finalists?

PROBLEM 12

The Drezners have a choice of three neighborhood supermarkets: Gamma Delta, Bill's, and Hewes. Five factors are important to the Drezners: (1) Location; (2) Overall Prices; (3) Cleanliness; (4) Ease of Parking; and, (5) Selection/Quality. The pairwise comparison matrices are shown below:

Location:

	GD	B	H
GD	1	1/2	4
B	2	1	3
H	1/4	1/3	1

Overall Prices:

	GD	B	H
GD	1	1/2	4
B	2	1	3
H	1/4	1/3	1

Cleanliness:

	GD	B	H
GD	1	1/2	4
B	2	1	3
H	1/4	1/3	1

Ease of Parking:

	GD	B	H
GD	1	1/2	4
B	2	1	3
H	1/4	1/3	1

Selection/Quality:

	GD	B	H
GD	1	1/2	4
B	2	1	3
H	1/4	1/3	1

a) Determine the priority vector for each of the criteria.

b) If all five criteria were equally important, what would be the overall supermarket priority vector?

Now assume the Drezners feel that:
1) Location and ease of parking have equal priority.
2) Overall price is moderately more important than cleanliness or selection, and is very strongly more important than location or ease of parking.
3) Cleanliness is strongly more important than ease of parking, very strongly more important than location, and moderately more important than selection.
4) Selection/quality are moderately more important than location and very strongly more important than parking.

c) Given these preferences, construct a criteria pairwise comparison matrix.

d) Calculate the consistency ratio for the criteria and comment.

e) Determine the overall priority vector for the Drezners.

PROBLEM 13

Abraham L. Ford is a lifelong Republican who has a dilemma in the upcoming election. In general, Mr. Ford very strongly prefers Republicans over Democrats and strongly prefers Republicans over Independents. He moderately favors Independents over Democrats.

However, in the upcoming election, on the issues he strongly to very strongly favors Democrat Fritz Carter over Republican Ron Nixon and strongly favors Fritz Carter over Independent George Anderson. He moderately favors Anderson over Nixon. He has decided that issues are moderately to strongly more important to him than party.

a) Determine the hierarchy for this problem.

b) Determine the pairwise comparison matrix for each alternative.

c) Determine the priority vector for the alternatives for each criterion.

d) Determine the consistency ratio for the issues criterion.

e) Determine a priority vector for the criteria.

f) Determine Mr. Ford's overall priority vector for the candidates.

PROBLEM 14

Terry's Trucking is trying to determine which database package to purchase for its microcomputer. It has narrowed its choices to BASE 8 and DATA RECORD. BASE 8 is very strongly to extremely preferred in price, but DATA RECORD is strongly to very strongly preferred for ease of use.

a) Determine the hierarchy for Terry's Trucking's decision.

b) Construct the pairwise comparison matrix for each criterion.

c) Determine the priority vector for the alternatives for each criterion.

d) Determine the overall priority vector if:
   (1) price is extremely preferred to ease of use; or if
   (2) ease of use is extremely preferred to price; or if
   (3) price and ease of use are equally preferred.

e) Approximately what relation between price and ease of use would give BASE 8 and DATA RECORD equal priority in an overall priority vector?

PROBLEM 15

Consider the following military application regarding the so called "star wars" or "strategic defense initiative". The overall goal is to maintain peace.

The criteria are: (1) strong defense; (2) international image; (3) U.S. - Soviet relations.

The decision alternatives are: (1) continue with "star wars" development; (2) scale down "star wars" development; (3) abandon "star wars" development.

a) Make up your own preferences and feelings regarding the criteria and alternatives. Determine an overall priority vector of the alternatives.

b) Comment on a possible limitation of this model with regard to the scale used for the pairwise comparison matrices.

TRUE/FALSE

16. A goal programming problem will always have more than one priority level.

17. The number of linear programs that must be sequentially solved to develop the solution to a goal program is determined by the number of goals in the objective function.

18. For each goal in a goal program, two variables are added: one for underachieving the goal and one for overachieving the goal.

19. It is not possible to have two penalties for the same goal, one for underachieving the goal and another for overachieving it.

20. For a particular goal program, the Phase 1 objective was Minimize d_1^+. The objective was not satisfied but underachieved by an amount of 50. Any solution to the Phase 2 problem of Minimize d_2^- must have $d_1^+ = 50$.

21. In the process of satisfying second-priority goals, improvement in the satisfaction of first-priority goals sometimes occurs.

22. Trade-offs among goals at the same priority level will not occur unless the goals have the same relative weight.

23. In the analytic hierarchy process, if the entry in row A for decision B is 2, the entry in row B for decision A is 1/2.

24. In the analytic hierarchy process, a consistency ratio of .99 is extremely good.

25. If the consistency index is .90, the consistency ratio is .90.

26. The analytic hierarchy process utilizes pairwise comparisons to establish priority measures for both the criteria and the decision alternatives.

27. The criteria priority vector for gum is: Price: .3, Taste: .7. For Price, BRAND A's priority is .8 and BRAND B's is .2. For Taste, BRAND A's priority is .4 and BRAND B's is .6. Overall BRAND A has a higher priority than BRAND B.

28. On the 1-to-9 pairwise comparison scale, a numerical rating of 9 means extremely preferred and 5 means equally preferred.

29. In the analylic hierarchy process, the hierarchy from top to bottom is overall goal, decision alternatives, and criteria.

30. A consistency ratio measures the consistency of a decision alternative's relative rank from one criterion to another.

Answers to Problems and True/False

CHAPTER 1

6) a) Management science can provide a quantitative methodology for deciding the job-machine pairings so that total job processing time is minimized.

b) How long it takes to process each job on each machine, and any job-machine pairings that are unacceptable

c) Decision variables: one for each job-machine pairing, taking on a value of 1 if the pairing is used and 0 otherwise.
Objective function: minimize total job processing time.
Constraints: each job is assigned to exactly one machine, and each machine be assigned no more than one job.

d) Stochastic: job processing times vary due to varying machine set-up times, variable operator performance, and more.

e) Assume that processing times are deterministic (known/fixed).

7) a) The company because of its size and the newness of its product should probably select the simplified model because of the reduced costs and the time period for attaining results. This first pass at the problem most likely will give a "ballpark" figure. The model can then be refined as more experience with production and demand is attained.

b) Because of the large volume and the national distribution, perhaps the more complete study should be done in this case. Additionally, since the firm is a conglomerate, a more complete justification of its policy to the stockholders may be required.

8) a)

$$\begin{array}{llllll}
\text{MAX} & 10s_1 + 10s_2 + 25s_3 & & & & \\
\text{S.T.} & 25s_1 & & & \le & 5{,}000 \\
 & & 50s_2 & & \le & 5{,}000 \\
 & & & 100s_3 & \le & 5{,}000 \\
 & 25s_1 & & & \ge & 1{,}000 \\
 & & 50s_2 & & \ge & 1{,}000 \\
 & & & 100s_3 & \ge & 1{,}000 \\
 & 25s_1 & + 50s_2 & + 100s_3 & \le & 10{,}000 \\
 & & s_1, s_2, s_3 \ge 0 & & &
\end{array}$$

b)

$$\begin{array}{llllll}
\text{MAX} & 1.4x_1 + 1.2x_2 + 1.25x_3 & & & & \\
\text{S.T.} & x_1 & & & \le & 5{,}000 \\
 & & x_2 & & \le & 5{,}000 \\
 & & & x_3 & \le & 5{,}000 \\
 & x_1 & & & \ge & 1{,}000 \\
 & & x_2 & & \ge & 1{,}000 \\
 & & & x_3 & \ge & 1{,}000 \\
 & x_1 & + x_2 & + x_3 & \le & 10{,}000 \\
 & & x_1, x_2, x_3 \ge 0 & & &
\end{array}$$

c) Both give the same result.

CHAPTER 1

9) a) $N = L/25$; $C = 8C_gN$; $C = .32C_gL$
b) $TC = C_n + .32C_gL$; if $L = 50$, $TC = \$260$; if $L = 65$, $N = 2.6$ guards, so it must be decided whether to use 2 or 3 guards during the day.

10) a) X_1 = number of seats CPI manufactures in quarter 1
X_2 = number of seats subcontracted in quarter 1
X_3 = number of seats held in inventory from qtr.1 to qtr.2
X_4 = number of seats CPI manufactures in quarter 2
X_5 = number of seats subcontracted in quarter 2
b) Minimize $10.25X_1 + 12.50X_2 + 1.50X_3 + 10.25X_4 + 13.75X_5$

11) a) $X_1 \leq 3800$ (1)
$X_4 \leq 3800$ (2)
$X_1 + X_2 - X_3 = 3700$ (3)
$X_3 \leq 300$ (4)
$X_3 + X_4 + X_5 = 4200$ (5)
b) The real problem is stochastic
c) Three decision variables must be introduced:
X_6 = number of seats held in inventory from qtr.2 to qtr.3
X_7 = number of seats CPI manufactures in quarter 3
X_8 = number of seats subcontracted in quarter 3
Addition to objective function: $+1.50X_6 + 10.25X_7 + 13.75X_8$
Adjustment to constraint (5) above: $X_3 + X_4 + X_5 - X_6 = 4200$
Three additional constraints:
$X_6 \leq 300$
$X_7 \leq 3800$
$X_6 + X_7 + X_8$ = 3rd quarter demand

12) a) $50s + 30c \leq 800$
$s \geq 5$
$c \geq 5$
b) (1) Max $s + c$; (2) Max $.03s + .05c$; (3) Max $6s + 5c$

13) a) Variable costs: Assembly labor = \$8, Packagin labor = \$1, Packaging material = \$11, Components = \$630
Fixed costs: Lease, utilities, etc. = \$5,000
Cost function: $c(x) = 650x + 5{,}000$
b) $r(x) = 700x$
c) 100
d) \$650
e) \$20,000

TRUE/FALSE

14. FALSE	15. TRUE	16. TRUE	17. TRUE	18. FALSE
19. TRUE	20. FALSE	21. FALSE	22. FALSE	23. FALSE
24. FALSE	25. FALSE	26. TRUE	27. TRUE	28. FALSE

CHAPTER 2

7) a) Let E_j = (# poor, # average, # excellent).
E_1 = (4,0,0), E_2 = (3,1,0), E_3 = (3,0,1), E_4 = (2,2,0),
E_5 = (2,1,1), E_6 = (2,0,2), E_7 = (1,3,0), E_8 = (1,2,1),
E_9 = (1,1,2), E_{10} = (1,0,3), E_{11} = (0,4,0), E_{12} = (0,3,1),
E_{13} = (0,2,2), E_{14} = (0,1,3), E_{15} = (0,0,4).
b) $\{E_7, E_8\}$
c) $\{E_9\}$
d) yes
e) no
f) yes

8) a) .357
b) .583

9) a) .15
b) .167
c) .56

10) a) .162
b) .37
c) .408
d) no

11) a) lower .095; same .469; higher .437
b) .604
c) .384

12) a) 6
b) {(G,S,B), (G,B,S)}
c) {(G,S,B)}
d) {(G,B,S)}

13) a) .25
b) .49
c) .12

14) a) .4225
b) .325
c) .06
d) .1925

15) .304

16) a) (1) .0121; (2) .7921 (3) .1958
b) .15
c) .571
d) No
e) P(Married Prefers) = P(Husband Prefers)P(husband)
+ P(Wife Prefers)P(Wife) = .145; more.

17) a) .234
b) .829
c) .133
d) yes
e) .987

TRUE/FALSE

18. TRUE	19. FALSE	20. FALSE	21. TRUE	22. FALSE
23. FALSE	24. FALSE	25. TRUE	26. TRUE	27. FALSE
28. FALSE	29. FALSE	30. TRUE	31. FALSE	32. TRUE

CHAPTER 3

9) a) (1) P(3) = 1/12, P(4) = 1/12, P(6) = 1/12, P(10) = 1/6, P(16) = 1/4, P(20) = 1/3, all other P(x) = 0.
(2) P(0) = 1/12, P(1) =1/6, P(2) = 1/6, P(3) = 1/6, P(4) = 1/3, all other P(y) = 0
(3) P(0) = 1/12, P(.05) = 1/12, P(.1875) = 1/6, P(.20) = 1/3, P(.25) = 1/6, P(.3) = 1/12, P(.333) = 1/12, all other P(z) = 0
b) all distributions are for discrete random variables
c) (1) the third; (2) the first; (3) the second.
d) 1/2 e) 5/12 f) 13.417 g) 2.583 h) 17.15% i) No

10) a) Relief m = 15, s^2 = 150; Comfort m = 15.25, s^2 = 6.19
b) Relief
c) Comfort

11) a) .3277
b) .2048
c) 300 minutes

12) a) 40 mph
b) .9332

13) a) 1/2
b) 1/2
c) 1
d) 0
e) (1) 0 (2) 1/2
f) (1) 1/2 (2) 1
g) 8:10

14) M- .6247
T- .3218
W- .1587
R- .3721
F- .6247
S- .2620

15) a) $30
b) $45.50
c) Yes, new daily profit = $71

16) a) $\mu = 4$, $\sigma^2 = 2.4$
b) .3822
c) 6
d) .2335

17) a) .0120
b) .0183

18) a) f(x) = 1.25 for 31.8 < x < 32.6, 0 otherwise
b) 0, .375, 0
c) no

19) a) 0, .5, .5, .1587
b) $2

20) a) Store 1
b) Store 1 - .1587, Store 2 - .2266
c) No - Store has larger stand. dev.

21) a) .0183, .0733, .1465, .7619
b) .0107
c) .8647

TRUE/FALSE

22. FALSE	23. TRUE	24. TRUE	25. FALSE	26. FALSE
27. TRUE	28. FALSE	29. FALSE	30. FALSE	31. TRUE
32. TRUE	33. TRUE	34. FALSE	35. FALSE	36. TRUE

CHAPTER 4

6) a) Stock C -- it dominates Stock B
   b) (1) Stock A; (2) Stock C; (3) Stock D
   c) Stock D

7) a)

		Rail Freight	
		Bid $470,000	Doesn't Bid
Transrail	Bid $500,000	0	$100,000
	Bid $460,00	$60,000	$ 60,000

   b) Bid $460,000
   c) Bid $500,000
   d) $15,000

8) a)

	Sales (in 1,000,000's)		
	100	50	1
Introduce	$1,000,000	$200,000	-$2,000,000
Do Not Introduce	-$400,000	-$400,000	-$400,000

   b)

	Sales (in 1,000,000's)		
	100	50	1
Introduce	$0	$0	$1,600,000
Do Not Introduce	$1,400,000	$600,000	$0

   c) (1) do not introduce; (2) introduce; (3) do not introduce
   d) Yes
   e) No

9) a) Introduce root beer; $p \leq .483$
   b) EVPI = $112,000
   NOTE: The answers to (c)-(e) are very sensitive to roundoff error. Figures in parentheses are for two decimal places only.
   c) Stanton - EVSI = $13,200 ($11,862)
   Efficiency = .118 (.106)
   New World - EVSI = $6,400 ($6,424)
   Efficiency = .057 (.057)
   d) hire Stanton (Stanton)
   e) hire New World (Stanton)

10) a)

Plan	Number of Subscribers 10,000	20,000	30,000	40,000	50,000	60,000
I	-550	-400	-250	-100	50	200
II	-520	-340	-160	20	200	380
III	-500	-300	-100	100	300	500
IV	-460	-220	20	260	500	740

(table in $1000)

CHAPTER 4

10) b) (1) Plan IV; (2) Plan IV; (3) Plan IV
    c) Plan II -- Expected Value = $11,000

11) a)

		Number of Clients Purchasing a Computer				
		0	1	2	3	4
Number of Computers Manufactured	1	-40	50	30	10	-10
	2	-70	20	110	90	70
	3	-80	10	100	190	170
	4	-70	20	110	200	290

(Payoffs are in $1,000's)

b) Build 4 computers
c) Nothing

12) a) Yes, Dollar should sell the store
    b) EVPI = $8,000
    c) No; the cost of the survey exceeds the EVPI

13) a)

	Number of Copies (in 1,000's per month)					
Plan	12.6	14.4	16.2	18.0	19.8	21.6
I	341.6	370.4	399.2	428.0	456.8	485.6
II	351.2	372.8	394.4	416.0	437.6	459.2
III	317.2	356.8	396.4	436.0	475.6	515.2
IV	363.0	372.0	381.0	390.0	399.0	408.0

b) (1) Plan III; (2) Plan IV
c) Plan IV

14)

		Demand For Ovens			
		0	1	2	3
Ovens Ordered	0	0	-25	-50	-75
	1	-70	80	55	30
	2	-140	10	160	135
	3	-210	-60	90	240

a) Order one oven -- EV = $25.00
b) EVPI = $63
c) Favorable: order 2; Unfavorable: order 0; No opinion: order 1
d) EVSI = $9.10

TRUE/FALSE

15. FALSE	16. TRUE	17. FALSE	18. FALSE	19. FALSE
20. FALSE	21. TRUE	22. FALSE	23. TRUE	24. FALSE
25. TRUE	26. TRUE	27. TRUE	28. FALSE	29. FALSE

CHAPTER 5

5) a) $1,075
   b) $5,000

6) a) Risk averse
   b) Produce root beer as long as $p \geq 60/105 = .571$
   c) Choose Stanton

7) a) Risk Taker -- Second Vice President
   Risk Avoider -- First Vice President
   b) First Vice President -- System I
   Second Vice President -- System III
   c) Risk Neutral Vice President -- System I

8) a) A risk avoider
   b)

Amount	Utility
- $40,000	32
$20,000	56
$100,000	72

   c)

Amount	Utility
- $40,000	16
$20,000	88
$100,000	136

   d) Decision is d_2; EV criterion decision would be d_1
   e) Paul should accept the offer since his utility of $20,000 is greater than the expected utility under the optimal decision

9) Buy 3 leases

10) b) I -- risk taker; II -- risk neutral; III -- risk avoider
   c) Risk avoider would pay 400; Risk taker would pay 200
   d) I -- d_1; II -- d_1; III -- d_1

11) Depends on your personal values

12) Depends on your personal values; Note in 12 (e) -- the utility for $d and $x is the same and hence their values should be identical.

TRUE/FALSE

13. TRUE	14. FALSE	15. TRUE	16. TRUE	17. FALSE
18. TRUE	19. FALSE	20. FALSE	21. TRUE	22. TRUE
23. TRUE	24. TRUE	25. FALSE	26. TRUE	27. FALSE

CHAPTER 6

PROBLEMS

6) a) 4 period weighted moving average; MSE = 408
   b) exponential smoothing -- \$298.48
      weighted moving average -- \$294.27

7) a) σ = .6 is better MSE (9.12); σ = .2 has MSE = 10.82
   b) For σ = .6, F_9 = 22.86; for σ = .2, F_9 = 21.72

8) Year 6: Quarter 1 -- 56; Quarter 2 -- 48; Quarter 3 -- 79; Quarter 4 -- 40

9) a) The 3 week moving average gives the better forecast (MSE = 16,337 vs a MSE = 17,911 for the 4 week moving average)
   b) 3 week moving average forecast for week 11 = 1,200
      4 week moving average forecast for week 11 = 1,158

10) a) Yes
    b) Week 17 -- 29.0; Week 18 -- 30.0; Week 19 -- 31.0; Week 20 -- 32.0

11) b) 141.44, 144.18, 119.44, 157.72, 111.93

12) a) F_t = 34.80 - 1.329t
    b) 26 months
    c) After 27 months sales will be approximately -1 cars; this is clearly impossible; the assumption of a continued linear decline must be in error.

13) 42.15, 70.14, 52.17; 43.46, 72.30, 53.76

14) a) y = 80.8757 + 5.3605(x)
    b) y = 80.8757 + 5.3605(33.5) = 260.45245 hours for a 3350 sq. ft. house.

TRUE/FALSE

15. TRUE	16. TRUE	17. FALSE	18. TRUE	19. FALSE
20. TRUE	21. TRUE	22. FALSE	23. TRUE	24. TRUE
25. FALSE	26. TRUE	27. FALSE	28. FALSE	29. FALSE

CHAPTER 7

9) $X_1 = 0$, $X_2 = 4$; $Z = 48$

10) a) $X_1 = 4$, $X_2 = 3/2$; $Z = 19$
    b) All points on the line $2X_1 + X_2 = 6$ between (3,0) and (24/13,30/13).

11) a-b) extreme points: (0,4), (1,2), (3,1) -- feasible region is unbounded.
    c) (1) optimal solution $X_1 = 3$, $X_2 = 1$, $Z = 1$
       (2) alternate optimal solutions on $X_1 - 2X_2 = 1$ above (3,1)
       (3) unbounded linear program

12) a) $X_1 = 3$, $X_2 = 4$; $Z = 29$
    b) No change. If only a single point is feasible, the slope of the objective function is inconsequential.

13) a) $X_1 = 10$, $X_2 = 15$, $Z = 230$
    b) Any point satisfying all the other constraints will also satisfy constraint 1
    c) $X_1 = 20$, $X_2 = 15$, $Z = 310$

14) a)
$$\begin{aligned} \text{MAX}\quad & 60X_1 + 43X_2 \\ \text{S.T.}\quad & X_1 + 3X_2 - S_1 = 9 \\ & 6X_1 - 2X_2 = 12 \\ & X_1 + 2X_2 + S_3 = 10 \\ & X_1, X_2, S_1, S_3 \geq 0 \end{aligned}$$
    b) line segment of $6X_1 - 2X_2 = 12$ between (22/7,24/7) and (27/10,21/10).
    c) Extreme points: (22/7,24/7) and (27/10,21/10). First one is optimal giving $Z = 336$.

15) a) $X_1 = 35$, $X_2 = 0$ $Z = \$630,000$
    b) $X_1 = 5$, $X_2 = 12$ $Z = \$630,000$
    c) $X_1 = 10$, $X_2 = 10$ $Z = \$630,000$

16) a) 100 dozen childs, 66 2/3 dozen professional, profit = $12,333.33; both slack variables equal 0.
    b) this point is an interior point in the original formulation

17) a) $X_1 = 2$, $X_2 = 4$, $Z = 32$
    b) $5 \leq C_1 \leq 10$; $3 \leq C_2 \leq 6$
    c) $X_1 = 0$, $X_2 = 6$
    d) 1; improvement in the objective function for an extra unit of iron
    e) The shadow price of zinc is 0 as long as this line does not determine the optimal point -- as long as its RHS ≤ 2.

18) a) 120 containers of jade figurines, 60 containers of linen placemats; Profit = $13,200
    b) Between $30 and $120
    c) (1) $6.67; (2) $16.67; (3) $0

CHAPTER 7

19) a) 105 minivans, 75 trailers; $673,500 profit
    b) $2812.50 $\le$ minivan profit $\le$ no upper limit,
       no lower limit $\le$ trailer profit $\le$ $5120.00
    c) Dual price for yardman hours is $1600. Thus, an increase of $1600 in monthly profit can be gained for each hour increase in the monthly availability of yardmen!

20) a) Put 10,000 miles on Harley; 35,000 miles on Hauler
    b) $15.00
    c) 7.5 cents

TRUE/FALSE

21. TRUE	22. TRUE	23. TRUE	24. FALSE	25. FALSE
26. FALSE	27. FALSE	28. FALSE	29. FALSE	30. TRUE
31. TRUE	32. TRUE	33. FALSE	34. TRUE	35. FALSE

CHAPTER 8

5) a) 1500 shares of airlines stock, 800 shares of insurance stock; the expected return is \$5400
   b) Between \$0 and \$2.40

6) a) 6 product 1, 4 product 2, Profit = \$540
   b) Between \$50 and \$75; at \$70 the profit is \$580
   c) No -- total % change is 83 1/3% < 100%
   d) Dual prices are the shadow prices for the resources; since there was unused copper (because S_2 = 2), extra copper is worth \$0
   e) \$30
   f) \$10; this is the amount extra man-hours are worth
   g) The shadow price is the "premium" for aluminum -- would be willing to pay up to \$10 + \$30 = \$40 for extra aluminum

7) a) Standard -- 33 1/3, Slim-Line -- 266 2/3, Z = \$1100
   b) \$5.60
   c) Standard -- 86 2/3, Slim-Line -- 213 1/3, Z = \$1180

8) a) No
   b) No
   c) Yes -- Sum of % changes > 100%
   d) \$10 -- Value of extra man-hours
   e) \$1 -- this is the "premium" value for the boxes; hence extra boxes are worth \$1.25
   f) They will stay the same -- Sum of % changes < 100%

9) a) 200 shares of James, 20 shares of QM, 40 shares of Delic. Total gain = \$3200
   b) Each dollar increase in the allowed minimum investment in QM will result in a \$.05 decrease in the total \$ gain.
   c) Constraint #1 dual price (.25) X 1000 = \$250
   d) No. It would be James Ind. (only stock with + dual price)
   e) Constraint #2 dual price (.15) X 1000 = \$150
   f) Allowed max. investment could be raised to \$8000
   g) No, cumulative change does not exceed 100%

TRUE/FALSE

10. TRUE	11. TRUE	12. TRUE	13. TRUE	14. FALSE
15. FALSE	16. TRUE	17. TRUE	18. TRUE	19. TRUE
20. TRUE	21. TRUE	22. TRUE	23. FALSE	24. TRUE

CHAPTER 9

10) a)

$$\begin{array}{lrrrrrrl} \text{MAX} & 1.5X_1 + & X_2 + & .75X_3 + & .5X_4 + & .75X_5 + & X_6 & \\ \text{S.T.} & 20X_1 + & 18X_2 + & 13X_3 + & 7X_4 + & 12X_5 + & 15X_6 & \leq 500 \\ & X_1 + & X_2 + & X_3 + & X_4 + & X_5 + & X_6 & \geq 40 \\ & X_1 + & X_2 + & X_3 - & 2X_4 - & 2X_5 - & 2X_6 & \geq 0 \\ & X_1 + & X_2 & & + & X_5 + & X_6 & \geq 20 \end{array}$$

$$X_j \geq 0 \; j = 1,\ldots,6$$

b) The variables must be integers.

11) P_i = the number of producers in month i (where i = 1,2,3)
T_i = the number of trainers in month i (where i = 1,2)
A_i = the number of apprentices in month i (where i = 2,3)
R_i = the number of recruits in month i (where i = 1,2)

$$\text{MIN } 3000P_1 + 3300T_1 + 2200R_1 + 3000P_2 + 3300T_2 + 2600A_2 + 2200R_2 + 3000P_3 + 2600A_3$$

s.t.

$$\begin{aligned} &.6P_1 + .3T_1 + .05R_1 \geq 20 \\ &.6P_1 + .3T_1 + .05R_1 + .6P_2 + .3T_2 + .4A_2 + .05R_2 \geq 44 \\ &.6P_1+.3T_1+.05R_1+.6P_2+.3T_2+.4A_2+.05R_2+.6P_3+.4A_3 \geq 74 \\ &P_1 - P_2 + T_1 - T_2 = 0 \\ &P_2 - P_3 + T_2 + A_2 = 0 \\ &A_2 - R_1 = 0 \\ &A_3 - R_2 = 0 \\ &2T_1 - R_1 \geq 0 \\ &2T_2 - R_2 \geq 0 \\ &P_1 + T_1 = 100 \\ &P_3 + A_3 \geq 140 \\ &P_j,\ T_j,\ A_j,\ R_j \geq 0 \text{ for all } j \end{aligned}$$

12) X_j = the number of instrument j produced; where j = 1(deluxe trumpet); 2(prof. trumpet); 3(deluxe cornet); 4(prof. cornet)

$$\begin{array}{lrrrrl} \text{MAX} & 80X_1 + & 160X_2 + & 60X_3 + & 120X_4 & \\ \text{S.T.} & 2X_1 + & 1.5X_2 + & 1.5X_3 + & X_4 & \leq 2000 \\ & X_1 + & 1.5X_2 + & X_3 + & 1.5X_4 & \leq 1800 \\ & X_1 & & & & \geq 500 \\ & & & X_3 & & \geq 300 \\ & & X_2 & & & \leq 150 \\ & & & & X_4 & \leq 100 \\ & X_1 + & X_2 - & 2X_3 - & 2X_4 & = 0 \end{array}$$

$$X_j \geq 0 \; j = 1,\ldots,4$$

CHAPTER 9

13) a)
$$
\begin{array}{ll}
\text{MAX} & 5X_1+12X_2+25X_3+4X_4+10X_5+18X_6+9X_7+16X_8 \\
\text{S.T.} & 1.8X_1+2.2X_2+3X_3+.74X_4+1.6X_5+2.2X_6+X_7+1.5X_8 \leq 300 \\
& 1.8X_1+2.2X_2+3X_3 \geq 75 \\
& 1.8X_1+2.2X_2+3X_3 \leq 120 \\
& .74X_4+1.6X_5+2.2X_6 \geq 75 \\
& .74X_4+1.6X_5+2.2X_6 \leq 120 \\
& X_7+1.5X_8 \geq 30 \\
& X_7+1.5X_8 \leq 75 \\
& .75X_1-.25X_2-.25X_3+.75X_4-.25X_5-.25X_6-.25X_7-.25X_8 \geq 0 \\
& X_j \geq 0 \quad j = 1,\ldots,8
\end{array}
$$

b) $X_1 = 0$, $X_2 = 0$, $X_3 = 40$, $X_4 = 41.28$, $X_5 = 0$, $X_6 = 33.84$, $X_7 = 0$, $X_8 = 50$, $Z = 2{,}574.28$

c) The variables must be integers.

14) X_{11} = pounds of chocolate used in Chompers
X_{21} = pounds of chocolate used in Smerks
X_{31} = pounds of chocolate used in Delicious Chocolate
X_{12} = pounds of caramel used in Chompers
X_{22} = pounds of caramel used in Smerks
X_{23} = pounds of peanuts used in Smerks
Y_1 = number of one ounce Chompers bars produced daily
Y_2 = number of one ounce Smerks bars produced daily
Y_3 = number of one ounce Delicious Choc. bars produced daily
Y_4 = number of one pound Delicious Choc. bags produced daily

MAX $.128Y_1+.148Y_2+.138Y_3+2.261Y_4-1.60X_{11}-1.60X_{21}-1.60X_{31}-.95X_{12}-.95X_{22}-1.40X_{23}$

$$
\begin{array}{lrcl}
\text{S.T.} & (1/16)Y_3 + Y_4 & = & X_{31} \\
& (1/16)Y_1 & = & X_{11} + X_{12} \\
& (1/16)Y_2 & = & X_{21} + X_{22} + X_{23} \\
& X_{12} & \geq & .18(X_{11} + X_{12}) \\
& X_{12} & \leq & .28(X_{11} + X_{12}) \\
& X_{22} & = & X_{23} \\
& X_{21} & \geq & .20(X_{21} + X_{22} + X_{23}) \\
& X_{21} & \leq & .40(X_{21} + X_{22} + X_{23}) \\
& Y_1 + Y_2 + Y_3 & \leq & 20{,}000 \\
& Y_4 & \leq & 1{,}000 \\
& Y_1 & \geq & 3{,}000 \\
& Y_2 & \geq & 3{,}000 \\
& Y_3 & \geq & 3{,}000 \\
& Y_1 - Y_2 & \leq & .10(Y_1 + Y_2) \\
& Y_2 - Y_1 & \leq & .10(Y_1 + Y_2) \\
& X_{11} + X_{21} + X_{31} & \geq & 1{,}000 \\
& X_{12} + X_{22} & = & 350 \\
& X_{23} & \leq & 500 \\
& X_{ij} & \geq & 0 \quad i = 1,2,3;\ j = 1,2,3 \\
& Y_j & \geq & 0 \quad j = 1,2,3,4
\end{array}
$$

CHAPTER 9

15) X_1 = number of bulldozers purchased for the year
X_2 = number of bulldozers leased for the year
annual cost = (purchasing) + (leasing) - (salvage) - (interest)
$= (40{,}000X_1)+(8000X_2)-(20{,}000X_1)-0.08(1{,}000{,}000 - 40{,}000X_1 - 8{,}000X_2)$
$= 23{,}200X_1 + 8{,}640X_2 - 80{,}000$. Thus,
MIN $23{,}200X_1 + 8{,}640X_2$
S.T. $4{,}000X_1 + 8{,}000X_2 \leq 1{,}000{,}000$
$8X_1 + 5X_2 \geq 240$ and $X_1, X_2 \geq 0$
Answer: Buy 0 bulldozers, lease 48; Annual cost= $334,720

16) X_j = \$ invested in investment j; where j = 1(Uni Eq.), 2(Col. Must.), 3(1st Gen REIT), 4(Met. Elec.), 5(Uni Debt), 6(Lem. Trans.), 7(Fair. Apt.), 8(T-Bill), 9(Money Market), 10(All Saver's)
MAX $.15X_1 + .17X_2 + .175X_3 + .118X_4 + .122X_5 + .12X_6 + .22X_7 + .096X_8 + .105X_9 + .126X_{10}$
S.T. $X_1 + X_2 + X_3 + X_4 + X_5 + X_6 + X_7 + X_8 + X_9 + X_{10} = 400{,}000$
$100X_1 + 100X_2 + 100X_3 + 95X_4 + 92X_5 + 79X_6 + 80X_8 + 100X_9 \geq 65(X_1 + X_2 + X_3 + X_4 + X_5 + X_6 + X_7 + X_8 + X_9 + X_{10})$
$60X_1 + 70X_2 + 75X_3 + 20X_4 + 30X_5 + 22X_6 + 50X_7 + 10X_9 \leq 55(X_1 + X_2 + X_3 + X_4 + X_5 + X_6 + X_7 + X_8 + X_9 + X_{10})$
$X_1 + X_5 \leq 60{,}000$
$X_1 + X_2 + X_3 \leq 160{,}000$
$X_4 + X_5 + X_6 \leq 160{,}000$
$X_3 + X_7 \leq 160{,}000$
$X_1 \leq 80{,}000$
$X_2 \leq 80{,}000$
$X_3 \leq 80{,}000$
$X_4 \leq 80{,}000$
$X_5 \leq 80{,}000$
$X_6 \leq 80{,}000$
$X_7 \leq 80{,}000$
$X_8 \leq 80{,}000$
$X_9 \geq 1{,}000$
$X_{10} \leq 15{,}000$
$X_4 + X_5 + X_6 \geq 90{,}000$
$X_8 \geq 10{,}000$
$X_j \geq 0 \quad j = 1,\ldots,10$

17) X_1 = amount invested in new soda advertising
X_2 = amount invested in traditional soda advertising
MAX $X_1 + 4X_2$ <==== $02(50X_1) + .04(100X_2)$
S.T. $X_1 + X_2 \leq 10{,}000{,}000$
$X_1 \geq 5{,}000{,}000$
$X_2 \geq 2{,}000{,}000$
$50X_1 + 100X_2 \geq 750{,}000{,}000$
$X_1, X_2 \geq 0$

Answer: spend $5,000,000 on new soda ad, $5,000,000 on traditional ad, profit is $25,000,000

CHAPTER 9

18) X_1-X_3 = number of students from NE to McHale,McCallum,McBride
X_4-X_6 = number of students from SE to McHale,McCallum,McBride
X_7-X_9 = number of students from SW to McHale,McCallum,McBride
X_{10}-X_{12} = number of students from NW to McHale,McCallum,McBride
X_{13}-X_{15} = number of students from Central to McHal,McCal,McBrid

MIN $1.5X_1+2.5X_2+.5X_3+4X_4+1.5X_5+3X_6+2.5X_7+3X_8+3.5X_9+.5X_{10}+4X_{11}+1.5X_{12}+1X_{13}+2X_{14}+1X_{15}$

S.T.
$X_1 + X_2 + X_3 = 700$
$X_4 + X_5 + X_6 = 1100$
$X_7 + X_8 + X_9 = 900$
$X_{10} + X_{11} + X_{12} = 600$
$X_{13} + X_{14} + X_{15} = 800$
$X_1 + X_4 + X_{10} + X_{13} \leq 1500$
$X_2 + X_5 + X_{11} + X_{14} \leq 1800$
$X_3 + X_6 + X_{12} + X_{15} \leq 1100$
$X_j \geq 0 \quad j = 1,2,...,15$

700 students from NE to McBride, 1100 from SE to McCallum, 500 from SW to McHale, 400 from SW to McCallum, 600 from NW to McHale, 400 from Central to McHale, and 400 from Central to McBride.

19) E = .968; Alabama store appears moderately inefficient

20) X_1-X_4 = number of full-time clerks starting at 8,9,10,11am
X_5-X_{11} = number of part-time clerks starting at 8,9,10,11am and 12,1,2pm
MIN $63X_1+63X_2+63X_3+63X_4+26X_5+26X_6+26X_7+26X_8+26X_9+26X_{10}+26X_{11}$

S.T.
$X_1 \geq 1$
$X_4 \geq 1$
$X_1 + X_2 + X_3 + X_4 \geq 4$
$X_1 + X_5 \geq 5$
$X_1 + X_2 + X_5 + X_6 \geq 4$
$X_1 + X_2 + X_3 + X_5 + X_6 + X_7 \geq 6$
$X_2 + X_3 + X_4 + X_5 + X_6 + X_7 + X_8 \geq 8$
$X_1 + X_3 + X_4 + X_6 + X_7 + X_8 + X_9 \geq 10$
$X_1 + X_2 + X_4 + X_7 + X_8 + X_9 + X_{10} \geq 9$
$X_1 + X_2 + X_3 + X_8 + X_9 + X_{10} + X_{11} \geq 7$
$X_2 + X_3 + X_4 + X_9 + X_{10} + X_{11} \geq 4$
$X_3 + X_4 + X_{10} + X_{11} \geq 7$
$X_4 + X_{11} \geq 5$
$X_j \geq 0 \quad j = 1,2,...,11$

TRUE/FALSE

21. FALSE	22. FALSE	23. TRUE	24. FALSE	25. TRUE
26. TRUE	27. TRUE	28. TRUE	29. FALSE	30. FALSE
31. FALSE	32. FALSE	33. FALSE	34. FALSE	35. FALSE

CHAPTER 10

8) a) $\text{MIN } Z = 2X_1 + 3X_2 + 8X_3$

S.T.
$$4X_1 + 2X_2 + X_3 - S_1 = 15$$
$$2X_1 + X_2 + 6X_3 - S_2 = 30$$
$$X_j \geq 0 \quad j = 1,2,3$$
$$S_j \geq 0 \quad j = 1,2$$

b) Cannot have negative numbers on RHS

c) $X_1 = 15$, $X_2 = 0$, $X_3 = 0$, $S_1 = 45$, $S_2 = 0$, $Z = 30$

9) $X_1 = 5$, $X_2 = 3/2$, $X_3 = 0$, $S_1 = 0$, $S_2 = 19/2$, $Z = 8$

10) $X_1 = 3$, $X_2 = 0$, $X_3 = 4\ 2/3$, $S_1 = 0$, $S_2 = 2\ 1/3$, $S_3 = 2$; $Z = 13\ 2/3$

11) a) Tableau infeasible at this stage, but cannot yet state whether or not the problem is feasible:

		X_1	X_2	X_3	S_1	S_2	S_3	A_2	
Basis	C_B	10	8	6	0	0	0	-M	
S_1	0	0	1	0	1	0	-2	0	4
A_2	-M	-1	0	0	0	-1	-1	1	6
X_3	6	1/2	1/2	1	0	0	1/2	0	5
Z_j		M+3	3	6	0	M	M+3	-M	-6M+30
$C_j - Z_j$		-M+7	5	0	0	-M	-M-3	0	

b) Optimal: $X_1 = 0$, $X_2 = 14$, $X_3 = 0$, $S_1 = 18$, $S_2 = 0$, $Z = 84$

c) Problem Unbounded: X_3 column is non-positive

d) Problem Infeasible: A_2 positive in this "optimal" tableau

e) Tableau is feasible, but not yet optimal

		X_1	X_2	X_3	S_1	S_2	
Basis	C_B	4	5	7	0	0	
X_3	7	0	0	1	0	0	12
S_2	0	0	0	0	-2/3	1	2
X_2	5	0	1	0	1/3	0	6
X_1	4	1	0	0	1/3	0	26
Z_j		4	5	7	3	0	218
$C_j - Z_j$		0	0	0	-3	0	

CHAPTER 10

12) a)

Basis	C_B	X_1	X_2	X_3	S_1	S_2	S_3	
		4	2	-1	0	0	0	
X_2	2	0	1	-1	6	0	1	10
S_2	0	0	0	4	2	1	1	20
X_1	4	1	0	0	-3	0	1	30
Z_j		4	2	-2	0	0	6	140
$C_j - Z_j$		0	0	1	0	0	-6	

b) $X_1 = 30$, $X_2 = 10$, $X_3 = 0$, $S_1 = 0$, $S_2 = 20$, $S_3 = 0$, $Z = 140$

c) increases by 1; increases by 3; unchanged; decreases by 12

d) X_3 enters; equations are:

$$X_2 - X_3 = 10 \quad (1)$$
$$4X_3 + S_2 = 20 \quad (2)$$
$$X_1 = 30 \quad (3)$$

(1) shows X_2 increases as X_3 increases. (2) shows S_2 decreases as X_3 increases, and (3) shows that X_1 is unchanged as X_3 increases. Thus ratio test is applied only to positive numbers in the entering column.

e) S_2 would become -20.

f) 5

g) New values: $Z = 145$; $X_2 = 15$; $S_2 = 0$; X_1 unchanged.

h)

Basis	C_B	X_1	X_2	X_3	S_1	S_2	S_3	
		4	2	-1	0	0	0	
X_2	2	0	1	0	13/2	1/4	5/4	15
X_3	-1	0	0	1	1/2	1/4	1/4	5
X_1	4	1	0	0	-3	0	1	30
Z_j		4	2	-1	1/2	1/4	25/4	145
$C_j - Z_j$		0	0	0	-1/2	-1/4	-25/4	

13) a)

Basis	C_B	X_1	X_2	X_3	S_1	S_2	S_3	
		5	2	1	0	0	0	
X_1	5	1	0	1/2	-3	1/2	0	4
X_2	2	0	1	-1/2	7	-1/2	0	0
S_3	0	0	0	- 2	15	-5	1	4
Z_j		5	2	3/2	-1	3/2	0	20
$C_j - Z_j$		0	0	-1/2	1	-3/2	0	

Solution: $X_1 = 4$, $X_2 = 0$, $X_3 = 0$, $S_1 = 0$, $S_2 = 0$, $S_3 = 4$, $Z = 20$.
Not optimal (a positive number is in $C_j - Z_j$ row).

CHAPTER 10

13) b)

Basis	C_B	X_1	X_2	X_3	S_1	S_2	S_3	
		5	2	1	0	0	0	
X_3	1	0	-2	1	-14	1	0	0
X_1	5	1	1	0	4	0	0	4
S_3	0	0	-4	0	-13	-3	1	4
Z_j		5	3	1	6	1	0	20
$C_j - Z_j$		0	-1	0	-6	-1	0	

Solution: Same as (a). This time, the $C_j - Z_j$ row indicates that this is an optimal solution.

c) When degeneracy occurs, an optimal solution may have been attained even though some $C_j - Z_j > 0$. Thus, the condition that $C_j - Z_j \leq 0$, is sufficient for optimality, but not necessary.

14) a) Produce 250 deluxe doors

b) There are many, including producing 200 standard and 100 deluxe doors

15) a)

$$
\begin{aligned}
\text{MAX } Z = \; & 2X_1 + 5X_2 + 5X_3 + 3X_4 \\
\text{S.T.} \quad & 10X_1 + 12X_2 + 10X_3 + 9X_4 + S_1 = 150 \\
& X_1 + X_2 + X_3 - S_2 = 12 \\
& -X_1 + X_2 + X_3 - X_4 + S_3 = 0 \\
& X_j \geq 0 \; j = 1,2,3,4 \\
& S_j \geq 0 \; j = 1,2,3
\end{aligned}
$$

b)

Basis	C_B	X_1	X_2	X_3	X_1	S_1	S_2	A_2	S_3	
		2	5	5	3	0	0	-M	0	
S_1	0	10	12	10	9	1	0	0	0	150
A_2	-M	1	1	1	0	0	-1	1	0	12
X_3	0	-1	1	1	-1	0	0	0	1	0
Z_j		-M	-M	-M	0	0	M	-M	0	-12M
$C_j - Z_j$		2+M	5+M	5+M	3	0	-M	0	0	

c) $X_1 = 4\ 1/3$, $X_2 = 0$, $X_3 = 7\ 2/3$, $X_4 = 3\ 1/3$,
$S_1 = 0$, $S_2 = 0$, $S_3 = 0$; $Z = 57$

TRUE/FALSE

16. TRUE 17. FALSE 18. TRUE 19. TRUE 20. TRUE
21. FALSE 22. FALSE 23. TRUE 24. TRUE 25. TRUE
26. FALSE 27. TRUE 28. FALSE 29. FALSE 30. FALSE

CHAPTER 11

8. a)

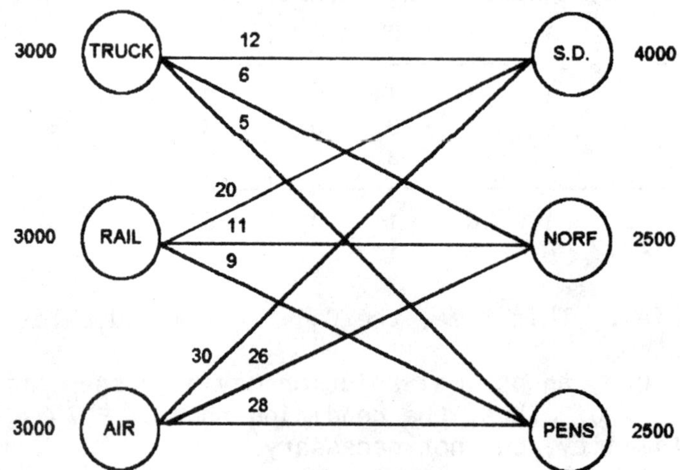

b) Truck - Pensacola 2500; Truck - Norfolk 500; Railroad - Norfolk 2000; Railroad - San Diego 1000; Airplane - San Diego 3000

c) Truck - San Diego 1000; Truck - Norfolk 2000; Railroad - Norfolk 500; Railroad - Pensacola 2500; Airplane - San Diego 3000

9) a) Newspaper - MR1 15; Newspaper - MR2 5; Newspaper - MR3 10; TV - MR2 15; Radio - MR2 5; Radio - MR4 20; Total Cost = $1,065,000

b) Newspaper - MR2 20; Newspaper - MR3 10; TV - MR1 15; Radio - MR2 5; Radio - MR4 20; Total cost = $1,065,000

c) Many answers. One with TV-MR1 = 5 is: Newspaper - MR1 10; Newspaper - MR2 10; Newspaper - MR3 10; TV - MR1 5; TV - MR2 10; Radio - MR2 5; Radio - MR4 20; Total cost = $1,065,000

10) Ace: 25 Sanitation and 5 Police; Band: 25 Parks and 15 Administration; QM: 20 Police and 10 Administration; Cost $1,035,000

11) LA-Denver 25; LA-NY 10; CHI-NY 30; NY-ATL 35; Profit $2,165,000

12) Abbey-Cabin3, Babbs-Cabin4, Carla-Cabin2, Diane-Cabin5, Ellsa-Cabin1; Performance rating total = 35

13) a) (diagram on next page)

b) Computer Town - P5; Computer World - P4; Universal - P1; Local Computer - P2 and P3; Total Cost $71,000

c) +M placed in matrix in row 2, column 5; no change in solution

d) +M's placed in assignment matrix row 2 column 4, and in row 2 column 5; Computer Town - P5; Computer World - P2; Universal - P1; Local Computer - P3 and P4; Total cost = $77,000

CHAPTER 11

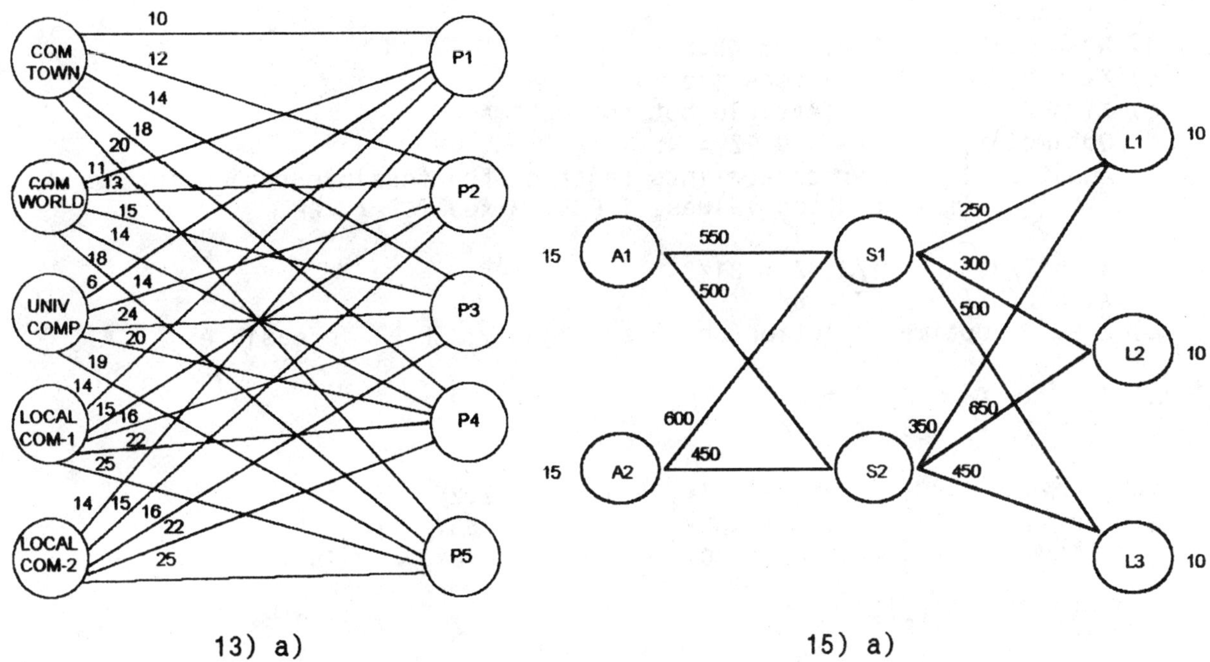

13) a) 15) a)

14) Division 1 - Bats; Division 2 - Golf Clubs; Division 3 - Racquetball Rackets; Division 4 - Tennis Rackets; Total 410

15) a) (above)
    b) Denote A1 as node 1, A2 as node 2, S1 as node 3, S2 as node 4, L1 as node 5, L2 as node 6, and L3 as node 7

$$
\begin{aligned}
\text{MIN } & 550X_{13} + 500X_{14} + 600X_{23} + 450X_{24} + 250X_{35} + 300X_{36} \\
& + 500X_{37} + 350X_{45} + 650X_{46} + 450X_{47} \\
\text{S.T.} \quad & X_{13} + X_{14} \le 15 \\
& X_{23} + X_{24} \le 15 \\
& X_{13} + X_{23} - X_{35} - X_{36} - X_{37} = 0 \\
& X_{14} + X_{24} - X_{45} - X_{46} - X_{47} = 0 \\
& X_{35} + X_{45} = 10 \\
& X_{36} + X_{46} = 10 \\
& X_{37} + X_{47} = 10 \\
& X_{ij} \ge 0 \text{ for all } i,j
\end{aligned}
$$

TRUE/FALSE

16. TRUE	17. TRUE	18. FALSE	19. TRUE	20. TRUE
21. FALSE	22. FALSE	23. FALSE	24. TRUE	25. TRUE
26. TRUE	27. FALSE	28. TRUE	29. FALSE	30. TRUE

CHAPTER 12

5) a) $X_1 = 2.8,\ X_2 = 3.4,\ Z = 48.8$
   b) $X_1 = 3,\ X_2 = 3$ -- infeasible
   c) $X_1 = 2,\ X_2 = 3$ -- feasible but not optimal
   d) Optimal $X_1 = 2,\ X_2 = 9,\ Z = 48 < 48.8$
   e) Additional integer constraints restrict the feasible region further; optimal solution values: ILP $\leq$ Mixed ILP $\leq$ LP.

6) a) $X_1 = 7/3,\ X_2 = 1/3,\ Z = 31/3$
   b) $X_1 = 2,\ X_2 = 0,\ Z = 6$
   c) L.P. -- optimal solution changes slightly; IP -- infeasible

7) a) $X_1 = 1,\ X_2 = 3,\ Z = 17$
   b) $X_1 = 1,\ X_2 = 3,\ Z = 14$

8)
$$
\begin{array}{llcccccccccccl}
\text{MAX} & Y_1 & + & 1.8Y_2 & + & 2Y_3 & + & 1.5Y_4 & + & 3.6Y_5 & + & 2.2Y_6 & & \\
\text{S.T.} & 20Y_1 & + & 55Y_2 & + & 47Y_3 & + & 38Y_4 & + & 90Y_5 & + & 63Y_6 & \leq & 175 \\
 & 15Y_1 & + & 45Y_2 & + & 50Y_3 & + & 40Y_4 & + & 70Y_5 & + & 70Y_6 & \leq & 150 \\
 & & & & & & & Y_4 & & & - & Y_6 & = & 0 \\
 & Y_1 & - & Y_2 & & & & & & & & & \geq & 0 \\
 & & & & & Y_3 & & & + & Y_5 & & & \leq & 1 \\
 & Y_1 & + & Y_2 & + & Y_3 & + & Y_4 & + & Y_5 & + & Y_6 & \leq & 3 \\
\end{array}
$$
$$Y_i = 0 \text{ or } 1$$

9)
$$
\begin{array}{llccccccclll}
\text{MAX} & 5.2X_1 & + & 3.6X_2 & + & 3.2X_3 & + & 2.8X_4 & & & \\
\text{S.T.} & .35X_1 & + & .50X_2 & + & .35X_3 & + & .50X_4 & \leq & 0.85 & \text{(FIRST YEAR)} \\
 & .55X_1 & + & .50X_2 & + & .40X_3 & & & \leq & 1.00 & \text{(SECOND YEAR)} \\
 & .75X_1 & & & + & .45X_3 & & & \leq & 1.20 & \text{(THIRD YEAR)} \\
 & X_1 & + & X_2 & + & X_3 & + & X_4 & = & 2 & \\
 & & - & X_2 & + & X_3 & & & \geq & 0 & \\
\end{array}
$$
$$X_i = 0 \text{ or } 1$$

10) a) 4/5 container of Grain A, 2 containers of Grain B, \$3960
    b) 2 containers of Grain A, 1 container of Grain B, \$3900
    c) (1) (0,2) feasible, not optimal; (2-3) (1,2) infeasible

11) a) $X_1 = 3,\ X_2 = 3.2,\ Z = 34.4$
    b) $X_1 = 2,\ X_2 = 4,\ Z = 36$

TRUE/FALSE

12. FALSE	13. TRUE	14. FALSE	15. FALSE	16. TRUE
17. FALSE	18. TRUE	19. TRUE	20. TRUE	21. FALSE
22. FALSE	23. TRUE	24. FALSE	25. FALSE	26. TRUE

CHAPTER 13

6) a)

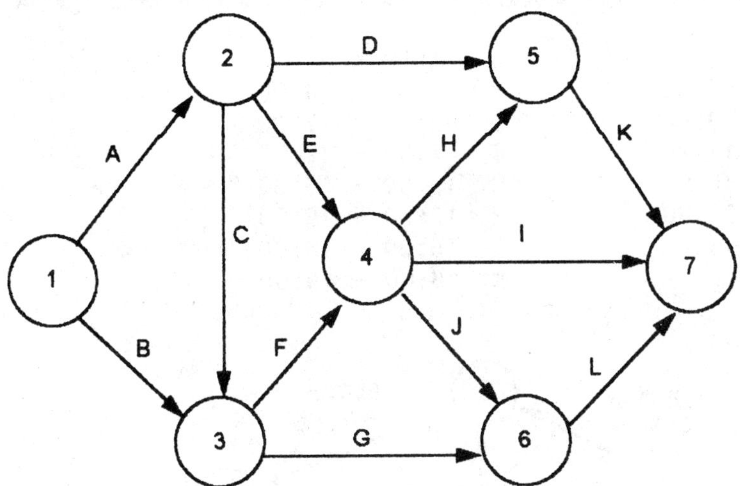

Expected Completion Time = 58; Critical Path = A - D - K

b) Yes
c) Yes
d) Slack on G = 7 hours; Slack on L = 4 hours
e) 4 hours; the slack times are not independent as G and L are on the same path.

7) a)

Activity	ES	EF	LS	LF	Slack
A	0:00	4:00	0:00	4:00	0
B	0:00	3:00	6:00	9:00	6
C	4:00	9:00	17:00	22:00	13
D	4:00	7:00	8:00	11:00	4
E	4:00	9:00	4:00	9:00	0
F	9:00	11:00	9:00	11:00	0
G	9:00	10:00	15:00	16:00	6
H	11:00	13:00	20:00	22:00	9
I	11:00	14:00	20:00	23:00	9
J	11:00	16:00	11:00	16:00	0
K	13:00	14:00	22:00	23:00	9
L	16:00	23:00	16:00	23:00	0

b) A - E - F - J - L; 23 hours

CHAPTER 13

7) c) There are many; here is one. Note that for Man 2, activity D must precede activity C (D's LS is 8:00 and C's EF is 9:00).

Intern 1			Intern 2	
A	0:00 - 4:00		B	0:00 - 3:00
E	4:00 - 9:00		D	4:00 - 7:00
F	9:00 - 11:00		C	7:00 - 12:00
J	11:00 - 16:00		G	12:00 - 13:00
L	16:00 - 23:00		H	13:00 - 15:00
			I	15:00 - 18:00
			K	18:00 - 19:00

8) a)

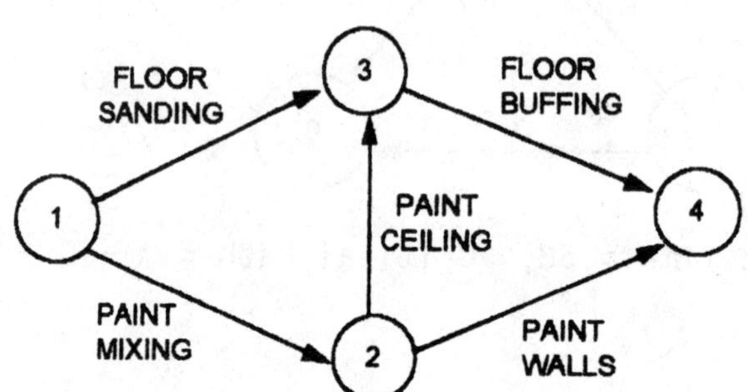

b) 8 hrs.
c) .8264

9) a)

Activity	ES	EF	LS	LF	Slack
A	0	6	1	7	1
B	0	8	0	8	0
C	6	7	7	8	1
D	6	9	9	12	3
E	8	11	9	12	1
F	8	12	9	13	1
G	8	18	8	18	0
H	8	13	10	15	2
I	11	14	12	15	1
J	12	13	14	15	2
K	12	17	13	18	1
L	14	17	15	18	1

b) Critical Path: B - G; Expected completion time = 18 weeks
c) Train its own employees

10) a) 16 weeks = August 21
b) About September 22 (20.66 weeks from May 1)
c) Do not accept the offer

CHAPTER 13

11) a) Expected Project Completion Time = 32; Standard deviation = 3.16
    b) Do not spend the money
    c) Activities off the critical path may vary enough so that a new critical path could be formed.

12) For this problem label the activities as follows:

A = Feasibility Study	F = Manufacturing Staff Hired
B = Building Purchased	G = Prototype Manufactured
C = Project Leader Hired	H = Production Run of 100
D = Advert. Staff Selected	I = Advertising Campaign
E = Materials Purchased	

a)

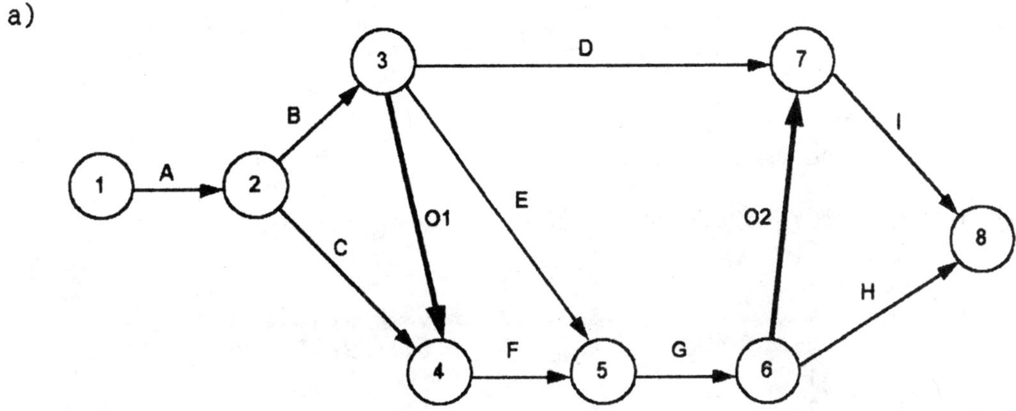

b) Define X_i = the time represented by node i
   Y_j = the amount of time activity j is crashed

MIN $20Y_A + 50Y_C + 50Y_D + 70Y_E + 60Y_F + 350Y_H + 75Y_I$ (in \$000)

S.T.

$X_8 \le 26$
$Y_A \le 1$
$Y_C \le 1$
$Y_D \le 3$
$Y_E \le 1$
$Y_F \le 3$
$Y_H \le 1$
$Y_I \le 4$

AND

$X_8 \ge X_7 + (8 - Y_I)$
$X_8 \ge X_6 + (6 - Y_H)$
$X_7 \ge X_6$
$X_7 \ge X_3 + (6 - Y_D)$
$X_6 \ge X_5 + 2$
$X_5 \ge X_3 + (3 - Y_E)$
$X_5 \ge X_4 + (10 - Y_F)$
$X_4 \ge X_3$
$X_4 \ge X_2 + (3 - Y_C)$
$X_3 \ge X_2 + 4$
$X_2 \ge X_1 + (6 - Y_A)$

$X_i, Y_j \ge 0$ for all i,j

12) c) The time reduction for each activity is proportional to the the crashing money that would be spent on that activity.
    d) Per-week reduction cost is shadow price for $X_8 \le 26$.

CHAPTER 13

13) The PERT network for this problem is:

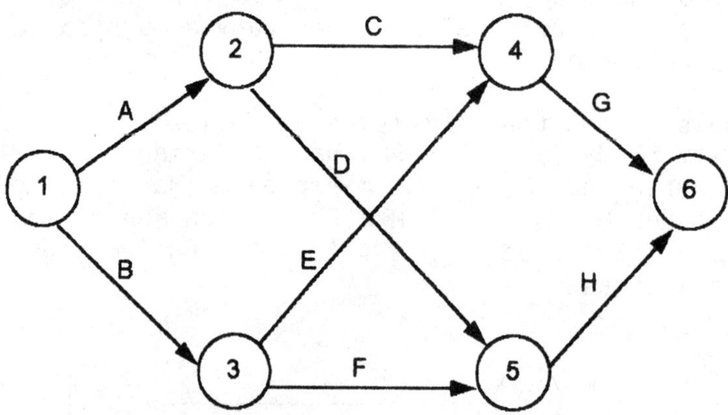

a) Define X_i = time represented by node i
Y_j = the amount of time activity j is crashed

MIN $1250Y_A+2000Y_C+500Y_D+500Y_E+2000Y_F+5000Y_G+6000Y_H$

S.T.

$X_6 \leq 16$		$X_6 \geq X_5 + (7 - Y_H)$
$Y_A \leq 4$		$X_6 \geq X_4 + (5 - Y_G)$
$Y_C \leq 4$		$X_5 \geq X_3 + (3 - Y_F)$
$Y_D \leq 2$	AND	$X_5 \geq X_2 + (4 - Y_D)$
$Y_E \leq 1$		$X_4 \geq X_3 + (2 - Y_E)$
$Y_F \leq 2$		$X_4 \geq X_2 + (10 - Y_C)$
$Y_G \leq 1$		$X_3 \geq X_1 + 3$
$Y_H \leq 2$		$X_2 \geq X_1 + (6 - Y_A)$

$X_i, Y_j \geq 0$ for all i and j

b) Same formulation as (a) except that the objective function is now: MIN X_6, and the first constraint is now:
$1250Y_A+2000Y_C+500Y_D+500Y_E+2000Y_F+5000Y_G+6000Y_H \leq 15,500$

14) a) No
b) Cost Overrun
c) Hopefully E could be sped up and costs reduced. Management should be told that a cost overrun is likely. The larger the cost overrun, the more likely the target date will be met.

TRUE/FALSE

15. TRUE 16. TRUE 17. FALSE 18. FALSE 19. TRUE
20. TRUE 21. FALSE 22. FALSE 23. FALSE 24. TRUE
25. TRUE 26. TRUE 27. FALSE 28. FALSE 29. TRUE

CHAPTER 14

9) a) 75
   b) Q* = 273.861, order 274
   c) $164.32
   d) Order every 4 months based on forecasted demand

10) a) 1) Buy from Harrison: Q* = 800; Total Annual Variable Cost = $1200; Total Annual Cost = $76,200.
       2) Manufacture themselves: Q* = 5345;Total Annual Variable Cost = $5,986.65; Total Annual Cost = $75,986.65.
    b) Harrison should manufacture displays; total cost is cheaper.

11) a) Q* = 109,544.5 or 109,545
    b) 9.13
    c) 13.33
    d) 115 days = 365 - (9.13)(13.33 + 14)

12) Order 2000 every week

13) a) (1) Q* = 16
       (2) 20 or when inventory reaches 4 and one order is pending
       (3) $47,840
    b) No; Yearly net profit under this policy is only $45,774

14) Q^* = 233, Total annual cost = $64,695.54

15) a) Order 648 every 3.08 weeks when supply reaches 42
    b) 12 spark plugs
    c) $6.60

16) 196

17) Z = 1.43 ===> Pr(Stockout) = .0764

18) Yes; Annual manufacture = $38,600; annual purchase = $40,800

19) a) Annual profit for machine I = $40,000 (operating at full capacity with no inventory); profit for mach. II = $41,520.
    b) For machine II, Q* = 92,582. Thus the firm has 3.24 cycles per year each lasting approximately 112.6 days. As the production time of the 92,582 pounds of luncheon meat is 33.8 days, some of the meat sold will be as old as 78 days. If Jim went to machine II, he would need more production runs per year thus incurring more setups and reducing his profit below the $40,000 he could earn from using machine I.

CHAPTER 14

20) a) Order 32 when inventory reaches 7
    b) Total annual variable cost = $1,301

21) a) .0951
    b) 299

22) a) 71,600 loaves
    b) 61,280 loaves

23) a) 46 pumpkins
    b) .525

24) Order 1000 tubes of lipstick each time

25) Choose Option III

26) a) order 100 units when the supply on hand reaches 172 units
    b) Total Annual Variable Cost = $24,024
    c) Initially order 272 units

27) Order 555 bags; safety stock = 105 bags

TRUE/FALSE

28. TRUE	29. FALSE	30. FALSE	31. FALSE	32. TRUE
33. FALSE	34. TRUE	35. TRUE	36. FALSE	37. FALSE
38. TRUE	39. FALSE	40. FALSE	41. TRUE	42. TRUE

CHAPTER 15

5)

ITEM:: ENGINE ASSEMBLY LEAD TIME: 1		WEEK						
LOT SIZE: L-F-L SAFETY STOCK: 0		6	7	8	9	10	11	12
GROSS REQUIREMENTS								1300
SCHEDULED RECEIPTS								
PROJECTED BALANCE							200	
NET REQUIREMENTS								1100
PLANNED ORDER RECEIPTS								1100
PLANNED ORDER RELEASES							1100	

ITEM:: MOTORS LEAD TIME: 1		WEEK						
LOT SIZE: L-F-L SAFETY STOCK: 500		6	7	8	9	10	11	12
GROSS REQUIREMENTS							1100	
SCHEDULED RECEIPTS								
PROJECTED BALANCE						500	500	
NET REQUIREMENTS							1100	
PLANNED ORDER RECEIPTS							1100	
PLANNED ORDER RELEASES						1100		

ITEM:: CARBURETOR LEAD TIME: 2		WEEK						
LOT SIZE: L-F-L SAFETY STOCK: 0		6	7	8	9	10	11	12
GROSS REQUIREMENTS							2200	
SCHEDULED RECEIPTS								
PROJECTED BALANCE						0		
NET REQUIREMENTS							2200	
PLANNED ORDER RECEIPTS							2200	
PLANNED ORDER RELEASES					2200			

CHAPTER 15

6)

Item	(a) Unit	(b) Week
Barbecue Grills	6000	15
Brolier	6000	14
Rack	12000	12
Electrical	6000	13
Element	24000	11
Plug	6000	12
Shell	6000	12
Lava Briquets	6000	14
Rotisserie	6000	14
Hardware	6000	12
Motor	6000	13

7)

ITEM:: LAVA BRIQUETS LEAD TIME: 1		WEEK					
LOT SIZE: 10000 SAFETY STOCK: 0		15	16	17	18	19	20
GROSS REQUIREMENTS		6000	9000	0	8000	6000	5000
SCHEDULED RECEIPTS		7000					
PROJECTED BALANCE	3000	4000	5000	5000	7000	0	6000
NET REQUIREMENTS		0	5000	0	3000	0	4000
PLANNED ORDER RECEIPTS			10000		10000		10000
PLANNED ORDER RELEASES		10000		10000		10000	

8) a)

ITEM:: ROTISSERIE LEAD TIME: 1		WEEK					
LOT SIZE: L-F-L SAFETY STOCK: 2000		15	16	17	18	19	20
GROSS REQUIREMENTS		6000	9000	0	8000	6000	5000
SCHEDULED RECEIPTS		7000					
PROJECTED BALANCE	2000	3000	2000	2000	2000	2000	2000
NET REQUIREMENTS		0	7000	0	8000	6000	5000
PLANNED ORDER RECEIPTS			7000		8000	6000	5000
PLANNED ORDER RELEASES		7000		8000	6000	5000	

CHAPTER 15

8) b)

ITEM:: ROTISSERIE	LEAD TIME: 1	WEEK					
LOT SIZE: L-F-L	SAFETY STOCK: 0	15	16	17	18	19	20
GROSS REQUIREMENTS		6000	9000	0	8000	6000	5000
SCHEDULED RECEIPTS		7000					
PROJECTED BALANCE	2000	3000	0	0	0	0	0
NET REQUIREMENTS		0	6000	0	8000	6000	5000
PLANNED ORDER RECEIPTS			6000		8000	6000	5000
PLANNED ORDER RELEASES		6000		8000	6000	5000	

9)

ITEM:: BROILER	LEAD TIME: 1	WEEK				
LOT SIZE: L-F-L	SAFETY STOCK: 0	11	12	13	14	15
GROSS REQUIREMENTS						6000
SCHEDULED RECEIPTS						
PROJECTED BALANCE					0	
NET REQUIREMENTS						6000
PLANNED ORDER RECEIPTS						6000
PLANNED ORDER RELEASES					6000	

ITEM:: ELECTRICAL UNIT	LEAD TIME: 1	WEEK				
LOT SIZE: L-F-L	SAFETY STOCK: 0	11	12	13	14	15
GROSS REQUIREMENTS					6000	
SCHEDULED RECEIPTS						
PROJECTED BALANCE				0		
NET REQUIREMENTS					6000	
PLANNED ORDER RECEIPTS					6000	
PLANNED ORDER RELEASES				6000		

CHAPTER 15

9)(con't)

ITEM:: ELEMENT LEAD TIME: 2	WEEK				
LOT SIZE: L-F-L SAFETY STOCK: 0	11	12	13	14	15
GROSS REQUIREMENTS			24000		
SCHEDULED RECEIPTS			16000		
PROJECTED BALANCE		0			
NET REQUIREMENTS			8000		
PLANNED ORDER RECEIPTS			8000		
PLANNED ORDER RELEASES	8000				

ITEM:: PLUG LEAD TIME: 1	WEEK				
LOT SIZE: L-F-L SAFETY STOCK: 0	11	12	13	14	15
GROSS REQUIREMENTS			6000		
SCHEDULED RECEIPTS		4000			
PROJECTED BALANCE		4000			
NET REQUIREMENTS			2000		
PLANNED ORDER RECEIPTS			2000		
PLANNED ORDER RELEASES		2000			

10) a)

ITEM:: HARDWARE LEAD TIME: 2	WEEK					
LOT SIZE: L-F-L SAFETY STOCK: 2000	15	16	17	18	19	20
GROSS REQUIREMENTS					6000	
SCHEDULED RECEIPTS						
PROJECTED BALANCE				0	2000	
NET REQUIREMENTS					8000	
PLANNED ORDER RECEIPTS					8000	
PLANNED ORDER RELEASES			8000			

CHAPTER 15

10) b)

ITEM:: MOTOR LEAD TIME: 1		WEEK					
LOT SIZE: L-F-L SAFETY STOCK: 1500		15	16	17	18	19	20
GROSS REQUIREMENTS						6000	
SCHEDULED RECEIPTS							
PROJECTED BALANCE					0	1500	
NET REQUIREMENTS						7500	
PLANNED ORDER RECEIPTS						7500	
PLANNED ORDER RELEASES					7500		

10) c)

ITEM:: HARDWARE LEAD TIME: 2		WEEK					
LOT SIZE: L-F-L SAFETY STOCK: 2000		15	16	17	18	19	20
GROSS REQUIREMENTS						6000	
SCHEDULED RECEIPTS						4000	
PROJECTED BALANCE					0	2000	
NET REQUIREMENTS						4000	
PLANNED ORDER RECEIPTS						4000	
PLANNED ORDER RELEASES				4000			

11)

Item	(a) Units	(b) Week
Food Processor	1500	14
Motor Assembly	1500	13
Motor	1500	10
Gear Unit	1500	12
Shaft	1500	11
Base Assembly	1500	12
Mixing Basket	1500	13
Cutters	9000	13
Screws	36000	11
Blades	18000	9

CHAPTER 15

12) a)

ITEM:: MIXING BASKET LEAD TIME: 1		WEEK					
LOT SIZE: 2500 SAFETY STOCK: 0		12	13	14	15	16	17
GROSS REQUIREMENTS		1600	1200	1500	1400	1800	2000
SCHEDULED RECEIPTS		2500					
PROJECTED BALANCE		900	2200	700	1800	0	500
NET REQUIREMENTS		0	300	0	700	0	2000
PLANNED ORDER RECEIPTS			2500		2500		2500
PLANNED ORDER RELEASES		2500		2500		2500	

12) b)

ITEM:: MIXING BASKET LEAD TIME: 1		WEEK					
LOT SIZE: 2500 SAFETY STOCK: 0		12	13	14	15	16	17
GROSS REQUIREMENTS		1600	1200	1500	1400	1800	2000
SCHEDULED RECEIPTS		2500					
PROJECTED BALANCE	600	1500	300	1300	2400	600	1100
NET REQUIREMENTS		0	0	1200	100	0	1400
PLANNED ORDER RECEIPTS				2500	2500		2500
PLANNED ORDER RELEASES			2500	2500		2500	

13) a)

ITEM:: BASE ASSEMBLY LEAD TIME: 2		WEEK						
LOT SIZE: 2000 SAFETY STOCK: 0		11	12	13	14	15	16	17
GROSS REQUIREMENTS			1600	1200	1500	1400	1800	2000
SCHEDULED RECEIPTS			2000					
PROJECTED BALANCE		800	1200	0	500	1100	1300	1300
NET REQUIREMENTS			0	0	1500	900	700	700
PLANNED ORDER RECEIPTS					2000	2000	2000	2000
PLANNED ORDER RELEASES			2000	2000	2000	2000		

CHAPTER 15

13) b)

ITEM:: BASE ASSEMBLY LEAD TIME: 2	WEEK						
LOT SIZE: 2000 SAFETY STOCK: 500	11	12	13	14	15	16	17
GROSS REQUIREMENTS		1600	1200	1500	1400	1800	2000
SCHEDULED RECEIPTS		2000					
PROJECTED BALANCE	800	1200	0	500	1100	1300	1300
NET REQUIREMENTS		0	500	0	1400	1200	1200
PLANNED ORDER RECEIPTS			2000		2000	2000	2000
PLANNED ORDER RELEASES	2000		2000	2000	2000		

14)

ITEM:: CUTTER LEAD TIME: 1	WEEK					
LOT SIZE: L-F-L SAFETY STOCK: 0	7	8	9	10	11	12
GROSS REQUIREMENTS						9600
SCHEDULED RECEIPTS						
PROJECTED BALANCE				0		
NET REQUIREMENTS						9600
PLANNED ORDER RECEIPTS						9600
PLANNED ORDER RELEASES					9600	

ITEM:: SCREW LEAD TIME: 2	WEEK					
LOT SIZE: L-F-L SAFETY STOCK: 0	7	8	9	10	11	12
GROSS REQUIREMENTS					38400	
SCHEDULED RECEIPTS						
PROJECTED BALANCE				0		
NET REQUIREMENTS					38400	
PLANNED ORDER RECEIPTS					38400	
PLANNED ORDER RELEASES			38400			

CHAPTER 15

14)(con't)

ITEM:: BLADE LEAD TIME: 4 / LOT SIZE: L-F-L SAFETY STOCK: 0		WEEK 7	8	9	10	11	12
GROSS REQUIREMENTS						19200	
SCHEDULED RECEIPTS							
PROJECTED BALANCE					4000		
NET REQUIREMENTS						15200	
PLANNED ORDER RECEIPTS						15200	
PLANNED ORDER RELEASES		15200					

TRUE/FALSE

15. TRUE 16. TRUE 17. TRUE 18. FALSE 19. TRUE
20. FALSE 21. FALSE 22. TRUE 23. TRUE 24. FALSE
25. FALSE 26. TRUE 27. FALSE 28. FALSE 29. TRUE

CHAPTER 16

10) a) $P(X = 0) = .1353$
    b) $P(T < 45 \text{ min.}) = .6321$
    c) $W_q = 2\ 1/4$ hours
    d) $P_3 = 27/256 = .105$

11) a) Yes; Total Cost = $70/day for computer vs. $90/day without computer
    b) Better off with computer; Total Cost for second employee is $86.18/day

12) 30 percent

13) a) $\lambda = 40$ per hour
    b) $L_q = 4/3$
    c) $L = 2$
    d) $1 - P_0 = \lambda/\mu = 2/3$
    e) $\mu = 97.2$ per hour

14) Purchase digital router; total cost = $204/day ($255/day without router)

15) a) $L_q = 1.04$ at each desk; Consolidated $L_q = .80$
    b) $P_0 = (3/8)(3/8) = .14$; Consolidated $P_0 = .23$
    c) $W = 1/3$ hour = 20 minutes; Consolidated W = 12.31 minutes
    d) P(both busy) = $(1-P_0)(1-P_0) = (5/8)(5/8) = .39$; Consolidated $P_W = .48$
    e) Yes if it will not result in a substantial loss in business. (average wait time (part c) decreases by 38% when two servers are consolidated.

16) No system: $49.20; System A: $50.00; System B: $47.20. Hence, install B.

17) a) George: W = 20 minutes; John: W = 3 1/3 minutes
    b) Total Cost: George -- $46.00; John -- $18.67. Hire John.

18) a) W = 6.22 minutes so total time in the store is 61.22 min.
    b) Yes; W = 6.01 minutes

19) a) .667
    b) .076 hrs = 4.56 mins.
    c) 1.43 vehicles
    d) .9772

20) a) no, 49.18%
    b) 18.03%

21) a) k = 4; $P_W = .021$
    b) $P_0 = .331$

22) a) $L_q = .15$
    b) $W = .028$ hr. = 1.7 minutes
    c) $P_W = .417$

23) a) $L_q = .7094$
    b) $W_q = 4.96$ days
    c) $1 - P_0 = .7151$

TRUE/FALSE

24. TRUE	25. FALSE	26. FALSE	27. FALSE	28. TRUE
29. TRUE	30. FALSE	31. FALSE	32. FALSE	33. FALSE
34. TRUE	35. TRUE	36. FALSE	37. FALSE	38. TRUE

CHAPTER 17

FOR ALL PROBLEMS IN CHAPTER 17, IT IS ASSUMED THAT THE FIRST RANDOM NUMBER IS 00. THE COLUMN HEADINGS FOR THE EACH SIMULATION ARE GIVEN TOGETHER WITH THE FIRST ROW IN THE SIMULATION. THEN THE ANSWER BASED ON THE SIMULATION IS GIVEN.

7)

Routes 5 - 57				Routes 55 - 91			
RN	Time On 5	RN	Time On 57	RN	Time On 55	RN	Time On 91
63	7	59	6	71	8	51	4
	etc.				etc.		

Freeways 5-57 have 62 mins.; Freeways 55-91 have 61 mins.; Select 55-91.

8)

Period	RN	Number of Arrivals	Service Free?	Number Waiting	RN	Service Time	Period When Service Completed
1	63	1	Yes	0	59	1	2
			etc.				

The average number of customers waiting in line for service is the average of the entries in the Number Waiting column. This average is 1.

9) a) Three critical paths with 17 weeks: B-C-F-G-H; B-D-G-H; A-F-G-H.
b) Five complete PERT analyses must be done. The first is as follows:

Job	RN	Change	Completion Time
A	14	-1	6
B	41	0	4
C	35	0	3
D	38	0	6
E	91	+1	6
F	78	+1	4
G	90	+1	4
H	18	-1	3

Critical path is B-C-F-G-H completion time = 18. Repeating 4 more times:

CHAPTER 17

9) Con't.

Trial	Critical Path	Completion Time
2	B-D-G-H	17
3	B-C-F-G-H	17
4	A-F-G-H or B-C-F-G-H	17
5	A-E-H	17

The average completion time of the five trials is 17.2 weeks.

10) a) Order 8 when inventory level reaches 2 units

b)

Day	Beg. Invent.	RN	Demand	End. Invent.	Order?	RN	Deliv. Time	Inv. Cost
1	6	59	2	4	No	--	--	$8

The average inventory cost per day is $13.00

11) a)

Week	Beg. Inv.	RN	Demand	End. Inv.	Avg. Inv.	Hold. Cost	Reord. Cost	RN	Lead Time	Stkout. Cost
1	5	51	3	2	3.5	$7	$40	80	2	--

The total cost for 8 weeks = $168.00

b)

Week	Beg. Inv.	RN	Demand	End. Inv.	Avg. Inv.	Hold. Cost	Service Charge	Stockout Cost
1	5	51	3	2	3.5	$7	$12	--

The total cost for 8 weeks = $194.00; Since this is more than $168.00, the company should keep its current policy.

12) a)

Per.	RN	# of Cust.	Cust.	RN	Here/ ToGo?	RN	Serv. Time	Compl. in Per.	# Cust. Pres.	Profit
1	63	0	--	--	--	--	--	--	0	--
2	88	1	1	59	ToGo	71	4	6	1	$.90

b) $3.04 c) 64% d) .84

13)

Day	RN	# of Cust.	Cust. Number	RN	Type Purch.	In Stock?	RN	Switch?	Remain. Invent. A L T
1	58	2	1	93	T	Yes	--	--	3 2 3
			2	63	L	Yes	--	--	3 1 3

Archie will sell out in 8 days in this simulation.

CHAPTER 17

14) a)

Day	RN	Number Rented	Car Rented	RN	Day Returned	Cost of Unused Cars	Shortage Cost
1	63	3	1	59	3		
			2	09	2		
			3	57	3	$5	--

The 10-day profit of this simulation is $885.

b)

Day	RN	Number Rented	Car Rented	RN	Day Returned	Cost of Unused Cars	Shortage Cost
1	63	3	1	59	3		
			2	09	2		
			3	57	3	$10	--

The 10-day profit of this simulation is $970.
Take the extra car.

15)

Per.	RN	# of Arr.	Serv. Area Free?	RN	Type Purch.	Serv. Time	# of Lost Cust.	# of Cust. Wait.	Serv. Compl. This Per.?	Prof.
1	63	1	Yes	59	Cone	30	0	0	Yes	$.12

a) Sum last column = $3.34
b) Divide total # lost customers by total # arrivals = 7/35 = 20%.
c) Divide the total # of cust. waiting by 30 periods = 65/30 = 2.17.

16) a)

A Last		B Last		C Last	
A	00 - 49	A	00 - 29	A	00 - 09
Next B	50 - 79	Next B	30 - 74	Next B	10 - 44
C	80 - 99	C	75 - 99	C	45 - 99

b)

Flight	RN	Next Airline
1	71	C
2	95	C

20% of flights on Airline A
48% of flights on Airline B
32% of flights on Airline C

TRUE/FALSE

17. FALSE 18. TRUE 19. FALSE 20. FALSE 21. TRUE
22. TRUE 23. TRUE 24. FALSE 25. FALSE 26. TRUE
27. FALSE 28. FALSE 29. TRUE 30. FALSE 31. FALSE

CHAPTER 18

8) a) Linear Programming constraints:

$$\begin{aligned} 3X_1 + X_2 &\leq 24 \text{ (total marketing employees)} \\ X_1 + X_2 &\geq 6 \text{ (minimum required ads)} \\ 50X_1 + 15X_2 &\leq 250 \text{ (Goal 1: Budget in \$1000's)} \\ 3X_1 + X_2 &\leq 12 \text{ (Goal 2: 50\% of marketing employees)} \\ X_1 &\geq 4 \text{ (Goal 3: TV ads)} \\ X_2 &\geq 4 \text{ (Goal 4: Radio ads)} \\ X_1, X_2 &\geq 0 \end{aligned}$$

There are no feasible points.

b) $\text{MIN } P_1(d_1^+) + P_2(d_2^+) + P_3(d_3^-) + P_4(d_4^-)$

$$\begin{aligned} \text{S.T. } 3X_1 + X_2 &\leq 24 \\ X_1 + X_2 &\geq 6 \\ 50X_1 + 15X_2 + d_1^- - d_1^+ &= 250 \\ 3X_1 + X_2 + d_2^- - d_2^+ &= 12 \\ X_1 + d_3^- - d_3^+ &= 4 \\ X_2 + d_4^- - d_4^+ &= 4 \\ X_1, X_2, d_j^-, d_j^+ &\geq 0 \text{ for all } j \end{aligned}$$

Optimal G.P. solution: 3 TV ads, 3 radio ads.
Priorities: $P_1(d_1^+) = 0$, $P_2(d_2^+) = 0$, $P_3(d_3^-) = 1$, $P_4(d_4^-) = 1$

c) The new objective function is:
$\text{MIN } P_1(d_1^+) + P_2(d_2^+) + P_3(2d_3^-) + P_3(d_4^-)$

Optimal G.P. solution: Produce 2.67 TV ads, 4 radio ads. Goal 3 is missed by 1.33 TV ads while the other goals are achieved.

9) $\text{MIN } P_1(d_1^-) + P_2(d_2^+) + P_3(d_3^-) + P_3(3d_4^-) + P_3(d_5^-)$

$$\begin{aligned} \text{S.T. } 3X_1 + 2.5X_2 + 2X_3 &\leq 200 \text{ (donation)} \\ X_1 &\geq 20 \text{ (athletic sch.)} \\ X_1 + X_2 + X_3 + d_1^- - d_1^+ &= 80 \text{ (P1, Goal 1: Total sch.)} \\ .75X_1 - .25X_2 - .25X_3 + d_2^- - d_2^+ &= 0 \text{ (P2, Goal 2: 25\% ath. sch.)} \\ X_1 + d_3^- - d_3^+ &= 25 \text{ (P3, Goal 3: desired ath. sch.)} \\ X_2 + d_4^- - d_4^+ &= 40 \text{ (P3, Goal 4: desired min. sch.)} \\ X_3 + d_5^- - d_5^+ &= 20 \text{ (P3, Goal 5: desired women sch.)} \\ X_j, d_j^-, d_j^+ &\geq 0 \text{ for all } j \end{aligned}$$

CHAPTER 18

9)(con't.)

Optimal: Award 20 athletic, 40 minority, and 20 women's scholarships. Goals 1, 2, and 4 are met. Goal 3 is underachieved by 5 athletic scholarships and Goal 5 is underachieved by 10 women's scholarships.

10) X_1 = # new non-minority hires
X_2 = # new minority hires
X_3 = # non-minority management promotions
X_4 = # minority management promotions

$$\begin{array}{lllr} \text{MIN} & 3d_1^- + d_2^- + d_3^+ + d_4^+ & & \\ \text{S.T.} & X_1 + X_2 & = & 17{,}520 \\ & X_3 + X_4 & = & 598 \\ & X_1 - d_1^+ + d_1^- & = & 19{,}680 \\ & X_3 - d_2^+ + d_2^- & = & 472 \\ & X_1 - d_3^+ + d_3^- & = & 11{,}680 \\ & X_3 - d_4^+ + d_4^- & = & 399 \\ & X_j,\ d_j^+,\ d_j^- \geq 0 \quad j = 1,2,3,4 & & \end{array}$$

11) Miss Northern State 18; Miss Central State 24; Miss Southern State 58.

12) a) Location: BG - .360; B - .512; H - .128
Price: BG - .589; B - .252; H - .159
Cleanliness: BG - .123; B - .320; H - .557
Parking: BG - .102; B - .612; H - .286
Selection: BG - .100; B - .713; H - .187

b) GD - .255; B - .482; H - .264

c)

	LOC	PRI	CLE	PAR	SEL
LOC	1	1/7	1/7	1	1/3
PRI	7	1	3	7	3
CLE	7	1/3	1	5	3
PAR	1	1/7	1/5	1	1/7
SEL	3	1/3	1/3	7	1

d) CR = .073 -- good consistency

e) GD - .340; B - .380; H - .280

CHAPTER 18

13) a) Goal: Choose the right candidate Criteria: Party, Issue
Alternatives: Carter, Nixon, Anderson

b)

Party

	C	N	A
C	1	1/7	1/3
N	7	1	5
A	3	1/5	1

Issues

	C	N	A
C	1	6	5
N	1/6	1	1/3
A	1/5	3	1

c) Party: C - .083; N - .723; A - .193
Issues: C - .707; N - .092; A - .201

d) .082 -- good consistency;

e) Party - .2; Issues - .8

f) C - .582; N - .218; A - .199

14) a) Goal: Choose the best database program
Criteria: Price; Ease of Use
Alternatives: BASE 8; DATA RECORD

b)

Price

	B8	DR
B8	1	8
DR	1/8	1

Ease Of Use

	B8	DR
B8	1	1/6
DR	6	1

c) Price: B8 - 8/9; DR - 1/9 Ease of Use: B8 - 1/7; DR - 6/7

d) (1) B8 - .81; DR - .19
(2) B8 - .22; DR - .78
(3) B8 - .516; DR - .484

e) Ease of use is slightly preferred to price.

TRUE/FALSE

16. FALSE	17. FALSE	18. TRUE	19. FALSE	20. TRUE
21. FALSE	22. FALSE	23. TRUE	24. FALSE	25. FALSE
26. TRUE	27. FALSE	28. FALSE	29. FALSE	30. FALSE

Appendices

APPENDIX A: Binomial Probabilities

Entries in the table give the probability of x successes in n trials of a binomial experiment, where p is the probability of a success on one trial. For example, with $n = 6$ trials and $p = 0.40$, the probability of $x = 2$ successes is 0.3110.

		p									
n	*x*	0.05	0.10	0.15	0.20	0.25	0.30	0.35	0.40	0.45	0.50
1	0	0.9500	0.9000	0.8500	0.8000	0.7500	0.7000	0.6500	0.6000	0.5500	0.5000
	1	0.0500	0.1000	0.1500	0.2000	0.2500	0.3000	0.3500	0.4000	0.4500	0.5000
2	0	0.9025	0.8100	0.7225	0.6400	0.5625	0.4900	0.4225	0.3600	0.3025	0.2500
	1	0.0950	0.1800	0.2550	0.3200	0.3750	0.4200	0.4550	0.4800	0.4950	0.5000
	2	0.0025	0.0100	0.0225	0.0400	0.0625	0.0900	0.1225	0.1600	0.2025	0.2500
3	0	0.8574	0.7290	0.6141	0.5120	0.4219	0.3430	0.2746	0.2160	0.1664	0.1250
	1	0.1354	0.2430	0.3251	0.3840	0.4219	0.4410	0.4436	0.4320	0.4084	0.3750
	2	0.0071	0.0270	0.0574	0.0960	0.1406	0.1890	0.2389	0.2880	0.3341	0.3750
	3	0.0001	0.0010	0.0034	0.0080	0.0156	0.0270	0.0429	0.0640	0.0911	0.1250
4	0	0.8145	0.6561	0.5220	0.4096	0.3164	0.2401	0.1785	0.1296	0.0915	0.0625
	1	0.1715	0.2916	0.3685	0.4096	0.4219	0.4116	0.3845	0.3456	0.2995	0.2500
	2	0.0135	0.0486	0.0975	0.1536	0.2109	0.2646	0.3105	0.3456	0.3675	0.3750
	3	0.0005	0.0036	0.0115	0.0256	0.0469	0.0756	0.1115	0.1536	0.2005	0.2500
	4	0.0000	0.0001	0.0005	0.0016	0.0039	0.0081	0.0150	0.0256	0.0410	0.0625
5	0	0.7738	0.5905	0.4437	0.3277	0.2373	0.1681	0.1160	0.0778	0.0503	0.0312
	1	0.2036	0.3280	0.3915	0.4096	0.3955	0.3602	0.3124	0.2592	0.2059	0.1562
	2	0.0214	0.0729	0.1382	0.2048	0.2637	0.3087	0.3364	0.3456	0.3369	0.3125
	3	0.0011	0.0081	0.0244	0.0512	0.0879	0.1323	0.1811	0.2304	0.2757	0.3125
	4	0.0000	0.0004	0.0022	0.0064	0.0146	0.0284	0.0488	0.0768	0.1128	0.1562
	5	0.0000	0.0000	0.0001	0.0003	0.0010	0.0024	0.0053	0.0102	0.0185	0.0312
6	0	0.7351	0.5314	0.3771	0.2621	0.1780	0.1176	0.0754	0.0467	0.0277	0.0156
	1	0.2321	0.3543	0.3993	0.3932	0.3560	0.3025	0.2437	0.1866	0.1359	0.0938
	2	0.0305	0.0984	0.1762	0.2458	0.2966	0.3241	0.3280	0.3110	0.2780	0.2344
	3	0.0021	0.0146	0.0415	0.0819	0.1318	0.1852	0.2355	0.2765	0.3032	0.3125
	4	0.0001	0.0012	0.0055	0.0154	0.0330	0.0595	0.0951	0.1382	0.1861	0.2344
	5	0.0000	0.0001	0.0004	0.0015	0.0044	0.0102	0.0205	0.0369	0.0609	0.0938
	6	0.0000	0.0000	0.0000	0.0001	0.0002	0.0007	0.0018	0.0041	0.0083	0.0156

Binomial Probabilities (*Continued*)

		p									
n	*x*	0.05	0.10	0.15	0.20	0.25	0.30	0.35	0.40	0.45	0.50
7	0	0.6983	0.4783	0.3206	0.2097	0.1335	0.0824	0.0490	0.0280	0.0152	0.0078
	1	0.2573	0.3720	0.3960	0.3670	0.3115	0.2471	0.1848	0.1306	0.0872	0.0547
	2	0.0406	0.1240	0.2097	0.2753	0.3115	0.3177	0.2985	0.2613	0.2140	0.1641
	3	0.0036	0.0230	0.0617	0.1147	0.1730	0.2269	0.2679	0.2903	0.2918	0.2734
	4	0.0002	0.0026	0.0109	0.0287	0.0577	0.0972	0.1442	0.1935	0.2388	0.2734
	5	0.0000	0.0002	0.0012	0.0043	0.0115	0.0250	0.0466	0.0774	0.1172	0.1641
	6	0.0000	0.0000	0.0001	0.0004	0.0013	0.0036	0.0084	0.0172	0.0320	0.0547
	7	0.0000	0.0000	0.0000	0.0000	0.0001	0.0002	0.0006	0.0016	0.0037	0.0078
8	0	0.6634	0.4305	0.2725	0.1678	0.1001	0.0576	0.0319	0.0168	0.0084	0.0039
	1	0.2793	0.3826	0.3847	0.3355	0.2670	0.1977	0.1373	0.0896	0.0548	0.0312
	2	0.0515	0.1488	0.2376	0.2936	0.3115	0.2965	0.2587	0.2090	0.1569	0.1094
	3	0.0054	0.0331	0.0839	0.1468	0.2076	0.2541	0.2786	0.2787	0.2568	0.2188
	4	0.0004	0.0046	0.0185	0.0459	0.0865	0.1361	0.1875	0.2322	0.2627	0.2734
	5	0.0000	0.0004	0.0026	0.0092	0.0231	0.0467	0.0808	0.1239	0.1719	0.2188
	6	0.0000	0.0000	0.0002	0.0011	0.0038	0.0100	0.0217	0.0413	0.0703	0.1094
	7	0.0000	0.0000	0.0000	0.0001	0.0004	0.0012	0.0033	0.0079	0.0164	0.0312
	8	0.0000	0.0000	0.0000	0.0000	0.0000	0.0001	0.0002	0.0007	0.0017	0.0039
9	0	0.6302	0.3874	0.2316	0.1342	0.0751	0.0404	0.0207	0.0101	0.0046	0.0020
	1	0.2985	0.3874	0.3679	0.3020	0.2253	0.1556	0.1004	0.0605	0.0339	0.0176
	2	0.0629	0.1722	0.2597	0.3020	0.3003	0.2668	0.2162	0.1612	0.1110	0.0703
	3	0.0077	0.0446	0.1069	0.1762	0.2336	0.2668	0.2716	0.2508	0.2119	0.1641
	4	0.0006	0.0074	0.0283	0.0661	0.1168	0.1715	0.2194	0.2508	0.2600	0.2461
	5	0.0000	0.0008	0.0050	0.0165	0.0389	0.0735	0.1181	0.1672	0.2128	0.2461
	6	0.0000	0.0001	0.0006	0.0028	0.0087	0.0210	0.0424	0.0743	0.1160	0.1641
	7	0.0000	0.0000	0.0000	0.0003	0.0012	0.0039	0.0098	0.0212	0.0407	0.0703
	8	0.0000	0.0000	0.0000	0.0000	0.0001	0.0004	0.0013	0.0035	0.0083	0.0176
	9	0.0000	0.0000	0.0000	0.0000	0.0000	0.0000	0.0001	0.0003	0.0008	0.0020
10	0	0.5987	0.3487	0.1969	0.1074	0.0563	0.0282	0.0135	0.0060	0.0025	0.0010
	1	0.3151	0.3874	0.3474	0.2684	0.1877	0.1211	0.0725	0.0403	0.0207	0.0098
	2	0.0746	0.1937	0.2759	0.3020	0.2816	0.2335	0.1757	0.1209	0.0763	0.0439
	3	0.0105	0.0574	0.1298	0.2013	0.2503	0.2668	0.2522	0.2150	0.1665	0.1172
	4	0.0010	0.0112	0.0401	0.0881	0.1460	0.2001	0.2377	0.2508	0.2384	0.2051
	5	0.0001	0.0015	0.0085	0.0264	0.0584	0.1029	0.1536	0.2007	0.2340	0.2461
	6	0.0000	0.0001	0.0012	0.0055	0.0162	0.0368	0.0689	0.1115	0.1596	0.2051
	7	0.0000	0.0000	0.0001	0.0008	0.0031	0.0090	0.0212	0.0425	0.0746	0.1172
	8	0.0000	0.0000	0.0000	0.0001	0.0004	0.0014	0.0043	0.0106	0.0229	0.0439
	9	0.0000	0.0000	0.0000	0.0000	0.0000	0.0001	0.0005	0.0016	0.0042	0.0098
	10	0.0000	0.0000	0.0000	0.0000	0.0000	0.0000	0.0000	0.0001	0.0003	0.0010
11	0	0.5688	0.3138	0.1673	0.0859	0.0422	0.0198	0.0088	0.0036	0.0014	0.0005
	1	0.3293	0.3835	0.3248	0.2362	0.1549	0.0932	0.0518	0.0266	0.0125	0.0054
	2	0.0867	0.2131	0.2866	0.2953	0.2581	0.1998	0.1395	0.0887	0.0513	0.0269
	3	0.0137	0.0710	0.1517	0.2215	0.2581	0.2568	0.2254	0.1774	0.1259	0.0806
	4	0.0014	0.0158	0.0536	0.1107	0.1721	0.2201	0.2428	0.2365	0.2060	0.1611

Binomial Probabilities (*Continued*)

n	x	p = 0.05	0.10	0.15	0.20	0.25	0.30	0.35	0.40	0.45	0.50
	5	0.0001	0.0025	0.0132	0.0388	0.0803	0.1321	0.1830	0.2207	0.2360	0.2256
	6	0.0000	0.0003	0.0023	0.0097	0.0268	0.0566	0.0985	0.1471	0.1931	0.2256
	7	0.0000	0.0000	0.0003	0.0017	0.0064	0.0173	0.0379	0.0701	0.1128	0.1611
	8	0.0000	0.0000	0.0000	0.0002	0.0011	0.0037	0.0102	0.0234	0.0462	0.0806
	9	0.0000	0.0000	0.0000	0.0000	0.0001	0.0005	0.0018	0.0052	0.0126	0.0269
	10	0.0000	0.0000	0.0000	0.0000	0.0000	0.0000	0.0002	0.0007	0.0021	0.0054
	11	0.0000	0.0000	0.0000	0.0000	0.0000	0.0000	0.0000	0.0000	0.0002	0.0005
12	0	0.5404	0.2824	0.1422	0.0687	0.0317	0.0138	0.0057	0.0022	0.0008	0.0002
	1	0.3413	0.3766	0.3012	0.2062	0.1267	0.0712	0.0368	0.0174	0.0075	0.0029
	2	0.0988	0.2301	0.2924	0.2835	0.2323	0.1678	0.1088	0.0639	0.0339	0.0161
	3	0.0173	0.0853	0.1720	0.2362	0.2581	0.2397	0.1954	0.1419	0.0923	0.0537
	4	0.0021	0.0213	0.0683	0.1329	0.1936	0.2311	0.2367	0.2128	0.1700	0.1208
	5	0.0002	0.0038	0.0193	0.0532	0.1032	0.1585	0.2039	0.2270	0.2225	0.1934
	6	0.0000	0.0005	0.0040	0.0155	0.0401	0.0792	0.1281	0.1766	0.2124	0.2256
	7	0.0000	0.0000	0.0006	0.0033	0.0115	0.0291	0.0591	0.1009	0.1489	0.1934
	8	0.0000	0.0000	0.0001	0.0005	0.0024	0.0078	0.0199	0.0420	0.0762	0.1208
	9	0.0000	0.0000	0.0000	0.0001	0.0004	0.0015	0.0048	0.0125	0.0277	0.0537
	10	0.0000	0.0000	0.0000	0.0000	0.0000	0.0002	0.0008	0.0025	0.0068	0.0161
	11	0.0000	0.0000	0.0000	0.0000	0.0000	0.0000	0.0001	0.0003	0.0010	0.0029
	12	0.0000	0.0000	0.0000	0.0000	0.0000	0.0000	0.0000	0.0000	0.0001	0.0002
13	0	0.5133	0.2542	0.1209	0.0550	0.0238	0.0097	0.0037	0.0013	0.0004	0.0001
	1	0.3512	0.3672	0.2774	0.1787	0.1029	0.0540	0.0259	0.0113	0.0045	0.0016
	2	0.1109	0.2448	0.2937	0.2680	0.2059	0.1388	0.0836	0.0453	0.0220	0.0095
	3	0.0214	0.0997	0.1900	0.2457	0.2517	0.2181	0.1651	0.1107	0.0660	0.0349
	4	0.0028	0.0277	0.0838	0.1535	0.2097	0.2337	0.2222	0.1845	0.1350	0.0873
	5	0.0003	0.0055	0.0266	0.0691	0.1258	0.1803	0.2154	0.2214	0.1989	0.1571
	6	0.0000	0.0008	0.0063	0.0230	0.0559	0.1030	0.1546	0.1968	0.2169	0.2095
	7	0.0000	0.0001	0.0011	0.0058	0.0186	0.0442	0.0833	0.1312	0.1775	0.2095
	8	0.0000	0.0000	0.0001	0.0011	0.0047	0.0142	0.0336	0.0656	0.1089	0.1571
	9	0.0000	0.0000	0.0000	0.0001	0.0009	0.0034	0.0101	0.0243	0.0495	0.0873
	10	0.0000	0.0000	0.0000	0.0000	0.0001	0.0006	0.0022	0.0065	0.0162	0.0349
	11	0.0000	0.0000	0.0000	0.0000	0.0000	0.0001	0.0003	0.0012	0.0036	0.0095
	12	0.0000	0.0000	0.0000	0.0000	0.0000	0.0000	0.0000	0.0001	0.0005	0.0016
	13	0.0000	0.0000	0.0000	0.0000	0.0000	0.0000	0.0000	0.0000	0.0000	0.0001
14	0	0.4877	0.2288	0.1028	0.0440	0.0178	0.0068	0.0024	0.0008	0.0002	0.0001
	1	0.3593	0.3559	0.2539	0.1539	0.0832	0.0407	0.0181	0.0073	0.0027	0.0009
	2	0.1229	0.2570	0.2912	0.2501	0.1802	0.1134	0.0634	0.0317	0.0141	0.0056
	3	0.0259	0.1142	0.2056	0.2501	0.2402	0.1943	0.1366	0.0845	0.0462	0.0222
	4	0.0037	0.0349	0.0998	0.1720	0.2202	0.2290	0.2022	0.1549	0.1040	0.0611
	5	0.0004	0.0078	0.0352	0.0860	0.1468	0.1963	0.2178	0.2066	0.1701	0.1222
	6	0.0000	0.0013	0.0093	0.0322	0.0734	0.1262	0.1759	0.2066	0.2088	0.1833
	7	0.0000	0.0002	0.0019	0.0092	0.0280	0.0618	0.1082	0.1574	0.1952	0.2095

Binomial Probabilities (*Continued*)

		p									
n	*x*	0.05	0.10	0.15	0.20	0.25	0.30	0.35	0.40	0.45	0.50
	8	0.0000	0.0000	0.0003	0.0020	0.0082	0.0232	0.0510	0.0918	0.1398	0.1833
	9	0.0000	0.0000	0.0000	0.0003	0.0018	0.0066	0.0183	0.0408	0.0762	0.1222
	10	0.0000	0.0000	0.0000	0.0000	0.0003	0.0014	0.0049	0.0136	0.0312	0.0611
	11	0.0000	0.0000	0.0000	0.0000	0.0000	0.0002	0.0010	0.0033	0.0093	0.0222
	12	0.0000	0.0000	0.0000	0.0000	0.0000	0.0000	0.0001	0.0005	0.0019	0.0056
	13	0.0000	0.0000	0.0000	0.0000	0.0000	0.0000	0.0000	0.0001	0.0002	0.0009
	14	0.0000	0.0000	0.0000	0.0000	0.0000	0.0000	0.0000	0.0000	0.0000	0.0001
15	0	0.4633	0.2059	0.0874	0.0352	0.0134	0.0047	0.0016	0.0005	0.0001	0.0000
	1	0.3658	0.3432	0.2312	0.1319	0.0668	0.0305	0.0126	0.0047	0.0016	0.0005
	2	0.1348	0.2669	0.2856	0.2309	0.1559	0.0916	0.0476	0.0219	0.0090	0.0032
	3	0.0307	0.1285	0.2184	0.2501	0.2252	0.1700	0.1110	0.0634	0.0318	0.0139
	4	0.0049	0.0428	0.1156	0.1876	0.2252	0.2186	0.1792	0.1268	0.0780	0.0417
	5	0.0006	0.0105	0.0449	0.1032	0.1651	0.2061	0.2123	0.1859	0.1404	0.0916
	6	0.0000	0.0019	0.0132	0.0430	0.0917	0.1472	0.1906	0.2066	0.1914	0.1527
	7	0.0000	0.0003	0.0030	0.0138	0.0393	0.0811	0.1319	0.1771	0.2013	0.1964
	8	0.0000	0.0000	0.0005	0.0035	0.0131	0.0348	0.0710	0.1181	0.1647	0.1964
	9	0.0000	0.0000	0.0001	0.0007	0.0034	0.0116	0.0298	0.0612	0.1048	0.1527
	10	0.0000	0.0000	0.0000	0.0001	0.0007	0.0030	0.0096	0.0245	0.0515	0.0916
	11	0.0000	0.0000	0.0000	0.0000	0.0001	0.0006	0.0024	0.0074	0.0191	0.0417
	12	0.0000	0.0000	0.0000	0.0000	0.0000	0.0001	0.0004	0.0016	0.0052	0.0139
	13	0.0000	0.0000	0.0000	0.0000	0.0000	0.0000	0.0001	0.0003	0.0010	0.0032
	14	0.0000	0.0000	0.0000	0.0000	0.0000	0.0000	0.0000	0.0000	0.0001	0.0005
	15	0.0000	0.0000	0.0000	0.0000	0.0000	0.0000	0.0000	0.0000	0.0000	0.0000
16	0	0.4401	0.1853	0.0743	0.0281	0.0100	0.0033	0.0010	0.0003	0.0001	0.0000
	1	0.3706	0.3294	0.2097	0.1126	0.0535	0.0228	0.0087	0.0030	0.0009	0.0002
	2	0.1463	0.2745	0.2775	0.2111	0.1336	0.0732	0.0353	0.0150	0.0056	0.0018
	3	0.0359	0.1423	0.2285	0.2463	0.2079	0.1465	0.0888	0.0468	0.0215	0.0085
	4	0.0061	0.0514	0.1311	0.2001	0.2252	0.2040	0.1553	0.1014	0.0572	0.0278
	5	0.0008	0.0137	0.0555	0.1201	0.1802	0.2099	0.2008	0.1623	0.1123	0.0667
	6	0.0001	0.0028	0.0180	0.0550	0.1101	0.1649	0.1982	0.1983	0.1684	0.1222
	7	0.0000	0.0004	0.0045	0.0197	0.0524	0.1010	0.1524	0.1889	0.1969	0.1746
	8	0.0000	0.0001	0.0009	0.0055	0.0197	0.0487	0.0923	0.1417	0.1812	0.1964
	9	0.0000	0.0000	0.0001	0.0012	0.0058	0.0185	0.0442	0.0840	0.1318	0.1746
	10	0.0000	0.0000	0.0000	0.0002	0.0014	0.0056	0.0167	0.0392	0.0755	0.1222
	11	0.0000	0.0000	0.0000	0.0000	0.0002	0.0013	0.0049	0.0142	0.0337	0.0667
	12	0.0000	0.0000	0.0000	0.0000	0.0000	0.0002	0.0011	0.0040	0.0115	0.0278
	13	0.0000	0.0000	0.0000	0.0000	0.0000	0.0000	0.0002	0.0008	0.0029	0.0085
	14	0.0000	0.0000	0.0000	0.0000	0.0000	0.0000	0.0000	0.0001	0.0005	0.0018
	15	0.0000	0.0000	0.0000	0.0000	0.0000	0.0000	0.0000	0.0000	0.0001	0.0002
	16	0.0000	0.0000	0.0000	0.0000	0.0000	0.0000	0.0000	0.0000	0.0000	0.0000
17	0	0.4181	0.1668	0.0631	0.0225	0.0075	0.0023	0.0007	0.0002	0.0000	0.0000
	1	0.3741	0.3150	0.1893	0.0957	0.0426	0.0169	0.0060	0.0019	0.0005	0.0001

Binomial Probabilities (*Continued*)

		p									
n	*x*	0.05	0.10	0.15	0.20	0.25	0.30	0.35	0.40	0.45	0.50
	2	0.1575	0.2800	0.2673	0.1914	0.1136	0.0581	0.0260	0.0102	0.0035	0.0010
	3	0.0415	0.1556	0.2359	0.2393	0.1893	0.1245	0.0701	0.0341	0.0144	0.0052
	4	0.0076	0.0605	0.1457	0.2093	0.2209	0.1868	0.1320	0.0796	0.0411	0.0182
	5	0.0010	0.0175	0.0668	0.1361	0.1914	0.2081	0.1849	0.1379	0.0875	0.0472
	6	0.0001	0.0039	0.0236	0.0680	0.1276	0.1784	0.1991	0.1839	0.1432	0.0944
	7	0.0000	0.0007	0.0065	0.0267	0.0668	0.1201	0.1685	0.1927	0.1841	0.1484
	8	0.0000	0.0001	0.0014	0.0084	0.0279	0.0644	0.1134	0.1606	0.1883	0.1855
	9	0.0000	0.0000	0.0003	0.0021	0.0093	0.0276	0.0611	0.1070	0.1540	0.1855
17	10	0.0000	0.0000	0.0000	0.0004	0.0025	0.0095	0.0263	0.0571	0.1008	0.1484
	11	0.0000	0.0000	0.0000	0.0001	0.0005	0.0026	0.0090	0.0242	0.0525	0.0944
	12	0.0000	0.0000	0.0000	0.0000	0.0001	0.0006	0.0024	0.0081	0.0215	0.0472
	13	0.0000	0.0000	0.0000	0.0000	0.0000	0.0001	0.0005	0.0021	0.0068	0.0182
	14	0.0000	0.0000	0.0000	0.0000	0.0000	0.0000	0.0001	0.0004	0.0016	0.0052
	15	0.0000	0.0000	0.0000	0.0000	0.0000	0.0000	0.0000	0.0001	0.0003	0.0010
	16	0.0000	0.0000	0.0000	0.0000	0.0000	0.0000	0.0000	0.0000	0.0000	0.0001
	17	0.0000	0.0000	0.0000	0.0000	0.0000	0.0000	0.0000	0.0000	0.0000	0.0000
18	0	0.3972	0.1501	0.0536	0.0180	0.0056	0.0016	0.0004	0.0001	0.0000	0.0000
	1	0.3763	0.3002	0.1704	0.0811	0.0338	0.0126	0.0042	0.0012	0.0003	0.0001
	2	0.1683	0.2835	0.2556	0.1723	0.0958	0.0458	0.0190	0.0069	0.0022	0.0006
	3	0.0473	0.1680	0.2406	0.2297	0.1704	0.1046	0.0547	0.0246	0.0095	0.0031
	4	0.0093	0.0700	0.1592	0.2153	0.2130	0.1681	0.1104	0.0614	0.0291	0.0117
	5	0.0014	0.0218	0.0787	0.1507	0.1988	0.2017	0.1664	0.1146	0.0666	0.0327
	6	0.0002	0.0052	0.0301	0.0816	0.1436	0.1873	0.1941	0.1655	0.1181	0.0708
	7	0.0000	0.0010	0.0091	0.0350	0.0820	0.1376	0.1792	0.1892	0.1657	0.1214
	8	0.0000	0.0002	0.0022	0.0120	0.0376	0.0811	0.1327	0.1734	0.1864	0.1669
	9	0.0000	0.0000	0.0004	0.0033	0.0139	0.0386	0.0794	0.1284	0.1694	0.1855
	10	0.0000	0.0000	0.0001	0.0008	0.0042	0.0149	0.0385	0.0771	0.1248	0.1669
	11	0.0000	0.0000	0.0000	0.0001	0.0010	0.0046	0.0151	0.0374	0.0742	0.1214
	12	0.0000	0.0000	0.0000	0.0000	0.0002	0.0012	0.0047	0.0145	0.0354	0.0708
	13	0.0000	0.0000	0.0000	0.0000	0.0000	0.0002	0.0012	0.0045	0.0134	0.0327
	14	0.0000	0.0000	0.0000	0.0000	0.0000	0.0000	0.0002	0.0011	0.0039	0.0117
	15	0.0000	0.0000	0.0000	0.0000	0.0000	0.0000	0.0000	0.0002	0.0009	0.0031
	16	0.0000	0.0000	0.0000	0.0000	0.0000	0.0000	0.0000	0.0000	0.0001	0.0006
	17	0.0000	0.0000	0.0000	0.0000	0.0000	0.0000	0.0000	0.0000	0.0000	0.0001
	18	0.0000	0.0000	0.0000	0.0000	0.0000	0.0000	0.0000	0.0000	0.0000	0.0000
19	0	0.3774	0.1351	0.0456	0.0144	0.0042	0.0011	0.0003	0.0001	0.0000	0.0000
	1	0.3774	0.2852	0.1529	0.0685	0.0268	0.0093	0.0029	0.0008	0.0002	0.0000
	2	0.1787	0.2852	0.2428	0.1540	0.0803	0.0358	0.0138	0.0046	0.0013	0.0003
	3	0.0533	0.1796	0.2428	0.2182	0.1517	0.0869	0.0422	0.0175	0.0062	0.0018
	4	0.0112	0.0798	0.1714	0.2182	0.2023	0.1491	0.0909	0.0467	0.0203	0.0074
	5	0.0018	0.0266	0.0907	0.1636	0.2023	0.1916	0.1468	0.0933	0.0497	0.0222
	6	0.0002	0.0069	0.0374	0.0955	0.1574	0.1916	0.1844	0.1451	0.0949	0.0518
	7	0.0000	0.0014	0.0122	0.0443	0.0974	0.1525	0.1844	0.1797	0.1443	0.0961

Binomial Probabilities (*Continued*)

		p									
n	*x*	0.05	0.10	0.15	0.20	0.25	0.30	0.35	0.40	0.45	0.50
	8	0.0000	0.0002	0.0032	0.0166	0.0487	0.0981	0.1489	0.1797	0.1771	0.1442
	9	0.0000	0.0000	0.0007	0.0051	0.0198	0.0514	0.0980	0.1464	0.1771	0.1762
	10	0.0000	0.0000	0.0001	0.0013	0.0066	0.0220	0.0528	0.0976	0.1449	0.1762
	11	0.0000	0.0000	0.0000	0.0003	0.0018	0.0077	0.0233	0.0532	0.0970	0.1442
	12	0.0000	0.0000	0.0000	0.0000	0.0004	0.0022	0.0083	0.0237	0.0529	0.0961
	13	0.0000	0.0000	0.0000	0.0000	0.0001	0.0005	0.0024	0.0085	0.0233	0.0518
	14	0.0000	0.0000	0.0000	0.0000	0.0000	0.0001	0.0006	0.0024	0.0082	0.0222
19	15	0.0000	0.0000	0.0000	0.0000	0.0000	0.0000	0.0001	0.0005	0.0022	0.0074
	16	0.0000	0.0000	0.0000	0.0000	0.0000	0.0000	0.0000	0.0001	0.0005	0.0018
	17	0.0000	0.0000	0.0000	0.0000	0.0000	0.0000	0.0000	0.0000	0.0001	0.0003
	18	0.0000	0.0000	0.0000	0.0000	0.0000	0.0000	0.0000	0.0000	0.0000	0.0000
	19	0.0000	0.0000	0.0000	0.0000	0.0000	0.0000	0.0000	0.0000	0.0000	0.0000
20	0	0.3585	0.1216	0.0388	0.0115	0.0032	0.0008	0.0002	0.0000	0.0000	0.0000
	1	0.3774	0.2702	0.1368	0.0576	0.0211	0.0068	0.0020	0.0005	0.0001	0.0000
	2	0.1887	0.2852	0.2293	0.1369	0.0669	0.0278	0.0100	0.0031	0.0008	0.0002
	3	0.0596	0.1901	0.2428	0.2054	0.1339	0.0716	0.0323	0.0123	0.0040	0.0011
	4	0.0133	0.0898	0.1821	0.2182	0.1897	0.1304	0.0738	0.0350	0.0139	0.0046
	5	0.0022	0.0319	0.1028	0.1746	0.2023	0.1789	0.1272	0.0746	0.0365	0.0148
	6	0.0003	0.0089	0.0454	0.1091	0.1686	0.1916	0.1712	0.1244	0.0746	0.0370
	7	0.0000	0.0020	0.0160	0.0545	0.1124	0.1643	0.1844	0.1659	0.1221	0.0739
	8	0.0000	0.0004	0.0046	0.0222	0.0609	0.1144	0.1614	0.1797	0.1623	0.1201
	9	0.0000	0.0001	0.0011	0.0074	0.0271	0.0654	0.1158	0.1597	0.1771	0.1602
	10	0.0000	0.0000	0.0002	0.0020	0.0099	0.0308	0.0686	0.1171	0.1593	0.1762
	11	0.0000	0.0000	0.0000	0.0005	0.0030	0.0120	0.0336	0.0710	0.1185	0.1602
	12	0.0000	0.0000	0.0000	0.0001	0.0008	0.0039	0.0136	0.0355	0.0727	0.1201
	13	0.0000	0.0000	0.0000	0.0000	0.0002	0.0010	0.0045	0.0146	0.0366	0.0739
	14	0.0000	0.0000	0.0000	0.0000	0.0000	0.0002	0.0012	0.0049	0.0150	0.0370
	15	0.0000	0.0000	0.0000	0.0000	0.0000	0.0000	0.0003	0.0013	0.0049	0.0148
	16	0.0000	0.0000	0.0000	0.0000	0.0000	0.0000	0.0000	0.0003	0.0013	0.0046
	17	0.0000	0.0000	0.0000	0.0000	0.0000	0.0000	0.0000	0.0000	0.0002	0.0011
	18	0.0000	0.0000	0.0000	0.0000	0.0000	0.0000	0.0000	0.0000	0.0000	0.0002
	19	0.0000	0.0000	0.0000	0.0000	0.0000	0.0000	0.0000	0.0000	0.0000	0.0000
	20	0.0000	0.0000	0.0000	0.0000	0.0000	0.0000	0.0000	0.0000	0.0000	0.0000

APPENDIX B: Poisson Probabilities

Entries in the table give the probability of x occurrences for a Poisson process with a mean λ. For example, when $\lambda = 2.5$, the probability of $x = 4$ occurrences is 0.1336.

x	λ 0.1	0.2	0.3	0.4	0.5	0.6	0.7	0.8	0.9	1.0
0	0.9048	0.8187	0.7408	0.6703	0.6065	0.5488	0.4966	0.4493	0.4066	0.3679
1	0.0905	0.1637	0.2222	0.2681	0.3033	0.3293	0.3476	0.3595	0.3659	0.3679
2	0.0045	0.0164	0.0333	0.0536	0.0758	0.0988	0.1217	0.1438	0.1647	0.1839
3	0.0002	0.0011	0.0033	0.0072	0.0126	0.0198	0.0284	0.0383	0.0494	0.0613
4	0.0000	0.0001	0.0002	0.0007	0.0016	0.0030	0.0050	0.0077	0.0111	0.0153
5	0.0000	0.0000	0.0000	0.0001	0.0002	0.0004	0.0007	0.0012	0.0020	0.0031
6	0.0000	0.0000	0.0000	0.0000	0.0000	0.0000	0.0001	0.0002	0.0003	0.0005
7	0.0000	0.0000	0.0000	0.0000	0.0000	0.0000	0.0000	0.0000	0.0000	0.0001

x	λ 1.1	1.2	1.3	1.4	1.5	1.6	1.7	1.8	1.9	2.0
0	0.3329	0.3012	0.2725	0.2466	0.2231	0.2019	0.1827	0.1653	0.1496	0.1353
1	0.3662	0.3614	0.3543	0.3452	0.3347	0.3230	0.3106	0.2975	0.2842	0.2707
2	0.2014	0.2169	0.2303	0.2417	0.2510	0.2584	0.2640	0.2678	0.2700	0.2707
3	0.0738	0.0867	0.0998	0.1128	0.1255	0.1378	0.1496	0.1607	0.1710	0.1804
4	0.0203	0.0260	0.0324	0.0395	0.0471	0.0551	0.0636	0.0723	0.0812	0.0902
5	0.0045	0.0062	0.0084	0.0111	0.0141	0.0176	0.0216	0.0260	0.0309	0.0361
6	0.0008	0.0012	0.0018	0.0026	0.0035	0.0047	0.0061	0.0078	0.0098	0.0120
7	0.0001	0.0002	0.0003	0.0005	0.0008	0.0011	0.0015	0.0020	0.0027	0.0034
8	0.0000	0.0000	0.0001	0.0001	0.0001	0.0002	0.0003	0.0005	0.0006	0.0009
9	0.0000	0.0000	0.0000	0.0000	0.0000	0.0000	0.0001	0.0001	0.0001	0.0002

x	λ 2.1	2.2	2.3	2.4	2.5	2.6	2.7	2.8	2.9	3.0
0	0.1225	0.1108	0.1003	0.0907	0.0821	0.0743	0.0672	0.0608	0.0550	0.0498
1	0.2572	0.2438	0.2306	0.2177	0.2052	0.1931	0.1815	0.1703	0.1596	0.1494
2	0.2700	0.2681	0.2652	0.2613	0.2565	0.2510	0.2450	0.2384	0.2314	0.2240
3	0.1890	0.1966	0.2033	0.2090	0.2138	0.2176	0.2205	0.2225	0.2237	0.2240
4	0.0992	0.1082	0.1169	0.1254	0.1336	0.1414	0.1488	0.1557	0.1622	0.1680
5	0.0417	0.0476	0.0538	0.0602	0.0668	0.0735	0.0804	0.0872	0.0940	0.1008
6	0.0146	0.0174	0.0206	0.0241	0.0278	0.0319	0.0362	0.0407	0.0455	0.0540
7	0.0044	0.0055	0.0068	0.0083	0.0099	0.0118	0.0139	0.0163	0.0188	0.0216
8	0.0011	0.0015	0.0019	0.0025	0.0031	0.0038	0.0047	0.0057	0.0068	0.0081
9	0.0003	0.0004	0.0005	0.0007	0.0009	0.0011	0.0014	0.0018	0.0022	0.0027
10	0.0001	0.0001	0.0001	0.0002	0.0002	0.0003	0.0004	0.0005	0.0006	0.0008
11	0.0000	0.0000	0.0000	0.0000	0.0000	0.0001	0.0001	0.0001	0.0002	0.0002
12	0.0000	0.0000	0.0000	0.0000	0.0000	0.0000	0.0000	0.0000	0.0000	0.0001

Poisson Probabilities (*Continued*)

	λ									
x	3.1	3.2	3.3	3.4	3.5	3.6	3.7	3.8	3.9	4.0
0	0.0450	0.0408	0.0369	0.0344	0.0302	0.0273	0.0247	0.0224	0.0202	0.0183
1	0.1397	0.1304	0.1217	0.1135	0.1057	0.0984	0.0915	0.0850	0.0789	0.0733
2	0.2165	0.2087	0.2008	0.1929	0.1850	0.1771	0.1692	0.1615	0.1539	0.1465
3	0.2237	0.2226	0.2209	0.2186	0.2158	0.2125	0.2087	0.2046	0.2001	0.1954
4	0.1734	0.1781	0.1823	0.1858	0.1888	0.1912	0.1931	0.1944	0.1951	0.1954
5	0.1075	0.1140	0.1203	0.1264	0.1322	0.1377	0.1429	0.1477	0.1522	0.1563
6	0.0555	0.0608	0.0662	0.0716	0.0771	0.0826	0.0881	0.0936	0.0989	0.1042
7	0.0246	0.0278	0.0312	0.0348	0.0385	0.0425	0.0466	0.0508	0.0551	0.0595
8	0.0095	0.0111	0.0129	0.0148	0.0169	0.0191	0.0215	0.0241	0.0269	0.0298
9	0.0033	0.0040	0.0047	0.0056	0.0066	0.0076	0.0089	0.0102	0.0116	0.0132
10	0.0010	0.0013	0.0016	0.0019	0.0023	0.0028	0.0033	0.0039	0.0045	0.0053
11	0.0003	0.0004	0.0005	0.0006	0.0007	0.0009	0.0011	0.0013	0.0016	0.0019
12	0.0001	0.0001	0.0001	0.0002	0.0002	0.0003	0.0003	0.0004	0.0005	0.0006
13	0.0000	0.0000	0.0000	0.0000	0.0001	0.0001	0.0001	0.0001	0.0002	0.0002
14	0.0000	0.0000	0.0000	0.0000	0.0000	0.0000	0.0000	0.0000	0.0000	0.0001

	λ									
x	4.1	4.2	4.3	4.4	4.5	4.6	4.7	4.8	4.9	5.0
0	0.0166	0.0150	0.0136	0.0123	0.0111	0.0101	0.0091	0.0082	0.0074	0.0067
1	0.0679	0.0630	0.0583	0.0540	0.0500	0.0462	0.0427	0.0395	0.0365	0.0337
2	0.1393	0.1323	0.1254	0.1188	0.1125	0.1063	0.1005	0.0948	0.0894	0.0842
3	0.1904	0.1852	0.1798	0.1743	0.1687	0.1631	0.1574	0.1517	0.1460	0.1404
4	0.1951	0.1944	0.1933	0.1917	0.1898	0.1875	0.1849	0.1820	0.1789	0.1755
5	0.1600	0.1633	0.1662	0.1687	0.1708	0.1725	0.1738	0.1747	0.1753	0.1755
6	0.1093	0.1143	0.1191	0.1237	0.1281	0.1323	0.1362	0.1398	0.1432	0.1462
7	0.0640	0.0686	0.0732	0.0778	0.0824	0.0869	0.0914	0.0959	0.1002	0.1044
8	0.0328	0.0360	0.0393	0.0428	0.0463	0.0500	0.0537	0.0575	0.0614	0.0653
9	0.0150	0.0168	0.0188	0.0209	0.0232	0.0255	0.0280	0.0307	0.0334	0.0363
10	0.0061	0.0071	0.0081	0.0092	0.0104	0.0118	0.0132	0.0147	0.0164	0.0181
11	0.0023	0.0027	0.0032	0.0037	0.0043	0.0049	0.0056	0.0064	0.0073	0.0082
12	0.0008	0.0009	0.0011	0.0014	0.0016	0.0019	0.0022	0.0026	0.0030	0.0034
13	0.0002	0.0003	0.0004	0.0005	0.0006	0.0007	0.0008	0.0009	0.0011	0.0013
14	0.0001	0.0001	0.0001	0.0001	0.0002	0.0002	0.0003	0.0003	0.0004	0.0005
15	0.0000	0.0000	0.0000	0.0000	0.0001	0.0001	0.0001	0.0001	0.0001	0.0002

	λ									
x	5.1	5.2	5.3	5.4	5.5	5.6	5.7	5.8	5.9	6.0
0	0.0061	0.0055	0.0050	0.0045	0.0041	0.0037	0.0033	0.0030	0.0027	0.0025
1	0.0311	0.0287	0.0265	0.0244	0.0225	0.0207	0.0191	0.0176	0.0162	0.0149
2	0.0793	0.0746	0.0701	0.0659	0.0618	0.0580	0.0544	0.0509	0.0477	0.0446
3	0.1348	0.1293	0.1239	0.1185	0.1133	0.1082	0.1033	0.0985	0.0938	0.0892
4	0.1719	0.1681	0.1641	0.1600	0.1558	0.1515	0.1472	0.1428	0.1383	0.1339

Poisson Probabilities (*Continued*)

	λ									
x	5.1	5.2	5.3	5.4	5.5	5.6	5.7	5.8	5.9	6.0
5	0.1753	0.1748	0.1740	0.1728	0.1714	0.1697	0.1678	0.1656	0.1632	0.1606
6	0.1490	0.1515	0.1537	0.1555	0.1571	0.1587	0.1594	0.1601	0.1605	0.1606
7	0.1086	0.1125	0.1163	0.1200	0.1234	0.1267	0.1298	0.1326	0.1353	0.1377
8	0.0692	0.0731	0.0771	0.0810	0.0849	0.0887	0.0925	0.0962	0.0998	0.1033
9	0.0392	0.0423	0.0454	0.0486	0.0519	0.0552	0.0586	0.0620	0.0654	0.0688
10	0.0200	0.0220	0.0241	0.0262	0.0285	0.0309	0.0334	0.0359	0.0386	0.0413
11	0.0093	0.0104	0.0116	0.0129	0.0143	0.0157	0.0173	0.0190	0.0207	0.0225
12	0.0039	0.0045	0.0051	0.0058	0.0065	0.0073	0.0082	0.0092	0.0102	0.0113
13	0.0015	0.0018	0.0021	0.0024	0.0028	0.0032	0.0036	0.0041	0.0046	0.0052
14	0.0006	0.0007	0.0008	0.0009	0.0011	0.0013	0.0015	0.0017	0.0019	0.0022
15	0.0002	0.0002	0.0003	0.0003	0.0004	0.0005	0.0006	0.0007	0.0008	0.0009
16	0.0001	0.0001	0.0001	0.0001	0.0001	0.0002	0.0002	0.0002	0.0003	0.0003
17	0.0000	0.0000	0.0000	0.0000	0.0000	0.0001	0.0001	0.0001	0.0001	0.0001

	λ									
x	6.1	6.2	6.3	6.4	6.5	6.6	6.7	6.8	6.9	7.0
0	0.0022	0.0020	0.0018	0.0017	0.0015	0.0014	0.0012	0.0011	0.0010	0.0009
1	0.0137	0.0126	0.0116	0.0106	0.0098	0.0090	0.0082	0.0076	0.0070	0.0064
2	0.0417	0.0390	0.0364	0.0340	0.0318	0.0296	0.0276	0.0258	0.0240	0.0223
3	0.0848	0.0806	0.0765	0.0726	0.0688	0.0652	0.0617	0.0584	0.0552	0.0521
4	0.1294	0.1249	0.1205	0.1162	0.1118	0.1076	0.1034	0.0992	0.0952	0.0912
5	0.1579	0.1549	0.1519	0.1487	0.1454	0.1420	0.1385	0.1349	0.1314	0.1277
6	0.1605	0.1601	0.1595	0.1586	0.1575	0.1562	0.1546	0.1529	0.1511	0.1490
7	0.1399	0.1418	0.1435	0.1450	0.1462	0.1472	0.1480	0.1486	0.1489	0.1490
8	0.1066	0.1099	0.1130	0.1160	0.1188	0.1215	0.1240	0.1263	0.1284	0.1304
9	0.0723	0.0757	0.0791	0.0825	0.0858	0.0891	0.0923	0.0954	0.0985	0.1014
10	0.0441	0.0469	0.0498	0.0528	0.0558	0.0588	0.0618	0.0649	0.0679	0.0710
11	0.0245	0.0265	0.0285	0.0307	0.0330	0.0353	0.0377	0.0401	0.0426	0.0452
12	0.0124	0.0137	0.0150	0.0164	0.0179	0.0194	0.0210	0.0227	0.0245	0.0264
13	0.0058	0.0065	0.0073	0.0081	0.0089	0.0098	0.0108	0.0119	0.0130	0.0142
14	0.0025	0.0029	0.0033	0.0037	0.0041	0.0046	0.0052	0.0058	0.0064	0.0071
15	0.0010	0.0012	0.0014	0.0016	0.0018	0.0020	0.0023	0.0025	0.0029	0.0033
16	0.0004	0.0005	0.0005	0.0006	0.0007	0.0008	0.0010	0.0011	0.0013	0.0014
17	0.0001	0.0002	0.0002	0.0002	0.0003	0.0003	0.0004	0.0004	0.0005	0.0006
18	0.0000	0.0001	0.0001	0.0001	0.0001	0.0001	0.0001	0.0002	0.0002	0.0002
19	0.0000	0.0000	0.0000	0.0000	0.0000	0.0000	0.0000	0.0001	0.0001	0.0001

	λ									
x	7.1	7.2	7.3	7.4	7.5	7.6	7.7	7.8	7.9	8.0
0	0.0008	0.0007	0.0007	0.0006	0.0006	0.0005	0.0005	0.0004	0.0004	0.0003
1	0.0059	0.0054	0.0049	0.0045	0.0041	0.0038	0.0035	0.0032	0.0029	0.0027
2	0.0208	0.0194	0.0180	0.0167	0.0156	0.0145	0.0134	0.0125	0.0116	0.0107

Poisson Probabilities (*Continued*)

	λ									
x	7.1	7.2	7.3	7.4	7.5	7.6	7.7	7.8	7.9	8.0
3	0.0492	0.0464	0.0438	0.0413	0.0389	0.0366	0.0345	0.0324	0.0305	0.0286
4	0.0874	0.0836	0.0799	0.0764	0.0729	0.0696	0.0663	0.0632	0.0602	0.0573
5	0.1241	0.1204	0.1167	0.1130	0.1094	0.1057	0.1021	0.0986	0.0951	0.0916
6	0.1468	0.1445	0.1420	0.1394	0.1367	0.1339	0.1311	0.1282	0.1252	0.1221
7	0.1489	0.1486	0.1481	0.1474	0.1465	0.1454	0.1442	0.1428	0.1413	0.1396
8	0.1321	0.1337	0.1351	0.1363	0.1373	0.1382	0.1388	0.1392	0.1395	0.1396
9	0.1042	0.1070	0.1096	0.1121	0.1144	0.1167	0.1187	0.1207	0.1224	0.1241
10	0.0740	0.0770	0.0800	0.0829	0.0858	0.0887	0.0914	0.0941	0.0967	0.0993
11	0.0478	0.0504	0.0531	0.0558	0.0585	0.0613	0.0640	0.0667	0.0695	0.0722
12	0.0283	0.0303	0.0323	0.0344	0.0366	0.0388	0.0411	0.0434	0.0457	0.0481
13	0.0154	0.0168	0.0181	0.0196	0.0211	0.0227	0.0243	0.0260	0.0278	0.0296
14	0.0078	0.0086	0.0095	0.0104	0.0113	0.0123	0.0134	0.0145	0.0157	0.0169
15	0.0037	0.0041	0.0046	0.0051	0.0057	0.0062	0.0069	0.0075	0.0083	0.0090
16	0.0016	0.0019	0.0021	0.0024	0.0026	0.0030	0.0033	0.0037	0.0041	0.0045
17	0.0007	0.0008	0.0009	0.0010	0.0012	0.0013	0.0015	0.0017	0.0019	0.0021
18	0.0003	0.0003	0.0004	0.0004	0.0005	0.0006	0.0006	0.0007	0.0008	0.0009
19	0.0001	0.0001	0.0001	0.0002	0.0002	0.0002	0.0003	0.0003	0.0003	0.0004
20	0.0000	0.0000	0.0001	0.0001	0.0001	0.0001	0.0001	0.0001	0.0001	0.0002
21	0.0000	0.0000	0.0000	0.0000	0.0000	0.0000	0.0000	0.0000	0.0001	0.0001

	λ									
x	8.1	8.2	8.3	8.4	8.5	8.6	8.7	8.8	8.9	9.0
0	0.0003	0.0003	0.0002	0.0002	0.0002	0.0002	0.0002	0.0002	0.0001	0.0001
1	0.0025	0.0023	0.0021	0.0019	0.0017	0.0016	0.0014	0.0013	0.0012	0.0011
2	0.0100	0.0092	0.0086	0.0079	0.0074	0.0068	0.0063	0.0058	0.0054	0.0050
3	0.0269	0.0252	0.0237	0.0222	0.0208	0.0195	0.0183	0.0171	0.0160	0.0150
4	0.0544	0.0517	0.0491	0.0466	0.0443	0.0420	0.0398	0.0377	0.0357	0.0337
5	0.0882	0.0849	0.0816	0.0784	0.0752	0.0722	0.0692	0.0663	0.0635	0.0607
6	0.1191	0.1160	0.1128	0.1097	0.1066	0.1034	0.1003	0.0972	0.0941	0.0911
7	0.1378	0.1358	0.1338	0.1317	0.1294	0.1271	0.1247	0.1222	0.1197	0.1171
8	0.1395	0.1392	0.1388	0.1382	0.1375	0.1366	0.1356	0.1344	0.1332	0.1318
9	0.1256	0.1269	0.1280	0.1290	0.1299	0.1306	0.1311	0.1315	0.1317	0.1318
10	0.1017	0.1040	0.1063	0.1084	0.1104	0.1123	0.1140	0.1157	0.1172	0.1186
11	0.0749	0.0776	0.0802	0.0828	0.0853	0.0878	0.0902	0.0925	0.0948	0.0970
12	0.0505	0.0530	0.0555	0.0579	0.0604	0.0629	0.0654	0.0679	0.0703	0.0728
13	0.0315	0.0334	0.0354	0.0374	0.0395	0.0416	0.0438	0.0459	0.0481	0.0504
14	0.0182	0.0196	0.0210	0.0225	0.0240	0.0256	0.0272	0.0289	0.0306	0.0324
15	0.0098	0.0107	0.0116	0.0126	0.0136	0.0147	0.0158	0.0169	0.0182	0.1094
16	0.0050	0.0055	0.0060	0.0066	0.0072	0.0079	0.0086	0.0093	0.0101	0.0109
17	0.0024	0.0026	0.0029	0.0033	0.0036	0.0040	0.0044	0.0048	0.0053	0.0058
18	0.0011	0.0012	0.0014	0.0015	0.0017	0.0019	0.0021	0.0024	0.0026	0.0029
19	0.0005	0.0005	0.0006	0.0007	0.0008	0.0009	0.0010	0.0011	0.0012	0.0014

Poisson Probabilities (*Continued*)

	λ									
x	8.1	8.2	8.3	8.4	8.5	8.6	8.7	8.8	8.9	9.0
20	0.0002	0.0002	0.0002	0.0003	0.0003	0.0004	0.0004	0.0005	0.0005	0.0006
21	0.0001	0.0001	0.0001	0.0001	0.0001	0.0002	0.0002	0.0002	0.0002	0.0003
22	0.0000	0.0000	0.0000	0.0000	0.0001	0.0001	0.0001	0.0001	0.0001	0.0001

	λ									
x	9.1	9.2	9.3	9.4	9.5	9.6	9.7	9.8	9.9	10
0	0.0001	0.0001	0.0001	0.0001	0.0001	0.0001	0.0001	0.0001	0.0001	0.0000
1	0.0010	0.0009	0.0009	0.0008	0.0007	0.0007	0.0006	0.0005	0.0005	0.0005
2	0.0046	0.0043	0.0040	0.0037	0.0034	0.0031	0.0029	0.0027	0.0025	0.0023
3	0.0140	0.0131	0.0123	0.0115	0.0107	0.0100	0.0093	0.0087	0.0081	0.0076
4	0.0319	0.0302	0.0285	0.0269	0.0254	0.0240	0.0226	0.0213	0.0201	0.0189
5	0.0581	0.0555	0.0530	0.0506	0.0483	0.0460	0.0439	0.0418	0.0398	0.0378
6	0.0881	0.0851	0.0822	0.0793	0.0764	0.0736	0.0709	0.0682	0.0656	0.0631
7	0.1145	0.1118	0.1091	0.1064	0.1037	0.1010	0.0982	0.0955	0.0928	0.0901
8	0.1302	0.1286	0.1269	0.1251	0.1232	0.1212	0.1191	0.1170	0.1148	0.1126
9	0.1317	0.1315	0.1311	0.1306	0.1300	0.1293	0.1284	0.1274	0.1263	0.1251
10	0.1198	0.1210	0.1219	0.1228	0.1235	0.1241	0.1245	0.1249	0.1250	0.1251
11	0.0991	0.1012	0.1031	0.1049	0.1067	0.1083	0.1098	0.1112	0.1125	0.1137
12	0.0752	0.0776	0.0799	0.0822	0.0844	0.0866	0.0888	0.0908	0.0928	0.0948
13	0.0526	0.0549	0.0572	0.0594	0.0617	0.0640	0.0662	0.0685	0.0707	0.0729
14	0.0342	0.0361	0.0380	0.0399	0.0419	0.0439	0.0459	0.0479	0.0500	0.0521
15	0.0208	0.0221	0.0235	0.0250	0.0265	0.0281	0.0297	0.0313	0.0330	0.0347
16	0.0118	0.0127	0.0137	0.0147	0.0157	0.0168	0.0180	0.0192	0.0204	0.0217
17	0.0063	0.0069	0.0075	0.0081	0.0088	0.0095	0.0103	0.0111	0.0119	0.0128
18	0.0032	0.0035	0.0039	0.0042	0.0046	0.0051	0.0055	0.0060	0.0065	0.0071
19	0.0015	0.0017	0.0019	0.0021	0.0023	0.0026	0.0028	0.0031	0.0034	0.0027
20	0.0007	0.0008	0.0009	0.0010	0.0011	0.0012	0.0014	0.0015	0.0017	0.0019
21	0.0003	0.0003	0.0004	0.0004	0.0005	0.0006	0.0006	0.0007	0.0008	0.0009
22	0.0001	0.0001	0.0002	0.0002	0.0002	0.0002	0.0003	0.0003	0.0004	0.0004
23	0.0000	0.0001	0.0001	0.0001	0.0001	0.0001	0.0001	0.0001	0.0002	0.0002
24	0.0000	0.0000	0.0000	0.0000	0.0000	0.0000	0.0000	0.0001	0.0001	0.0001

	λ									
x	11	12	13	14	15	16	17	18	19	20
0	0.0000	0.0000	0.0000	0.0000	0.0000	0.0000	0.0000	0.0000	0.0000	0.0000
1	0.0002	0.0001	0.0000	0.0000	0.0000	0.0000	0.0000	0.0000	0.0000	0.0000
2	0.0010	0.0004	0.0002	0.0001	0.0000	0.0000	0.0000	0.0000	0.0000	0.0000
3	0.0037	0.0018	0.0008	0.0004	0.0002	0.0001	0.0000	0.0000	0.0000	0.0000
4	0.0102	0.0053	0.0027	0.0013	0.0006	0.0003	0.0001	0.0001	0.0000	0.0000
5	0.0224	0.0127	0.0070	0.0037	0.0019	0.0010	0.0005	0.0002	0.0001	0.0001
6	0.0411	0.0255	0.0152	0.0087	0.0048	0.0026	0.0014	0.0007	0.0004	0.0002
7	0.0646	0.0437	0.0281	0.0174	0.0104	0.0060	0.0034	0.0018	0.0010	0.0005
8	0.0888	0.0655	0.0457	0.0304	0.0194	0.0120	0.0072	0.0042	0.0024	0.0013

Poisson Probabilities (*Continued*)

	λ									
x	11	12	13	14	15	16	17	18	19	20
9	0.1085	0.0874	0.0661	0.0473	0.0324	0.0213	0.0135	0.0083	0.0050	0.0029
10	0.1194	0.1048	0.0859	0.0663	0.0486	0.0341	0.0230	0.0150	0.0095	0.0058
11	0.1194	0.1144	0.1015	0.0844	0.0663	0.0496	0.0355	0.0245	0.0164	0.0106
12	0.1094	0.1144	0.1099	0.0984	0.0829	0.0661	0.0504	0.0368	0.0259	0.0176
13	0.0926	0.1056	0.1099	0.1060	0.0956	0.0814	0.0658	0.0509	0.0378	0.0271
14	0.0728	0.0905	0.1021	0.1060	0.1024	0.0930	0.0800	0.0655	0.0514	0.0387
15	0.0534	0.0724	0.0885	0.0989	0.1024	0.0992	0.0906	0.0786	0.0650	0.0516
16	0.0367	0.0543	0.0719	0.0866	0.0960	0.0992	0.0963	0.0884	0.0772	0.0646
17	0.0237	0.0383	0.0550	0.0713	0.0847	0.0934	0.0963	0.0936	0.0863	0.0760
18	0.0145	0.0256	0.0397	0.0554	0.0706	0.0830	0.0909	0.0936	0.0911	0.0844
19	0.0084	0.0161	0.0272	0.0409	0.0557	0.0699	0.0814	0.0887	0.0911	0.0888
20	0.0046	0.0097	0.0177	0.0286	0.0418	0.0559	0.0692	0.0798	0.0866	0.0888
21	0.0024	0.0055	0.0109	0.0191	0.0299	0.0426	0.0560	0.0684	0.0783	0.0846
22	0.0012	0.0030	0.0065	0.0121	0.0204	0.0310	0.0433	0.0560	0.0676	0.0769
23	0.0006	0.0016	0.0037	0.0074	0.0133	0.0216	0.0320	0.0438	0.0559	0.0669
24	0.0003	0.0008	0.0020	0.0043	0.0083	0.0144	0.0226	0.0328	0.0442	0.0557
25	0.0001	0.0004	0.0010	0.0024	0.0050	0.0092	0.0154	0.0237	0.0336	0.0446
26	0.0000	0.0002	0.0005	0.0013	0.0029	0.0057	0.0101	0.0164	0.0246	0.0343
27	0.0000	0.0001	0.0002	0.0007	0.0016	0.0034	0.0063	0.0109	0.0173	0.0254
28	0.0000	0.0000	0.0001	0.0003	0.0009	0.0019	0.0038	0.0070	0.0117	0.0181
29	0.0000	0.0000	0.0001	0.0002	0.0004	0.0011	0.0023	0.0044	0.0077	0.0125
30	0.0000	0.0000	0.0000	0.0001	0.0002	0.0006	0.0013	0.0026	0.0049	0.0083
31	0.0000	0.0000	0.0000	0.0000	0.0001	0.0003	0.0007	0.0015	0.0030	0.0054
32	0.0000	0.0000	0.0000	0.0000	0.0001	0.0001	0.0004	0.0009	0.0018	0.0034
33	0.0000	0.0000	0.0000	0.0000	0.0000	0.0001	0.0002	0.0005	0.0010	0.0020
34	0.0000	0.0000	0.0000	0.0000	0.0000	0.0000	0.0001	0.0002	0.0006	0.0012
35	0.0000	0.0000	0.0000	0.0000	0.0000	0.0000	0.0000	0.0001	0.0003	0.0007
36	0.0000	0.0000	0.0000	0.0000	0.0000	0.0000	0.0000	0.0001	0.0002	0.0004
37	0.0000	0.0000	0.0000	0.0000	0.0000	0.0000	0.0000	0.0000	0.0001	0.0002
38	0.0000	0.0000	0.0000	0.0000	0.0000	0.0000	0.0000	0.0000	0.0000	0.0001
39	0.0000	0.0000	0.0000	0.0000	0.0000	0.0000	0.0000	0.0000	0.0000	0.0001

APPENDIX C: Areas for the Standard Normal Distribution

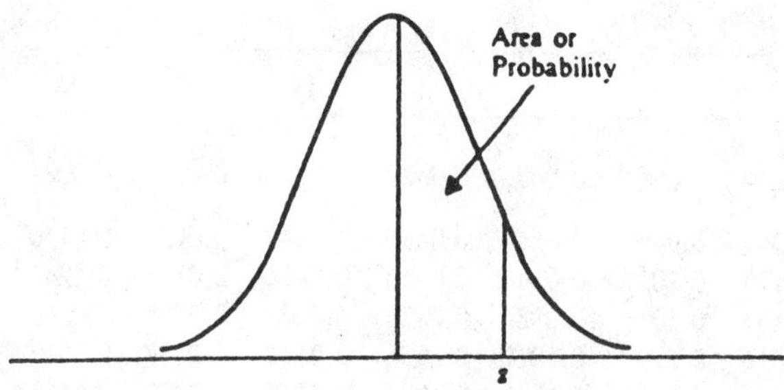

Entries in the table give the area under the curve between the mean and z standard deviations above the mean. For example, for $z = 1.25$, the area under the curve between the mean and z is 0.3944.

z	0.00	0.01	0.02	0.03	0.04	0.05	0.06	0.07	0.08	0.09
0.0	0.0000	0.0040	0.0080	0.0120	0.0160	0.0199	0.0239	0.0279	0.0319	0.0359
0.1	0.0398	0.0438	0.0478	0.0517	0.0557	0.0596	0.0636	0.0675	0.0714	0.0753
0.2	0.0793	0.0832	0.0871	0.0910	0.0948	0.0987	0.1026	0.1064	0.1103	0.1141
0.3	0.1179	0.1217	0.1255	0.1293	0.1331	0.1368	0.1406	0.1443	0.1480	0.1517
0.4	0.1554	0.1591	0.1628	0.1664	0.1700	0.1736	0.1772	0.1808	0.1844	0.1879
0.5	0.1915	0.1950	0.1985	0.2019	0.2054	0.2088	0.2123	0.2157	0.2190	0.2224
0.6	0.2257	0.2291	0.2324	0.2357	0.2389	0.2422	0.2454	0.2486	0.2518	0.2549
0.7	0.2580	0.2612	0.2642	0.2673	0.2704	0.2734	0.2764	0.2794	0.2823	0.2852
0.8	0.2881	0.2910	0.2939	0.2967	0.2995	0.3023	0.3051	0.3078	0.3106	0.3133
0.9	0.3159	0.3186	0.3212	0.3238	0.3264	0.3289	0.3315	0.3340	0.3365	0.3389
1.0	0.3413	0.3438	0.3461	0.3485	0.3508	0.3531	0.3554	0.3577	0.3599	0.3621
1.1	0.3643	0.3665	0.3686	0.3708	0.3729	0.3749	0.3770	0.3790	0.3810	0.3830
1.2	0.3849	0.3869	0.3888	0.3907	0.3925	0.3944	0.3962	0.3980	0.3997	0.4015
1.3	0.4032	0.4049	0.4066	0.4082	0.4099	0.4115	0.4131	0.4147	0.4162	0.4177
1.4	0.4192	0.4207	0.4222	0.4236	0.4251	0.4265	0.4279	0.4292	0.4306	0.4319
1.5	0.4332	0.4345	0.4357	0.4370	0.4382	0.4394	0.4406	0.4418	0.4429	0.4441
1.6	0.4452	0.4463	0.4474	0.4484	0.4495	0.4505	0.4515	0.4525	0.4535	0.4545
1.7	0.4554	0.4564	0.4573	0.4582	0.4591	0.4599	0.4608	0.4616	0.4625	0.4633
1.8	0.4641	0.4649	0.4656	0.4664	0.4671	0.4678	0.4686	0.4693	0.4699	0.4706
1.9	0.4713	0.4719	0.4726	0.4732	0.4738	0.4744	0.4750	0.4756	0.4761	0.4767
2.0	0.4772	0.4778	0.4783	0.4788	0.4793	0.4798	0.4803	0.4808	0.4812	0.4817
2.1	0.4821	0.4826	0.4830	0.4834	0.4838	0.4842	0.4846	0.4850	0.4854	0.4857
2.2	0.4861	0.4864	0.4868	0.4871	0.4875	0.4878	0.4881	0.4884	0.4887	0.4890
2.3	0.4893	0.4896	0.4898	0.4901	0.4904	0.4906	0.4909	0.4911	0.4913	0.4916
2.4	0.4918	0.4920	0.4922	0.4925	0.4927	0.4929	0.4931	0.4932	0.4934	0.4936
2.5	0.4938	0.4940	0.4941	0.4943	0.4945	0.4946	0.4948	0.4949	0.4951	0.4952
2.6	0.4953	0.4955	0.4956	0.4957	0.4959	0.4960	0.4961	0.4962	0.4963	0.4964
2.7	0.4965	0.4966	0.4967	0.4968	0.4969	0.4970	0.4971	0.4972	0.4973	0.4974
2.8	0.4974	0.4975	0.4976	0.4977	0.4977	0.4978	0.4979	0.4979	0.4980	0.4981
2.9	0.4981	0.4982	0.4982	0.4983	0.4984	0.4984	0.4985	0.4985	0.4986	0.4986
3.0	0.4986	0.4987	0.4987	0.4988	0.4988	0.4989	0.4989	0.4989	0.4990	0.4990

APPENDIX D: Values for $e^{-\lambda}$

λ	$e^{-\lambda}$	λ	$e^{-\lambda}$	λ	$e^{-\lambda}$
0.05	0.9512	2.05	0.1287	4.05	0.0174
0.10	0.9048	2.10	0.1225	4.10	0.0166
0.15	0.8607	2.15	0.1165	4.15	0.0158
0.20	0.8187	2.20	0.1108	4.20	0.0150
0.25	0.7788	2.25	0.1054	4.25	0.0143
0.30	0.7408	2.30	0.1003	4.30	0.0136
0.35	0.7047	2.35	0.0954	4.35	0.0129
0.40	0.6703	2.40	0.0907	4.40	0.0123
0.45	0.6376	2.45	0.0863	4.45	0.0117
0.50	0.6065	2.50	0.0821	4.50	0.0111
0.55	0.5769	2.55	0.0781	4.55	0.0106
0.60	0.5488	2.60	0.0743	4.60	0.0101
0.65	0.5220	2.65	0.0707	4.65	0.0096
0.70	0.4966	2.70	0.0672	4.70	0.0091
0.75	0.4724	2.75	0.0639	4.75	0.0087
0.80	0.4493	2.80	0.0608	4.80	0.0082
0.85	0.4274	2.85	0.0578	4.85	0.0078
0.90	0.4066	2.90	0.0550	4.90	0.0074
0.95	0.3867	2.95	0.0523	4.95	0.0071
1.00	0.3679	3.00	0.0498	5.00	0.0067
1.05	0.3499	3.05	0.0474	5.05	0.0064
1.10	0.3329	3.10	0.0450	5.10	0.0061
1.15	0.3166	3.15	0.0429	5.15	0.0058
1.20	0.3012	3.20	0.0408	5.20	0.0055
1.25	0.2865	3.25	0.0388	5.25	0.0052
1.30	0.2725	3.30	0.0369	5.30	0.0050
1.35	0.2592	3.35	0.0351	5.35	0.0047
1.40	0.2466	3.40	0.0334	5.40	0.0045
1.45	0.2346	3.45	0.0317	5.45	0.0043
1.50	0.2231	3.50	0.0302	5.50	0.0041
1.55	0.2122	3.55	0.0287	5.55	0.0039
1.60	0.2019	3.60	0.0273	5.60	0.0037
1.65	0.1920	3.65	0.0260	5.65	0.0035
1.70	0.1827	3.70	0.0247	5.70	0.0033
1.75	0.1738	3.75	0.0235	5.75	0.0032
1.80	0.1653	3.80	0.0224	5.80	0.0030
1.85	0.1572	3.85	0.0213	5.85	0.0029
1.90	0.1496	3.90	0.0202	5.90	0.0027
1.95	0.1423	3.95	0.0193	5.95	0.0026
2.00	0.1353	4.00	0.0183	6.00	0.0025
				7.00	0.0009
				8.00	0.000335
				9.00	0.000123
				10.00	0.000045

APPENDIX E: Random Digits

63271	59986	71744	51102	15141	80714	58683	93108	13554	79945
88547	09896	95436	79115	08303	01041	20030	63754	08459	28364
55957	57243	83865	09911	19761	66535	40102	26646	60147	15702
46276	87453	44790	67122	45573	84358	21625	16999	13385	22782
55363	07449	34835	15290	76616	67191	12777	21861	68689	03263
69393	92785	49902	58447	42048	30378	87618	26933	40640	16281
13186	29431	88190	04588	38733	81290	89541	70290	40113	08243
17726	28652	56836	78351	47327	18518	92222	55201	27340	10493
36520	64465	05550	30157	82242	29520	69753	72602	23756	54935
81628	36100	39254	56835	37636	02421	98063	89641	64953	99337
84649	38968	75215	75498	49539	74240	03466	49292	36401	45525
63291	11618	12613	75055	43915	26488	41116	64531	56827	30825
70502	53225	03655	05915	37140	57051	48393	91322	25653	06543
06426	24771	59935	49801	11082	66762	94477	02494	88215	27191
20711	55609	29430	70165	45406	78484	31639	52009	18873	96927
41990	70538	77191	25860	55204	73417	83920	69468	74972	38712
72452	36618	76298	26678	89334	33938	95567	29380	75906	91807
37042	40318	57099	10528	09925	89773	41335	96244	29002	46453
53766	52875	15987	46962	67342	77592	57651	95508	80033	69828
90585	58955	53122	16025	84299	53310	67380	84249	25348	04332
32001	96293	37203	64516	51530	37069	40261	61374	05815	06714
62606	64324	46354	72157	67248	20135	49804	09226	64419	29457
10078	28073	85389	50324	14500	15562	64165	06125	71353	77669
91561	46145	24177	15294	10061	98124	75732	00815	83452	97355
13091	98112	53959	79607	52244	63303	10413	63839	74762	50289
73864	83014	72457	22682	03033	61714	88173	90835	00634	85169
66668	25467	48894	51043	02365	91726	09365	63167	95264	45643
84745	41042	29493	01836	09044	51926	43630	63470	76508	14194
48068	26805	94595	47907	13357	38412	33318	26098	82782	42851
54310	96175	97594	88616	42035	38093	36745	56702	40644	83514
14877	33095	10924	58013	61439	21882	42059	24177	58739	60170
78295	23179	02771	43464	59061	71411	05697	67194	30495	21157
67524	02865	39593	54278	04237	92441	26602	63835	38032	94770
58268	57219	68124	73455	83236	08710	04284	55005	84171	42596
97158	28672	50685	01181	24262	19427	52106	34308	73685	74246
04230	16831	69085	30802	65559	09205	71829	06489	85650	38707
94879	56606	30401	02602	57658	70091	54986	41394	60437	03195
71446	15232	66715	26385	91518	70566	02888	79941	39684	54315
32886	05644	79316	09819	00813	88407	17461	73925	53037	91904
62048	33711	25290	21526	02223	75947	66466	06232	10913	75336

This table is reproduced with permission from The Rand Corporation, *A Million Random Digits*, The Free Press, New York, 1955 and 1983.